Turkey and the Crimean War

TURKEY AND THE CRIMEAN WAR:

A NARRATIVE OF HISTORICAL EVENTS.

BY

REAR-ADMIRAL SIR ADOLPHUS SLADE, K.C.B.

(MUSHAVER PASHA).

"Methinks, the Truth should live from age to age,
As 'twere retail'd to all posterity,
Even to the general all-ending day."——Shakspeare.

LONDON:
SMITH, ELDER AND CO., 65, CORNHILL.
1867

TO

ADMIRAL W. A. BAILLIE HAMILTON,

MANY YEARS SECRETARY OF THE ADMIRALTY

WITH HONOUR TO HIMSELF AND ADVANTAGE TO THE SERVICE :—

The following Pages are Dedicated

WITH PLEASANT MEMORIES OF EARLY DAYS,

BY HIS OLD MESSMATE,

THE AUTHOR.

PREFACE.

The reforms wrought by Sultan Mahmoud II.—in effect a Moslem social revolution,—disturbed the foundations of the edifice reared by his ancestors, and altered the relations of Turkey with Christendom. Previously isolated, with her hand against everybody and everybody's hand against her, Turkey then entered the comity of nations, but on invidious terms,—the terms of a step-child in a numerous family. Drawn irresistibly within the sphere of alien influences exercised by diplomatists variously inspired, she gravitated now towards one now towards another centre of attraction, with unstable equilibrium. No longer self-reliant, she viewed apprehensively the ambition of a neighbour and uneasily the aspirations (encouraged by classic sympathies) of quondam subjects: ill reassured in regard of the former by international jealousy, and with respect to the latter by political incapacity.

Irresolute between antagonistic pretensions, the Porte allowed a dispute at Jerusalem between members of the Latin and Oriental churches to ripen into a "question;"

which opened a way for the French ruler to raise the tone of his army and thereby replace France in her natural position, abdicated by his predecessor, in the front rank of nations. Leading England, while seeming led by her, to concur in his policy, and Turkey to believe in his sincerity, he secured their active alliance, and so ably played his cards in the ensuing game of war as to derive from it a maximum of "glory" with a minimum of obloquy. Russia's ardent foe in the Crimea, France sat at the council table at Paris her genial advocate.

A sketch of Sultan Mahmoud's reforms, and—direct consequence—the attitude of diplomacy at Constantinople, preceded, for the sake of comparison, by an outline of the conditions of Turkish power when that power was formidable to Europe, has seemed to the author a fitting commencement of a narrative which embraces, with other topics, remarks on the Crimean war remotely flowing therefrom.

Having briefly touched on those subjects, the author indicates in the following pages the influences brought to bear on the Porte preceding and during the Crimean war, and gives deferentially a qualified Turkish view, essential for the completion of the picture, of some of the events of that war: moved by a legitimate desire to show cause for the untoward action of the Anglo-French alliance on the prestige of the Ottoman power; and also, by a sense of the moral obligation of every one in a position of observation during that period to contribute, in the degree of his lights and opportunities, materials for the elucidation of a probable subject of controversy in later times, the miscarriage in the main of a remarkable league formed for the purpose of depressing one and ostensibly sustaining another empire.

Within eight years of the Peace of Paris Russia dared to irritate her recent vanquishers. Heedless of the urbane remonstrances of one, of the traditional sympathies of the other, she stamped out Polish nationality with her heel, and, careless about public opinion, plucked, remorseless, Caucasian independence up by the roots. The Khans of Turkistan have since admitted her supremacy, and the Ameer of Bokhara has sued for her graces. Within eleven years of that peace the Eastern question, which enthusiasts fancied had been laid under the Malakof for a century, reappears looming on the horizon, hazy, indistinct, like the genius freed by the fisherman in the Arabian Nights. Like that curious Arab watching amazed the condensation of the portentous vapour into form and substance, politicians and philosophers are watching with speculation in their eyes for an outline of the features of the Apparition. In view of a possible menacing aspect, monarchies are arming, cabinets are scheming, nationalities are stirring, and propagandism is active. England alone, the most interested after Turkey, *the outwork of her Asiatic Empire,* in that question, sits in the chair of self-complacency, fanned by the breeze of commercial prosperity.

The thesis that no race, whether Christian or Moslem, *in* the Turkish empire can succeed the Ottomans as the rulers of it, may be disputed by phil-Hellenists and philo-Sclavs, and the theorem that Egypt cannot exist as a sovereign Moslem state is apparently ignored by the actual viceroy: they are, nevertheless, the reality of the Eastern question; and although in the opinion of some it matters but little to England whether an Othman, a Romanof, or a Hapsburg rule on the banks of the Bosphorus, it does in the opinion of all concern her much whether a Turk or a Frank rule in the valley of the Nile.

London, March 1, 1867.

CONTENTS.

CHAPTER I.

CHAPTER II.

CHAPTER III.

CHAPTER VII.

CHAPTER VIII.

CHAPTER IX.

CHAPTER X.

CHAPTER XI.

CHAPTER XII.

CHAPTER XX.

CHAPTER XXI.

CHAPTER XXII.

CHAPTER XXIII

CHAPTER XXIV.

CHAPTER XXV.

CHAPTER XXVI.

CHAPTER XXVII.

CHAPTER XXVIII.

APPENDIX.

ERRATA.

Page 123, line 30, *for* "uncensured" *read* "uncensored."
Page 133, line 6, *for* "the Egyptian *Hassan Pasha*" *read* "the Egyptian Admiral Hassan Pasha."
Page 138, line 23, *for* "Certainly not" *read* "Certainly."

TURKEY

AND

THE CRIMEAN WAR.

CHAPTER I.

Origin of the Ottoman Nation—Othman Founder of the Turkish Monarchy—Sultan Amurath I. defeats the Sclavonic League—Bajazet subjugates Asia Minor—He is defeated and taken Captive by Tamerlane—Mahomet I. and his Descendants consolidate the Empire—Syria and Egypt subdued by Selim I.—Amurath IV. captures Bagdad—Eastern Empire of the Turks—Policy of the House of Othman—Reign of Sultan Mahomet IV.—Power of the Sultans—Policy of Sultan Mahmoud—The Janissaries and their Organization—Their Destruction and its Consequences—The Reforms of Sultan Mahomet II.—Fires in Constantinople—Pertef Pasha—Death and Burial of Sultan Mahmoud.

The Ottoman nation, like other nations which have achieved greatness, rose from a small beginning. A few hundred Turcoman families, living in tents, like the Turcomans and Kurds of the present day, formed its nucleus. Under their chief, Ertogrul, they led a pastoral life, in the dominions of the Sultan of Roum; whose capital, originally Nice until its capture by the Crusaders (A.D. 1097), was Iconium. The kingdom of Roum was a fragment of the empire, extending from Samarcand to Egypt, consolidated by Alp Arslan, a lineal descendant of Seljuk, which, breaking up on the death of Malek Shah, resolved itself into four states, each ruled by a prince of the Seljukian line.

Othman, the son of Ertogrul, entered early the military service of the Sultan of Roum; he acquired favour and influence there, and on the abdication of his suzerain succeeded to the throne, A.D. 1299. The fallen dynasty retained wealth and spiritual honours, and its representative, the Mollah-Hunkiar, has since enjoyed the right to gird with the sabre of power every sultan of Turkey on his accession. Othman, the son of Ertogrul, was the founder of the Turkish monarchy, and the Turks by birth or adoption have since been styled Ottomans or Osmanleys.

The Ottomans looked upon the dissolving Eastern empire as their inheritance. Vigorously led, brave, and united by a fervent religious belief, they despised alike the arms and sophistry of the Greeks, who betrayed their sense of weakness by sending in nominal marriage a daughter of the imperial house to Sultan Orchan. In the course of three generations they transferred their capital, first to Brussa, next to Adrianople. Their neighbourhood disturbed the repose of the Byzantines, and roused the Bulgarians, Servians, and Albanians to arms; but the tardy valour of the latter was of no more avail than the processions of the former. Amurath I., the founder of the Janissaries, overthrew their army, and broke the Sclavonic league formed against him, at the battle of Kossova, A.D. 1390. As the victor surveyed the field of battle on the following day, a Servian started up from among a heap of slain and revenged his comrades by a blow of his yataghan, of which the Sultan died, in the seventy-second year of his age and the thirty-first of his reign. The tide of success continued to flow on under his son Bajazet, surnamed Ilderim (lightning). He curbed the aspirations of the emirs of Anatolia, who ill bore the ascendancy of the house of Othman; he subjugated the country from the Hellespont to Mount Hæmus; and he vanquished a confederate army under Sigismund, king of Hungary, at the battle of Nicopolis. The hour then arrived for the salutary trial of adversity; that ordeal which developes the virtues of a race and discloses its tendencies. Every nation which has acquired eminence has been early tempered by that trial. The want of it proved fatal to the empire whose capital had known neither infancy nor adolescence. Born of a master will, "new Rome" sprang at once, untrained, untutored, into adult existence, with the wealth of nations at command to gratify the passions of a corrupt age. Success had made Bajazet arrogant, and his arrogance had aroused the jealousy of Tamerlane, popularly known as Timour the Tartar. Mutual reproaches and defiance led naturally to war. The Tartar and Turkish armies, both of common origin, met on the plain of Angora, each led by its sovereign in person and animated by his rancour. In the battle which ensued, July, 1402, victory remained faithful to her favourite. The Turkish army was routed; Bajazet was taken prisoner, and Asia Minor lay at the feet of the conqueror. The fruit of a century of toil and courage, the work of Othman, Orchan, and Amurath, seemed lost in a day. But the Ottomans had not accomplished their allotted task; the promise of Mohammed of Constantinople for the "faithful" had to be fulfilled. Tamerlane, therefore, satisfied with success and revenge, retired to his dominions beyond the Caspian, leaving the Turkish empire to be contended for by the four sons of Bajazet, the eldest of whom, Mahomet, after ten years of civil strife, remained the victor and ascended the throne of his father at Adrianople. Mahomet I. reconsolidated the Ottoman empire; his son, Amurath II., strengthened its foundations by wise legislation; and his grandson, Mahomet II., by the aid of a monster cannon, wrought by a Venetian, throwing 600-pound balls, crowned the edifice by the conquest of Constantinople, 29th May, 1453. Mournful day! when the last Constantine fell nobly in the breach, slain by a vulgar hand; and the first cathedral, reared before the birth of *Islam*, rung with the praises of Mohammed.

This catastrophe revealed to central Europe the existence of a great and menacing Moslem power, and showed the Italian republics the folly of having allowed their policy to be shaped solely by mercantile considerations. Hungary with Transylvania became the battle-field of the German and Turkish empires; while the Venetians and Genoese sank from their haughty position under the Greek emperors to the humble condition of suitors for commercial favours at the feet of a slave of the Sultan. Selim I., the third in succession from the conqueror, subduing Syria and Egypt, dethroned together with the Mamlouk dynasty the titular caliph of the Fatimite line, seated in mock state at Cairo, and transferred, A.D. 1516, the relics of the Prophet and other insignia of the caliphate from his palace to the imperial seraglio. The eleventh in descent, Amurath IV., the last Sultan who took the field in person, wrested Bagdad from the Persians. In possession of the "holy cities," and the famous seats of the caliphate, the house of Othman, invested thereby with the religious and historic associations dear to Islam, became lustrous in the eyes of the Moslem world, and but for its Scythian origin the lofty title of "Commander of the Faithful" * might have been awarded by common consent to its chief.

The tenacious hold of the Eastern Empire by the Turks, encamped amidst disaffected peoples with whom fusion was next to impossible, and menaced by powerful neighbours animated by religious hostility, forms a remarkable passage in history. They had taken that empire literally in pieces. They reconstructed it. They reannexed to it the Mesopotamian provinces ceded, with part of Armenia, to the Persians by the Emperor Jovian, as the price of his retreat from the Tigris with the remnant of Julian the Apostate's army. They added to it the African presidencies, part of the Western Empire, also Dacia, never ruled firmly even by Rome; and, with garrisons in Hungary, they included in their dominion the extreme point of Arabia, far beyond the Roman sway, Aden—the refuge of Cain, according to the Arabs. With their power recognized East and West, they sent, during

* "Commander of the Faithful" was one of the titles of the Caliph, and in virtue of it his name was mentioned in the Khoutbey (Friday noon prayer) in every mosque. That distinction ceased with the fall of the Abbassides. Since then each state has mentioned only its own sovereign in the Khoutbey. Moslems in countries ruled by sovereigns of another faith mention as Commander of the Faithful the Sultan of Roum (Turkey) in their Khoutbey.

the reign of Solyman the Magnificent, in a fleet built expressly at Suez, an army to India against the Portuguese; and their diversion in Hungary and Naples in favour of France, leading Charles V. to raise the sieges of Marseilles and Arles, and retire with his forces behind the Var, readjusted the European balance of power. Haireddin Pasha (Barbarossa), with the ambassador of the eldest son of the Church for his guest, the negotiator of the treaty of alliance defensive and offensive between Francis I. and the Ottoman Porte, carried away captive in his galleys on that occasion many thousand Italians from Brindisi and Otranto.

The House of Othman avoided dynastic complications and evaded that rule of inheritance which gives precedence to the eldest of the race—fecund source of Asiatic civil discord—by usages calculated to prevent collateral extension and facilitate direct succession. The princes of the blood, state prisoners virtually from the hour of their father's death, were given concubines for toys, and the princesses of the blood were married, for little more than form's sake, to pashas who were generally relegated to distant governments, with the charge of maintaining their royal wives' establishments. The issue of these unions, if female, might be reared; but the duty of perpetuating the imperial race devolved upon the Sultan. No son, traditional testimony leading to that conclusion, born to or of any other member of the family, survived to gladden its mother's heart with its prattle; nor did the exception, proving the rule thus far, occur until the reign of the thirtieth Sultan, Mahmoud II. His eldest daughter's son attained the age of five years and then died. His heir, Sultan Abdul

Medjid, was equally tolerant of his brother, who, on his accession, produced a son four years old, whose existence had been a family secret; but the boy was then recognized, and registered at the Porte as a prince of the imperial race. Infanticide, however, was rare, recourse being had to an expedient to which allusion is sufficient; and which, becoming with such high sanction interwoven with the domestic economy of private harems, may be considered one of the causes (precocious marriage aiding) of the dis proportionate female mortality among the Moslem population of the capital.

Thus the Ottoman dynasty became, like the Nile among rivers, a solecism: a stately stem without branches, as the other is a noble stream without affluents. The direct succession of the first fourteen Sultans is proof that each of them survived his uncles; whether fairly or unfairly cannot, in regard of all, be affirmed. History only records three Sultans guilty of the death of their brothers, the number of whom in one instance exceeded fifty; and in the absence of evidence we may be allowed to assume that the princes in general died naturally: some of them, perhaps, of *tedium vitæ*. They were sensually pampered, intellectually starved; they had no healthy pursuits, no manly diversions; they had much to fear, nothing to hope for; their society was composed of treacherous eunuchs, fawning pages, dissolute buffoons, and fanatic mollahs. When sickness oppressed them why try to combat it with nauseous drugs and insipid diet? Better lie down and die. Moslem resignation is often the indifference to life generated by mental and physical languor, and sometimes the impatience of it, born of "the law's delay," and "the insolence of office." The nation approved of an arrangement the advantages of which it shared without the responsibility; all it required was, security for the succession, in case of the Sultan having no son, or one of tender age.

The fortunes of the Ottomans culminated in the reign of Sultan Mahomet IV. That reign witnessed the conquest of Crete; the phenomenon of a series of able, upright grand viziers of one family—the Kiuproglous, whose still respected tomb faces the column erected by the first Constantine in the centre of his forum,—and the siege of Vienna, A.D. 1683. The Turkish army before Vienna clamoured for an assault for the sake of plunder; its commander, Kara Mustapha, temporized for a capitulation for the sake of ransom: the plunder would belong to the troops, the ransom to their general and his friends in the capital. This hesitation gave time for Sobieski and his Poles to arrive to the rescue. The tide then turned, and, sweeping the Ottomans out of Hungary, where their horsetails had floated in the breeze for above a century, it continued to ebb slowly and fitfully, occasionally checked by a transient breeze of prosperity, until it reached low-water mark in the reign of Sultan Mahmoud II.; of which I shall speak more at length, since out of its events grew the Eastern question. In that reign, for the first time, revolt was successful, and peace was accompanied by humiliation. The Greeks, cheered in their struggle and finally aided by Western Europe, gained independence, and the Russians exacted a pecuniary indemnity at the peace of Adrianople; and then, organized by an aspiring rebel, the despised fellahs of Egypt, crossing the Taurus, overthrew the imperial army at Konia, the cradle of the monarchy. Their further advance, beyond Kutaieh, was deterred by the disembarkation, in February, 1833, of a Russian army on the Asiatic shore of the Bosphorus: direct evidence of the distress of the monarchy, thus reduced to crave aid from its hereditary foe —the foe destined, in its own opinion, to deal by the Turkish as the Turks had dealt by the Lower Empire.

Sultan Mahmoud's reign was a prolonged struggle with his people for power. Theoretically absolute, the power of the Sultan of Turkey had for generations been practically limited by custom; which in the East has the force of law: often more. *Adet dir* (it is the custom) is the excuse and the apology for abuses and anomalies whose name is legion. The Sultan might, unquestioned, decapitate individuals and confiscate their goods; but he dared not oppress the community nor levy taxes unauthorized by law. He might fill his harem with strange women, but he dared not peer through the harem lattice of the meanest of his subjects. The seduction of a Turkish lady by Sultan Ibrahim filled the measure of his unpopularity and determined the storm which deposed him. The Tartar race, which sprang into notice under Othman, regarded him as their chief, tacitly elected. They swore fealty for themselves and posterity to the family of the founder of the dynasty; but reserved the right to choose the worthiest of it to reign. When the line of conquering Sultans, followed joyously by the nation, ended, their effeminate successors found themselves circumscribed by institutions silently grown out of the traditions of their nomade ancestors, of which the *Kourshaltai* was prominent. The Turkish nation, unable to free itself from the obligation of passive obedience ordained by the Koran, placed that volume beside the throne, and empowered the Scheick ul Islam, the chief of the Ulema, to interpret its meaning to the Sultan, and remind him of his obligation also to govern according to law. This restraint, aided by the domestic arrangement before spoken of, has caused the comparative stability of the Ottoman family among Moslem dynasties, the cohesion of the heterogeneous elements composing the vast empire under its sway. The Caliphate had been nearer the fountain of Islam, invested moreover with a sacred character; yet each of its branches having run through the cycle of conquest, torpor and decay sank under the withering influence of a despotism which none dared gainsay. The Ottoman monarchy—solecism in the East—possessed a constitution: defective, and in a state of chronic disorder, but still a roughly balanced system.

The tragedy enacted at Constantinople by the Janissaries and Mustafa Bairactar * which terminated with the

* In 1807 the Janissaries deposed Selim III. in favour of Mustafa, the eldest of his two nephews, the sons of Sultan Hamid. On hearing of the fall of his patron, Mustafa Bairactar, the pasha of Rudschuk, raised an army of Albanians and marched on Constantinople to reinstate him. Overawing the city, he traversed it with his force to the outer wall of the seraglio. Chamberlains met him there, and demanded, in the name of Sultan Mustafa, his object. "I know no other Sultan than Selim; let him appear and I will give an answer," said the Bairactar. Sultan Mustafa sent word to him in rejoinder to wait a little and Sultan Selim would appear. In half-an-hour the Bairactar was admitted into the outer court, and there saw the dead body of the unfortunate Selim, victim to his zeal. He at once stormed the inner courts, deposed Sultan Mustafa, and transferred his brother Mahmoud from the recess in which, it is said, the architect of the palace had concealed him, to the throne. Sultan Mahmoud II. made Mustafa Bairactar the grand vizier; but he did not long fill that post. The Janissaries in revenge soon afterwards set fire to his residence, in the flames of which he perished.

accession, A.D. 1808, of Sultan Mahmoud II. over the bodies of his uncle Selim III. and his brother Mustapha III., was of a nature to make him ponder over cause and effect. Mahmoud came to the conclusion that the disorganization of the empire was due to institutional checks on the sovereign's will—in the shape of *Deré-beys*, or feudal nobles, some of whom were of older standing in the land than the reigning house; of the *Timarlees*, a tithe-endowed gentry; of the Ulema, a religio-legal establishment; and more than all, of a popular element, the Janissaries. He resolved to remove those checks. He pursued that resolve imperturbably; he bent every consideration to it; and by remaining the last of his race during many years was free from seditious interruption. He cut off, with few exceptions, the Deré-beys; some by force, some by treachery, and impoverished their families by confiscation of their estates. He dispersed the Timarlees, and he suppressed the popular voice by his celebrated act, the destruction of the Janissaries. He shattered the idols of his nation as his prophet had shattered the idols of the *Caaba*; but less effectively. Religious idols broken drop at once into the limbo of oblivion, while social idols overthrown leave memories behind them. To weaken these, he proscribed, so far as he dared, the national garb and traditional usages. The Ulema alone of the noticeable classes were allowed to follow their fathers' fashions: they continued to wear turbans and yellow slippers, to sit cross-legged on sofas and speak oracularly of the signs of the times. But deprived of their right arm, the Janissaries, their influence became of the kind termed moral; which self-willed monarchs in general make light of.

The Janissaries have been likened to the Pretorian guards at Rome, but the resemblance is only specious. The Pretorians were mercenary troops of various races, quartered apart from the people; they sold the empire to the highest bidder, or to him from whom they expected most indulgence; they made whom they pleased emperor—an illiterate Illyrian, a sedate Spaniard, or a polished Italian; and when their choice turned out good, the merit was scarcely theirs. The Janissaries, on the contrary, were, during the greater part of their existence, composed exclusively of Turkish citizens, and they never looked outside the house of Othman for a sovereign. If the prince elevated by them to the throne proved no better than his predecessor, the fault was not theirs, for they had no other choice. They were in their origin an army of converted Christians, given, when children, as tribute to the conquerors; but this tribute, being at variance with the letter and spirit of the Koran, soon ceased, and *kharadj* was paid instead. Native-born Turks took their place. In time the body expanded into a national guard of armed citizens, pursuing, with martial habits, their respective avocations in peace, and ready to follow the Sultan in war. They aided the tent sultans to build up the empire; they prevented the harem sultans from pulling it to pieces. Their credit led the people, high and low, to inscribe their names in one or other of their *ortas*, with preference for those distinguished in the wars of the empire. They were divided into numerous ortas of unequal strength. Each orta had an *oda* (guard-house) at Constantinople, with a permanent staff and a sufficient number of citizens for police and garrison duty. An *ulufé* (gratification) of ninety *paras* a head was given once in three months, and on the accession of a Sultan, to the active force: which received also rations. Their chief, the Janissary Aga, held the second rank in the hierarchy of the empire, and with his two lieutenants had the right to attend at the Sultan's stirrup on Friday. Each Janissary was indelibly marked on the arm with the number and emblem of his orta, which facilitated recognition of the slain in battle: a fish, for example, was the emblem of the 25th, the favourite orta, which generally numbered 20,000 names on its roll. The 31st and 64th ortas were also popular. In the provinces, registration in an orta, though less observed than in the capital, was general; so much so, that Janissaries and the adult male Turkish population were nearly convertible terms. The practice of civic virtue, as it entails inconvenience, is never zealous. The home-loving Constantinopolitans made no exception to the rule, and therefore in the course of time the guard-house and garrison service fell into the hands of a low, idle set, apt materials for demagogues to work with, who often made themselves as odious to the peaceable citizens as to the seraglio. Strangers, prone everywhere to see the abuse and overlook the use of an institution, saw in them the Janissaries, and took no note of the vast organization of which they were the exaggerated expression. When their discontent was popular, they were the citizens of Constantinople; when unpopular, they stood alone. Such was their position as their fatal hour drew near.

The Ulema and the people, enlightened by the discredit of the Grecian war of independence, concurred with the Sultan in the state necessity of a reorganization of the Janissaries, and the Sheick ul Islam gave his *fetwah*, sanctioning compulsion. With this moral support, Sultan Mahmoud—himself enrolled, like his predecessors, in the first orta of the Janissaries—invited them to submit to rules and discipline conducive to military efficiency. Distrust marred the negotiation which ensued between the seraglio and the ortas. The Janissaries suspected ulterior designs, and misled by their aga, who had been gained over to the imperial side, under-estimated the force ready to be arrayed against them. On their final refusal to come to terms, with arms in their hands and their soup-kettles reversed, the Sultan, displaying the holy standard, summoned the citizens to rally round it or remain in their houses; then, 26th June, 1826, he attacked the mutineers (who, dismayed by their isolation, made a sorry resistance) with the *topchis*, *galiondgis* and a body of *zeymens*, and destroyed them with grapeshot, sword, and fire. Many hundreds perished in the flames of their odas on the Etmeidan. Daily, during a month afterwards, citizens accused of reactionary tendencies were brought before a commission, sitting *ad hoc* in a tent pitched in the Hippodrome. Their interrogatory was short, their condemnation inevitable. After the form of an inquiry, they were strangled then and there, and their bodies, collected at sunset, were conveyed in a cart to Akher Kapou, and thrown into the Propontis. Similar scenes on a smaller scale were enacted in the chief provincial cities. Many fell victims to revenge; several were strangled for their wealth.

Sultan Mahmoud was then master of the situation; as every one in the East is who strikes a heavy unexpected blow. He might then have reorganized the institution, had he chosen to make the attempt; following the example of the most sagacious of his ancestors, Soliman I., after the suppression of the revolt of the Janissaries excited by their jealousy of his creation of the corps of Bostandgis. He might then have regenerated Turkey in a Turkish sense: the sense most becoming an Ottoman's consideration. No one could affirm that the Janissaries, as an institution, had proved detrimental to Turkey; their grasp of the Eastern Empire of the Cæsars, with extended frontiers, was evidence of their loyalty and devotion during centuries: all that could be said was, that a faction, making its will prevail over reason, had long defied all attempts to adopt their organization to altered circumstances. With Janissaryism the Ottoman dynasty had traversed five centuries, defiant and self-reliant: without it, in the course of thirteen years (between 1826 and 1840) it was twice on the brink of destruction, and was saved each time from falling into the abyss by the friendly arm of foreign intervention. With the institution unreformed, rational government might demonstrably be despaired of: without it, in one form or another, Turkey, it might be apprehended, would become a Byzantine empire; an estate to feed a luxurious capital.

History inclines us to think that a nation's progress or regeneration is mainly conditional on adherence to the rule or principle of its growth, tempered in practice to modified social relations; because that, harmonizing with popular instincts and traditions, is intelligible to the mass. Peter the Great, despotic by the suppression of the Strelitzes, respected Muscovitism embodied in the boyards and the priesthood. The Anglo-Americans, with independence, remained English at heart, with the representative and municipal institutions of the old country. Both Russia and the United States, faithful to tradition, have since progressed with great strides in power and consideration. Spain, on the contrary, discarded her cortes and fueros, and ridden by the Inquisition retrograded from a high to an inferior place in the scale of nations. The greatest of reformers, Mohammed, while touching everything Arabian with a refining rod, respected social usage. He found the Arabs idolatrous, he made them devout; he elevated their thoughts from the worship of images to the adoration of an invisible, eternal Being; but he left them the excitement of their fantastic whirl round the Caaba, and their belief in the mystic virtues of zem-zem water, drawn from the well at which they believe Hagar filled her bottle for the lad Ishmael; and though he disturbed custom by eliminating from their calendar its intercalary days, deference for the Mosaic arrangement reconciled them to the innovation. He found them discordant tribes addicted to internecine strife, he left them a nation of warriors united by the stimulus of the glory of propagating their faith by the sword. He found them polygamists, he left them such, but he gave woman rights. He found them slave-owners, he left them such, but he enjoined kind treatment of the slave, with manumission after seven years' faithful service; and, animated by his example, Omar, the second Caliph, who collated the pages of the Koran, ordained the freedom of the bondswoman pregnant by her master, with the legitimacy of her offspring. He proclaimed the equality of Moslems before God; but he recognized the pre-eminence of the tribe of Koreish, and the merit of ancient lineage in man as well as horse. An exception appears. He found the Arabs dirty, he made them cleanly by religious obligation. One hundred and forty millions of Moslems worshipping one God with like forms, all prostrate, thrice or oftener a day, with clean hands and feet, their faces turned towards Mecca, attest the vitality of his legislation in the thirteenth century after his death; and the absence of worldly distinctions in the mosque reveals its fraternal spirit. Black and white, rich and poor,—the Ethiopian and the Tartar, the jewelled sirdar and the uncombed fakir,—kneel down side by side on the same carpet, and listen together to prayer recited in the old Arabian dialect. The seraglio, with closed portals jealously guarded, is the shrine of autocracy; but the mosque, with its doors wide open from dawn till after sunset, inviting all to enter for repose, meditation, or prayer, is the temple of democracy. The Sadr'azam enters with viziral attendance; no one regards, no one makes room for him: the mendicant is at home, is his equal there.

Writers on Turkey, in dilating on the excesses of the Janissaries, have seldom paused to examine if some justification may not have been pleaded. One of their earliest recorded risings, that in the reign of Amurath III., merits notice for the moral, more recently applicable, to be drawn from it. Their motive on that occasion was the debasement of the coin of the realm, the favourite resource of improvident governments until the discovery of an ingenious substitute—inconvertible paper money. They demanded the head of the vizir who had sanctioned the measure, of the master of the mint who had struck the base coin, and of the defterdar who had paid the troops with it. The sacrifice of those heads appeased the sedition, and this example long retarded the depreciation of the money. Writers also have been in the habit of connecting the current ills of Turkey with the Janissaries, and in particular have invariably attributed to their malice the fires of Constantinople. No theory has ever been more controverted by the logic of facts. Fires have raged, as frequently since as in their time, in the capital and the provinces. Every year has been marked by fires more or less calamitous. Pera, with its churches and embassy hotels, was burnt to the ground six years after their fall; and the greatest fire seen at Constantinople for half a century—called, for distinction, *harik kibir* (the great fire)—occurred in August, 1865, consuming in its progress, during twenty-three hours, across the city from Hodja Pasha on the Golden Horn to Yeni Kapou on the Propontis, a score of mosques, some churches, many public establishments, and more than 2,000 dwellings.* In the ensuing months of March, April, and May, 1866, three other fires in Constantinople, respectively at Psamatia, Balata, and Bakché Kapousou, consumed together more than 2,000 houses or shops, with several mosques and other public edifices. The wonder is not that there are so many fires, but that

* D'aprés les documents presentés par le comité, le grand incendie de Hodja pacha a consumé vingt-sept quartiers qui contenaient 1879 maisons, 751 boutiques, 13 khans, 7 bains, 22 mosquées, 3 *tékés*, 18 écoles, 7 *médressés*, 3 églises, 2 *imarets*, 5 corps de garde, 37 fontaines, et 4 *sébils*. Si l'on ajoute à ces chiffres celui des pertes immobilières causées par trois autres incendies, savoir: 13 maisons et 87 boutiques brûlées à Ortakeuy; 73 maisons et 48 boutiques, à Balat; 57 maisons et 41 boutiques, à Yédik-pacha, le nombre total des constructions de toutes sortes réduites en cendres dans ces quatre incendies s'élève à 3,020.—*Official Paper.*

they are not more numerous at Constantinople, considering the materials of the houses, the carelessness of their inmates, the deficiency of water, and the absence of organization. In olden days the fountains ran freely, and the Grand Vizir attended on the spot with means to stimulate zeal and deter plunderers; his purse-bearer distributed gold to some, his cavasses dealt blows to others. The fire service of Constantinople is become in some respects worse than formerly. It is composed of the *élite*, not of the unwashed, for there are none in a land where the bath is an institution, but of the rabble of the city; dare-devil lads, who rush, on the cry *yanghen var*, to the various pump-stations, in light racing costume, *i.e.*, with bare arms, legs, and necks. Their progress through the streets, at the top of their speed, to the fire from all quarters, the pump-bearers being relieved every five minutes, is a veritable stampedo. The halt and the blind slink into corners on their approach, and old women cry *aman!* as they pass. Their services are voluntary; their remuneration is precarious, being derived, it is said, from those on whose houses they favourably pump, when water is procurable. They, the street dogs, and the eunuchs form the visible link between the past and the present. The Janissaries may have set fire occasionally—the fire spreading—to an obnoxious functionary's *konak;* but they had recognized modes of showing discontent, other than kindling a conflagration likely to devour their own houses. They formed the guard of honour lining the streets on the Sultan's Friday progress to and from mosque; and while fans borne aloft by pages screened the imperial countenance, theirs was open to the inquisitive scrutiny of the imperial suite. If indications of ill-humour appeared, discreet inquiries would be made into the cause. They had also the *aiyak divan*, rarely resorted to—an open-air "meeting," clamorous for redress on some capital point, before the seraglio gates.

The situation created by the destruction of the Janissaries soon made itself felt. The observation, Who now will restrain the Sultan? cost the poet Izzet Mollah his head.

Sultan Mahmoud had by his side in Pertef Pasha, commonly styled the last of the Turks,—of the Turks who were loyal without flattery, hospitable without ostentation, self-respectful without arrogance, and who with the vices possessed the virtues of a dominant race,—the man to aid him in the task of reforming Janissaryism and germane institutions. Pertef Pasha aimed at the devélopment of an Eastern civilization, based on respect for national usages and predilections. An Eastern civilization consisted in adapting existing institutions to modern requirements, in purifying tradition of error by education, and seeking knowledge everywhere, even (in the words of the Koran) in China. The refinement and prosperity attained by the Moorish kingdom of Cordova under the Omeyah dynasty was on record to show the compatibility of eminence in arts, science, and agriculture with the tenets of the Koran. The Córdovan schools were famous throughout Europe, particularly the school of medicine founded by Abdurrahman III. Instinct may have told him that a civilization, the result of an amalgamation of usages derived from antagonistic principles, would prove inherently weak and superficial. An Oriental polish seemed to him preferable to a Western varnish. Pertef Pasha, however, did not long retain favour. He saw idolatry in the honours ordered to be paid to the Sultan's portrait, and impolicy in the course pursued towards Mehemet Ali pasha of Egypt. His enemies took advantage of his outspoken frankness on these tender points. They represented him to the Sultan as one kneaded with the old leaven. They attained a decree for his exile to Adrianople, and soon afterwards, fearing his return, an order to the governor of that city to send his soul "back to its eternal abode."

Sultan Mahmoud had a dominant passion—revenge, and a prominent defect—incapacity to regard an object from two points of view. Their combined operation had made him, in earlier life, attack out of season Ali Tepelen, pasha of Yanina, and it drove him into his disastrous second Egyptian war, in the course of which his troubled reign terminated. His velleity for Ali Tepelen's head blinded him to the danger, greater than that of any satrap's contumacy, of a Grecian revolt, and his animosity against Mehemet Ali, making him resent pacific counsel as treason, led to consequences subversive of Oriental faith in Ottoman infallibility. He was spared the sorrow of draining the cup of bitterness to its dregs by dying a few hours before the news of the battle of Nezib, fatal to the Turkish arms, reached Constantinople. He had sent an order to Hafiz Pasha, the Grand Vizir, to give battle on a certain day, named auspicious by the court astrologer, but, before the bey entrusted with it reached the scene of action, the battle had been fought, and Hafiz was a fugitive. Next followed the defection of the Turkish fleet under Achmet

Pasha; whose rise in a few years from the position of stroke-oarsman in the imperial caik to the post of Capitan pasha, had excited jealousy. On his sovereign's death, Khosrew Pasha, Achmet's enemy, sent the nazir of the naval arsenal to the Dardanelles with an order for the immediate return of the fleet to the Bosphorus; sending also by the same hand instructions to the capitana bey to strangle his chief, if contumacious, and take the command. Achmet Pasha, however, intercepted the nazir on his way to the capitana bey's ship. His departure in a steamer to save his life would have been viewed indulgently; but his taking the fleet with him to Alexandria was unpardonable.* . . .

Sultan Mahmoud expired in a kiosk, at Scutari, June 30, 1839. Having throughout his reign wielded the executioner's blade vigorously, and the warrior's sabre feebly, he was not regretted. His remains, after ablution, were conveyed over the water to the old seraglio, and laid out on a mat, symbolic of the Moslem sense of equality in death. His son, Abdul Medjid, having looked at them, ordered their interment—the first and indispensable act of sovereignty; then proceeded to the *Koub'alti* for the ceremony of *beeat* (submission). This ceremony, which takes place in one of the vast courts of the seraglio, surrounded by structures of all forms and ages, is Asiatic. The Sultan stands alone, unguarded, while the dignitaries of state successively, on bended knees, kiss his feet; and in that

* Ahmed Pasha, surnamed firari (deserter), remained in Egypt after the treaty of 1841; and died there soon afterwards from the effects of poison: administered to him, it is said, by Mehemet Ali Pasha, in a cup of coffee. His two sons are well placed in the service of the Porte at Constantinople.

abject posture—regarded with as much indifference by the spectators as by the dogs at their feet or the storks above their heads—do not receive a glance from the object of their adoration. A few paces off, in a kiosk beyond the "gate of felicity," the dead Sultan's body has been in the meanwhile encoffined, as simply as a mendicant's; and when his successor turns his back on his lieges, pages carry it through the throng of anxious courtiers who the day before were at its feet to the imperial gate, when the people take it and bear it on their shoulders to the mausoleum prepared for its reception, mounted eunuchs in advance scattering money right and left.

CHAPTER II.

Sultan Abdul Medjid—The Tanzimat and its Results—Abrupt Transitions in the Administration—The Army and Conscription—Brigandage—Lenity of the late Sultan—Official Corruption—Redshid Pasha—His Policy—The Medjlises, or Boards—Authority and Power of the old Vizirs—Mode of dealing with rebellious Vizirs—Government without an Army—Decentralization of Finance—The Navy—Effects of Centralization—Conciliation of the Rajahs advisable—Retrospect of an ancient Turk.

By the subversion of the ancient Turkish constitution, Sultan Mahmoud, uniting all the powers of the State in his own person, became, as an Arabian caliph, Mohammed's vicegerent, responsible for his acts to none on earth. He transmitted this terrible power to his son, Abdul Medjid Khan, then eighteen years of age, to use or abuse as he might see fit. Brought up by his Georgian mother with other sentiments, Sultan Abdul Medjid was, nevertheless, of the race of Othman—a race prone to, and with difficulty restrained from, the abuse of power; being taught by flattery to believe in its divine right. The people, wearied by foreign and domestic strife, watched with intense anxiety for indications of his policy. Another five years of his father's rule would have exhausted the empire, morally and physically. He did not long keep them in suspense. He tranquillized their fears, and justified their hopes, by his tanzimat (reforms) proclaimed four months after his accession

This famous proclamation, conceived in a spirit of clemency and tolerance, inaugurated a new era for Turkey. The direct power of death by decapitation was taken from scores of vizirs; the indirect power of death by vexation, from hundreds of inferior station. Oriental ductility was severely tested. An ensanguined nation was ordered to be gentle, and the order was obeyed. Pashas used to rule with the sabre were required to rule by exhortation. Mudirs and agas, wont to admonish rayas with the stick, were enjoined to be civil to them. The exhaustion of the nation, after twenty years of unparalleled suffering, favoured the experiment: anything for quiet was the universal aspiration. The Ottomans, with the instincts of a dominant race, adapted themselves to altered circumstances; they leant upon their prestige, and it did not fail them. Fatalists, they were not sorry to see their Sultan cease, of his own accord, to be the direct instrument of fate in regard of them.

The tanzimat, skilfully drawn up by Redshid Efendi, afterwards Redshid Pasha, so as not to alarm the susceptibilities of the Moslems, nor unduly excite the expectations of the rayas, shadowed forth rather than indicated organic changes. It embodied a declaration of sorrow for the past, with an assurance of improved government for the future. It deplored the excesses of delegated authority, and the abuse of monopolies, and it promised protection to life, honour, and property thenceforwards: a promise which has been fairly kept. It left every one free to draw his own deduction from its tenour, and gave no one the right to say that the Sultan and his advisers had bound themselves to any definite course.

This has been the sum and substance of the famous Hatti Sherif proclaimed at Gul-baneh, in the face of the world, Nov. 3, 1839. Under its healing influence, trade and agriculture revived, while the charm of luxuriating in yalis on the banks of the Bosphorus, without seeing the sword of Damocles suspended overhead, has reconciled the upper class to diminished personality.

But the transition from one extreme to the other proved too abrupt. The infliction of death, recklessly resorted to for centuries, and exciting no keen terror among a people hardily nurtured, some under the dogma, some under the idea of predestination, was suddenly abolished in a country without the knowledge of secondary punishment other than the bastinado: also forbidden by the tanzimat, though still occasionally irregularly administered. The administration, hitherto systematically decentralized, was centralized now, in an empire without roads, a post-office, or newspapers;* save two salaried gazettes, in Turkish and French respectively, of limited circulation among officials. Legislation went far in advance of the age. Redshid Pasha's political philosophy, gleaned in courtly European circles, had not taught him that every state of society, as well as every age, has its appropriate scale of punishment; and that the treatment unduly harsh in one, may be wholesomely severe in another. It had not taught him that centralization, while it may be expansive in the West, must be absorbent in the East. The

* Since that period Turkey, still deficient in roads, has organized a letter post connecting the principal cities, and a telegraph system. Since then newspapers in various languages, in English, Italian, German, French, Armenian, Greek, Bulgarian, Turkish, and Arabic, are published at Constantinople.

transition, moreover, coincided with a period of social disquietude; with disaffection in every class, including the military.

The Nizam (regular force), in place of the Janissaries, was long odious to the Turkish people, and with reason. Violence, guided by ignorance, long formed and organized it. Young men, the single and married alike, were, on the call for a levy, seized in the provinces, wherever they were found, were handcuffed, and driven to the nearest town. They were retained there some days, amidst filth and vermin, to allow time for acting a counterpart of the recruiting scene (minus its humour) in Justice Shallow's house. They were then sent to the coast for embarkation; and on their arrival in the capital, sea-sick and home-sick, were told off to regiments or ships, for life. Felons sent to the bagnio had fairer prospects. Their food was bad and insufficient, their apparel scanty, and their treatment brutal. A captain of a frigate might be named who had his cook beaten to death, in return for a bad dinner. Their doctors in those days were charlatans; their hospitals charnel-houses, where patients perished of heat and neglect in summer, of cold and neglect in winter.* Numbers of men, also, were frozen every winter in the barracks and ships, until the introduction, in 1850, of stoves in both, with port sashes in the latter. But this picture happily belongs to the past: like impressment, with its attendant misery, in another

* The military and naval hospitals at Constantinople were duly organized in the reign of Sultan Abdul Medjid. In regard of space and ventilation they are now superior to most, and in regard of comfort inferior to few, European hospitals.

land. Eighty per cent. of the levies made during that gloomy period of transition never saw their homes again, but died at their post miserably, like galley-slaves at the oar. Deserters avoided their villages through fear of discovery; they went to the hills and joined others who had fled from the conscription. In the brigand's garb they had self-respect and were respected. Those retaken, sentenced to receive a given number of blows, one-third on the soles of the feet, one-third on the posteriors, and one-third on the belly, were beaten to death in the presence of their comrades. Strong men became insensible under the first and generally expired under the second series of blows. One man, a negro sailor, is noted for having survived the third series.

Brigandage, ever recognized in Turkey, has never been considered disreputable there. The exploits of noted brigands have formed the theme of popular chaunts; and, in the Grecian provinces, Klephte and fine fellow have long been synonymous terms. Never political, confined to certain hilly districts in Europe and Asia, it was vexatious, without giving umbrage to authority. Occasionally serving the views of rival or recalcitrant beys, it rarely aimed at more, on its own account, than the interception of traders in ill-guarded passes, or the lifting a troublesome proprietor's sheep. The fate—impalement, or the hook—reserved sooner or later for a brigand-hero, unless timely transformed into a *derbent aga*, deterred all but the desperate or the innately depraved from the career. The Turk reviled by a pasha's minion, till he turned and struck, and the Greek crossed in love by a primate's sensuality, might shake hands at a cavern's mouth, and, banded with the reprobates of the neighbourhood stained with vulgar crime, swear revenge upon society; but the simply idle and wayward might find congenial occupation in feudal service, or loiter away their existence parasitically in towns. Social revolution swelled the ranks of brigandage with men of another stamp, outlaws from necessity. Emboldened by the tanzimat, it descended into the valley, no longer dominated as of yore by an armed gentry and yeomanry. One band under Yanni Catergi frightened Smyrna out of its propriety during two years, and another, led by Moomgi Oglou, long infested the plain of Adrianople. These worthies in time found their way to the bagnio, where they remained several years, the admiration of the incarcerated public, chained, exceptionally, each by the leg to a corner of their cell.

With restored order, and limited military service with fair treatment, brigandage resumed its normal proportions, and its quietude for a while gave hopes of its disappearance. Those hopes have been disappointed. Lulled by the din of the Crimean war, it has revived since the Peace of Paris, re-inforced by an active contingent from the Circassian immigration, giving constant anxiety to provincial governors, and harassing occupation for their police. Its audacity went the length, in 1865, of twice plundering the Imperial post carrying treasure respectively near Silybria and Ismid. We have not to go deep for the cause. Taxation has increased of late years in a greater ratio than national wealth, while the exercise of charity and hospitality—the cardinal virtues of the land during centuries, and still remarkable—has been sensibly on the decline; both in combination tending to produce the embarrassment felt in parts of Christendom on the suppression of monasteries, when men sought to obtain by force or importunity the relief they had been used to receive, with kind words, for the asking.

This, however, was the lesser of two evils developed into unusual proportions by the lenity of the system inaugurated by Sultan Abdul Medjid; who, in the first twelve years of his reign, is said to have sanctioned only two executions, one of a relapsed Armenian renegade, the other of a citizen of Kastambol, convicted, partly on his wife's evidence, of blaspheming the Prophet: the only crime which Mussulmans have agreed to consider heinous and unpardonable. Brigandage on the hill and in the plain continued to be held in check, more or less, by incarceration in noxious prisons; whence some with money or friends might escape, but where many sickened and died, without the negative merit of having served as an example.* But in other regions, with euphonious names, its urban foster-brother revelled free and fearless. Those with places, promotion, monopolies, or contracts to give, and in their default, those in a position to influence them, yielded to seduction in every form which ambition or avarice could suggest to render it acceptable; and so general became the weakness, giving point to the

* In 1858 capital punishment was partially resorted to, with a wholesome effect, in Thessaly. Orientals are moved to reflection through the medium of their senses. The sight of one brigand hung on the theatre of his exploits has more effect than the report of a hundred brigands wasting away in chains in the bagnio. Whatever may be advanced against public executions, it will be admitted that punishment without example has the taint of vengeance—a reproach sure to be levelled in time against the cloistral imprisonment of the 19th century; the horrors of which cannot be imagined, nor conveyed even faintly to the imagination by the pen of a Sterne or a Dickens. Public execution

proverb, *Mal miri deniz dir itchmein domouz dur,** as to lead, in a few years, to the formation of the Tanzimat Council: the rules emanating from which, with a remedial view, showed its gravity. Chamberlains and kislar agas traded with their influence; the kiayas and secretaries of chiefs of departments sang the praises of wide-awake aspirants for favours; cabinet ministers' ladies listened graciously to fair suppliants for marital or filial advancement. The Janissaries in their day had battled with the hydra—official corruption, and, by occasionally lopping off some of its heads, circumscribed its action within comparatively narrow limits. The bare mention of their name, after an interval of forty years, makes the monster hiss with all its tongues. Under the old régime only imperial favourites and a few aspiring spirits willing to stake life against the Aladdin's lamp wealth dared openly indulge in malversation; and retribution, the poetical justice adored in the East, generally lighted on them sooner or later. Some purchased forbearance by expending part of their gains on public works, or on pious endowments.

Allowance may in fairness be made for the necessities of the position. The men who had floated to the surface on the wreck of the orthodox Turkish party were in general needy, unillustrated by descent. They had to acquire wealth to gain influence and make partisans, in default of which they would be mere bubbles on a troubled sea. Each in enriching himself had to wink

is the only guarantee for the mass that criminals of a certain quality do suffer death, and in times of social excitement, that criminals of another stamp are becomingly dealt by.

* The public treasury is a sea, who does not drink of it is a pig.

at his colleague's infirmity, and partisans could only be retained on like conditions. The old nobility, profuse and open-handed, lived on their estates: their ovens were never cool; their pilaf cauldrons never empty. The State was the estate of the new nobility. Redshid Pasha inspired their policy; and on his return in 1846 from his second mission to Paris—an ostracism to allow time for certain jealousies to subside—became their leader, retaining that post with slight intermission until his death in 1858. He, the son of a muderris of Beyazid's mosque, realized in that interval an Oriental's brightest dream of prosperity, unaccompanied by the usual drawback. With the highest honours, with widespread lands and sumptuous palaces, with domestics, slaves, horses and jewels on a profuse scale, he enjoyed imperial and civic favour. Every man in his shadow, said an enthusiastic admirer, became rich. Redshid Pasha had acquired, while representing the Porte abroad, an insight into other forms of government. He admired the system, bating popular control over the national purse, which practically limits the sovereign's prerogative to the faculty of choosing his ministry from a given set, with possibly dissonant views but with common interests. He adopted the phrase, "*Le Roi règne et ne gouverne pas,*" roughly applicable under the old régime, when a Sultan could rarely retain a vizir long in office against the popular voice. Redshid Pasha doubtless saw the distinction between the right to accept a ministry indicated by public opinion, and the power to choose one independent of it; but he may not have clearly noted that the machinery of parties unbased on representation, when understood by the Sultan, would give him mild absolute authority, free from care and trouble. With a pensioned ministry out, eager to supplant the ministry in power, the Sultan would find accord on one point—the will to propitiate his royal favour.

Out of this policy grew the imperial extravagance, of world-wide resonance. Out of it grew the multiplication of offices beyond the requirements of centralization, with the transformation of the Turks from a place-avoiding to a place-seeking people. And out of it grew the medjlis—ingenious contrivance for veiling despotism with the semblance of deliberation and screening responsibility with the show of collective decision. A medjlis (Anglicè, "board,") became attached to every department in the capital, and to every provincial administration. In the capital the members are salaried; in the provinces, though honorary, the position is self-beneficial. Spread like a net over the empire, the medjlises have given occupation and profit to the ruling classes, and maintained mildly their supremacy. In other respects their action has been mediocre, productive of no actual mischief and leading to no positive result. The medjlis has effaced personal responsibility, without affording security against misbehaviour. The chief, if resolute, impresses the members with respect for his position; if timid, he admits their respectful persuasion; if corrupt, he finds abettors; if scrupulous, his credit is undermined by intrigue. Generally speaking, a compromise is effected. The rayas, disappointing legitimate expectations, have shown themselves animated by Byzantine traditions. Some experience in the ways of medjlises has taught the author, with sorrow, that the rayas members are the least, and, with surprise, that the muphti of a medjlis is the most, to be depended upon by the chief, to aid him in spoiling a job or baffling an oppressor. With the progress of centralization, the value of seats in metropolitan medjlises became estimated less by obvious than indirect advantages. Dignity, patronage, and influence, enjoyed with the breezes and views of the Bosphorus in the Sultan's shadow, have made them objects of ambition. Expectant ministers bide their time in a medjlis. Youthful damads learn the art of combining much talk and little work in a medjlis. Dismissed chamberlains find refuge in a medjlis; blessing Allah for non-transportation to a distant pashalic. Men of rank, as a rule, place their sons in one or other of the kalems (public offices); which have again become, as in the days of the Lower Empire, the avenues to wealth and power.

The Tartar conquerors of the Lower Empire saw nothing worth copying in Byzantine centralization. They judged the tree by its fruits, and avoided it. Their ruling idea was to combine metropolitan predominance with modified provincial autonomy. Their ruling policy was to retain the superior administrative functions and military authority in their hands, leaving every community, every sect, every town, every village, to manage its own affairs. They organized their empire in such a guise that it resembled a federation; or rather a congeries of states bound to co-act with the sovereign, for imperial objects. They gave *eski adet* (old custom) the force to resist despotism. Vizirs, imperial delegates, ruled the provinces; potentates within them, but responsible to the lord paramount for ruling according to law and usage. Invested themselves with the power of life and death, they were liable to be bowstrung on the strength of a simple mandate. Brought up in the imperial shadow, their sense of personal dignity and decorous manners impressed the provincials with respect. Wild Albanians, crafty Arabs, and supple Armenians admitted the moral superiority, the instinct of command, of the Ottoman. Each vizir was a Sultan in miniature. The notables of his province kissed the hem of his garment, and stood before him with crossed hands till bidden to sit. They sent him, on his arrival, horses and arms in token of good-will. Their attitude was defensive. The vizir had to obtain all he could, the province to resist giving more than custom sanctioned. The vizir had a right to all fines: a right suggesting incrimination, and nearly sure to be abused, if not by himself, by subordinates in his name. He also shared with the cadi *ilam parasi*, *i.e.*, five per cent. of adjudicated claims, paid by the winner. The provinces supplied, by custom, the viziral abode with provisions and forage for bountiful hospitality, and entertained couriers and others travelling on Government account: a source of irritation in the villages, since those gentry expected *dich parasi* (teeth money) besides. The province also found labour gratis for public works. This obligation, termed *angaria*, gave rise to oppression; but, being in accordance with immemorial Eastern custom, never led to disturbance. Although discountenanced by the tanzimat, *angaria* still exists in a less obtrusive but equally exacting form. The inhabitants of a district, for example, are invited to build barracks for troops, a village for Caucasian immigrants, or a lazzaretto for cholera suspects. Having completed the work, they press for payment, and are put off from month to month with fair words. After a while, making a merit of necessity, they renounce their claim, and are rewarded by seeing their "patriotism" and "devotion" duly lauded in the official Gazette. A loan extracted from the provincials in 1860 was repaid with like coin.

The vizir's residence contained within its precincts the symbols of authority—the armoury, the treasury, the guard-house, and the prison. He had a chamberlain in his kiaya, a minister of the interior in his divan-efendisi, a minister of finance in his defterdar, a minister of police in his tchiaushbashi, a master of the horse in his ser-akhor, and a keeper of the robes in his tchamasha agasi—all domestics, but each with domestics of his own, each with his little circle of parasites, and each intent on filling a purse during his lord's term of office. He had also his body-guard of Albanians, a council (when he chose to convene it) of ayans and ulema, and, more important than all, he had his representative in the capital in his kapou kiaya, through whom he communicated officially with the Porte. The kapou kiaya, necessarily chosen from among the literate efendis of Constantinople, was expected by his employer to inform him of sinister designs, and by the Porte to betray him when necessary.

The vizir came to his province like a Roman proconsul, intent on raising money. He bought his place during the reign of the series of feeble Sultans, when black eunuchs were more esteemed at court than white sages, and was therefore farmer of the revenue, as well as governor. The amount was based on a rough estimate of the revenue derivable from the salian (property-tax), the tithe on sheep, and the unappropriated tithe on wheat and barley. This tithe in many districts belonged to the timarlees and spahis, who, forming in the vigorous days of the monarchy a permanent yeomanry above 100,000 strong, had the reputation of being traditionally content with less than their dues: a distinction never accorded to any other class of tithe recipients, lay or clerical. Celebrated for their skill with the sabre, they were formidable in the Hungarian and Persian wars, and, with the resident gentry, kept up the breed of horses. If the vizir raised the revenue within the limits of custom, he was considered a man with the fear of Allah before his eyes. The amount sufficed to repay his debt to his sarraf, with a balance over for his temporary *rahat* (repose) at Constantinople and the propitiation of his patron in the seraglio: less than is needful now for such objects being required in days of simplicity, when pashas drank water out of brass goblets and their ladies rode to the "sweet waters" in arabas. Arabian horses and Circassians, the chief luxuries, were cheap, so long as India imported but few of the former, and the slave-dealers were freely supplied with the latter. Unusual exaction exposed the vizir to be petitioned against, in terms representing him oppressive in regard of the poor; and, unless he were exceptionally backed, the petition would be attended to, the more readily since the confiscation likely to follow would benefit the privy purse. His loyalty was, as a rule, guaranteed by provincial antagonism and metropolitan ties. But sometimes it happened that a vizir, seduced by acquired popularity, declined a successor; or a deré-bey of influence arrogated to himself the right to ignore the Sultan's delegate, and govern the province himself. In addition to the insult, the audacious mortal might withhold the revenue. The Porte then had to consider whether it was politic to vindicate its authority by sending for his head, or save appearances by confirming his usurpation; the former means being in general first resorted to. The kapougi bashi, bearer of the firman of death, would experience no difficulty, if able to reach the provincial capital; respect for the Sultan's herald would protect and aid him: even the rebel's guard would lower their arms at sight of the imperial firman. The rebel, therefore, advised by his friends at Constantinople of the view taken of his proceeding, endeavoured to have the kapougi bashi waylaid on the road, as if by brigands. If a second herald were thus served, the Porte would then probably send a third to him, with the firman of investiture, and bide its time. It would lure him by flattery or ensnare him by deceit; and, if these arts failed, wait till his errors enabled it to attack him openly. At the worst his power would not survive him. Rebellion was simply local and personal, with all the forms and protestations of loyalty: a demonstration to avert danger, or to extort recognition of office. The dynasty was not menaced, nor conterminous provinces affected by it. One bad man had made it, and his removal quelled it. Neither vengeance nor proscription followed; for the Porte never admitted that the people had rebelled: they had been misled, nothing more. The Ottoman dynasty respected national institutions and usages, and was *pro tanto* respected. Hence the rare spectacle of a vast heterogeneous empire kept together during centuries, by a government often vicious and contemptible, and without a regular army. The Barbary regencies, apparently exceptions, are not so really. Appendages, rather than provinces, of the empire, they had slipped away insensibly from metropolitan control. Their distance made the Porte indifferent to more than the forms of vassalage and the payment of tribute, while their uninterrupted state of hostility—*dar ul harb*—to the "infidel" gave them the air of champions of Islam.

Decentralization also characterized the public expenditure. Every service had its distinct, inalienable revenue, derived from territorial sources. The state domain maintained the imperial dignity. The *vacoofs* (endowments) supported the mosques, the *medressehs* (colleges), the *imarets* (almshouses), the *mektebs* (parish schools), the cemeteries, the fountains, and the pavement of cities; in fine, all the pious and beneficent establishments. The *vacoofs*, previously administered locally under state supervision, were consolidated in Sultan Mahmoud's reign, and placed under the administration of a minister of state (*evcaf naziri*). The aggregate revenue has not been diverted into secular channels; but it is remarked that the *salathin* (royal mosques) obtain more than their share of it, for reparation and decoration, at the expense of humbler objects, as parish mosques, fountains, &c., in disregard of founders' intentions. The unassigned tithes, the salian, and the kharatch defrayed the expenses of the central government, the artillery, the fortresses, and the enrolled Janissaries. A district near the capital defrayed the expense of the gunpowder manufactory. The Navy—justly esteemed the right arm of an empire with coasts bathed by the Mediterranean and the Indian Ocean, by the Red and the Black Seas, by the Persian and Venetian Gulfs, with numerous islands, some of them kingdoms in ancient days—was endowed with vast means, and its chief, the Capitan Pasha, held the third rank in the empire. It was endowed with the revenues of Maina and of the sandjaks of Lepanto and the Negroponte, of the Thracian Chersonesus, of Biga, Codja-eili and Sighala, rich maritime provinces of Asia Minor, and of the Cyclades and Sporades in the Archipelago. A capitan pasha then, ordered to build ships or construct docks, or reproached for keeping the seamen in arrears of pay, would have idly pleaded in excuse want of money—the excuse often justly pleaded since by successive capitan pashas. Had the Turkish navy possessed in 1821 the slightest organization, the Grecian revolt would have been crushed the first year; and had it possessed in latter times its ancient resources, the neutralization of the Black Sea would not have been thought of. Favoured spots in Scio and other islands supplied the ladies of the imperial harem with aromatics and cosmetics. Works of general utility, such as dykes, mountain passes, *bendts* and bridges, were kept in order, and mines were worked, by local personal service given in lieu of taxation with exemption from military requisition. The value of the privilege ensured cheerful fulfilment of the conditions; as long appeared in the comparatively flourishing condition of various communities.

This self-acting machinery, combining despotic power with municipal freedom, and providing ways and means independent of the calculations of a finance minister, was eminently fitted for an empire made up of various races, each tenacious of its own customs, with a traditional right of exemption from fiscal novelties. Purified of its manifold abuses, this system would, in conjunction with the humanizing spirit of the tanzimat and a regular organized police force, have given lustre to the throne, contentment to the people, and maintained the services of the empire on a becoming scale : that is, with the exaction, indispensable in an Oriental state, of personal responsibility. Centralization has proved an inadequate substitute. Ministers virtually irresponsible may favour one department at the expense of the other, the capital at the expense of the provinces; may yield to the solicitations, pressed with varying urgency, of the favourite of the day; may defer to another the necessary expenditure of the current year; while, dependent on the sovereign's favour, they rival each other in obsequious deference to his wishes. There have been, however, obstacles more than sufficient to prevail against the firmest will, coupled with energetic perseverance. Financial ability, statistical data, facile communications, and agents to carry out any scheme of a comprehensive character, have been wanting. Fraud, incompetence, and indolence have not had the check or the spur of publicity; they have, on the contrary, been encouraged by the cuckoo note of the official journals : all is for the best in the best of all possible empires. Moreover, centralization is absorbent in the East; of which the ornamentation of the banks of the Bosphorus, during the last twenty years, with palaces, mosques, kiosks, and yalis, representing untold millions, is ocular evidence to the crowds who daily pass up and down that celebrated strait in the Shirket Hairié steamers. Under the head of public works, little beyond imperial abodes, barracks, and state manufactories have been cared for. The Golden Horn remains as it was before the development of its trade by steam, with indifferent accommodation in the way of quays, landing-places, &c. :

though it is fair to say in extenuation, that European merchant vessels, the general carriers, do not, in virtue of antiquated treaties, pay port or anchorage dues.* Reservoirs, bridges, mines, &c., have deteriorated, through inability or indisposition to hire labour in lieu of the personal service spoken of. Even the bendts in the shadow of royalty, formerly tended by the inhabitants of the adjoining village of Bakché-keuy, have been neglected, so as to cause frequent distress of late years to populous quarters dependent upon them for water. The coal-fields lying within 200 miles of the Bosphorus, on the edge of the Black Sea, ought to furnish motive power for every steamer in the Mediterranean and Euxine; yet they are so ill worked, through want of labour, that their produce is undersold at Constantinople by coal brought from Newcastle. The iron and copper mines respectively of Samakof and Tocat are also comparatively unremunerative. Passing over intermediate districts, each presenting more or less evidence of the inability of the central government to supply the want of self-administration and custom, the dyke of Djezair, formerly under local supervision, has given way, and the

* European vessels pay no port or anchorage dues in any provincial harbour of the Turkish empire. At Constantinople they pay, without reference to tonnage or length of sojourn, dues varying from one to two shillings per vessel, according to her flag. For example: the *Great Eastern* might lie in the Golden Horn for a year and her anchorage due would be twelve piastres. Twelve piastres, once representing as many dollars, now represent two shillings. In 1864, the Porte, at the instance of its admiralty, proposed to improve the harbour accommodation on consideration of a graduated moderate scale of anchorage dues, and in expectation of assent, suitable buoys with mooring chains were brought from England. The European legations declined the proposition.

stagnant water, with malaria resulting therefrom, has completed the desolation of Bassorah, the happily-placed city near the confluence of the Tigris and Euphrates, whose inhabitatants, in the days of the caliphate, prayed in a hundred mosques and bathed in a thousand baths.

Centralization, with divided civil and military authority—the system initiated by Constantine, and perfected by Theodosius—has undoubtedly strengthened the hands of the Porte in regard of its subjects in general; has given it means to deal temperately with disturbances, and quell in a forbearing spirit insurrection; but it may be doubted if it possesses equal ability to repel invasion, counting upon disaffection within. Under the ancient system the nation and the army were identical. The forces on the frontier might be defeated; but the nation, with rights and liberties to defend, was behind. The population, armed from childhood, and skilled in the use of their arms, was sufficiently organized under hereditary nobles to hold strong positions, and to harass troops in a roadless sparsely-peopled country interspersed with morasses. An invader, with spahis on his flanks, with the villages on his path abandoned, and their flocks and herds driven away, found his difficulties increase at every stage. Under the modern system, the army is the measure of national defence; and this expression, applicable elsewhere as well, has peculiar force in an empire with no ties of kindred and few bonds of sympathy with the outer world.

Viewing dispassionately the altered conditions of its rule, the Porte would conciliate those sections of the rayas who, unimbued with "grand ideas," have little more than social aspirations. The Armenians, with Asiatic habits, reading in an antiquarian spirit the history of Armenia, and the placid and industrious Bulgarians, with no traditions worth dwelling upon, would as citizens become loyal subjects, and be a counterpoise to the irascible Greeks; with whom their sympathy, created in other days by common oppression, is on the wane: Greek vanity is more intolerable to them than Turkish pride. Formation of Armenian and Bulgarian regiments—military service being the only reliable bond in an empire composed of various races—should be the first step in the process. Comradeship under one banner, in the absence of marked physical or intellectual differences, assuages sectarian antipathies. The prevalence of Turkish speech would render amalgamation easier than might be supposed. The Armenians speak that language like their own; the Jews speak it as well as Spanish; the easy class of the Sclavic tribes speak it for practical purposes, more or less; and the Greeks in many inland districts of Asia Minor speak no other. The Arabs, exalting the language of the Koran above all dialects, are, with the Kurds, as a rule, least acquainted with Turkish of any part of the population. When, however, so disposed, they easily master a language into the literary composition of which Arabic enters largely; though no amount of practice ever gives them the euphonious Ottoman accent. Arabian recruits soon pick up vulgar Turkish.

An ancient Turk, looking back to the days of his youth, might draw conclusions from the survey not altogether unfavourable to the mixed government of Sultan, Beys, Ulema, and Janissaries. Under it Turkey governed herself (badly he would admit), in her own way, and fought unaided her own battles; than which national pride has no higher aspiration. Under it Turkey was a lightly-taxed and a cheap country. With a reserved fund for war expenses, she never had recourse to usurers to defray current expenditure, and never gave people the trouble to call twice for payment of just claims. With a reasonable income, the old seraglio, one summer palace of modest dimensions, and a few plain kiosks, sufficed for the accommodation and recreation of the imperial family. In those days Turkey clothed her population, and equipped her troops, ships, and fortresses, chiefly with native products. Her gentry then loved the chase, and the exciting game of jerreed, which requires a strong arm, a sure eye, self-possession, and expert horsemanship; and her citizens, led by imperial example, relaxed themselves often with archery on the Okmeidan. The ancient Turk would bid his son note that under that form of government Algiers was a dependency of the empire, Greece an integral portion of it, Egypt a nomination pashalic, and the vassalage of Moldo-Wallachia and Servia something more than nominal. If slightly acquainted with history, he would further remark, with bitterness, that since its subversion the Franks had sat down in Pera and Galata somewhat after the fashion of the Genoese and Venetians in the later days of the Lower Empire, while their ambassadors, far from bringing gifts to the Sultan from their respective courts, as of yore, received instead presents from him for themselves and relatives. *Ai de mi Alhambra!*

CHAPTER III.

Ambassadors at Constantinople, under the Old and the New Régime—Position of Diplomatists at Constantinople—Effect of Obsolete Commercial Legislation—Turkish Manufactures supplanted by Cheap Foreign Fabrics—Novel Attitude of Diplomacy towards the Divan—Presents to Foreign Diplomatists—Oriental Ideas of Presents—Usury, the Cancer of Turkey and Cause of the Low State of Agriculture—Education—Parish Schools—Colleges—Military and Medical Schools—Quarantine—The European Crisis of 1848—Dilemma of the Porte as to Hungarian Fugitives—The Montenegrin Insurrection—Demands of Austria acceded to—Similarity of Turkish and Austrian Policy—Ball given by the French Ambassador in honour of the Second Empire.

With Sultan Abdul Medjid's reign commenced the intermittent sway of European ambassadors at Constantinople. Their position alone showed the significance of the change, effected within a few years, in the relations of Turkey with Christendom. Under the old régime, an ambassador had been tolerated rather than recognized in the capital of the successor of the caliphs. His presentation at court to deliver his credentials was a comedy. Presumed to be hungry, he and his suite were preliminarily regaled at the Sultan's expense, when their awkwardness in eating with their fingers *lokmas*, *kadaif*, and other oriental delicacies, with their unbecoming mode of squatting round the *sinni* (tray), drew from the attendants remarks of pity for their defective education. Possibly the infidels might become excited in the presence of the prophet's vicegerent, and, therefore, in precaution, their swords were taken from them; and to render their appearance tolerable to oriental eyes, their uniforms were covered by pelisses. The cortège was augmented on its way to the seraglio by the ambassador's compatriots in the capital; who, arrayed variously, went to see a show and made one themselves. Thus garnished, the "representative of the most powerful of the kings of the adorers of Jesus," was led into a dimly lit chamber, at one end of which the Sultan sat on a sofa, and having delivered his little oration, more or less faithfully translated by his dragoman, was honoured in return by a stare. He was regarded during his sojourn in Turkey as an accredited spy; and as such, on a declaration of war with his sovereign, was sent to the Seven Towers. In his rare interviews with the Grand Vizir, he sat lower than that functionary, and his dragoman, wearing a *calpak*, knelt at his highness's feet.

An ambassador, under the new régime, has had nothing to complain of on the score of etiquette; he has no longer been stuffed with *moalebbi* and *pilaf*, nor sprinkled with rosewater. He has stood, with sword by his side and cocked hat in his hand, face to face with the Sultan; he has lounged on the same sofa with the Grand Vizir; and his dragoman has smoked amicably with the Reis Efendi, thenceforwards ycleped minister for foreign affairs. The mission of ambassadors under the new régime was ostensibly to encourage or observe Turkey in the new path traced for her by fate. Some of them came out with theories ready cut and dried for her regeneration, and moulded facts to suit; others came with objects in reference to her, and wove theories to justify them. Either process was easy; for Levantines have the art to divine the bias of a man's mind, and the tact to adapt their conversation to it. An influential man in the East, be he Christian or Moslem, may give what shape he likes to the passing cloud—a camel, a weasel, or a whale; he will always find a Polonius ready to echo him. Thence, in part, arises the difficulty of a diplomatist at Constantinople losing a wrong scent. Socially isolated, in a country devoid of periodical literature, he has not opportunities, as in other lands, to correct or confirm his views by friendly intercourse with natives of various callings and opinions. Remarks incidentally dropped in familiar conversation over a chibouque, throw light on doubtful points, suggest further inquiry, and sometimes vexatiously upset a pet theory based on misapprehension or hasty generalization. He has no intercourse with the ruling race, excepting ministers of state, conversing with those ignorant of a western language through an interpreter, when words are weighed and sentences measured; nor with the rayas, beyond a select few who thrive upon their footing at embassies. The dinners of the minister of foreign affairs, at which diplomatists and state dignitaries mingle, give him no insight into national manners; for the table is Parisian, the conversation vapid, and the Faithful drink as though the prophet had enjoined, not forbidden, indulgence in wine. At his dinners, given in return, the guests, leaving prejudices with their slippers at the door, discourse politely with unveiled ladies, and, blandly declining ham in conjunction with turkey, see merit in punch *à la Romaine*.

Schools, hospitals, prisons, factories, tribunals, &c.,

evidences of the degree of a people's civilization, lie not in his way. The Ramazan, key of many riddles, annually cementing the bonds of Islam under a lunar sign, and making the followers of Mahommed during thirty days one family—the newest fashions being replaced for the time by the most ancient usage—seems only an irksome penance; and the Bairam ceremony, in which the Sultan figures in his regal and sacerdotal character, is viewed simply as a brilliant spectacle. The diplomatist resides in winter at Pera, a nondescript suburb peopled by a loosely knit assemblage of various races, whose choicest pastime is gaming, and whose favourite topic of conversation is the demerits of the Turks, the source of their prosperity; and in summer at Therapia or Buyukdereh, pleasant villages on the Bosphorus, where the muezzin's chant is not heard. Outside these chosen spots he sees little with his own eyes. He visits as a matter of course the show mosques and the tekieh of the "dancing dervishes;" strolls in the bazaars; rows in spring up the meandering Lycus to Kiat-haneh, and in summer down the Bosphorus to Ghiok-sou; rides, with reminiscences of Constantine and Belisarius, from Yedi Koulé to Eyoub, the ancient Greek wall or a Turkish cemetery on either hand; and goes perhaps, in duty bound, to Khalki to see the tomb of an ambassador interred in that fragrant island. A talented Oriental on a mission to the court of St. James's or the Tuileries, located in Leicester Square or in a corresponding quarter of Paris, in habitual communication with disaffected natives and prejudiced foreigners, would occupy somewhat an analogous position; and if we might fairly expect to read in his despatches, mingled with shrewd remarks on social anomalies, direful forebodings drawn from conversation with sanguine Fenians or morbid socialists, we should cease to smile at strange tales in blue or yellow books: we should cease to wonder at the ever recurring announcement during a century, by wise men from the West, of the imminent collapse of the Turkish empire, and should ascribe it to a careful notation of the fissures in the edifice, with inobservance of its ivy-covered props.

Ambassadors under the new régime, how much soever disagreeing on some points, have cordially agreed with each other in enforcing the commercial legislation founded on treaties applicable to bygone days, which has made Turkey virtually a colony after the old colonial fashion, bound to admit the products of every European state, *without reciprocity*, at a uniform low rate of duty,* reduced lower by partial tariffs and by a system of smuggling from which she is not allowed to protect herself; † and they with other foreign counsellors have, in their wisdom, led her in a few years through the cloudy maze of financial

* The treaties of commerce between Turkey and European states, based on the original treaty between Solyman II. and Francis I., were merged in the treaty of Balta Liman, 1841. Until then, foreign products had been charged in Turkey 3 per cent. duty. This import duty was increased 2 per cent., Turkey consenting at the same time to abolish interior transit dues, which had been arbitrary and vexatious, and restrict herself to one export duty of 12 per cent. In 1862 another commercial treaty was made between Europe and Turkey, enabling Turkey to levy 8 per cent. duty on imports and 8 per cent. on exports, the latter to be reduced annually 1 per cent., till it fall to 1 per cent. This is a great improvement; but, in the name of free trade, one might ask, why has not Europe granted reciprocity to Turkish products in her markets?

† European merchant vessels in Turkish ports are, by a strained interpretation of treaties, free from the visit of custom-house employés.

expediency to the Austro-Hispano-Italian platform of an annual deficit and increasing debt. Free trade, in that sense, has ruined Turkey's manufactories, and politico financial economy has brought her to a chronic state of pecuniary embarrassment.

Various causes had contributed to render the Turks commercially indifferent about their capitulations with Europe until early in the present century, when Greek traders pointed out a field for enterprise in Turkey, and imparted to the manufacturers of the West the tastes of her inhabitants. Turkish manufactures flourishing in the memory of man then began inevitably to decay, throwing out of employment permanently those classes, always existing in old communities, unable to devote themselves to the production of raw materials. The muslins of Aleppo, the silks of Brussa and Damascus, the cottons of Tocat and Kastambol, the cloths of Tirnova and Selivria, the shawls of Angora, the shalis, muslins, and embroidery of Constantinople, have become in great part replaced by wares got up for the Eastern market. The people, at first, captivated by the difference of price, exulted, but found out too late that cheapness in a country unswayed by fashion ill compensates for durability. Garments made from their own rich manufactures wore becomingly to the last, while those made with cheap foreign materials wear shabby from the first. The army has specially suffered by the change, which favours collusion between officials and contractors. The manufactures of arms in Sparta (ancient Pisidia), Damascus and Constantinople have sunk under the competition of Liége and Birmingham. The manufacture of Turkey carpets still flourishes, but is beginning to be affected by the cheap bright-coloured carpets of the West.

The divan was at first perplexed by the novel attitude of diplomacy. It seemed menacing. An ambassador might speak his mind to the Sultan about his ministers, and represent Turkey in any light he pleased to his court. He might write ugly despatches on the report of a disappointed dragoman, or of a provincial consul out of humour with his pasha. But the divan after a while discovered, to its great relief, that diplomatists, like ordinary mortals, could inhale voluptuously the fumes of the moral opium of the East—adulation, and accept smilingly tokens of imperial munificence, and were, therefore, it thought, unlikely to be hypercritical : as events showed. Every minister of state under the new régime who has benefited himself and friends more than usual by office has had an ambassador for his friend and embassy dragomans for panegyrists.

The readiness of diplomatists to accept presents from the Sultan for themselves or friends, and ask favours from the Porte for their satellites, must be ascribed to misapprehension of Oriental habits of thought. The objections to similar condescension in the West exist with infinitely greater force in the East, where the line between a present and a bribe is not sharply defined, and where everything is estimated at its money's worth. An Oriental conveys to his hearers an idea of a woman's beauty, or a child's comeliness, by stating the price which one or the other would fetch, if a slave, in the market. An Oriental knows nothing of ideal values. His sovereign's portrait is valued for its setting; and as for a lock of a lady's hair, even Hafiz the

Persian Anacreon would have preferred a bunch of roses to it. A gift of a rare manuscript or a bas-relief from an ancient sarcophagus would, through Oriental indifference to ideal value, excite no remark; not so diamonds or Arabian horses, which directly represent money. The highest type of a present in the East is money; in which form the Sultan gratifies docile chamberlains or assiduous ministers of State. An Oriental, whatever his station, is equally flattered by a present of a purse of gold or a snuff-box of like value. He would probably, being eminently practical, prefer the former: a view shared not many years ago by an ambassador, who, on being informed that Sultan Abdul Medjid had in token of his esteem ordered a snuff-box worth 1,000*l.* to be given him, sent word to say he would rather have the money. Versed in the ways of the court jeweller, his Excellency guessed that, although the Sultan's account would be debited the full amount, the box would be of less value. The presents given to, or out of regard for, diplomatists, supplemented by offerings to distinguished persons on special missions, or on their travels, during the last twenty years, represent a large sum. The amount of this tribute to necessity, as it may be termed, cannot be accurately stated, but is believed to be approximately known, and, in face of the habitual indebtedness of every department, has excited comment from natives and foreigners. Incurred in a constitutional country, such expenditure would suggest questions.

There is another point from which the question has to be viewed. An Oriental, seeing a man accept presents from one, argues his readiness to accept them from any other quarter, and one might as soon persuade him to the contrary as make him believe in more than a shade of distinction between waltzing ladies and dancing girls; therefore when he sees an ambassador press a claim of the Pacifico kind, he suspects a personal motive: his Excellency accepts diamonds from the Sultan, what should restrain him from taking diamonds, or their equivalent, from any other person? Two pashas were conversing one day during Sultan Abdul Medjid's reign about a bribe believed by them to have been given to an embassy to induce it to urge a compensation claim on the Porte, which even the claimant's compatriots thought exaggerated: they even specified the amount given respectively to the ambassador, the secretary, and the first dragoman. At this stage, a European present in the room interposed with—"Gently, Efendis, this is impossible: that embassy is not to be bribed, directly or indirectly." "My friend," rejoined one of the pashas, "your ambassador is a clever man, so is his secretary, and his dragoman is sharp-witted; is it likely they would back a claim of that kind for nothing? be quiet, we are not asses." An Oriental has no great respect for human law, but he has a sense of equity. He will give a man credit for doing justice, but never injustice, gratis. Another trait is worthy of note. Bribes taken by an inferior functionary are believed in the East to be shared by his superior, on the principle of prize money.

The commencement of Sultan Abdul Medjid's reign was a favourable opportunity to lead Turkey forward in the thorny path of civilization, of which she had only tasted the bitter fruits, conscription and taxation, before *eski adet* (old custom) should partially renew its sway. The nation was pliant through exhaustion, and humbled by misfortune; but not broken in to view innovation with apathy. The young Sultan was auspiciously disposed. His father's ministers and courtiers had cast their lot in with reform, and dared not retrograde: reaction would have been their ruin. Unfortunately her patrons looked down upon her from the height of their own civilization, and urged upon her conditions of progress beyond her powers. They should have looked back to the history of Europe at that period when convictions were realities, free-thinking was heresy, and intolerance was a virtue, when astrology was esteemed a science, when spirits were exorcised and witches burnt, when the evil eye was shunned and comets were portents, and have asked themselves how their ideas would then have been received. The minister of the day, in advance of his age, while admitting the abstract merit of his interlocutor's theories on tolerance, imprisonment, slavery and civil rights, would have said:—"Go to yonder priest, yonder soldier, yonder mechanic, yonder farmer, and hear what they have to say: each of them has to be convinced."

Religious disabilities, requiring tact and patience to deal with in all countries, slavery—the slavery arrayed in shawls, interwoven with the affections of society from the sovereign born of a slave downwards—and civic inequality, were delicate subjects. Inveighing against them at that period was simply talking to the wind. But there were other topics to dwell upon, involving no religious or sentimental feelings. Turkey has still one paramount evil—usury; and two pressing wants—popular education and medical aid. Usury, sordid unscrupulous usury, is the cancer preying on the vitals of Turkey. Bad enough in the cities, where wit meets wit, it revels oppressively in the rural districts. Individuals, under the denomination of *selem*, taking advantage of the peasants' ignorance of the state of markets, lend them money on the security of their forthcoming crops; they add together the sum advanced and the stipulated interest—often three per cent. per month—and, setting an arbitrary value on the crops, force repayment, in money or in kind as suits their convenience. The lender is in some instances in league with the aga of the district, or with a trading consul; he may be the aga or the consul himself, lending in his private and recovering in his official capacity. Herein lies the secret of the low state of agriculture: the cultivators require advances which are only to be obtained on onerous conditions; the usurer, the tithe-farmer, and the tax-gatherer combine against them, and often, to satisfy the demands of the last, they are forced to listen to the offers of the first.

Education, though neglected, has ever been prized in Turkey. Mahalleh (parish) schools were established in the towns and boroughs in the reign of Soliman II., 300 years ago. They still exist, but with no higher objects. The children of each parish, rich and poor, mingle in them, and the first day of a child going to school is a family *fête*. The little novice, his fez ornamented with gold coins or his mother's diamonds, is escorted in triumph by his future companions from his home to the school, and the juvenile procession, the prettiest sight of Constantinople, is regarded by the spectators with affectionate interest. A pasha's son is generally attended in the school by a black slave boy of his own age. Nothing is learned there beyond the rudiments of Turkish, and docile manners. The *Rushdieh* schools, of recent creation in the cities, teach only oriental literature; yet with a trifling annual expenditure for educational appliances and competent salaried teachers, they as well as the *mahalleh* schools might be elevated to a level with the requirements of the age. The imperial pages' school, distinguished by its comparatively refined tone, would admit of development into an oriental Eton. The medressehs (colleges) might possess other than theological chairs. With means elsewhere for preparatory education, the imperial military, naval, and medical schools—where every expense, including pocket-money, is defrayed by the Government —would produce more than a showy result. Much time is passed in them in gaining elementary knowledge, acquired in Europe by private tuition. The scholars have in general to learn their own native language, involving a smattering of Arabic, and gather some knowledge of history and geography, before commencing the study of special sciences. The military schools have had a further disadvantage in the sons of influential individuals obtaining high rank while students.* These favoured youths have no other than abstract motives for study, and their example acts banefully on their companions, who thus too early learn the shortest road to advancement. In the medical schools the scholars have first to

* In 1853 there were in the military school at Constantinople among the scholars under twenty years of age, one lieutenant-general, two major-generals, one colonel, sons of ministers of state. One of the said major-generals, Mahzar Pacha, left the school in 1854 to command a brigade of cavalry in Bulgaria.

learn some French, through the want of appropriate Turkish terms. Although alive to the value of military and medical knowledge, the Porte has not seen fit to encourage popular instruction. The attentive group in the mosque gathered round a muderris expounding the Koran and the Hadis might listen eagerly to a professor of natural philosophy; and the earnest crowds hanging on the lips of the impassioned Ramazan preachers might have ears for a political discourse. In its apprehension of the possible effects of diffusion of knowledge among the dominant race, the Porte has overlooked the impatience likely to be generated by superior scholastic attainments in the subject races.

The friends of Turkey might have thundered against usury, taking for their text this verse of the Koran: "They who live by usury will rise on the day of resurrection like one whom Satan has soiled by his touch,—they who, warned of the iniquity, abandon usury, will obtain pardon for the past,—they who relapse into usury will be cast into the fire and remain there eternally." They might have urged the improvement of schools, the amelioration of prisons and the creation of hospitals, with the Koran in their hands; and then the people, benefited morally and physically by civilization, would have learned to appreciate the motives of its propagators. Quarantine, the undoubted boon of civilization, has been sceptically viewed from the outset. Death in the shape of plague has seemed kept out by it, but in the form of cholera it has leaped the barrier and seized its prey notwithstanding.

More than all, Turkey required a long period of repose, to habituate her people to the new system, to lessen the pressure of military service on the Turkish race—one cause of its comparative numerical decline—and to restore her finances by the gradual development of the resources of the country: a natural result—unless checked by war's alarms—of the security for life and property guaranteed by the tanzimat. The duty of every friend of Turkey was to counsel her to avoid giving needlessly any cause of offence either to Austria or Russia. With respect to Russia, the motives for preserving good neighbourhood with her were self-evident. With respect to Austria, they were less obvious, but more valid in a moral sense. Austria had long been a loyal friend to Turkey; she had spared her in the day of triumph; had never since Tekeli's time fomented insurrection among her rayas; and had no presumed designs on any part of her territory. The integrity of the Ottoman Empire had been a canon of faith with Prince Metternich, and respect for it in 1814 had perpetuated the complication of Austrian and Turkish interests at either extremity of the Ragusan territory. This duty became apparent when, with reviving strength, with habitual indifference to past sufferings, and with a fairly-drilled army, the Ottomans—a warrior race, imbued with the traditions of their conquering period, and descended from ancestors who gave their children arms for playthings—after some years of inaction, began again to indulge in flattering dreams. The chief feature of the Ottomans, as of every dominant race, has ever been pride: their bane has been self-commendation. Believing themselves the elect of Islam, devoid of the means of comparison with other nations by travel and study, they have ignored their defects, and have discredited rumour thereon. The sword of Ali, Mahomet's first and truest follower, remains in their possession, and they have long fancied themselves as able as ever to wield it. Unaccustomed to reason on cause and effect, they refer everything to predestination or special providence. Allah had sorely chastised them, but he had pardoned them. Nearly all the provinces of their vast empire were tranquil under the gentle rule of Sultan Abdul Medjid. Mecca rejoiced in an increased annual pilgrimage, unmolested by heretic Wahabites. Plague had departed from the land. The Turks felt new born. In this mood the European crisis of 1848 found them. They heard of crowns falling, of states rocking on the wave of revolution, of ministers who had ruled the feverish masses of civilization fleeing in dismay from their homes. Tranquil themselves, outside the storm circle, they gloried in their prophet's institutions.

As the flame spread in Hungary, they watched its progress with intense interest. Why might they not rebuild the fallen mosque at Ofen? They sympathized with the Hungarians, their Christian cousins. They opened communication with the patriots through their agents at Widdin, encouraged in their equivocal course by a "friendly" embassy. The hearts of Turks and Greeks for once beat in unison, for success to Hungary. In vain. Betrayed by their jealousies, and oppressed by Russia, the Hungarian leaders and their immediate followers closed a noble struggle by a sorry flight. After having harangued like kings and striven like knights, they crossed the Danube, fugitives, and claimed Turkish hospitality; as their ancestors had often done before them. It was accorded without hesitation, but with misgivings. Rightly advised, the Porte would have had steamers stationed in time at Varna to convey them far away, after the purgation of their quarantine at Widdin. That would have dulled the edge of Austria's demand for their surrender, if then made, and have saved Turkey the expense and waste of life incurred by calling out the first division of the *rediff* to be ready to support her refusal. Austria, backed by Russia, demanded their surrender, in virtue of a treaty for giving up deserters and refugees from either side, excepting apostates. The Porte saw, in the exceptional clause, a mode of escape from the dilemma created by the opposing claims of international obligation and civic duty. She held out to the refugees congregated at Schumla inducements to conversion. The shining example of the French taken at the battle of Nicopolis—who remembered the divine warning, "Whoever shall deny me before men, him also will I deny before my Father which is in heaven," and who all suffered decapitation, save a few nobles reserved for ransom—was unheeded. The majority of the Hungarian refugees embraced Islamism; the minority, a distinguished few, were conveyed, according to agreement, to Kutaieh, where they remained sequestered a year, honourably and liberally maintained at the Porte's expense.

Thus far Turkey had acted well; had reconciled policy with humanity. Thus far, England's representative had merited applause in recommending his Government to send a demonstrative squadron to the Hellespont, and in throwing the weight of his personal influence on the side of the unfortunate. Both, in their zeal, went further. Not content with the merit of having shielded the Hungarian refugees from political vengeance, one advised conferring and the other showered honours upon them. Several were created pashas, and many received field-officer's rank in the Turkish service. One might draw a parallel by supposing high rank in the British navy conferred upon the commanders of the *Alabama* and *Shenandoah*, on their taking refuge in England. Austria saw with vexation, easily imagined, the coveted title of pasha, withheld from the noblest rayas, accorded to men termed rebels by her. She saw with indignation officers recently in arms against her, enrolled in the army of her ally. Russia felt equally this violation of international decorum, but was silent thereon. The Porte measures weakness by quiescence under scorn or ill-usage. She knew the gravity of the insult offered to Austria, and attributed her placidity, if not to fear, to inability to back her words with deeds. Thenceforwards, during three years, Austria was treated like a second-rate power in discredit. Austria's claims were neglected: Austrian influence became a by-word in the circles of Pera and Galata.

Austria at length roused herself, on the occasion of a feud between the Montenegrins and the Hirzegovinians for the disputed territory of Zetta and Crajova; which, long tacitly considered neutral ground for common pasturage, had been claimed by the Pasha of Scodra in 1848 as Turkish soil, and as such entitled to protection. The Montenegrins, bent on annexation, had overbearingly abused the common right. The Porte thought the hour arrived for reading a lesson to Montenegro—perennial source of irritation, nucleus of disaffection in the northern provinces—and encouraged by an influential embassy, set about the task in earnest, and in a way which indicated an intention of reduction rather than repression, such as the case demanded. She sent in the autumn of 1852 an army from Monastir to the disaffected region under Omar Pasha; who, zealous for his adopted faith, promised (it is said) the Sultan to extract from the Montenegrins the arrears of *kharadj* due since their last revolt. That revolt had occurred in 1767, and is briefly mentioned by Wassaf Efendi, historiographer of the empire, thus: "The Montenegrins, A.H. 1181, excited by detestable priests, and led on by a bad individual, refused to pay their *kharadj*. The affair having been examined into, the Scheick ul Islam issued his *fetwah* that if they did not submit the men should be made an example of, and the women and children be carried into slavery. This *fetwah* was communicated to the mountaineers; and on their refusal to submit, the Porte ordered Mehemet Pasha of Bosnia, and Mehemet Pasha of Roumelia, to carry out the sentence. They assembled troops and munitions of war, and attacked the mountains in two columns." The Turks, after their success, again abandoned the mountain, carrying away some women and children. The inhabitants, most of whom had fled, then returned, and from that time Montenegro had remained practically independent. The Porte sent also a light squadron to the Adriatic, to blockade the coast, and aid in provisioning the army. Concurrently, about sixty Montenegrins * at Constantinople were arrested as a precautionary measure, and

* There are generally above a thousand Montenegrins at Constantinople under their own chiefs; they work chiefly as gardeners, and after a few years return with their earnings to their families in the Black Mountain.

thrown into prison ; whence they were in time released through the good offices of the Russian legation. Turkey, misinformed about the temper of Christendom on certain points, underrating the effect of pseudo-religious sympathy, had made a false move ; and, instructed by it, her campaign against the Montenegrins ten years later, conducted more warily and with avowed reasonable views, proved successful in a military sense. Austria was ill-disposed to see the mountain overhanging the waters of Cattaro ruled by a pasha. Western Europe was ill-prepared to see a community self-administered the greater part of a century, reduced to the condition of kharatch-paying rayas. The vladika was Russia's pensioner.* Austria being the nearest interested, espoused the cause of the Montenegrins, and made that the opportunity to settle a long account with the Porte. She sent Field-

* Prince Daniel (Vladika), born in 1823, succeeded to the princedom in 1851. He went to Petersburg the ensuing year, and was acknowledged by the Emperor Nicholas, who pensioned him, secular prince of Montenegro.

October, 1854, a Russian envoy came to Cettigno, and tried without success to induce Prince Daniel to organize a Christian insurrection in Bosnia and the Hirzgovin.

The Turkish plenipotentiary to the peace conference at Paris, 1856, maintained the Porte's rights over Montenegro. In that year Prince Daniel, in a memoir addressed to the cabinets of Europe, demanded for Montenegro recognition of independence, and possession of the port of Antivari with the intermediate coast. The following year Prince Daniel went to Paris to solicit French protection, which was promised.

13th August, 1860. Prince Daniel was assassinated in revenge at Cattaro, and was succeeded by his cousin, Prince Nicolas. Prince Nicolas, encouraged by France, from whom he expected material aid, made war against the Porte in 1861-62, and was signally defeated. He declared himself, by the treaty of Cettigno, Sept. 1862, the sultan's vassal, and consented to the construction of a military road through his territory, with a Turkish fort at either extremity. Through French influence the construction of the road and forts is given up.

Marshal Count Leiningen, in January, 1853, to Constantinople with a friendly autograph letter from the Emperor to the Sultan, and a list of demands for the consideration of the divan. This list comprised:—1. Abandonment of the intention to build a fort on Sutorina, the strip of Turkish soil dovetailed into Dalmatia, connecting Le Bocche di Cattaro with Bosnia. 2. Recall of the Montenegrin expedition. 3. Non-employment of Hungarian refugees with the army of the Danube. 4. Consideration for Austria's treaty right to protect the Roman Catholics of Bosnia and Albania. 5. Indemnity for damages caused to Austrian subjects by the forays of Turkish borderers,* and for exaction of excessive dues by local authorities from the Austrian company licensed to fell timber in Bosnia:—a licence, it may be observed, much abused by that company, with irreparable damage to the forests, giving rather Turkey the right to claim compensation from it. 6. Respect for the exception to the treaty of Balta Liman in Austria's favour. Count Leiningen held out the prospect of war as the alternative, while the Austrian embassy packed up ready for departure. The Porte hesitated at compliance, and talked boldly of calling out 100,000 rediff. Turkey would have made a good figure in a war with Austria alone, taking into account the elements of disaffection in various parts of the Austrian dominion ever watching for their opportunity.

* By an ancient treaty between Austria and Turkey, the Porte engaged to make good losses sustained by Austrian subjects through the acts of Barbary corsairs. In case of failure therein, Austria to have the right to compensate them by forays on the Turkish territory. The Turks, unwilling to be thus vicariously chastised, naturally retaliated when that right was exercised. Hence arose the hereditary border feud between the two empires.

But Russia's concurrence with Austria was undisguised; her co-operation loomed in the distance; the Western Powers were silent. So Count Leiningen obtained the substance of his demands except in regard of the fifth, which was balanced by counter Turkish claims for border outrages; and the Constantinopolitans, whose credulity is marvellous, readily persuaded themselves that the object of his visit had been to obtain the Sultan's permission for the young emperor's coronation. The Turkish official newspaper announced his arrival and departure in one paragraph, and merely stated for the information of the public that he had come to Constantinople on a particular mission. His prompt success was facilitated by the impending mission of Prince Mentchikoff; though, if Russia had reckoned as part of her game the continuance of Austria's rancour, she deceived herself. Satisfied with *her* gain, Austria, on the return of her envoy, directed her agents in the Levant to refrain from displaying exultation, and to endeavour to re-establish amicable feelings between the two empires. Austrian and Turkish statesmen understand each other; each has the same evasive, dissembling, procrastinating policy, derived from ruling respectively an ill-assorted empire, peopled by various races some in antagonism to others, and therefore each is inclined to make allowances for the other's position.

The Montenegrin expedition cost Turkey a grievous expenditure of men and horses, through their exposure with scanty food and clothing to inclement weather; and its recall, at foreign dictation, when in occupation of the passes leading to Cettigno, with an advanced guard of irregulars within five hours' distance of that city, weakened the wholesome effect which its advance had produced on the minds of the Bosnians and Hirzegovinians.

The sojourn of Count Leiningen at Constantinople was marked by an event which, though of a social character, was, nevertheless, a sign of the times. The French ambassador threw open his saloons, freshly decorated with impannelled N's and eagles each surmounted by an imperial crown, and gave a grand ball in honour of the inauguration of the second empire. The preceding ball given in them had been in honour of the inauguration of the second republic; and sixty years earlier, the French ambassador of that day had assembled his countrymen at the same spot to celebrate the Revolution; when, according to local tradition, the guests, excited by champagne and patriotism, sung the Marseillaise in chorus, and, led by their host, danced half frenzied the Carmagnole round a tree of liberty planted in the garden near the chapel of St. Louis. Pera has many associations with departed glories. Polish Street recalls to mind the time when the King of Poland had his representative at the Sublime Porte, and the Austrian internuncio inhabits the palace inhabited of yore by the Venetian Bails. The Italians at Pera look upon that palace as theirs by right, and in the excitement of '48 caballed over their cups in coffee-houses, theatrically vowing to go and take it; the rumour of which, alarming the internuncio, made him send to the Porte for an armed force to protect his residence. The assemblage of the Turkish ministers and other functionaries of high rank in gala costume at the ball shewed the change which had come over their thoughts, in regard of France, since the period of Louis Philippe's vacillating reign: and there was reason for their deference to the representative of French power, for the cloud long floating over Jerusalem, formed of vapour exhaled by the heat of the second Napoleonic era, now cast an ominous shadow on Constantinople.

CHAPTER IV.

Louis Napoleon's Choice of a War Policy — The Rival Christian Powers in the East—The Firman restoring to the Roman Catholics the Holy Places—The Porte summoned to carry it into Effect —Menacing Attitude of France—Weakness of the Turkish Policy —The Matter in Dispute—Attitude of England—Question of the Holy Places—Russian Intervention—Mission of Prince Mentchikoff—Passive Attitude of the Porte—English View of the Situation.

Louis Napoleon, in adopting the rule of his illustrious uncle's internal policy, foresaw the external consequences. Preparing for war from the outset of his presidency, the question was, where to make it when the hour should arrive for encircling the foreshadowed imperial crown with a military halo? Three courses presented themselves. First, war with Germany for the Rhine boundary. But that, with his power unconsolidated, would arouse Europe: isolation and dethronement might follow, without the preamble of a splendid drama like that closed with the drop-scene of *les adieux de Fontainebleau*. Secondly, war with England. But that, although an hereditary passion with his people, would be equally hazardous. England might again rally nations to her banner, again marshal a royal crusade against dangerous doctrines. Thirdly, war with Russia. Distance, inadequate maritime resources, and sad but not dishonouring recollections, were deterrent considerations. Nevertheless it appeared the only choice.

A motive and an ally were required. The problem was, to irritate Russia and invert England's normal attitude with respect to France. There was but one field, Turkey; and in that field but one spot where the solution could be found, Jerusalem. The means were, to excite the jealousy of Russia in regard of her influence in Turkey, and make that react on the susceptibility of the English in regard of the integrity of the Ottoman Empire; to place Russia in the dilemma of surrendering her ascendancy in Turkey, or of sustaining it in a manner admitting of construction into designs on the Sultan's rights. War once lighted in the East, none could discern ulterior consequences; and be they what they might, France in alliance with England might reasonably expect to leave off a gainer. Louis Napoleon chose that course, and made the Roman Catholic religion his instrument to prepare the way.

During a long period the Roman Catholic religion, under French protection, had acted a part in Turkey analogous to the part since acted by the Greek religion, under Russian protection. But as the Catholics in the East were comparatively few in number, it had caused no uneasiness to the Porte, then too powerful to heed Christendom, and had simply proved vexatious to rival powers. The Protestant powers of that day combated Catholicism in the East with the Greek religion, which the Jesuits were attempting to undermine, and showed their influence occasionally by carrying the nomination of a meritorious churchman to the patriarchal chair: pre-eminently of the learned Cyril Lucari, brightest ornament of the Oriental church since the Moslem conquest of Constantinople. Turkey and Europe would both have gained if England and Holland had resumed that lucid policy on renewing their intercourse with Turkey after the civil and international troubles of the seventeenth century. Free from the sectarianism of the East—for only in latter days have they attempted to plant Protestantism in an ungenial soil—they might then have proved instrumental in purifying the Greek church of many abuses, and might have competed with Russia in the field of protection. They might have prevailed upon the Porte, in its own interests, to consent to the nomination of the Greek patriarch and primates for life, and thus have prevented the development of a system of unexampled simony.

In other days, long previously, French ascendancy in the Holy Land, fruit of the Crusades, had deprived the Greeks of the position which their numbers and the edicts of Omar and succeeding caliphs rendered incontestable. But only for a while. With the resumption of Moslem rule in Syria the Greeks recovered it. In their turn they made the Catholics taste the bitterness of religious intolerance, and were naturally indifferent about the preservation of monuments commemorative of their rival's ascendancy. The Ottoman conquerors confirmed the edicts of the caliphs in their favour. The feud between the Greeks and the Latins in Palestine has continued ever since, a scandal to Christianity and a jest to Islam.

Thus things were, when, in 1740, the French ambassador at the Porte obtained a firman from Sultan Mahmoud I., to restore to the Roman Catholics sundry holy sanctuaries at Jerusalem (not particularized) alleged to have been usurped by the Greeks; against whom a charge of desecration of the tombs of Godfrey de Bouillon, of Guy de Lusignan, and of others, were urged as a further and particular grief. Generally speaking, an unscrupulous ambassador and a complaisant vizir have sufficed to obtain a firman for any purpose not militating against the letter of the Koran; and the one in question may have sprung from such a combination. Be that as it may, the said firman remained a dead letter, like many others: war and revolution gave France other matters to think about; and, as if it were non-existent, many firmans concerning the Holy Places were subsequently given, down to the reign of Sultan Mahmoud II., confirmatory of the rights of the Greeks.

Louis Napoleon brought that firman to light, and menacingly summoned the Porte to act up to its tenor. Circumstances, however, had widely changed in the interval. The subjects of the Porte of the Oriental church had increased in numbers, wealth, and intelligence; many of them, the Moldavians, Wallachians, and Servians, had acquired self-administration; and Russia had gained an importance in the European scale with a preponderance in regard of Turkey which naturally constituted her the officious advocate of her co-religionists. Circumstances had strangely altered since Sully, speaking of his doubt of Russia consenting to join St. Pierre's projected peace association,* said: "Si le grand duc de Muscovie ou Czar

* The Abbé St. Pierre, in the reign of Henri IV., committed to paper a vision of universal peace among Christian nations by arbitration, which was seriously entertained by that monarch and his minister. A dispute between two nations was to be submitted to the arbitration of all. In case of the party declared in the wrong proving refractory, he was to be proceeded against in accordance with the award of the international Areopagus and compelled to submission.

de Russie, que l'on croit être l'ancien knés de Scythie, refuse d'entrer dans l'association, on doit le traiter comme le Sultan de Turquie, le depouiller de ce qu'il possède en Europe et le releguer en Asie, où il pourra, sans que nous nous en melions, continuer tant qu'il voudra la guerre avec les Persans et les Turcs."

The zeal of the czars in behalf of their co-religionists in Turkey may have been a cloak to cover ambitious projects with; but it reflected the sympathies of the Russian nation, and thereby became an apparent duty from which they might, when convenient, plead inability to exonerate themselves. Nevertheless, they cannot fairly claim credit for disinterestedness at any period in regard of the Turkish Greeks. Twice during the eighteenth century the Czarina excited them to revolt with promises of aid, and each time abandoned them to the vengeance of their incensed masters; and during the civil war from 1820 to 1827, in the Morea and Attica, when they were exposed there and elsewhere in the Turkish dominions to the excesses of a dominant race, stung in its pride and stimulated by fanaticism, the Czar remained a tranquil spectator of their exertions and their sufferings: not through any misapprehension of the nature of the struggle, for his ambassador at Constantinople had, as early as July, 1821, expressed in a note to the Porte his sovereign's fear lest the "measures of the Ottoman government should give the revolution the character of a legitimate defence against the total destruction of the Greek nation and its religion;" but out of deference to the tenets of the "Holy Alliance," which made no distinction between a patriot fighting for his cause in the face of heaven and a carbonaro armed with the assassin's blade.

For the sake of the doubtful claims of a Roman Catholic minority, France called upon the Porte to irritate the feelings of ten millions of her subjects of the Oriental church, and to subject Russia to the mortification of seeing her influence lessened in their eyes and in the eyes of Europe. This was the able scheme devised to place Russia in the alternative of surrendering her prestige or of provoking war. Intimidation, and instilling into the mind of the divan an exaggerated idea of France's power under a Buonaparte, were resorted to as subordinate action. A French fleet threatened to bombard Tripoli on an ignoble pretext; * other Turkish towns were menaced with similar visits, and the French ambassador at the Porte talked of solving the Holy Places question summarily by occupying Jerusalem with a French army. The Porte was thus led to believe in the peril of offending France. Alarmed, she lost her presence of mind. Instead of making a candid appeal to the enlightenment

* Two French soldiers having deserted from Algiers in 1852, came to Tripoli; these became Moslems, and were enrolled, with the knowledge of the French consul, in the Turkish army. They found the fast of Ramazan unpalatable; they infringed it, and were punished accordingly. Escaping then from the barracks, they went to the French consulate, proclaimed themselves Christians, and claimed protection. The pasha of Tripoli demanded them from the consul, but in vain. He could not seize them under the French flag; but the delinquents having one day left its protection to go to a grog-shop in the neighbourhood, were laid hold of by the police and reconveyed to the barracks. The French consul demanded their surrender, and being refused, reported the affair to Paris. Three weeks afterwards a French fleet arrived at Tripoli with orders to bombard the city if the men in question were not on board in twenty-four hours. Its commander invited the European inhabitants to place themselves in safety on board ship. Thus summoned, the pasha had no choice. The men were given up, and the pasha was recalled from his post as a further satisfaction to the French government.

of Europe, to extricate her from the strait in which opposing forces compressed her, she tried to wriggle out of it. She advised the Sultan to promise the Czar the maintenance of the *status quo* at Jerusalem, and afterwards evaded performance. She ostensibly reviewed favourably the claims of the Greeks, and gave to the Latins the key which opened the gates of Janus. It seems very like fiction, but it is true, that a key, a porter, and a star were the elements out of which grew the late eventful war with Russia: the question being if the Latins should possess a key to the principal door of the church at Bethlehem, if the Moslem porter, the modern *Shallum*, should be empowered to restrain Christians of a certain denomination from entering the church at given hours, and if the merit of replacing a star over the tomb of the Virgin Mary, in lieu of one abstracted a few years previously, should belong to the Greeks or to the Latins. This question was left to the decision of the Porte, who referred it to a council of ulema and efendis. Fairly might they exclaim, "God is great and Mohammed is his prophet!" since Christians were willing to defer to their judgment a question concerning places hallowed by the acts and sufferings of their Saviour. England was in a position to decide it. Her Protestant and neutral character would have enabled her to decide authoritatively whether a firman, obtained no one could say through what influence, never acted on, never even cited during a hundred years, were or were not valid in equity to deprive the Greeks of possessions and privileges enjoyed by them for centuries. Her common sense would not have required two volumes of despatches to show her the different effect on the dignity of France and Russia, respectively, between replacing the Latins in the *status quo* of the days of the Frank monarchy in Palestine, and depriving the Greeks of the position occupied by them long before Russia had acquired European importance. England, far from desiring to mediate, early resolved to look on and enjoy the fight. It began in 1850. In June of that year, Sir Stratford Canning is desired to watch and report the progress of the contest which he considers likely to arise between the Latin and Greek churches in Turkey, but to abstain at present from taking any part in it. His Excellency replied in a letter to the Secretary of State as follows: "Mindful of your lordship's instructions, I confine myself to the duty of watching from a distance any movement that may occur in the antagonists' camps. A Christian having no immediate concern in the dispute might reasonably wish to see the removal of a contention between the two churches which arrogate an exclusive guardianship of places sanctified by our common religion. But no Englishman, alive to the importance of a true European policy in the East, could witness without regret and anxiety the triumph of a political influence which would always be ready to overflow its bounds."

During the ensuing two years, the Holy Places question went up and down like the mercury of a barometer; now announced in despatches from Constantinople to be insolvable, now announced as on the point of solution. It did not admit of earnest settlement, since England had manifested a bias for the Latins. Louis Napoleon knew that, and let the process work itself out. Ostensibly, at length, a compromise was made. France forewent part of her claims for the Latins;* Russia yielded a portion of the Greeks' vantage-ground. Russia had betrayed indecision, and thereby lost caste in the eyes both of Christians and Moslems. She soon felt this. In the hope of recovering it, she prepared a pompous embassy to send to Constantinople, to demand some concession for the Oriental churches, in order to show the world that her influence still preponderated in Turkey. Rumour thereon, magnifying her object, produced unwonted agitation at Constantinople. The Turks saw, in imagination, the realization of prophecies connecting the year of the Hegira, 1270, with national disaster; and the Greeks anticipated nothing less than the re-elevation of the Cross in St. Sophia at the ensuing Easter.

With the capital in this mood, Prince Mentchikof arrived in the Bosphorus, 28th February, 1853, with a numerous suite, including naval and military officers of rank to survey the position. His arrival excited the rayas, and flurried the diplomatic body. Greeks thronged the main street of Pera before the gates of the Russian embassy, at which Russian sentries were posted, from morn till night, to catch a glimpse of the "liberator," and others passing them made the sign of the cross. The representatives of minor courts exchanged significant glances with the pregnant remark, "*L'eau chauffe.*" The English and French chargés-d'affaires held midnight councils, and declared Turkey in danger. One wrote for the British

* France had in reserve a distinct claim, said to be based also on the firman of 1740, viz., the right to hoist the French flag at Jerusalem. This claim was brought forward during the war, was conceded, and in September, 1855, the French flag was hoisted on the French consulate at Jerusalem, in the presence of the pasha and of the Moslem and Christian notables.

fleet at Malta, and the other suggestively for the French fleet at Toulon, to repair to Vourlah. By their request, an English officer with Turkish rank waited on the Grand Vizir, to urge the adoption of defensive measures. He found his Highness indisposed to view affairs as desperate. *Bakalum* had yet to play its accustomed part. He consented only to sanction silent preparations: to prepare the squadron, laid up dismantled as usual in winter, as far as could be done without attracting notice; and he enjoined discretion in conversing on the subject with Franks. The Porte had made up its mind to listen to Prince Mentchikof with an air of entire trust in the purity of his sovereign's intentions.

In England Prince Mentchikof's mission was considered ominous. Ministers felt more than they avowed: Publicists implied more than they wrote. All concurred in thinking Lord Stratford de Redcliffe, then in England on leave, the man for the emergency; and accordingly he was directed to return to his post.

CHAPTER V.

Prince Mentchikof's injudicious Conduct—Russian Demands—Position of the Greek Church in Turkey—Russian Objects—Prince Mentchikof's "Note"—European Misconception of its Object—Feelings of the Turks towards Russia—Death of the Sultan's Mother—The Funeral Ceremonies—Her Character and Influence over the Sultan—Change of Ministry—Redshid Pasha's Policy—Antagonistic Feelings of the Ministers—The Russian "Note" rejected by the Council of State—Rupture of Diplomatic Relations with Russia—Departure of Prince Mentchikof and the Russian Legation.

Prince Mentchikof reposed three days at Pera, in seclusion. Reports of the state of public feeling flowed in that interval to his residence like flies to a spider's web. On the fourth day his serene Highness made his official début, inauspiciously. He went, knowing an all but regal reception awaited him, to the Porte—region of formal etiquette—in plain undecorated costume; and having smoked the calumet with the Grand Vizir, declined to visit the minister for foreign affairs, who, in uniform, with pipes, coffee, and sherbet ready, sat expecting him in his apartment, a few paces off, under the same roof. This demeanour might have suited the atmosphere of a saray in Turkestan, but was indiscreet in a capital under the eyes of Europe. He gained his end; but at the expense of dignity. The slighted minister, since decorated with the cordon of a Russian order, tendered two days afterwards his resignation; which was weakly accepted. The Porte might thus early have made a stand with the concurrence of every crowned head except one. Supposing Fuad Efendi to have dissembled with Russia (as stated) on the Holy Places question, in excess of the licence of statecraft, Prince Mentchikof might on his arrival have intimated in a becoming manner his reluctance to transact business with him: as Viscount Ponsonby, when representing England at Constantinople, had conveyed in a "note" his desire to cease intercourse with Akif Efendi, the minister for foreign affairs of that day, for having deliberately sanctioned the arbitrary imprisonment of an Englishman; but the prince lost sight of decorum when he read the Sultan a lesson, as it were, by offering a public slight on unappreciable grounds to one of his ministers, so timed that it could not be avoided. This injudicious proceeding aroused personal feelings on which his diplomatic opponents worked. His serene Highness afterwards made another mistake, showing ignorance of the Oriental mind, by warning the Porte to beware of disclosing the nature of his negotiation to the French or English embassy. He thereby betrayed a sense of apprehension, and so defeated his object; whereas affected indifference about their opinions would have ensured discretion on the part of Rifaat Pasha, the new Minister for Foreign Affairs.

Prince Mentchikof first intimated his sovereign's wish to revive the treaty of Hunkiar Iskellesi; engaging, if it was acceded to, for Russia to assist Turkey with an army whenever required. With two shepherds at hand, the representatives of France and England, this was playing the wolf too openly. He next suggested a convention to give increased honour and dignity to the Greek

Church in the person of its patriarch. The patriarch, named according to custom, by the Sultan, to be immovable, unless for treason; in the appreciation of which the Czar might, it was hinted, expect to have a voice: the patriarch to continue to nominate in synod, subject to the Sultan's approval, the sub-patriarchs and the bishops, also for life. This proposition taxed the Porte inferentially—its weak point—with the odium of interference in spiritual matters, and aimed—its real object—at the power of the synod. The action of the Porte, whatever it may be in substance, in regard of the nomination of the patriarch or other dignitary of the Church, is in form confirmatory of the national will expressed apparently by the synod and the council of notables. Its *congé d'élire* is general. The Porte may unostensibly influence the election of a patriarch; has occasionally refused to confirm one; but as a rule its prerogative has been used to prevent the election of a given individual rather than favour that of any one in particular. The proposition, though deemed unacceptable, was good. No scheme short of life nomination will give dignity and moral tone to the Greek Church in Turkey,—seeing the tendency of the synod to suscitate and entertain charges of dereliction of duty or venality against the patriarchs and primates, to augment the chances of preferment, and the disinclination of influential individuals in another sphere to forego the advantages derivable therefrom. Patriarchates and bishoprics have, like pashaliks, been objects of competition, and, as the douceurs have till recently been considerable, frequent mutations have pleased all parties except the flocks ultimately sheared. Two Fanariots, the *capou-kiayas* of Moldavia and

Wallachia, much caressed in political and diplomatic circles, monopolized during many years preceding the war the credit of adjusting the interests of this simoniacal traffic. Russia conferred a notable service on religion by obtaining life occupancy of their sees for the bishops in the Danubian principalities. She accorded that also to the spiritual head of the Armenians, the patriarch of Etchmiazin, a Russian subject since the peace of Adrianople; an example which, aided by the good sense of his nation, has practically given permanence to the resident Armenian Patriarch at Constantinople.

The anomalous position of the Greek Church in Turkey — a religio-civil establishment with municipal and judicial attributions—has rendered the Porte, persuaded of Russia swaying the rayas through their clergy, averse to increase its prestige by the surrender of the right of spiritual degradation. Western Europe seems by its silence to have allowed itself to be influenced in the same sense. But though the apprehension of the Turks, seeing a natural-born foe in every Greek, might obscure their vision, Europe should have taken a larger view of the question. The Greek Church, occupying an honourable independent position, might care less for foreign protection, than now, when exposed to intrigues within itself and to the vagaries of a dominant race. The Patriarch of Constantinople would not be a genuine priest if he should antepose another to his own Church. He remembers that one of his predecessors, Jeremiah, consecrated the first Russian patriarch. Even in his sorry state under the Porte, he has never admitted the supremacy of the synod of

Moscow.* He has ever regarded himself as the head of the Oriental Church, and Russia, by increasing his prestige, might be arming him against herself. A celibate churchman, on attaining the object of his ambition, is an arrogant mortal, ready to "make his cap co-equal with the Crown." As if anticipating this tendency, Russia has endeavoured to introduce a Slavic element into the synod of Constantinople. Her success would be justice to the Bulgarians and a check on Fanariote aspirations; but it might give tone to Panslavism, viewed by some as one of Russia's objects. On this point the Greeks are at variance with her. Pre-eminent, in a religious sense, over the races of the Oriental Church in Turkey—as the Ottomans are pre-eminent over the Moslem races within its limits—the Greeks have jealously opposed the elevation of the Bulgarian clergy on whom only three or four mitres have fallen, through Russian influence.

Prince Mentchikof, abandoning successively his idea of a treaty and of a convention, reduced his demands to the famous "note," and sent it to the Porte as his ultimatum, May 7, 1853. He accorded three days for a categoric answer, which delay was extended to the 18th of May. The interval was passed in deep anxiety by the

* While the Lower Empire lasted, the Patriarch of Moscow depended spiritually on the Patriarch of Constantinople. But after the fall of that empire the inconsistency was seen of the Russian Church owing obedience to a patriarch named by a Moslem sovereign. Iwan the Terrible, having married a daughter of the house of Palæologos, fancied he inherited thereby the spiritual rights of the Byzantine emperor; he therefore formally separated his church from Constantinople and became the head of it. The orthodox Greek of every other land regards the Czar as the protector only of his church: the spiritual head of it in his eyes is the Patriarch of Constantinople.

public. Diplomatic and state machinery was set in motion to influence the result. The Roman people never watched more excitedly for the curl of white smoke from the Hall of Conclave than the Constantinopolitans for an indication of the deliberation on the "note." It was a momentous pause. The "note," impartially tested, was not alarming. It embodied a demand for an engagement by the Sultan, in confirmation of his promise to that effect, to maintain the rights and immunities of the Greek Church on the existing basis; to give to that Church all the rights and advantages which might be conceded to any other Church in Turkey; to maintain and cause to be respected the ancient rights of the Greek Church at Jerusalem without prejudice to other Christian communities, native or foreign; and to maintain the *status quo* of the sanctuaries at Jerusalem, held by the Greeks either exclusively or in common with other sects. The "note" contained less in wording and substance than three treaties—the treaties of Carlowitz, Belgrade, and Sistowa—had accorded to Austria on behalf of the Roman Catholics of Turkey, and it implied no more than France had claimed to exercise in favour of them since the days of Francis I., and had effectively exercised of late years: notably in the reign of Charles X. and with more energy during the presidency of Louis Napoleon. Charles the Tenth's ambassador obtained by importunity the Porte's concession to the nomination of a Roman Catholic Armenian patriarch; which, involving partial secular jurisdiction over his flock, gave offence to the Gregorian Armenians, in number forty to one. Louis Napoleon's ambassador, on the occasion of a dispute between the Roman Catholic Armenians and their patriarch—the former appealing to the Porte, the latter to Rome—supported the Papal authority, and desired the Porte, in virtue of "France's right to protect the Roman Catholic faith in Turkey," to abstain from interference in the matter.

But Europe, misled by those who should have known better, imagined the "note" would transfer the Sultan's authority over the rayas to the Czar. Russia had owed her influence with the rayas to community of religion and of enmity to the Turks. The "note" would not have added anything to those titles; it would simply, as intended, have set her right with the Oriental Christians in regard of the check she had experienced on the Holy Places question. The Turks had abundant reasons for feeling angry with Russia, but shrank from the consequences of a rupture with her. Revenge, however, prevailed, and made them listen to the counsellors who whispered, "Fear not, the Western Powers are with you; together you will reduce Russia to the condition of a second-rate power." Prudence ever and anon gained the ascendant. They knew that the "note" contained nothing fatal to their dominancy over the rayas,—the one thing prominent in their minds. It did not ask for non Mohammedan evidence to be admitted in the *mekkiemehs* (tribunals). It did not ask for rayas to share in posts of dignity and hold commissions in the army. It did not ask for bells to be rung in churches for prayers. The "note," less explicit than the Hatti Humayoun of 1856, would have left matters materially as they were. No astuteness on Russia's part could have extracted anything practical from it, beyond showing the Greeks that France had not supplanted her in the Porte's estimation. Reflecting Turks saw danger to their law and their independence in a war with allies. They feared that if Turkey became the cause of a European conflict she might by an easy transition become the object of it; and, stopping short of that consummation, they saw looming in the distance emancipation of their rayas, as the remuneration to be demanded for the alliance at once desired and dreaded. They instinctively apprehended that a war waged by Christian powers on behalf of a Moslem race, dominant over many millions of Christians invoking rights, would prove a snare and a delusion, so far as they were concerned, and develope designs, already latent, more fatal to their race than the "amity" of Russia. They had divined, before the publication of the "Confidential Despatches," the aversion of Russia, how well soever disposed towards the Greeks, from the revival of the Lower Empire. Left unbiassed to their own inspirations, the Turks would have considered the "note" in an acquiescent spirit. Reluctantly, they would have acquiesced in it; for much had passed of that which blinds men and leads them on in dangerous courses. Prince Mentchikof's demeanour had been arrogant, his language haughty. Calm reflection was required to mitigate their effect.

In the midst of these troubles the Sultan sustained the affliction deepest felt by a Mussulman, in the death of the Valideh Sultana, his mother. Whatever may be thought of the wife's position in the East, that of the mother is unexceptional: she is in all respects the mistress of her son's house and the confidant of his sorrows, in every class of life. Female screams at dawn in the palace of Beshik-tash, one morning early in May, announced his bereavement to the guard-boats and passing caiks, and bade farewell to the body which at that early hour was conveyed in the imperial caik, followed by other caiks with the deceased lady's suite, to the old seraglio. It was there washed and perfumed according to usage, and laid on a bier covered with clothes of gold and silver. Preceded by incense-bearers and choristers, it was then brought forth from the interior of the palace and deposed under the shade of trees in the centre court for a few minutes, while the court imam recited a prayer for the soul of the departed. During its recital, the spectators, taking off their slippers, stood on the soles up-turned: a sign of deep respect.

The procession was then formed. Military pashas on horseback, in single file, flanked by their grooms and *tchiaushes* on foot, led the way, followed by a compact body of Arabian dervishes chanting lustily. Then rode three legal dignitaries, also in single file, the *cazi-askers* of Europe and Asia with the *evcaf nazir.* A body of *Khademes* (royal domestics) marched next in order. Then the ministers of state rode in single file; the three last being the Capitan Pasha, the Scheick ul Islam, and the Grand Vizir. After them rode a body of the Sultan's eunuchs, the chief of whom, the kislar agasi, an aged melancholy-looking Nubian, immediately preceded the corpse. The eunuchs of the deceased lady, scattering new-coined silver money among the crowd, closed the procession. As the procession passed along the streets, lined at intervals with troops, numerous female spectators in open spaces sobbed audibly; and although Eastern women have ever tears as well as smiles at command those shed on this occasion were sincere, for the sex had lost that day an advocate, the poor a friend. The procession halted in front of the garden of the Mahmoudieh mausoleum, where, on an elevated slope, the boys of adjoining schools, chanting hymns, were drawn up, and being reformed on foot moved on through gilded gates and rose-beds, slowly to the tomb. As its portals swung open, screams from the valideh's women gathered in the interior of the edifice to pay the last tribute of respect to their kind mistress issued forth, sad and plaintive; to mingle, strangely harmonious, with the chants of dervishes and the neighing of led horses. The body was buried beside that of Sultan Mahmoud II.

The deceased lady, a native of Georgia, brought to the seraglio when a child, died aged forty-six, having survived her lord fifteen years. During her widowhood she had devoted her large income to pious and charitable works, and strenuously espoused the cause of her sex, high and low. She built two mosques, and a civil hospital—the only one deserving the name in the empire—for Moslem poor, but which since her death has declined in usefulness. She had exercised her influence with her son for his good and the good of the State. Freed from her gentle restraint, Sultan Abdul Medjid gave way to those excesses which brought him to a premature grave: if that expression is admissible in regard of a fatalist. During the valideh's last illness, the physician in attendance, seeing the Sultan's grief, begged to be relieved from responsibility on account of his treatment. "Do what seems proper to you," replied the Sultan; "if my mother lives it will be with the consent of God; but if her hour is arrived your skill will avail nought."

A few days after his mother's interment the Sultan gave Prince Mentchikof a private audience; then shuffled his ministry. He removed Mehemet Ali Pasha from the Grand Viziriat to the seraskiriat (war department); installed Kiridli Mustafa Pasha in his room; turned out the Hassa Mushiri (general of the guard) to make place for the ejected seraskir; and brought in Redshid Pasha as minister for foreign affairs, his predecessor becoming the president of the council. Save a few aware of the influences at work against the "note," people in general including the Russian party expected conciliatory counsel from Redshid Pasha, the soul of the Porte whatever office he might hold. More clearly than most men he saw the hazards of a war such as the one foreshadowed. But he was not a free agent. Ambitious, he had to choose between leading the war party or leaving that to his rival, the husband of the Sultan's surviving sister, and the assumed representative of orthodox principles. The hand of the Sultan's eldest daughter, chief prize of the state, was shortly to be given away; the aspirants for it being one of Redshid Pasha's sons and Mehemet Ali Pasha's son by a former wife (divorced, as a matter of course, on his marriage with a sultana), and though promised to the former the promise might be revoked. Redshid Pasha felt this and trimmed his sails accordingly. He expected Russia, though she might suspend diplomatic relations with Turkey, would compromise difficulties at last rather than break with the Western Powers. He hoped to talk war and maintain peace. He miscalculated the popular temper in both climes. He underrated the strength of individual will.

The principal members of the said heterogeneous ministry bore no love to each other. Redshid Pasha, when Grand Vizir, had turned Mustafa Pasha, the actual holder of the seal of state, out of the government of Candia—which post, held by him for twenty-five years, had made him one of the richest men in the empire; and Mehemet Ali Pasha, having previously supplanted Redshid Pasha in the Grand Viziriat, had striven to involve him in the imputed delinquency of Djezairli Migriditch, the head of the customs: a weapon which Redshid Pasha afterwards turned against him with more success, if not with more justice. Two ex-Grand Vizirs rivals for power under a new man, a stranger to the capital, made an unmeaning coalition on which nobody counted. The ministry was considered embodied in Redshid Pasha, regarded as England's nominee. He soon became the head of it.

May 17th.—A council of dignitaries and ulema, forty-six in number, met under the presidency of Redshid Pasha to deliberate on a foregone conclusion—the answer to the "note." Forty-three members voted for its rejection; three for its acceptance. After the council Redshid Pasha repaired to the British embassy and remained there until midnight.

May 19th.—The cessation of diplomatic relations between Russia and Turkey was announced to the public. Prince Mentchikof had already embarked in a steamer and was lying at Buyukdereh, detained by a thunder-storm. That evening the representatives of Austria, England, France, and Prussia met to reconsider the question, in the hope of finding a less menacing solution; and next day two of them rowed up the Bosphorus to make a final appeal to the prince's feelings. To no purpose. On May 21st his serene Highness steamed into the Euxine, and next afternoon the eagles were removed from the gates and façade of the Russian embassy in the presence of a crowd of Greeks excited into silence. They looked as though they expected the carved birds to fly away of their own accord to "Holy Russia." They blessed their descent. That night was *lelei berat** (record-night). Every pious Greek gazing on the beautiful city, as it lay tranquil in the moonlight with feasting in its palaces, its thousand minarets wreathed with lamps tracing the contour of the hills and valleys in their vast extent, from the Propontis to the Golden Horn, from the seraglio to the Golden Gate, thought of the "handwriting on the wall."

The ordinary Russian legation left Constantinople May 26th, leaving Russian subjects to the good offices of the Prussian legation. A fortnight afterwards a Russian secretary arrived at Constantinople with a letter from Count Nesselrode to the Porte, approving of Prince Mentchikof's proceedings, and inviting it to reconsider its refusal of his ultimatum; and on June 17th he steamed back to Odessa with a confirmation of that refusal. War remained undecided. People continued to hope against hope.

* *Lelei berat* is the night on which the *kiramen kiatibin* (recording angels) make up their accounts for the year. Every Moslem is supposed to have two angels constantly in attendance, one on his right shoulder noting down his good, the other on his left shoulder noting down his bad actions. It is to be feared that in these degenerate days the angel on the right shoulder has little to occupy his pen dipped in azure.

CHAPTER VI.

The Porte takes defensive Measures—The Castles on the Bosphorus—The Turkish Fleet—Dangers from the Vicinity of European Merchant Vessels—Harbour-masters of Foreign Consulates—Turkish Captains under Restrictions—Fear of the Porte to give Umbrage to Russia—Readiness and Activity of Sailors and Soldiers—Military Preparations of the Porte—Self-devotion of the People—Troops marched to the Frontiers—Influence of the English and French Press—Addresses of the Greek and Armenian Patriarchs—Mussulman Distinctions applied to the Western Potentates—Arrival of the English and French Fleets—The Turks supposed them to have been hired by the Sultan—Moslem Belief in a special Providence watching over them—Foreign Orders and Decorations profusely conferred on Turkish Officials.

Having done the deed, the Porte felt like a merchant who has embarked his all in a hazardous venture. With misgivings it began to think about defensive measures. There appeared to be no time to lose. Russia might any day issue a declaration of war and send it with her fleet to the Bosphorus. A social panic would ensue; the bewildering effect of which, only surmised then, was seen twelve years later on the appearance of cholera. The spirit which animated the Turks in 1807 to prepare to resist the English fleet under Sir John Duckworth's command, then in sight from Galata Tower, had died out under depressing influences. The castles of the Bosphorus, on either side of a straight broad reach, were inadequate for its defence. They could hardly, if duly armed and manned, have checked a fleet impelled by the summer north-east wind; *à fortiori*, with guns of mingled calibres deficient in accessories, and with gunners unpractised in firing. Whenever attention had been invited to their inefficiency the authorities had spoken contemptuously of the idea of a fleet attempting the passage: it would be sunk, they said; but, confident as they then had been, they were now depressed. In face of the danger self-delusion vanished. Baron de Tott, the designer of most of those castles, had overlooked, if unrestricted in his choice, the defensible points of the Bosphorus—three salient points lower down, where the stream flows narrow and sinuous, indicated by Mehemet II.'s castles, built four centuries ago, and still remaining, quaint picturesque monuments of his military judgment. Many Venetian vessels were sunk or stopped by them during the last siege of Constantinople. Heavy-armed batteries on those points would render the passage of the Bosphorus problematic even with screw-propelled ships.

As things were little argument was required to show the dependence of Constantinople on its fleet, but much persuasion was required to overcome the reluctance of the Porte to betray to its own people an apprehension of war by stationing it in an indicative locality. The fleet had left the Golden Horn towards the latter end of April, to be ready to co-operate with the military in repressing Greek demonstrations, apprehended as likely to occur during Easter week, on the shores of the Bosphorus, in honour of Prince Mentchikof. Four steamers and thirty guard-boats had been employed on this precautionary service day and night. After the saturnalia, which had passed off with little more than the usual amount of noise and merriment, the fleet remained at its summer anchorage off Beshik-tash; giving leave as in ordinary times to officers and men, in a position, as it might have turned out, of delusive security. A swarm of Cossack galleys had burned Buyukdereh in the reign of Amurath IV.; why might not a Russian fleet venture as far in Abdul Medjid's reign? This contingency being admitted the fleet was towed up the Bosphorus during the first week in June, and moored between Saryieri and Therapia; its broadsides, when sprung, bearing on the entrance of the Black Sea. The Umouryeri bank, with two line-of-battle ships moored inside, rendered the position remarkably strong. The Turkish fleet then answered for the defence of the Bosphorus against any naval force in the power of Russia to send. Block-houses were erected on the hills commanding Buyukdereh Bay; signal stations were established between the outer castles and the city; and a service of steamers and guard-boats was organized to keep watch near the mouth of the Bosphorus and between the inner castles, to prevent a surprise, and frustrate incendiary attempts traditionally dreaded by the Turkish navy.

Danger, however, in that shape, seemed more likely to be hatched at Constantinople under the wing of the lax police exercised over European merchant vessels. Such vessels are free from native supervision, whereby gunpowder is frequently landed contrabandwise. Much damage was done in Salonica a few years ago to life, limb, and property, by the explosion of gunpowder stored in large quantities, unknown to the authorities, in a

French merchant's warehouse; and every maritime town in the empire has been constantly, of late years, exposed to similar danger. A Greek vessel was detected, in 1860, in the inner port of Constantinople—a piece of water surrounded by wooden structures, and crowded with shipping—with 120 half barrels of gunpowder concealed under her declared cargo; and guided by this indication several depôts of gunpowder were then found in European stores near the harbour. Each consulate has its own harbour-master to attend to the affairs of its shipping, and whatever his business may be it is hardly his interest to denounce smuggling. In accordance with the rule of contrary, omnipotent in most affairs in the East, the choice of men, whose reports on collisions, salvage, derelicts, foul berths, &c., form the basis of judicial proceedings, is rarely determined by nautical considerations. The English, for instance, have made their harbour-master out of a servant in search of a place, out of a ship-chandler in difficulties, out of a hydropathic doctor in want of patients, but never out of a sailor; and the example has not been lost upon the consuls of other nations.

During the interval between the suspension of relations between Turkey and Russia and the declaration of war, any Hellenic or other vessel might have fitted herself clandestinely as a fire-ship with the materials at hand at Galata, might have ascended the Bosphorus with a southerly wind, unnoted among a crowd of vessels, and have anchored with them at Buyukdereh among the Turkish fleet, each ship of which, beside its powder and shells, had on board carcasses or fire-balls, ten per gun. Vessels anchored there how and where they pleased: some hooked men-of-war's cables and swung alongside.

The Turkish captains were restrained from exercising the right of keeping clear water round them—exercised by men-of-war in every part of the world, exercised freely afterwards by the allied fleet in Beikos Bay,—by fear of misrepresentation. All any of them ventured on in case of suspicious proximity was to place a guard on board the offending vessel. The naval reader will exclaim indignantly, "Why did not Hassan Bey or Ali Bey weigh Captain Tomkins' or Captain Lefevre's anchor and let him drift to the devil if he pleased?" I will tell him why. Captain Tomkins or Captain Lefevre would have made a report to his consul, who would have forwarded it with elucidatory remarks to his ambassador; who in his turn would have sent a dragoman to the Porte with a demand for pecuniary compensation to Captain Tomkins or to Captain Lefevre for the anxiety and ill-usage he had suffered by his own statement, and a request for the dismissal of Hassan Bey or Ali Bey from his ship for over zeal.

Few can imagine the anxiety of serving an irresolute government. Notwithstanding repeated representations the co-operation of the European legations could not be obtained to make their respective merchant vessels anchor clear of the lines of the Turkish fleet; a slight return for the order and discipline maintained among 10,000 men during their wearisome sojourn in the waters of Buyukdereh. Not a child was scared nor a bunch of grapes plucked in any of the neighbouring villages or vineyards: no leave was granted except to Constantinople for the sake of the Franks; and the small-arm men were drilled on barren hills in the morning before they had risen. The navy would have profited much by having a squadron of all rates, as earnestly recommended, out in the Euxine during the fine season of 1853, half the crews being new-raised men and the other half little better; but the fear of the Porte to accelerate events by giving, as it fancied, cause of umbrage to Russia, overcame nautical considerations. Only two light vessels, afterwards increased to four, were allowed to cruise. They cruised seventy miles in either direction from the Bosphorus, that Russian vessels might not set emissaries ashore unnoticed among the Greeks.

The Capitan Pasha objected to reefing and shifting sails at anchor, out of regard for the Sultan's feelings in case men should fall from aloft. He averted his eyes from the prospect of winter cruising in the Black Sea. Allah was expected to make sailors. To propitiate his favour, the men were enjoined to miss none of the prescribed daily prayers; and the *Sourei Fethi Sheref* (war hymn) was chanted every evening on the lighted decks by the imams of the fleet. In one respect the men were pre-eminent. Sleeping, more or less dressed, on their mattresses spread on the decks, they were able to clear for action at night, load, and stand ready to fire under five minutes. The garrisons of the castles of the Bosphorus with similar habits displayed equal alacrity. We have rowed to one or the other of the castles at uncertain hours of the night, and in six minutes seen the guns manned, the gunners looking eagerly through the embrasures for the expected enemy. The soldiers, at the sound of the trumpet, rushed half asleep out of their barracks, and ran full speed along the ramparts to their quarters.

Military preparations were also attended to. A body of engineers was sent to Silistria, Widdin, and Routschuk, to set their works in order; siege-guns and field-batteries were sent to Trebizonde for transmission to Erzeroom and Kars; activity was imparted to the cannon-foundry and the powder-mills; and orders were sent to the provinces to call out the first division of rediff. Withal, the word was passed, "Avoid display, do the needful quietly." The spirit of the people required no rousing. All were ready to march, and waited for the order patiently. Resolution is always calm. The earnestness and self-devotion of the Turkish people in 1853 were remarkable: they showed themselves descendants of a conquering race, worthy of being better led than it was their lot to be. Europe had fancied religious enthusiasm weak, union impossible. The bureaucracy of Constantinople, misled by its own indifferentism, were even more astonished than Europeans at the ardour of Islam. During the summer of 1853, 60,000 troops from various parts of the empire were conveyed quietly, scarcely noticed by the public, through the Bosphorus, in the steamers of the Ottoman navy, and were landed at Varna in high condition. Thence they marched to the lines of the Danube and the Balkan, reinforced by troops from Albania, Bosnia, and Macedonia. Thirty thousand troops, besides irregulars, were collected on the Asiatic frontier.

Steam had given Turkey a marked advantage over Russia at the outset of war, by enabling her to assemble an army on the Danube without wear and tear. In previous wars the two empires had been on equal terms in that respect, each having had long distances to march to the frontier. Turkey was not allowed to profit by this novelty. Russia's good fortune also restrained the allies afterwards from duly availing themselves of the exclusive possession of screw-propelled line-of-battle ships and minié rifles.

While preparing for war the Porte did not abandon hopes of peace, and thereby, instead of leading the movement, exposed itself to be led by it. The Porte was equally indisposed to view war as inevitable, as to make up its mind to profit by the contrast of a blithe, elated Turkish army in Bulgaria with a footsore dusty Russian army in Bessarabia. Its prime councillor contributed to this indecision by sending the minister for foreign affairs articles extracted from the Western press, eulogizing Turkey, depreciating Russia. Unused to free discussion, their own newspapers being strictly censored, the Turkish ministers were unable to discriminate justly between the government and the press. Innately suspicious, they may readily have fancied collusion. The warlike articles of sundry English and French journals weakened the effect of foreign offices' pacific despatches. They were decidedly more palatable. The latter alluded to social aberrations and rayas' rights; whereas the former made no allusion in that day to such delicate topics. On the contrary, their editors seemed ready to smoke their pipes with any efendis and join chorus with them in abuse of the Greeks.

Soon after the rupture of relations, the Greek and Armenian patriarchs were persuaded to send addresses to the Sultan, breathing sentiments of devotion and gratitude, in return for a firman recently issued, which confirmed anterior firmans in favour of the rayas and enjoined on the Moslems fraternal treatment of them, though not having been read in the mosques it was unknown to the public. The Porte could not consistently proclaim its love for the rayas while exciting the Moslems to a holy war. Fulsome addresses, inexpressive of the feelings of their flocks, both of whom nourished disaffection in their hearts, one being on the verge of rebellion, they were *bosh lakerdeh* (empty words), intended solely for the ear of Europe. Now for the first time the epithet *hazretleri* (highness), instead of *djenableri* (excellency), was subjoined in the Turkish Gazettes to the names of the French and English sovereigns: a distinction previously reserved for native dignitaries.

The Turks have been accustomed in public and private documents to distinguish non-Mussulmans from Mussulmans, except of late years those with Turkish rank when no distinction is made during life. On death it reappears. Let two functionaries, one Mussulman the other Christian, die the same day, the death of the former would be recorded in the Gazette thus: "The hour marked by destiny having arrived, he returned to his eternal abode." Of the latter, thus: "He ceased to live." In common parlance, the vulgar say a Mussulman dies; a non-Mussulman perishes. The innovation caused a marked sensation. Every one reading the exclusive epithet, when it first appeared in the Gazette in connection with Louis Napoleon's name, stopped surprised, and rubbed his eyes or wiped his spectacles. Also the prefix *hashmetly* (splendid) was accorded, the higher qualification, *shevketly* (majestic), being reserved for the Sultan. When Austria showed a disposition to co-operate with the Western Powers, the epithet was given to her Emperor. The King of Sardinia next obtained it; and soon all potentates, including the Pope, were thus honoured: except the Czar, who was simply styled Nicolas or Alexander, until the peace; and King Otho, for whom *djenableri* was deemed sufficient distinction. On the resumption of peaceful relations the arbiter of state trifles displayed capriciousness in the application of the said epithet, but after some oscillation it was applied to all crowned heads and their heirs apparent, and exceptionally for a while to the Grand Duke Constantine and the Imperial Prince Napoleon. As if in apprehension, however, of the people ceasing thereby to regard the Sultan as the king of kings, the dispenser of crowns, a marked distinction of style has lately been revived in the Turkish Gazettes.

The arrival of the English and French fleets at Beshika Bay and the unfaltering tone of the Western press encouraged the Turks in their bold career, and confirmed them in the belief, variously generated, of Europe being under a destined necessity to abet their interests. Not gratuitously, however. The people imagined the Sultan had hired those fleets. Some officers seriously asked the author how many purses his majesty had agreed to pay per month for their services, and were courteously jocose on his avowal of ignorance of the transaction, averring, in corroboration of their notion, that he had paid for the use of the English fleet in 1840 against Mehemet Ali, Pasha of Egypt. Allah, said the Constantinopolitans, showed his regard for the chosen race by inclining the hearts of infidels towards them. This sentiment explained to them the anomaly of Christians being about to wage war on a Christian power on behalf of Moslems. Thus reasoned the middle and lower classes, with whom religion is something more than a banner. The upper class accounted for it by the antagonism between the occidental and oriental churches. Much has occurred in various ages to root in Moslems' minds the belief in a special Providence watching over them. The Crusades, destined apparently to confine Islam within the limits of Arabia, weakened instead the Greek empire, and paved the way for its overthrow by Moslem arms. The capture of Bagdad and the subversion of the caliphate by Holokou Khan gave Islam a shock such as might well have seemed impossible to recover from; but the development soon afterwards of the Turkish power—then unforeshadowed—reinvigorated it, and planted its minarets beyond the Danube. And in recent days, whenever a rebellious satrap or an ambitious neighbour has menaced the first Moslem empire—the stronghold of Islam—Christian powers have armed or interposed in its defence. Arguments in the mouths of missionaries, drawn from Revelation, are weak beside such practical evidence of a superintending Providence. Mohammed promised his followers the aid of legions of angels when overmatched in battle with the infidels. They reverently believed him; but they would have listened incredulously to the prediction of a time when the infidels themselves would fight their battles; and had he foretold the day when Christian potentates would vie with each other in giving their orders of chivalry to Moslems, the mantle of prophecy would have seemed slipping off his shoulders.

The profusion of orders conferred of late years on Turkish civilians by foreign potentates, in singular contrast with the opinions of their representatives at Constantinople respecting some of them, has excited comment and somewhat impaired their prestige. To the question, For what services have they been given? echo in most cases answers, "For what!" Are they duly appreciated? "Scarcely," would be the answer prompted by the indisposition to wear them at native ceremonies or in the Sultan's presence. What, then, it might be asked, has influenced the donors and the recipients? They are given at times to gain partisans for a policy, and at times to reward cheaply services or complaisances. The French Government, in exemplification of the latter category, gave in 1853 five orders of the Legion of Honour to dockyard officials at Constantinople, for repairs done to one of its ships; and a few years later, in return for an entertainment given by a high functionary to the Duke de Brabant, Belgian decorations were sent to his principal domestic officers. Cabinet ministers and ambassadors receive grand cordons presumedly *ex officio*; and inferior badges are acceptable to a certain class of officials as giving them a colourable claim on the good offices, in case of need, of an embassy, with invitations to its fêtes. The motives which have led minor sovereigns uninterested in the Eastern question, as the King of Saxony, the Grand Duke of Baden, and the Grand Duke of Weimar, to follow the example of interested great Powers in that respect, is inexplicable. What are Baden and Weimar to Turkey, and what is Turkey to them? Baden and Weimar doubtless relish the figs and raisins of Turkey; and Turkey, unconscious perhaps of the glory of Weimar, Goethe, has heard of the gaming-houses of Baden. Denmark, still further off, can nevertheless adduce a motive. She persuaded Turkey, whose flag had rarely floated outside the Mediterranean, and never north of the Thames, to pay her 4,000*l.* in exemption from Sound dues, and marked her sense of the conciliatory temper of the officials engaged in the negotiation with her minister at Constantinople by sending each of them a Danish order. The New World has also contributed its quota of decorations. Some crosses of Nuestra Señora of Guadaloupe have found their way to the Bosphorus, and several of the newly-fledged Mexican eagles have flown across the Atlantic to alight at the Sublime Porte. The hidalgo spirit has kept Old Spain's orders from being thus indiscriminately disposed of. The order which, from its name and origin, might have seemed specially reserved from Turks, the Grecian Order of the Saviour, has been the most liberally bestowed upon them. A shower—one of many—of sixteen crosses fell at Constantinople in November, 1865; and none of the recipients, we venture to say, have dared avow services past or prospective in return for the honour.*

* Voici la liste des décorations que S. M. le roi des Hellènes a bien voulu conférer aux ministres et fonctionnaires de la Sublime Porte dont les noms suivent:—

Les Insignes de la Grande Croix de l'Ordre du Sauveur.—À S. Exc. Halil Pacha, ministre de la marine; à S. Exc. Edhem Pacha, ministre du commerce; à S. Exc. Saïd Effendi, *mustéchar* du ministère des affaires étrangères; à S. Exc. Kiamil Bey, introducteur des ambassadeurs.

Les Insignes de Grand Commandeur du même Ordre.—À S. Exc. Naïzi Effendi, *Beylikdji*, et à S. Exc. Aarifi Bey, drogman du divan impérial.

Les Insignes de Commandeur.—À Mehmed Effendi, *kiatib* du ministère des affaires étrangères; à Chevketi Effendi, *mektoubdji* du même ministère; à Fuad Bey, fonctionnaire du bureau de l'*Amedi*; à Munif Effendi, premier traducteur de la Sublime Porte, et à Serkis Effendi, chef du bureau de la correspondance étrangère.

Les Insignes de Chevalier.—À Nouri Bey, *muavin* du *Techrifatdji:* Mehemet Bey, Sead Oullah Bey, Shogoumon Effendi, et Hatchik Effendi, fonctionnaires du ministère des affaires étrangères.—*Journal de Constantinople*, 25th November, 1865.

CHAPTER VII.

Passage of the Pruth by the Russians—The Sultan dismisses his Ministers, but recalls them—Decision of a Council of State—Position of Russia weakened—Dilemma of the Porte—Delusion of the People—The Vienna Note—Advice respecting it—Sir Stratford Canning and Redshid Pasha—The Porte's Refusal of the Vienna Note—Warlike Preparations of Turkey—The Porte in the Meshes of Diplomacy—The Ruling Class of Turkey Past and Present—Frankish Turks.

NEWS of the passage of the Pruth by the Russians, July 5th, 1853, reached Constantinople July 8th, and on the evening of the latter day a Russian frigate and a steamer hove in sight, ten miles from the outer castles of the Bosphorus: the first seen by us since the rupture of relations. The coincidence of their appearance with the advance of the Russian army seemed calculated: they might be the look-outs of a fleet. Two frigates were accordingly sent out next day to reconnoitre, with orders on no account to fire unless fired upon. They fell in at midnight with two strange frigates, and the excitement of mustering at quarters revived their qualmish crews. In the morning they saluted the Russian flag with twenty-one guns, a courtesy which remained unresponded to, and soon afterwards returned to port, driven in by a summer gale. Closed to them since twenty years, the Black Sea was not a lake for Turkish ships.

The day of the arrival of the news of the passage

of the Pruth the Sultan dismissed the Grand Vizir, and the minister for foreign affairs, Redshid Pasha, from office: an abrupt act, the cause of which did not transpire, though shrewdly surmised. But the representations of the representatives of friendly Powers on the impolicy of unsettling the Government at a critical conjuncture, aided by the difficulty of choosing successors, led to their reinstatement next day. The public had expected Aali Pasha to be summoned to the foreign department; but having been recently recalled from the government of Smyrna, at the instance of the internuncio—for having taken a liberal view of a quarrel there between Hungarian refugees and Austrian naval officers, which led tó a departure from the law of nations derogatory to the Austrian flag by an American corvette in the harbour—his appointment to a ministerial post would have ruffled Austria's temper. In her character of mediator in the Russo-Turkish dispute, her susceptibilities demanded consideration.

July 11th a council sat at the Porte to consider on the matter of the passage of the Pruth. The council agreed to consider it a violation of treaties, short, however, of a *casus belli;* to protest against it in the face of Europe and remain on the defensive. Wishing to gain time, the Porte accepted, by the advice of her friends, the novel doctrine of a distinction between war and invasion. On the other hand, Russia had made a false move and weakened her position in a moral, political, and military sense. She had committed a wrong; she had insulted public opinion; she had given up the vantage-ground of an incompleted menace. By remaining on her own side of the Pruth, giving Europe no cause for action, she would have disconcerted Austria's manœuvring and have wearied the Porte, with its hands tied, into an accommodating temper. Determined on occupying the Danubian principalities, her wisest and manliest course was to have preceded it by a declaration of war. We leave out of consideration her right. She had, at all events, more right to declare war than to trespass with an army on her neighbour's territory.

The toleration of the seizure of the "material guarantee" (Moldavia and Wallachia) having been included in the programme of the drama, the event scarcely excited comment among the Constantinopolitans (accustomed, moreover, to hear of the presence of the Russians in those provinces), and did not influence the march of affairs either domestic or foreign. The double action of canvassing for peace and preparing for war continued. The Porte, however, about this time began to apprehend a novel complication. Having roused the spirit of the nation, it now feared inability to control it in case of the avoidance of war becoming desirable. The language of the metropolitan softas in their annual provincial migration and of the seyah (roaming dervishes) had stirred the Moslem soul to its depths. The people believed that Russia designed to substitute Christians for them in the rule of the land: they saw in idea their mosques converted into churches, their rayas revelling in their konaks and tchiftliks. Better die first! Pains were therefore taken to keep the people ignorant of the character of pending negotiations and make them believe that the maintenance of peace, if maintained, would proceed solely from the Czar's awe of the Sultan. The people readily credited the flattering tale and much more. The Czar, they said, had sent the Czarina incognita to Constantinople to intercede for him; he had offered to reimburse Turkey the expense of her war preparations; but that would not suffice; he must give up the Crimea also. Such was the idle talk in the cafés of the capital. Thus the Porte at once sustained and controlled the excitement.

In the meanwhile Prince Mentchikof's "note," cause of the tribulation of Europe, having been stirred in the political crucible, came out as the "Vienna Note." In that form, approved of by Europe and accepted (reluctantly) by Russia, it was sent to Constantinople, scarcely any one anticipating opposition in that quarter. Had Vienna and Constantinople possessed then electric intercommunication none would probably have been offered effectively. But it arrived too late. The "Vienna note" reached Constantinople after the incubation of another variety of the original "note" by the representatives of the mediating powers, and being preferred to their bantling by their respective Governments seemed defective in their eyes. The Porte, beginning to weary of acting a subordinate part in a play where its interests were principally at stake, was disposed to accept the "Vienna note," and only required friendly pressure to allay its pride, chafed by the wording rather than by the substance of it. Three months had raised the hopes of the Turkish nation, but had not increased the confidence of the Porte in the result of an appeal to arms.

Few persons who have considered the subject now doubt that Turkey, in her own interests, viewing her dependence on eventualities beyond her guidance, ought to have accepted the "Vienna note;" stating frankly her objections to it, and waiving them out of deference to the wishes of her allies. She would then have secured the continuance of peace on honourable terms, and would have had her integrity ensured by the respect of Europe and by her own unimpaired strength and dignity, far better than by the formal guarantee afterwards given on implied conditions, and which has been rendered derisive since by the demeanour, incompatible with the ordinary notions of sovereign rights, of one or more of the guarantors in various parts of the empire. She might not then have heard the chords, tuned by her allies, of Roumanian independence and of Sclavic nationality vibrated in the ears of the world. She would not have been humiliated by the occupation of part of Syria by a French army, because her troops were said to have looked on while two semi-barbarous tribes, variously instigated, amused themselves in traditional fashion. She would not have been drawn into the vortex of foreign indebtedness. She would not have lost 120,000 men, the flower of the Turkish race. Her army, unimpaired by disease and contumely, would have returned to their homes or their barracks, proud in the conviction of having by their gallant attitude forced Russia to recede, and her people would have escaped the gaze in no friendly spirit of myriads of strangers on their faults and their deficiences.

The English ambassador, in accordance with his instructions, advised officially acceptance of the "Vienna note," and in accordance with his idiosyncracy advised officiously its rejection; or, to speak more accurately, allowed his personal view of it to transpire. The Prussian minister was said to have also dissociated his individual and official character. In regard of the latter this may have been surmise, based on the impression abroad of Russia's objection to the "note," but with respect to his noble colleague the evidence is less inconclusive. Meeting the seraskir, the representative of the war party, at a ball at the French embassy, he entered into conversation with him through a chance interpreter—an unusual condescension,—and alluding to the "Vienna note," just then arrived, said that in his opinion, speaking in his individual capacity, it was unacceptable. That turned the scales, balanced by acceptance and rejection, in favour of the latter. In those days the Porte cared less for reading by its own lights the despatches of the British Government than for ascertaining its distinguished representative's reading of them. His Excellency's dislike of the Czar Nicolas was no secret: he seemed bent on seeing that autocrat humbled; and long experience had made the Turks believe in the adoption sooner or later of his views on Eastern policy by his Government.

The Porte at that time was for international negotiation impersonated in Redshid Pasha, the Turkish statesman *par excellence:* the first who had conciliated diplomatic favour, given him seven years previously at the critical point of his career, when, with all eyes fixed on him, an imperial smile or frown might make or mar him. He might legitimately aspire to guide the policy indicated by himself; he might through rivals' intrigues be consigned to obscurity in the form of a provincial governor. He comprehended the position; he saw the necessity of external support, and found it in an alliance with Sir Stratford Canning. Those eminent individuals—who in their mutual relations might in some respects bear faint comparison with Rufinus the prefect of the East and Eutropius the great chamberlain at the court of the Emperor Arcadius—aided each other many years to retain the objects of their ambition, respectively political ascendancy and diplomatic preponderance. They left the stage on which they had acted important parts within a few weeks of each other; one for the other world,* the other for dignified repose in his own country. What, it might be asked, should have induced his Excellency to disclose himself thus unreservedly on a vital point to the seraskir, a man decried and always politically thwarted by him, the rival of his friend? Presumedly to give the war party weight in the council and keep Redshid Pasha in hand. Redshid Pasha, like M. Drouyn de Lhuys and Lord Clarendon, was anxious to avert, with honour to all parties, a war whose preliminaries foreshadowed indecision and cross purposes,—a war which, ostensibly undertaken for the sake of Turkey, would aggravate in no ordinary degree her financial difficulty, the rock in her course,—a war which, if stopping short of its logical conclusion, letting Russia off with passing under the caudine forks, would leave her the gainer by the lessons of its teaching, and her antagonist the loser by the

* Redshid Pasha died suddenly, January 7, 1858, in the post of Grand Vizir for the sixth time; and the concourse of citizens at his obsequies next day showed the general esteem which his affability, kindness, and liberality had acquired for him. He left five sons, thus placed. The eldest was ambassador at Paris with the rank of *bala* [Bala is the second rank (for civilians) in the official hierarchy]; the second was a *mushir* and member of the Supreme Council; the third was a *damad*, and a minister of state; the fourth was a member of the Supreme Council with the rank of *bala*; the fifth was a *ferik* (lieut.-general). Redshid Pasha and his sons drew in salaries and allowances about 4,000*l.* a month; and his second wife, a Circassian, had a treasury pension of 25,000 piastres (220*l.*) a month settled on her.

incidents of its perturbation. But Redshid Pasha was an Oriental. Seeing others ready to play the game if he threw up the cards he wrote a despatch in answer to the "Vienna note," worthy rather of a special pleader than of a statesman.

Intellect playing off rivalries one against the other formed a prominent group in the political cartoon of 1853.

August 20th, a Tartar left Constantinople for Belgrade, bearer of the Porte's refusal to accept the Vienna note unless with modifications, which Russia had already declared inadmissible be they what they might. That matter might therefore be considered settled. Then was the time for Turkey to declare war. Towards the end of August Turkey's preparations were tolerably complete. The Danube was lined with good troops, provided with excellent artillery. Schumla, Silistria, and Varna were stronger than they had ever been in previous wars. A numerous but indifferently commanded army was collected on her Asiatic frontier. The Egyptian contingent had arrived. The Tunisian contingent was expected. The pulse of the nation beat high with religious zeal and hope. From all parts of the empire, from every Moslem sect and race, addresses and offerings flowed in. The season was favourable for troops dependent by their equipment on serene weather for extended operations. As much as cold would numb the Turks would it nerve the Russians. The Turkish navy could only hope to keep the sea in fine weather, without disaster. With due appreciation of the case as it stood between Turkey and Russia, and of the case impending between Europe and Russia, statesmen would not have held back Turkey till the eve of winter. Turkey was making a supreme effort for independence: Europe was weaving a coalition to curb Muscovite ambition. On first moves much would depend.

At the commencement of September the Turkish army was in a condition for active service; light clothing and simple rations increasing its efficiency. On the other hand, long marches, heat, and drought had seriously demoralized the Russian army. Statesmen had worked well for Turkey up to the period of the Vienna note; and in her interest they should then have left her the free exercise of her own discretion. Having displayed far more energy and resources than her most sanguine partisans had given her credit for she had the option between two courses: either of sending an envoy to St. Petersburg with the prospect of a gracious reception or of taking the field with the certainty, humanly speaking, of occupying the principalities in a few weeks. But in order to adopt either course, it would have been necessary first to send the friendly ambassadors (figuratively) to the Seven Towers. Their Excellencies seemed resolved not to let Turkey escape from their protectorate; neither negotiate without them nor commence war on terms which might free her from their dictation. Misled by their implied assurances, their avowed predilections, by the sustained war-cry in Europe, and the demonstrative attitude of the Anglo-French fleet in Beshika Bay, the Porte clung to the hope of England and France drawing the sword together with her, and so remained in the entanglement of diplomacy, frittering away precious time. The quotation:—"There is a tide in the affairs of men," &c., became then applicable.

The ruling class of Turkey in that day were unequal to the position and did not clearly understand it. Wanting popular antecedents, they inspired little confidence: wanting earnest convictions, they failed to comprehend the enthusiasm of the nation. As much as the nation trusted in itself did they apparently distrust it. In olden days those only who had led armies in the field, or had ruled turbulent provinces, dared aspire to the dangerous honour of wielding the powers of the State in troublous times. They knew what the nation could do and with all their misreckonings they were never wanting in stubborn self-reliance. Their Epicurean successors, the bland smooth-tongued efendis of Constantinople, knew little of the nation from intercourse and the nation knew little of them save by report. They were, moreover, impressed more or less with the ideas of the men inlaid in every department, who had as youths been sent to Europe for education, to become the mirror for young Turkey. These youths had not been selected from the scions of the old race, with names to uphold and nursery traditions of their country's glory to dwell upon; they had been selected from among the slaves of pashas or the sons of obscure denizens of Constantinople. The young Circassians had no patriotic feelings and their companions aspired to no higher felicity than to live and die, as they had been born and bred, in the Sultan's shadow. After some years passed by most in desultory studies and idle pleasures, admiring the superstructure but giving no heed to the foundations of civilization, they returned home neither Franks nor Turks: without the knowledge of the former or the instincts of the latter. Their traditional contempt for the infidel had been succeeded by envy, mingled with discouragement. They had in general schooled themselves into neglect of their Prophet's self-denying ordinances and had weaned themselves from the practice of their national virtues. They had learned to view everything European with Turkish and everything Turkish with European eyes. Some may be deemed worthy of their rapid elevation, but their countrymen would assuredly liken many to those Florentines whose souls Dante, in his visit to the lower regions, found—

> Mischiate a quel cattivo coro
> Degli angeli che non furon ribelli,
> Nè fur fideli a Dio ma per se foro.

CHAPTER VIII.

Arrival of the Egyptian Contingent—Their close Stowage and scanty Fare—Story of the Egyptian Contingent—Self-mutilation in Mehemet Ali's time to escape Military Service—Desertion and its Penalty—Their Inspection by the Sultan—His Reception and Largesse—Embarkation of the Egyptian Troops—Their soldierly Spirit—Galata Newsmongers' Canards—Sanguinary Rumours credited by the French and English Ambassadors—Groundless Alarm—Four War Steamers summoned by the Ambassadors—Calmness of the Sultan—Protection afforded by the Porte to Foreigners—Governmental Authority in Constantinople—Loyalty of the Soldiery—Their Isolation from the Civilians.

During the month of August, 1853, the first Egyptian contingent, 14,000 troops, arrived from Alexandria in an Egyptian squadron, composed of three line-of-battle ships, four frigates, three corvettes, two steamers, and several transports,—a magnificent offering from a tributary prince. This force had been twenty-eight days on their passage, during which the soldiers, stowed literally like sheep, had received for sustenance 1½ lb. of biscuit each a day, and one drink of water served out in the evening. To economize the water, measured in a tub for each mess, the men imbibed it by turns through a reed as more fortunate mortals imbibe "sherry-cobbler." Notwithstanding this abstinence and want of space, not more than twenty men had died on board, and about 300 only were hospital cases on their arrival in the Bosphorus. When they landed at the Sultan's Valley, where a camp had been pitched for them with provisions and cooks, their first cry was for water, their first act was to rush into a stream with the zest of amphibious animals after a promenade in the rushes. Their camp occupied the spot where the Russian army, invited by Sultan Mahmoud to aid him in his first Egyptian war, had been encamped twenty years previously; and, by a happy coincidence, their pasha's tents were pitched beside the stone erected on *Selvé Bouroun* to commemorate the presence of the Russians in that valley.

The tale of the enrolment of the Egyptian contingent is sadly characteristic. The soldiers composing it were veterans of Ibrahim Pasha's army, several of them having served under him in Greece during the war of independence, and all had shared in the toils and triumphs of his Syrian and Anatolian campaigns. Disbanded about the year 1843, they had returned to their villages to recommence the life of fellahs; had married, and become fathers of families. When the Sultan demanded aid of his vassal ten years later, Abbas Pasha, declining to part with his embodied troops, cast his eyes on the veterans, none of whom assuredly had ever expected to shoulder a musket again. The required number were seized wherever they happened to be, in their fields or in their cabins, and were driven chained in pairs to Cairo. There, cavalry, infantry, and artillerymen, non-commissioned officers and privates, were commingled in one mass, and then subdivided into six regiments, 2,400 strong each. After being clothed they were sent to Alexandria for embarkation. While at Alexandria many deserted, of whom six were retaken and shot before the fleet sailed. None of the men seemed under thirty, while the beards of several indicated nearly double that age.

Some of them had sacrificed the forefinger of the right hand, others the right eye. The severity of discipline in Mehemet Ali's time had led to the practice of self-mutilation, in the hope of thereby escaping from the service. At first, the forefingerless were sent to labour in the dockyard at Alexandria, but that possessed no deterring effect; for as the convicts used to be liberated for joy on the launch of a ship of war, then of annual occurrence, many soldiers preferred the loss of a finger and limited convictism to military service. Perceiving this, Mehemet Ali ordered such to be retained in the ranks. Those afflicted with nostalgia then deprived themselves of the right eye, by scooping out or arsenic. They were also retained by their ruthless master. The desperate then put out both eyes, but with no better result; they were set to pick oakum. We saw several ancient soldiers minus thus a finger or an eye in the Egyptian camp in the Sultan's Valley in 1853, and heard their tale from their own lips. It soon became necessary to station a body of Turkish police at the camp to prevent desertion. Some deserters were retaken, and as an example could not be made of them near Constantinople the general expressed his intention of showing his sense of discipline by having them shot on the line of march in Bulgaria. We trust he kept his qualified promise to us to spare them. "Killing no murder" spoilt Oliver Cromwell's rest; and another pamphlet might be written in an inverse sense to show that killing men thus arbitrarily impressed for attempting to escape from their bondage *is* murder. Part of the crews of the Egyptian ships were also veterans of Mehemet Ali's time and had been employed in the excavation of the Mahmoudieh Canal,—a work which cost the lives of 20,000 labourers.

Abbas Pasha agreed to pay his men during the war; the Porte to feed them and renew their clothing. He had sent them to Constantinople destitute of many necessaries; so much so, that the seraskiriat had to supply them with great-coats, cloth trousers, and tents: also water horses, one per company. As soon as ablutions and good food had removed the dirt and squalor of their wearisome cruise the Sultan honoured them with a visit. Their joy at beholding the successor of the caliphs repaid them for their troubles; and as his majesty passed through their ranks, extending from Hunkiar Iskellesy to the imperial tents, many were heard praying in subdued tones for his welfare. The Sultan gave each of the generals a diamond-set snuff-box, and to every officer, non-commissioned officer, and private, a gratification of a month's pay. His imperial father had on the same spot, twenty years earlier, distributed medals to the Russian troops spoken of. Ill-advised, Sultan Abdul Medjid never inspected any of his own devoted troops, either on going to or returning from the war.

A few days after this pleasing ceremony the Egyptian troops were again stowed on board ship as closely as the most ingenious method of folding men into each other would admit of. Six Turkish paddle-steam frigates, with as many transports in tow, and two Egyptian steamers, carried them with their baggage. Four of the steamers embarked 2,000 men each. The only possible posture was sitting, each man with his knapsack on his back and his musket between his knees, each having besides a loaf or two of bread and some onions, bought with his own money, to supplement his slender rations. They landed at Varna, and marched thence, some to Babadagh and Issatcha, and some to Schumla. These veterans, thus cruelly seized, thus abruptly torn from their homes, with their children's cries ringing in their ears, transported from the banks of the sunny Nile to the swamps of the dismal Danube, sustained to the last the true soldierly spirit. Whether in Bulgaria or elsewhere, they were distinguished for courage in battle and resignation under hardships. Alas! half their number had taken their last look at Egypt.

Soon after their departure the newsmongers of Galata, stirred by the presentation of a petition to the Sultan on his way to mosque one Friday by some ardent softas, circulated an ugly rumour of a projected massacre of Christians at the ensuing bairam; adding, in confirmation, that the Egyptians, who might have been relied on to oppose "Turkish fanaticism," had been sent away on purpose. These gentlemen had found a mole-hill and manipulated it into a mountain, according to their wont. The preceding summer one of the fraternity, who had always visions of truculent Janissaries and feline eunuchs before his eyes, hearing of a body floating between Seraglio Point and Tophana, which turned out to be that of a missing German, wrote in hot haste to an embassy at Therapia, to say the revolution had commenced and the harbour was already covered with headless corpses. That canard had died as soon as hatched, but the one in question lived a while. The rayas, who might, supposing the rumour founded, have been in jeopardy, gave little heed to it; but the Franks and the Levantines fancied themselves doomed to act the part of sheep at the sacrifice, each to have his or her throat cut by a zealous Moslem. The French and English ambassadors accredited the rumour, and increased the panic by sending to Beshika Bay for war steamers. The former allowed himself to be ludicrously mystified, and recorded his *bonhomie* in a despatch, writing thus to his Government: "La position du gouvernement Turc s'aggrave de plus en plus, et les choses sont au point de faire craindre une catastrophe dont les habitants rayas ou Européens seraient les premières victimes, et qui menacerait même le trône du Sultan."

M. Delacour was new to Turkey, and his credulity was, therefore, in some measure excusable; for he had yet to learn that every statement made there should be submitted to the test of probability before adoption. Those in the way of being correctly informed, with no party or stock exchange purposes to serve, assured their Excellencies of the groundlessness of the alarm, and commented upon the bitter effect of bringing up steamers for the protection of their countrymen; who would in case of need, as truly observed, find refuge, men, women, and children, in the Turkish barracks and ships. The softas' petition, expressing discontent at the state of affairs, had simply arraigned the Government for not declaring war against Russia. The instinct of the people is in general true. Those uneducated men saw the approach of war, stealthily but surely, and felt the danger of procrastination. The Porte replied to the petition, saying that it was equally desirous for war, that it had sent proposals to Russia becoming the honour of Turkey, and, in case of her rejecting them, there would be war. Interrogated by the Sheick ul Islam, the petitioners disclaimed all ideas of disaffection: they had only, they said, spoken in the spirit of their holy law, which enjoined war with the infidel, when provoked by him and ready to meet him.

Excited, the French and English ambassadors summoned four war steamers from Beshika Bay, in order, quoting from the despatch of the latter on the subject, "to have sufficient resources at hand to protect their compatriots, and even, in case of need, to give aid to the Sultan, if the movement provoked by the war party should go to the extent of menacing his authority." Their Excellencies should have been consistent, and have summoned the combined fleets: not a vessel too many for the apprehended emergency. They were sanguine in regarding four steamers "sufficient resources" for protecting their compatriots located in Pera hemmed in by Turkish quarters, or scattered in villages along the Bosphorus, and for giving "aid to the Sultan." There were then at Constantinople eighteen battalions, two regiments of cavalry, artillery, and a fleet with crews trained in infantry movements. This force would have acted either for or against the Sultan's authority. If for it, four steamers were a mockery; if against it, a folly. They were just sufficient to give a superfluous sense of security to a few individuals fenced round by the law of nations. Two of them anchored off Therapia and kept their boats ready to bring off the inmates of the French and English embassies at any hour of the day or night. The other two remained off Tophana, to protect the French and English in general and give aid to the Sultan!

During that vision of alarm, Sultan Abdul Medjid was seen going about more than usual, by land or water, with his ordinary slender suite, unconscious of anything menacing either his authority or public order.

The Franks and Levantines had had the excitement to themselves, and they incurred the ridicule when the bubble burst. They had altogether, in their fright, forgotten history. Foreigners, styled in Turkey *misafir* (guests), have always been protected as such. A foreigner, provided with the Sultan's firman or a Vizir's *bouyouroul-tou* and accompanied by a Tartar, travelled safe in the worst times in all parts of the country. More tourists have been waylaid or intimidated from pursuing their objects in the little kingdom of Greece since its establishment than in the vast Turkish empire during its existence. In periods of trouble, suggestive of anti-Christian feelings—the civil war in the Morea, the destruction of the Janissaries, the battle of Navarino, the war of 1828-29—the Franks and Levantines had not only been unmolested, but their safety had been specially cared for. Ought they, then, on any hypothesis, to have apprehended molestation when their Governments had come forward as the friends of Turkey, and were expected to co-operate with her?

The Turks were scandalized at this manifestation of distrust, and surprised at the local ignorance betrayed by it. In no capital is authority so paramount as in Constantinople. Means of concert and action are wanting there. The attitude of the Government is suspicion: its rule is espionage. There are no papers uncensured; no criers unlicensed; no places of meeting tolerated. The mosques, the cafés, and the gates of the city are closed two hours after sunset. The habits of the people are early and domestic. The police can seize suspected or obnoxious individuals without notice or inquiry, and sequester them; and in a few hours embark them, if necessary, in a steamer for a distant island. No one in the East inquires after a man struck by fate. By the agency of the *imams* and *mooktars* of the parishes the Government knows, hour by hour, if it please, all what is passing in the city, and thus exercises complete control over the population. No popular émeute could readily occur at Constantinople; occurring, it would be easily quelled. The Janissaries, in their day the only troops in the capital, except the artillery and the galiondgis, had been the sword of the Ulema to enforce compliance with the holy law, and to punish ministerial delinquency; and with them ended fear of popular commotion at Constantinople. Their successors, the *nizam*, all drawn from the provinces, are not learned in the holy law, are indifferent about corruption, and their rallying cry is, "Long live the Sultan!"—a heartfelt sentiment, not mere lip homage. In his shadow they receive their pay and rations, and they feel grateful to him. Their faculties belong to the state during their period of service. They know this, and resign themselves to a monotonous existence. The men never sleep out of their barracks or guard-houses. Their only recreation is the bath and an occasional promenade. The Sultan's uniform, instead of being a passport for the officers, is a social disqualification. Their steps are noted by informers. They dare not visit men of rank in opposition. They may not frequent others than assigned cafés. They may not accept invitations to dinner in a foreign house without permission. They are forbidden to mingle with the gay and promiscuous crowds at Kiathané and Ghioksou, the Hyde Park or Bois de Boulogne of Constantinople. Between the military and civilians, in a word, non-intercourse is enforced.

CHAPTER IX.

Russia refuses the Porte's Modifications of the Vienna Note—The Porte declares War—Prince Gortchakoff invited to evacuate the Principalities—Honours conferred by the Sultan on the Greek Patriarch—A Turkish Squadron sent to the Black Sea returns to the Bosphorus—Condition of the Turkish Navy—The Author's Suggestion to the Capitan Pasha—It is overruled—Sinope, the only safe Roadstead, exposed to Attack—The Navy in a transition State—Two Parties in the Service—Its low Tone—Forebodings of Disaster—A Russian Squadron reported—The frigate *Nuzretieh* ordered to Sea—Representation of Mushaver Pasha—Strange Order of the Capitan Pasha—The *Nuzretieh* in the Black Sea—Orders given to the Turkish Squadron—Omar Pasha's Victory at Oltenitza—Successes and Reverses of the Turks in Asia—Valour of the Troops and Misconduct of their Officers—Exultation of the Turks.

INTELLIGENCE of Russia's refusal to accept the Porte's modifications of the "Vienna note" having reached Constantinople on September 21st, the grand council, convoked on extraordinary occasions, composed of the principal functionaries, religious, civil, and military, in the capital, about 200 members in all, met to deliberate on the question of peace or war. They sat two days, and decided nearly unanimously for war. In consequence, on the first day of Moharrem, 1270, corresponding to October 4th, 1853, the Porte issued a temperate manifesto to the nation, which explained the state of affairs and declared the existence of war between Turkey and Russia. Although expected, the declaration of war created, nevertheless, deep sensation. Turkey had committed herself, single-handed, to war with Russia on a religious question. The antagonistic principles of Christianity and Islamism were again about to come into conflict. The backwardness of the Western Powers to declare themselves now excited painful comment. Some termed it treachery; others ascribed it to the effect of their religion.

The Porte sent orders to the commander of the army of the Danube to invite Prince Gortchakoff by letter to evacuate the Principalities in fifteen days, and to warn him, in case of refusal, that he would be attacked at the expiration of that delay. Reinforcements were sent to the army of Asia Minor.

Concurrently, to propitiate the Greeks, their newly-elected patriarch, Anthimos, was invested, with ceremonies in abeyance since the execution of the Patriarch Parthenius for imputed treason. His holiness went from the Fanar with a priestly cortège to the imperial palace; received investiture at the Sultan's hands; then proceeded to the Porte, where due honours awaited him; and was reconducted to the patriarchal residence with viziral pomp. Too late!

A squadron of frigates and smaller vessels was sent into the Black Sea under the command of —— Pasha, who received a month's extra pay to animate him, but who returned without orders two days before war commenced, and never left the Bosphorus afterwards until able to steam under convoy of the allied fleets. This was a bad omen and a worse example. Raw crews, stormy weather, cold, and want of ports of refuge, made the Turkish navy regard an order to cruise in the Euxine as tantamount to a sentence of exposure to wreck or destruction by the foe. Their taunt-rigged ships and scantily-clothed sailors were adapted only for summer work, and they had not enjoyed much of that. They had never navigated in winter even the Mediterranean, where ports abound, and they had to learn their task in the "icy Pontick," where fog and currents confuse the reckoning, and where running for the land on an uncertain course was eminently hazardous in those days, through deficient lightage. The vaunt of having a squadron at sea as well as the Russians prevailed with the Porte over the prudence of retaining the sailing vessels in the Bosphorus, keeping up communications with the outports with steamers.

Seeing the risk for a few cruisers, we proposed to the Capitan Pasha, on his coming up to Buyukdereh to announce war to the navy, to let the entire fleet go to sea for the remaining few days of comparatively fine weather, and then act according to circumstances indicated by the movements of the Anglo-French fleet,—either proceed to Sinope or return to the Bosphorus; but keep together. We were the more anxious for a short cruise, to shake things into their places, knowing the liability of the fleet to be ordered out any day. In general slow in deliberation, dilatory to a fault, the Porte can decide on impulse, and order ships to sail or troops to march in disregard of wind or weather. Our proposition was overruled by an apprehension that the appearance of the Turkish fleet at sea would entice the Russians out. The position of Sevastopol might have been reckoned on for restraining the enemy from going far away, with the chance of bringing on a general action off a lee-shore; while a few frigates out would be a bait to draw him to our coasts. The Capitan Pasha a few days afterwards ordered the naval pashas to indicate a place in the Black Sea for a light squadron to winter in. The council, after deliberation with pilots and others, reported Sinope to be the only roadstead in which vessels could lie safely in regard of weather; but, viewing its proximity to Sevastopol, they added the expression of their opinion that they would lie exposed there to an attack from the enemy. The council was snubbed for their addendum: they were told they had exceeded their powers, their opinion having been asked on the nautical question only.

The Turkish navy at that time, like everything else in Turkey, was in a state of transition. The forms of two systems were in presence without the substance of either. The fitful energy of one had not been succeeded by the regulated forces of the other. Open vests, shalwars and sashes had given way to buttoned-up coats and strapped-down trousers; but under a Russian garb there lurked the galiondgi, reckless and indolent. Modern ideas of uniformity were at issue with prayers and ablutions at the option of the devout. You looked round in a squall for the men stationed at the top-gallant sheets and halyards, and you saw them on their knees absorbed in prayer. Ramazan, turning night into day, mocked the routine of the other eleven months. The officers were divided into two sets, the educated and the uneducated, each led by an admiral; and the latter were then in the best places. The educated talked slightingly of practice, and fancied crude notions on the theory of storms sufficient to enable one to grapple with the reality. The uneducated declared science spoiled the sailor, and some of them made it a point of conscience to set their chronometers in harbour to Arabic time. Rules to guide patronage and laws to measure offences, irrespective of position, were yet desiderata; and as the bastinado, and on an emergency the bowstring, had not been replaced by the independent court-martial, slander, the undermining element of Oriental society, and passive resistance, the potent weapon of the East, were unchecked. A vicious system of promotion during many years joined with slender appointments had lowered the tone of the service, while compulsory retirement from time to time, to make room for favourites, had deprived the navy of several good officers. The Capitan Pasha of that day, a nominal soldier, was as ready to take inspiration from his tchiaoushes as from his captains, and shared the reluctance of his countrymen in every sphere of life to seek advice until a crisis arrived: then generally too late. His council sat to echo his words and register his decrees. Withal there was a confusion of powers coupled with an absence of responsibility, and a pressure from without through unseen influences. The Porte, hugging itself to the last moment with the hope of receiving valid aid from its allies, had rushed into war scarcely knowing the meaning of the word. It sought no professional counsel. It listened alike to a chamberlain of the palace, to a scribe of the council, to a dragoman of an embassy. Thus a position was created which may be described by the word bewilderment. The armies (there being no telegraph) were out of its reach, but the navy was not. Every officer and man consequently felt in his heart a sense of impending disaster. They looked forward to certain defeat or wreck, and many expressed envy of their "fortunate comrades in the Archipelago."

Towards the end of October, a few days after the commencement of hostilities, a steamer from the Black Sea reported a Russian squadron of three line-of-battle ships, two frigates, and a steamer, cruising 120 miles from the Bosphorus. Whereupon the Capitan Pasha sent orders to the fleet at Buyukdereh to select one of two heavy frigates to send out next morning, to reinforce a light squadron of frigates and corvettes which had sailed three days earlier; and he added his desire, if the *Nuzretieh* should be selected, for Mushaver Pasha to go in her. The *Nuzretieh*, a long frigate with first-rate's spars, had scarcely been thought of for winter cruising, and was therefore deficient in many respects. One hundred of her best men had been lent to vessels at sea: they were at once replaced from the squadron at Buyukdereh, naturally with indifferent hands. While her captain occupied himself with completing his crew, getting on board also those on leave who could be found, and using his eloquence with his brother captains to obtain a few indispensable stores from their ships, the dockyard being drained, Mushaver Pasha repaired to Constantinople, and represented to the Capitan Pasha the rashness of exposing frigates to unequal contest, reminding him that ship for ship of nominal force the Russians were superior, and he recommended him to send out two line-of-battle ships as well. The Capitan Pasha replied that the Porte having ordered out one frigate only it would ill become him to discuss that question; but in regard of his further recommendation (in the propriety of which he entirely concurred), to have the next squadron, the squadron intended to winter at Sinope, composed of line-of-battle ships and frigates, instead of frigates and corvettes as ordered, he promised to submit it to the Porte's consideration. The Capitan Pasha concluded the interview by giving Mushaver Pasha a written order to abstain from firing first in case of meeting the enemy. "Are we not at war?" asked the latter. "We are," he replied; "but such is the Porte's order." Mushaver Pasha excused himself from undertaking to comply with it, since the first broadside from a ship in position might decide an action. "That is your affair," replied the chief. "I have given you the order and that suffices me."

The first heaving of the Black Sea under the *Nuzretieh* showed unmistakeably many of her crew to be on their trial cruise; and a judicious helmsman was not forthcoming, although several had apposite ratings. Her captain proposed at once to fit gratings to the hatchways. "They are to prevent the men running below in action," he said. "Is that likely?" "Likely! it is sure if the hatches are left open." That was simply a class prejudice. Throughout the war, whether ashore or afloat, the men, with nothing to gain, displayed more zeal than the officers, with honours and promotion in view. Next day the *Nuzretieh* spoke the *Pervaz* steamer, which had been sent out to look for the cruising squadron, but had not found it. She had heard at Varna of firing in the direction of Issatcha, and having nothing further to communicate steamed on to the Bosphorus. Her luck was bad. Sent soon afterwards to Ereghli, she fell in with a Russian squadron, by which she was captured, with her captain and half her crew slain, after a gallant running fight.

On the second evening after leaving the Bosphorus the *Nuzretieh* joined the squadron, and was hailed with the signal "Welcome" flying at the masthead of the Egyptian *Hassan Pasha*. Mushaver Pasha found that officer and every captain of the squadron in possession of an order to refrain from opening fire on meeting the enemy, and on inquiry ascertained that his own captain had received the same injudicious order. Two days afterwards, Hassan Pasha, apprehending a gale—he feared no other foe—telegraphed, "Is it right for us to remain at sea, or to bear up for the Bosphorus?" The *Reala*, Pir Bey, telegraphed in support, "It looks truly like a storm." The *Nuzretieh* answered, "It is right to remain at sea." And well it was she did, for otherwise the squadron would have been embayed on a lee shore. Before night the squadron was under low sail, with top-gallant masts on deck. A succession of gales followed, with rain, sleet or snow; the snow lying one night (November 11th) several inches on deck. Those gales proved very distressing: they made several vessels leak seriously, and the *Nuzretieh's* masts and rudder-head complain sadly. Pressed one night by north-west squalls and a heavy sea, apprehensive of losing a mast or the use of her rudder, the *Nuzretieh* was on the point of bearing up: one of her consorts, the *Kaid*, did bear up, finally reached Sinope, and was destroyed there.

One dark night, the squadron being under close-reefed topsails and reefed foresail, one of the corvettes mistaking the signal "Wear in succession" for "Wear together," placed herself in jeopardy of being run over, and barely escaped that consummation by hoisting with marvellous promptitude numerous lanterns and burning blue-lights stem and stern. The recent adoption by the Capitan Pasha of coloured lights led more than once to confusion in misty or snowy weather. The sufferings of the crews of the squadron, nearly all more or less sea-sick, with diarrhœa prevalent among them, excited mingled pity and admiration. Theirs was no ordinary trial of fortitude. None had flannels; few had stockings; many were still in white trowsers, the winter clothing in store being deficient; each had only one cottony blanket to cover him at night on a mattress not much thicker than a hearth-rug; and their coats were made of cloth through which the stars might be seen. Biscuit, rice, olives and water composed their sustenance, in insufficient quantity to allay hunger, much less afford due nourishment. None ever swerved, none shirked his duty; but many were carried below, exhausted by cold and wet. We may not criticize the Porte for the destitution of its navy. Within three months it had trebled its military and naval armaments, and could not face the needful expenditure. But we may regret its having inconsiderately ordered its ships to keep the sea for the point of honour, regardless of other considerations.

On his return to the Bosphorus, Mushaver Pasha mournfully reproached his chief for having composed the Sinope squadron, which had sailed ten or twelve days earlier, of only frigates and corvettes. The Capitan Pasha excused himself: he had done all that depended on him to carry out Mushaver Pasha's views, by representing them to the Porte soon after his departure. Entirely approving of them, the Porte had ordered him to prepare line-of-battle ships for sea, and they were nearly ready to sail when a counter-order came to the Admiralty: given, he said, by the desire of the British ambassador. "Inshallah!" he added, with a sigh, "our frigates will be safe." He had done his best on their behalf, by culling the best men of the fleet for them. Moreover the Anglo-French fleet had arrived at Beikos. The Turks fancied it came to fight their battles, and doubted the pluck of the Russians to leave port with that host in the neighbourhood. Instead, therefore, of dwelling on anticipation of disaster, the Capitan Pasha busied himself with doing the honours of the Bosphorus to his guests. He gave a banquet on board the *Mahmoudieh*, remarkable for the variety and quantity of viands and wines consumed, to the admirals and captains of the expected allied fleets, in company with the pashas and beys of his own fleet. With the champagne, he read a speech in Turkish—translated, after delivery, into French, for the benefit of the strangers, by the chief dragoman of the Porte—on the balance of power and the integrity of the Ottoman Empire. The healths of the Sultan, of the Queen, and of the Emperor, were then drunk with reiterated applause. The health of the English and French admirals, prefaced by thanks for their promptitude in coming to Turkey's aid, was next drunk with due honours. The jovial party then ascended to the quarter-deck, transformed for the occasion into a brilliant saloon, to listen to a concert by the artistes, male and female, of the Pera Italian Opera. The Capitan Pasha and the two admirals sat during the performance, in silent dignity, side by side, on a sofa, smoking long pipes, and their subordinates, picturesquely grouped about the deck, followed their example. Tea and cakes were handed round at intervals to the company by a score of *laquais de place*, in black coats and white neckcloths. All was "alla Franca." After the departure of the guests, amidst a blaze of blue-lights from the Turkish squadron, the scene changed. The deck was swept; the pianoforte removed; and on came, smiling and salaaming, *kutchek* (dancing boys) with *tchalghigiler* (native musicians).

The Capitan Pasha's statement, listened to with incredulity, of the ambassador having prevented his sending line-of-battle ships to Sinope, was corroborated by the blue book.* On its appearance his Excellency said, in explanation, he had vetoed their departure by the advice of Admirals Hamelin and Dundas; and to the question, asked with amazement, why he had relied for such a matter on the opinion of men unacquainted with circumstances and localities, he observed that the rank and command given them by their respective Governments left him no choice. The Secretary of State approved of his veto, with the following trustful words, in his despatch of November 21, 1853,—"The Turkish

* *From Mr. Pisani to Lord Stratford de Redcliffe. Pera, Nov.* 3, 1853.

[*Extract.*]

"The Turkish squadron, with the exception of the three-deckers, is to proceed into the Black Sea, and will probably be ready on Sunday."

From Lord Stratford de Redcliffe to the Secretary of State for Foreign Affairs. Therapia, Nov. 5, 1853.

[*Extract.*]

"I have succeeded in dissuading the Porte from sending a detachment of line-of-battle ships and frigates into the Black Sea at this moment."

Government, if it understands its own interests, will readily defer to the sound judgment of your Excellency and the practical experience of Admiral Dundas." In nine days from that date the flames of Sinope illuminated the horizon. The gallant admirals may have conscientiously expressed doubts about the fitness of Turkish ships for winter cruising: their own well-found, ably-manned ships did not relish it. That, however, was not the point. The point was, the Porte considering its dignity concerned in keeping a squadron in the Euxine, to have that squadron sufficiently strong to take care of itself at the anchorage designed for it.

War had already commenced in earnest on both continents. Omar Pasha had laid a clever decoy at Oltenitza, into which the enemy, underrating his opponents, had fallen. Satisfied with having furnished the public with an agreeable topic of conversation, he sat down at Schumla for the winter. Some have thought that, by following up his success, he would have wintered in Bucharest; perhaps without another blow. In Asia the Turks captured the Russian frontier post, Shekvetil, on the coast of Mingrelia, October 28, and Abdi Pasha won the battle of Beyendir, November 3. These advantages were balanced by the battle of Akiska, fought November 14, in which the Turks, under Ali Pasha, were defeated with the loss of twelve guns; and by the battle of Kedicleer, lost also by the Turks, under Ahmed Pasha, with several guns, November 18.

These battles, all but unheeded in Europe, where attention was fixed on the operations on the Danube, were not on the whole discouraging. The valour of the troops in the two latter engagements had been as conspicuous as the incompetence of their leaders (who were afterwards recalled and exiled to Cyprus) had been glaring. The delusion that the Sultan confers with high rank corresponding ability is the only excuse that can be offered for the Porte having made so wretched a selection of men for commands, in a quarter where she had no one else to rely upon; and where, owing to distance, it was difficult to arrive at the truth of what occurred. Asia was Russia's weak point; war found her there unprepared, with disaffection on every side. Had the Turks been ably led at the outset in that quarter, the current of success would have set in steadily in their favour, and have carried them to Tiflis. All that seemed to be required was a pasha willing to advance at the head of his columns.

The successes in Europe and in Asia gave the Sultan the title of ghazi (victorious), and led his Majesty to announce an intention to fix his headquarters at Adrianople in the ensuing spring. They wonderfully excited the spirit of Islam. The Turkish Gazette, alluding to the slain, said: "Drinking the sherbet of martyrdom, they gained eternal life." A pasha inquired of the author if he thought the Turks would be allowed to march to St. Petersburg the following year? Certainly not, was the reply. He mused awhile, then said: "I see how it is; Europe will not allow the Russians to come to Constantinople nor the Turks to go to St. Petersburg."

CHAPTER X.

The Turkish Squadron at Sinope—A Russian Squadron in the Offing—Choice of Measures for the Turkish Commander—An Opportunity of Retreat—Reappearance of the Russian Squadron—Position of the Turkish Ships—Shore Batteries of Sinope—The Russian Ships enter the Bay—Flight of the Governor of Sinope and the Moslem Inhabitants—Vacillation of the Turks—The Fire of the Russian Squadron—Total Destruction of the Turkish Ships—Terrible Loss of Life—Gallantry of some Turkish Officers—Indulgence of the Porte—Escape of the Taif—The Capitan Pasha reproaches the French and English Governments—Opinions of their Ambassadors—Sinope after the Battle—Pusillanimity of the Governor—Sufferings of the Survivors—Pitiable State of the Wounded—Their Joy at the Prospect of Removal to Constantinople.

But the memorable, the decisive event of the campaign of 1853 was naval. All conspired to class the battle of Sinope in the category of predestined events.

Scattered by a gale of wind on the way, Osman Pasha's squadron, the flag-ship with her mainyard sprung, ran for and re-assembled at Sinope. All the ships had suffered much wear and tear, and their crews, ill-provided with winter clothing, were so beaten by cold and wet as to be unable, for several hours after coming to anchor, to go aloft to furl their sails. The appearance in the offing of a Russian squadron the day after the arrival of the last Turkish ship, coupled with the facility, then clearly recognized, of its receiving reinforcements from Sevastopol, 180 miles distant, indicated the prudence of running for the Bosphorus when the coast should be clear. There were two chances to one in favour of a successful run. The enemy might not reappear; or if reappearing might be outsailed. At the worst, a squadron, composed of six frigates, a ship sloop, two corvettes, and two small steamers, might hope to sustain creditably a running fight with three line-of-battle ships, a frigate, and a steamer—the force which originally hove in sight to count heads in the trap. But Osman Pasha, distrusting the ability of his captains to keep their stations, allowed the possible contingencies of the third course to outweigh the other two. In his opinion, as he afterwards said, an action under way would have entailed the loss of all hands: moreover, the weather had affected his nerves; leading him to avow his preference to await the enemy at anchor, rather than face another gale of wind.

A surer chance of retreat yet presented itself. Four Turkish steam frigates, on their way home from landing ammunition for the Circassians at Vardan on the coast of Abasia, called at Sinope a day or two after the reconnoitring Russian squadron had stood away out of sight in a north-easterly direction. Their commander, by virtue of his higher rank, might have relieved Osman Pasha from the sense of responsibility which oppressed his judgment, and have towed the squadron clear of the bay—the chief effort—and further. The united force, six steamers and nine sail ships—four of the former well armed and some of the latter good sailers—would, if declining action, have distanced the Russians. Judged by the event, he was reproached afterwards for remissness; but if he had taken that step with no other authority than his perception of its necessity, his enemies —and who has not got them in the East?—insinuating the improbability of the attack, would have blamed him for over-zeal. Moreover, a fillip was wanting to rouse Europe, loth to plunge into war. So Mustapha Pasha, ruled by fate, leaving one of his steamers at Sinope, continued with the remainder his voyage to Constantinople, where he arrived November 24, and made known the unpromising aspect of affairs at Sinope. He had seen no Russians on the way.

The Russian squadron reappeared off Sinope the day after the steamers' departure, and remained in sight from the neighbouring promontory during the ensuing gale. It was then, November 27, reinforced by ships from Sevastopol, making a total of three three-deckers, three two-deckers, two frigates, and three steamers. They stood on and off for three days, waiting for moderate weather. During that anxious interval, the doomed Turkish squadron took up its final position in fifteen fathoms, on a curve before the town, its left supported by a sorry five-gun battery served by local gunners; which, nevertheless, did excellent service in the action, and with impunity, owing to its unobtrusive form and admirable position on the edge of a low cliff. The ground around it was literally ploughed with the enemy's shot, itself being unharmed. The guns of this battery were 14-pounders and 19-pounders—three of them old Genoese guns. Of three similar batteries, the fire of one was masked by its own ships, and that of another soon ceased through want of cartridges. These were the "respectable batteries" of Sinope, thus styled by Tophana (the ordnance department); and they were not exceptions to a general rule. From the Bosphorus to Batoom on the one hand, and from the Bosphorus to the Danube on the other, there was not on the coast of the Black Sea, when war commenced, a battery deserving of the name, nor a trained artilleryman, except at Varna. The Turkish squadron, mounting collectively 430 guns, many of them 32-pounders, did not make the most of circumstances. It ought to have moored in five or six fathoms water, from one and a half to two cables' length off shore, have established flanking batteries on the adjoining cliff with some of its inboard guns, and have landed its light spars, sails, and boats—inflammable and splintering matter. Presumedly, the Russians would not then have attacked it; or attacking, they would probably have been repulsed.

About noon of November 30, 1853, the Russian squadron, leaving its steamers outside to cut off the escape of any of the intended prey, stood into the Bay of Sinope under all plain sail, wind light at E.S.E., each ship towing her boats astern. It was thought at the time that the Russians, expecting the Turks to surrender at discretion, had manned their boats to take possession of them; but it seems more likely they had been lowered to keep them intact, ready to lay out or replace springs. Seeing the approach of the enemy, the governor of Sinope, Husseyin Pasha, who had kept his horses saddled since the commencement of the blockade, mounted, rode away from the town, and never halted till he reached a place fourteen hours distant. The Moslem inhabitants fled also. The Greeks, seeing friends in the Russians, remained. Conversing a few days later with some of the former, we commented on their flight. "When the pasha runs, can the people remain?" was the aphoristic answer. Thus ever in the East; the example of the chief is contagious.

The Turks, with customary vacillation, deferred firing until the enemy had approached within half range; or it may be their commander let himself be fettered by the suicidal order spoken of. The signal of the *Navik* for leave to fire was disregarded. The *Nizamieh* with the flag of the second in command, thinking the enemy about to double on them, first opened fire; her example being followed directly by the whole line. Whereupon the Russians rounded to, clewed up, and anchored with springs on their cables; three-deckers opposite the two pashas' frigates. During this manœuvre some of their ships suffered much by the Turkish fire; and had that fire been opened earlier, while the enemy was slowly bearing down, he would have had no easy victory to boast of. The enemy's fire at first was ineffective. Having given his guns too much elevation, his missiles during half an hour passed chiefly over the bulwarks of the Turkish ships, cutting away masts and yards; while it is deducible from the unimportant injury inflicted by them during that interval, that the Turkish gunners had, through inattention to their quoins, lost the aim obtained before smoke obscured their vision. A breeze then scattering the smoke enabled the enemy to correct his sights. Awful execution followed; inevitable with line-of-battle ships armed with 68-pounders pouring broadsides into frigates and corvettes. Some of the Turkish ships were unable to fire three rounds afterwards. In one frigate, in a few minutes, six iron guns were split, and several brass guns bent. In all, the supply of ammunition was checked by the slaughter among the powder-boys. Many hundreds of men were drowned endeavouring to escape in boats or on broken spars. "The devil was on one side, and the deep sea on the other." Turks do not, but Egyptians do swim like fish; hence the crew of the *Dimiat* frigate, remnant of the Egyptian squadron at Navarino, who took to their boats or jumped overboard after discharging a few broadsides, saved above 300 of their number.

Unable to resist the iron storm, the Turkish ships slipped their cables, when not cut away, and drifted on shore. The *Nizamieh* (60), in flames, fell on board the *Kaid* (50), and both were consumed together. In an hour and a half the action was decided, and if Admiral Nakhimof then, unheeding straggling shot from desperate hands, had ceased fire, there would have been no alloy to the credit of having ably performed the critical operation of attacking with sail-ships a squadron on a lee shore. But he continued to keep up a merciless fire of shot, shell and carcasses, which killed numbers of unresisting men, and burnt the Turkish quarter of the town. He did not cease firing till every Turkish ship save one was a stranded bilged wreck. The Russians took possession of the *Nesim* frigate, in hopes of saving her for a trophy; but making water rapidly, she was run ashore next day and burnt with carcasses. The *Farsly Ilah*, one of the destroyed frigates, had, under the name of *San Raphael*, been captured from the Russians in 1829.

The battle of Sinope, in which 2,700 Turks lost their lives out of 4,200, displayed vivid contrasts of character. Ali Bey, a fine fellow, became early excited: saying he never would be a prisoner, he bade his men try to save themselves, then went below to the magazine and blew up his ship the *Narik*. Otherwise inspired, the captain of the—— left her in a boat ere a shot was fired; deaf to the remonstrances of his pasha, who remained in her, wounded, till next day. The second captain of the —— also rowed ashore early in the action and narrowly escaped being hit by a shot fired after him by his indignant captain, who fell on his quarter-deck. These traits came out at the examination of survivors before the Naval Council. The inquiry also brought to light the devotion of the imams of the squadron, five of whom were slain out of eleven; the gallantry of Husseyin Pasha, who commenced his career at Navarino and closed it at Sinope; the gallantry of the Syrian Kadri Bey, drowned in swimming from his stranded burning ship towards the shore; and the valour of Izzet Bey, captain of the *Faisi-Marbout*, who passed through the ordeal unscathed.

Neither praise nor reproach was attached to the incidents of the battle of Sinope, regarded apparently as the decree of fate. The wary captains recovered favour after a few months' reclusion in their homes on full pay; and the prudent governor of Sinope was appointed the following year to a more lucrative government. The second captain of the ——, who fought the ship while his captain noted the working of the engines, forgetting the proverb, "Speech is silver but silence is gold," was passed over. This indulgence, more or less shown throughout the war—a deviation from the pole-star of a warrior race—proceeded from the predominance of the civil element in the rule of the land. In previous wars the Sultan's lieutenants—the Grand Vizir, and the Capitan Pasha,—had led in person the forces of the empire, armed with sovereign authority. Punishment was then terrible and reward ample, both on the spot, in the face of approving thousands. No poltroon then returned to the capital, and with lies and largess passed himself off for a hero; no brave man then had his character whispered away in ante-rooms. In the late war the nation fought in the shade of a bureaucracy.

Just before the action commenced, the *Taif* slipped her cable, steamed round her consorts in the direction of Gherzeh, had a running fight with Russian steamers outside, saw the flames of Sinope in the evening, made a detour in the Black Sea, and arrived in the Bosphorus with the stunning news in the afternoon of a stormy day, December 2, 1853, the day of the departure of the destroying Russian squadron for Sevastopol.

The Capitan Pasha's countenance the following morning showed traces of a restless night. His distress for the loss of his squadron was aggravated by a prohibition to appear in the Sultan's presence. He vented reproaches against the French and English Governments for their delusive attitude: "They bade us arm," he said, "resist Russia, and now in the hour of our need their fleets look calmly on!" A naval pasha present offered, by way of consolation, to go out with two steam frigates to reconnoitre the enemy, and communicate, if possible, with Sinope; but as an officer of superior rank had just declined that service with four steamers, the Capitan Pasha could not, out of consideration for the other's feelings, accept the offer. Intelligence, however, of some kind or other, was indispensable, and therefore the Capitan Pasha desired him to wait on the English and French Ambassadors, and ask them to send a French and an English steamer to Sinope, accompanied by a Turkish steamer.

His envoy found their Excellencies at the French embassy in conference with Admirals Dundas and Hamelin about the catastrophe; the circumstances of which, as far as then ascertained, he related to them. General Baraguay d'Hilliers frankly observed it was an incident of war, and seemed to attach no great importance to it. Lord Stratford de Redcliffe professed his ignorance, till within a few days, of a Turkish squadron out in the Black Sea, and the gallant admirals expressed themselves much to the same effect. Their innocence of knowledge on a subject of general painful anxiety, the chief topic of conversation in every konak and café, was only so far remarkable that the squadron had sailed from Buyukdereh in sight of Therapia and Beikos. The ambassadors objected to Turkish steamers going alone to Sinope, from apprehension of further disaster, and they objected to a Turkish steamer accompanying the English and French steamers they agreed to send there, because they said the sight of the Turkish flag might compromise their Governments. Carrying out that idea to its extreme limit, Lord Stratford de Redcliffe objected also to a Turkish officer going in the English steamer; his colleague, however, overruled his scruples, on the ground of the service he might render, and his lordship yielded the point, with the proviso that he should doff his fez if the Russians were still there, and keep his followers out of sight. The envoy's further request for extra surgeons and appliances to be sent with the combined steamers, prefaced by an exposition of deficiencies on the spot, was acceded to: he had made it hesitatingly; half expecting to hear that the sight of French and English surgeons dressing the wounds of Turkish sailors would be compromising.

December 4, 1853.—The *Retribution* and the *Mogador* steamed into the Black Sea, still heaving from the effects of the late gale, and in fifty hours anchored in the Bay of Sinope. The Russians had left there indubitable marks of their visit. The shore of the bay was lined with wrecks and strewed with corpses. Havoc had done her worst. Not a mast was standing, not a timber was left whole. The Czar, believing the Turkish squadron at Sinope intent on supplying the Circassians with ammunition, had ordered its destruction, and he had been literally obeyed. One vessel only, the *Taif*, escaped, and she alone had been thus employed. On landing we found Sinope like a town after an assault: disorder and confusion everywhere; the bakeries closed and provisions rare. Our arrival restored some order and confidence. We collected the valid Turkish officers and seamen in the town, and made them useful. There were thirteen officers and 120 men. Five officers, including the commander of the late squadron, and about 150 men had been carried away prisoners by the Russians. Many officers and about 1,000 men had gone off into the interior the evening of the battle.

The Governor, who had returned to his post, tried to excuse himself in our eyes for his pusillanimity; but no rational excuse could be framed for it. His defection had caused the flight of the Moslem inhabitants, and thence the destruction of their quarter of the town, thus left without hands to extinguish the nascent flames; it had also contributed to the neglect of the wounded, to a scarcity of provisions, and to general demoralization. The captains who had fled inland as far as Baibout, twenty hours distant, merited also reproach: they ought to have remained in or near the town, where their presence was much required, to collect stragglers and attend to the wounded; in a word, to supply the absence of the missing authorities. They had been punished, as we afterwards heard from their lips, by their sufferings from cold and fatigue on the way. Had boats put off to the wrecks in the night, after the action, many lives would have been saved. Many men sunk and died in them from exhaustion. Others survived through sheer hardihood. The Bash-hodja, for example, of one of the stranded frigates, and three others remained on the wreck three days and nights, and lived to tell the tale. The smouldering timbers, they said, warmed the water inside, and enabled them to bear semi-immersion nearly all that while. Soon after the ships had stranded, officers and men dropped themselves overboard and struck out for the shore, with the aid of barrels or pieces of timber. Many perished in that short transit, drowned or struck by the enemy's missiles. Husseyin Pasha reached the shore, only to die there of exhaustion. His body was recognized next day, and was interred at the *tekieh* above the city, near the tomb of Seiti Belal,* a Moslem saint in great repute with mariners. Most of those who

* Tradition says that Seiti Belal came to Asia Minor with the Persians in the 11th century. He was slain in a battle with the ruler of Sinope. His body was removed from the spot where first interred to the *tekieh* by the Turks. He is popularly considered to have been descended from Ali; but this is improbable. All *seyahs* (travelling dervishes) visit his tomb, where lamps burn at night. It is customary for the captains of Turkish vessels touching at Sinope to send presents of oil for the lamps.

succeeded in setting their feet on shore, apprehending pursuit, started immediately inland, and never stopped till out of sound of the guns. Wounded men, who under ordinary circumstances would have fancied themselves incapable of movement, managed to reach villages several hours off. We saw some of them brought thence to Sinope on horses or in carts, and marvelled how they had ever reached them. We particularly remarked three badly hurt men brought in in a cart from Gherzeh, six hours distant, whither they had crawled after the action. They explained their feat thus: freshly wounded, their limbs were not rigid, and mental excitement overcame physical suffering.

Our first care had been to look for the wounded. We found above a hundred in various cafés, in every stage of suffering: some in agony, many of them frightfully disfigured by explosions. They were stretched on the floors or on the estrades, without beds or coverings; the wounds of some had not been dressed. Two medical men of the destroyed squadron, a Pole and an Armenian (the others were missing), were in attendance, and showed zeal and devotion; but having lost everything in the catastrophe they were unable to afford much alleviation to the sufferers. Six days having elapsed since the action, and it being necessary to keep the windows closed to exclude the cold air, the stench was sickening: with the best hearts, our nerves could scarcely resist it. Gallant tars present were moved to tears at the sight of such unmitigated, unmerited suffering. When the poor fellows saw me they looked joyful; and those able to speak said, "Welcome, father! We have now hope!" On hearing that Captains Drummond and La Vallé had consented to convey them in their steamers to Constantinople they almost forgot their pains. That announcement was their best medicine.

The surgeons of the *Mogador* and the *Retribution*, and their coadjutors, took the sufferers in hand, and well performed their task of mercy. With much persuasion some of the wounded submitted to amputation; but they might as well have been spared the pain, for tetanus generally supervened. None who saw them can easily forget the distressing scenes in those dingy cafés,—their first glimpse of war's disillusory feature. Several wounded men were brought in from neighbouring villages, on the news of our arrival spreading. More being spoken of, we left two native doctors with two Turkish naval officers and ten sailors to attend upon them, with necessary surgical appliances; and next afternoon we embarked the survivors of the battle then at Sinope, excepting a few at death's door. God was merciful to the wounded: He gave them fine weather and smooth water on their voyage to the Bosphorus. A request came off from the authorities, on the *Retribution* and *Mogador* coming to anchor off Tophana, to defer landing the wounded until evening, that the people might not see them.

CHAPTER XI.

The Turkish Fleet preparing for Sea—The Author summoned to the Porte—Reception by the Divan of the Defeat at Sinope—Report of a Repulse of the Russians—Unwelcome Counsel—The Author's Representations prevail—His Suggestions for the Erection of Redoubts at Sinope overruled—Impracticable Suggestions made to the Porte—Turkish Policy in yielding to them—Gradual Progress safest for Nations—Result of Inquiry into the Disaster of Sinope—Blame unjustly thrown on the Porte—The Grand Council ready to treat for Peace—Warlike Demonstration of Softas calmed down—Manifesto of the Porte—Redshid Pasha's Note to the Four Powers—Lord Clarendon's Reply—Action of the Western Powers—The combined Squadrons enter the Black Sea—Notification of the Allies' Admirals to the Russian Admiral.

We found the Turkish fleet hurriedly preparing for sea, it having been ordered out on the impulse of the sensation excited by the battle of Sinope. The dejection of the navy was profound; but none dared give utterance to it. —— Pasha said to the author, "If you will prevent the fleet from going out, I and all the captains will kiss your feet."

Summoned there for the purpose, the author went to the Porte to relate the details of the battle to the ministers. Their cheerful cushioned apartment and sleek fur-robed persons deepened in imagination, by the force of contrast, the gloom of the dingy cafés of

Sinope with their writhing occupants. They listened, apparently unconcerned, to the woful tale; they regarded composedly a panoramic view of the Bay of Sinope, taken a few days after the action by Lieutenant O'Reilly of the *Retribution.* A stranger, ignorant of the *nil admirari* of Ottomans, would have fancied them listening to an account and looking at a picture of a disaster in Chinese waters. The mention, however, of the flight of the Pasha of Sinope elicited a spark of the old Turkish spirit. Redshid Pasha, in whose household he had formerly served, attempted to excuse his conduct: "He could not," he naïvely remarked, "be expected to remain in the way of cannon balls." On which Kiridli Mustafa Pasha gave him a scowl pregnant with meaning. No notice was taken of it, but it was not forgotten. Kiridli Mustafa Pasha had been given the seal of Grand Vizir as a lay figure, the real power lying with Redshid Pasha, the minister for foreign affairs. Within a few weeks of that scornful glance the former resigned and the latter took his place.

I had scarcely finished the sad recital when a minister of State rushed into the room joyous and announced the arrival of a Tatar from Kastambol, bringing news of the repulse of the Russians by the Turkish squadron at Sinope, with the loss of two ships. A few gloomy words from his colleagues calmed his exuberance. I then, with due regard for national susceptibility, disclosed to them the state of their fleet and its prospects at sea. Four or five thousand of its best men had just perished or been dispersed at Sinope; and the remainder, chiefly new levies, inadequately fed and clothed, were deeply discouraged. If the Fleet encountered the enemy, it would be defeated; if a storm, it would be wrecked. Either would be equally a triumph for the Russians. Such language sounded as harsh as it was novel to men ordinarily under the influence of self-delusion. But facts were stubborn. They had just lost one squadron—through presumption; they were at war without allies; so, after some vaporing for form's sake, they admitted the prudence of nursing their fleet in port until the return of spring with renewed confidence.

Bent, however, on showing a bold face, like one half stunned by a blow who still shakes his fist and cries "Who's afraid?" the Porte two days afterwards ordered the Capitan Pasha to run round the Black Sea with four steam frigates. This was, if possible, more objectionable. A corpulent landsman propped up by cushions, giving distracting orders, was the pleasantest feature of the prospect. Those steamers had been employed as troop or pilgrim ships for more than a year, with barely time allowed them to wash their decks. There was no harbour of refuge to run for in case of an accident; no depôts of coals on the coast. The Capitan Pasha signified his desire for the author's company on the cruise, at the same time expressing freely his sense of its folly, and unable officially to raise objections, desired him to represent them officiously in the right quarter: which he did. "If," it was observed to Redshid Pasha's secretary, "there is any object in view, let them circumnavigate the Euxine by all means, and no one will shirk the service, but do not send them out merely to show their flag. You have already lost two corvettes by this kind of bravado. Your frigates are too valuable to risk the loss of: you will require them all, and more, in spring, to carry troops and munitions of war."

The steamers were countermanded.

The defenceless state of the coasts of the Euxine being then tardily recognized, the author was ordered to confer with the council of Tophana on the subject. Premising the policy, in due season, of making Sinope a fortified arsenal, he recommended for the present the erection on given spots of the bay of four redoubts, trenched, mounting each ten guns; also similar batteries at Ereghli, Sampsoun, Trebizond, Ignada, and at the anchorages in the Gulf of Bourgas and in the Bay of Kavarna, one at each place. Armed anchorages are the condition for the weaker belligerent keeping cruisers at sea and carrying on its coasting trade. This plan, simple and inexpensive, was accepted, and a minute made for its speedy execution. Materials and labour were on the spots, and appropriate ordnance was in store at Constantinople. In another month the Turks would have been able to send cruisers out and let merchant vessels leave port, unanxious about their safety. But a diplomatist, whose lightest word in that day was law, interposed his veto: he desired the Porte to wait for a report from a competent authority, whom he proposed to send to the indicated places. Accordingly, two months later, an English and a Turkish engineer officer went to Sinope and Trebizonde on that errand, under his auspices. Their report, with corresponding designs, was worthy of their Woolwich education; but being too elaborate for the rough needs of actual war it remained a dead letter.

The misadjustment of means to ends has caused many suggestions to fail in Turkey. This had been more strikingly exemplified shortly before the war, by advice from the same eminent quarter to make a carriage-road from Trebizond to Erzeroom; an undertaking more arduous than the construction of the roads over Mount Cenis and the Simplon combined. Whenever the Porte agrees to an impracticability to please a friend it shuts its eyes to a job or acquiesces in a mystification. Four miles of that road on the side of Trebizond were made, absorbing in the process 25,000*l.*, when the enterprise was abandoned for want of funds; whereas had the Porte been advised to repair the existing bridle-road from end to end, the money might have been advantageously expended, and the road would then have proved invaluable during the war for military and subsequently for commercial purposes. Many other similar cases of the preference for the costly and problematic to the facile and requisite might be cited.

What Turkey can do is rarely suggested: what she cannot do is frequently urged. She is told to draw on European boots and run at the risk of breaking her neck: she is not allowed to walk briskly in her slippers, as inclined to do. Where a boat camber, for example, daily wanted, would at a trifling expense save annually hundreds of boats and much merchandise from loss, a breakwater for shipping is advocated. Where a few miles of paved road over a miry district or through a defile, of easy construction with local means, would connect fertile provinces with the sea or with each other, railways with high guaranteed interest are projected.* Where

* The guaranteed interest on Turkish railways, calculated on a capital in excess of the estimated outlay, is about 10 per cent. In the course of 1867 three railways—single lines—measuring col-

fountains lack water, spirit-shops abound; the vendors being foreigners, licensed by their respective chanceries. Where grammar-schools are deficient, a palace is built for a polytechnic university. Where whitewash, a prison dress, and improved drainage would suffice to relieve the administration from reproach, a prison *à la Pentonville* is designed; and for declining to lodge forgers, burglars, and murderers better than artisans, the Turks are termed impracticable.

Turkey might, with the money idly laid out during the last thirty years on dubious undertakings, have given her harbours quays and boat havens, bridged her rivers, and opened hundreds of miles of fluvial navigation in Asia Minor and Roumelia, by clearing the Saccaria, the Kysil Irmak, the Marizza, the Meander, the Cydnus, &c., of obstructions in their courses or at their mouths. Turkey, in yielding against her convictions, may yet deem herself wise in her generation. She sees special correspondents abroad, and hears of tourists "taking notes" at Pera or Therapia. For them and other celebrities she lights gas, patronizes learned institutions, copies Gallic codes, concocts budgets, subsidizes newspapers, and grants lucrative concessions. For them she pins on the ruffles of civilization. Nations do not progress by jumps or runs, but by steps. Macedonia, in ancient days, subdued Asia from the Hellespont to the Indus in a reign, and lost it in a day; but Rome

lectively 290 miles, will be open; respectively from Varna to Rudschuk, from Smyrna to Aidin, and from Smyrna to Cassaba. The guaranteed interest on those railways amounts to 294,000*l*. a year. Less than the annual expenditure of that sum on bridges, roads, and defiles would suffice to maintain a general healthy circulation throughout the empire.

welded her mighty dominion stroke by stroke. Modern Greece passed at a bound from subjection to an Oriental despotism to the exercise of constitutional liberty, and the deplorable result is too obvious to need illustration here. Napoleon overran Europe with his legions, and left France narrower than he had found her. Warned by the example, his imperial nephew contented himself with a ramble in Northern Italy, and extended her frontier to the crest of the Cottian Alps. Then, giddy with success, he took a leap into Mexico and sprained his ankle.

Next, to appease public indignation by hitting a blot somewhere—anywhere but in the right place—a council sat at the Porte to inquire into circumstances in connection with naval administration before the Battle of Sinope. A trial, in the East, often records a foregone conclusion. Much "dirt" was eaten on that occasion. Jealousies and animosities long pent up found vent. The Capitan Pasha accused his feriks, one of cowardice and disobedience, the other of remissness and error in judgment. The feriks making up their quarrel for the nonce, joined against the common foe, who had shown want of tact in not restricting his animadversions to one. They accused him in turn of incapacity and giving contradictory orders. The naval captains, seeing him the doomed scapegoat, sided with the admirals. Accordingly, the forms of inquiry having been complied with, Mahmoud Pasha was dismissed the capitan-páshalik and sent out of sight to Borloz, in Asia Minor.

The British ambassador, in a despatch to the Secretary of State for Foreign Affairs, dated 17th December, 1853, threw the blame directly on the Porte, and indirectly on other parties. He could not, he said, conceal from himself that "the destruction of so many Turkish vessels at Sinope would probably never have occurred if the ships of France and England had been sent there at an earlier period; not that he would throw the blame of that disaster anywhere but on the Porte and its officers. They alone, or their professional advisers, were cognizant of the miserable state of the land defences of Sinope. They alone were answerable for the obvious imprudence of leaving so long in helpless danger a squadron exposed to attacks from hostile ships of far superior force." His Excellency did not think of his own glass-house while throwing those stones. The French and English fleets were more or less under the direction of their ambassadors at Constantinople; and it has not appeared that *previous* to the battle of Sinope a wish had been expressed by them for any French or English ships to enter the Black Sea. The state of the defences, not only at Sinope but in every part of the empire, ought to have been familiar to men who claimed the right to dictate to the Porte its war operations, deeming it superfluous to counsel preliminarily with any of its military or naval officers; and who, with consuls at outports and contingent service money, had ready means for obtaining special information. The Capitan Pasha, the Porte's professional adviser, had recommended sending line-of-battle ships into the Black Sea, to obviate the exposure of a squadron of frigates and corvettes "to attacks from hostile ships of far superior force;" and his recommendation, approved by the Porte, had been overruled.

A more important council, the Grand Council, next sat to deliberate on peace, two months after it had met to deliberate on war. It sat on the 16th and 18th December, 1853, and deliberated on an identic note, drawn up by the representatives of Austria, England, France and Prussia, at Constantinople. Redschid Pasha was, as before, the spokesman; but in an inverse sense. The lay members voted with him, but the Ulema were less tractable. The council voted readiness to treat for peace on the basis of the evacuation of the Principalities, the maintenance of Turkey's sovereign rights, and a guarantee from the Four Powers for her independence, as understood in a "note" already presented by their representatives. The divulging of pacific views excited a few muderris and many softas to make an anti-demonstration (exaggerated in the correspondence of the day) at Sultan Suleyman's mosque. The seraskir met them there. Admonished by him, they gave up their arms. Interrogated afterwards at the Porte, some of them pertinently said, "If you want peace now, why did you declare war two months ago?" The most turbulent were told that, as they were warlike, they might go to the frontier. They replied to this sarcasm that their avocation was to pray, not to fight; the war was holy, and angels would assist them. Above a hundred of them were shipped next day and sent to Candia; there to meditate on the Koran and learn that all knowledge is contained in its pages for those who know how to read them. Each exile was allowed for maintenance four piastres (eightpence) and two pounds of bread a day.

The Porte then issued a manifesto, published in the State *Gazette*, December 23, 1853, and read in the mosques, to the effect that the Grand Council had unanimously decided to consider peace desirable, but with the maintenance of sovereign rights and territorial integrity; that it had come to this decision in consequence of the frequently manifested desire of Russia for peace, and by the advice of the four allied Powers. War would not be relaxed during negotiations. It warned the nation that if any one should dare to utter a word against the decision of the council, he would instantly receive condign chastisement. On the 31st December, Redshid Pasha addressed a note to the representatives of the Four Powers, acquainting them with the acceptance by the Porte, under the Sultan's sanction, of the terms of the identic note, since they contained nothing prejudicial to the sacred rights of the Ottoman Empire, and with the readiness of his Majesty to conclude a peace in the manner indicated by his allies. Lord Clarendon, in his despatch dated 17th January, 1854, to Lord Stratford de Redcliffe, said her Majesty's Government considered the said "note" quite satisfactory, and added the expression of a hope that Russia, alive to her own interests and those of Europe, would agree to the reasonable terms now offered to her. Too late! The cannon of Sinope had re-echoed in Europe and given a definite direction to public opinion; and that finally overcame the irresolution of the Western Powers: which had, in truth, seemed unchivalrous from the hour of Turkey drawing the sword. The French and English Governments had already written to their ambassadors at Constantinople, to inform them that the French and English fleets were to protect the Turkish flag and territory in the Black Sea, and to require all Russian vessels of war to return to Sevastopol or the nearest port; and to remove any doubts from the admirals' minds, Lord Stratford de Redcliffe, subsequently, in a despatch to Admiral D. Dundas, desired him to bring into the Bosphorus every Russian ship declining to comply with the requisition.

Peace could not reasonably be expected after this warning. The wonder is that it should still have been harped upon.

We will now recur to the steps taken with respect to the allied fleets on the news arriving of the battle of Sinope. Two days afterwards Redshid Pasha, in a letter addressed to the British ambassador, after observing "that the salutary object of the French and English fleets in the Bosphorus is to protect the Turkish coasts," intimates the desire of the Porte for active efforts on the part of the allies in the Black Sea; and the Secretary of State for Foreign Affairs, in his despatch to his Excellency, dated 17th December, 1853, expresses the conviction of the British Government that the allied fleets had been directed by the English and French ambassadors, on the return of the steamers sent to Sinope, to enter the Black Sea. General Baraguay d'Hilliers and Lord Stratford de Redcliffe had endeavoured to persuade Admirals Hamelin and Dundas to sail, and differences of opinion thereon had produced coolness among those distinguished individuals. The reluctance of the gallant admirals to quit their picturesque anchorage at Beikos during the month of December, 1853, remains a mystery, since no credit can be attached to the rumour in circulation that they had expressed themselves apprehensive of the Russians seizing the Dardanelles during their absence. There was no longer a squadron to save, but there was the duty of depriving the Black Sea of the character of a Russian lake. During the month which elapsed between the return of the combined steamers from Sinope and the entrance of the combined fleets into the Black Sea, the Russians might have disturbed the repose of every town (except Varna) on the shores of that sea.

Hesitation was at length finally overcome by the arrival, December 25th, 1853, of a despatch from the French Government, written on an understanding with the English Government, ordering the French fleet into the Black Sea. Ten days were still required to prepare the fleets for sea; those noble fleets, one of which, the Turks had been told, lay ready to sail even for China at twenty-four hours' notice. At length they sailed, and the ambassador announced their departure to the Secretary of State by the following pithy sentence, in his despatch of 5th January, 1854:—"The combined squadrons succeeded at length in making good their entrance into the Black Sea at an early hour yesterday morning." While they ran in two lines, with a fair wind, along the coast of Anatolia, with a few Turkish steamers under their convoy, her Majesty's ship *Retribution* steamed to Sevastopol with a letter from the allied admirals to the Russian admiral, to inform him that the object of their presence in the Black Sea was to protect the Turkish flag and territory from any aggression or act of hostility; of which they apprised him, they added, with the view of preventing any collision prejudicial to the friendly relations between their Governments and the Russian Government. No answer was returned to their letter.

CHAPTER XII.

Unexpected Return of the combined Fleets to Beikos Bay—They are mistaken for the Russian Fleet by the Capitan Pasha—The Russians again Masters of the Black Sea—Consequences of imperfect Accord between the Allies' Ambassadors and Admirals—Turkish Steamers with Troops under Convoy enter the Black Sea—Patience of the Soldiers under their Privations—Distress from Overcrowding—Former Instances—The Turkish Convoy anchor at Sinope and at Trebizond—Readiness of the Troops—Shiftlessness of Regular Troops when not cared for—Mortality in the Turkish Army—Confidence at Trebizond in the Allies—A native Preacher's Prophecy for English Unbelievers—Turkish Ideas of English Protestants—Invalid Troops at Batoom—Georgian Bashi Bazouks and their Leader—Troops under Canvas—Error in adopting European Clothing for Turkish Troops—Advantages of the old Turkish Costume—Re-adoption of Oriental Uniforms by the present Sultan—Foreigners wonder at the hardihood of Turkish Soldiers—The Secret explained—Habits of the Turkish Peasant fit him for enduring Hardships—Promises of Mohammed to Soldiers—Influence of patriotic or religious Sentiment—Comforts for Soldiers and Sailors of recent Date—Initiation in England by Royalty—Extent of Improvements in the British Navy—Former Condition of the Sailors—Unhealthiness of Batoom—Turkish reverses in that District—A Westerly Gale in the Black Sea—Disasters to the Steamer *Faisi-bari*—No Assistance rendered by other Steamers.

The combined fleets did not remain long out in the Euxine. Within three weeks of their departure, while the public were speculating on the chance of their meeting with the Russians, they were again moored in Beikos Bay. They had sailed to Sinope in three days, lain there eight, and sailed back in six days. Thus ended this memorable cruise, which had assuredly caused more talking and writing than the voyage of the Argonauts had given rise to. The admirals returned, on their own suggestion, uninvited, nearly unheralded. Admiral Hamelin did intimate to General Baraguay d'Hilliers the probability of his early return; but Admiral Dundas omitted to write a word on the subject to his ambassador, and his Excellency's disbelief of the rumour thereon, based on a private letter, led him to tell the Capitan Pasha the day before the fleet's reappearance in the Bosphorus that they were still at Sinope, with no intention of coming away. I was in the gallery of the *Mahmoudieh*, with the Capitan Pasha, when the fleets hove in sight, and, on the faith of the ambassador's statement, his Excellency thought they were the talked-of Russian fleet, chasing in a French and an English steamer in advance. A signal from the outer castles at that moment saved him from the jest of signalizing his fleet to haul on their springs and prepare for action. The Russians were again masters of the Black Sea, and profited by their luck (little to be expected after the notice given) to remove some exposed garrisons from the coast of Abasia, which the slave-dealers took advantage of. They may have seen in the retreat of the combined fleets an indication of vacillation on the part of the French and English Governments, since their ideas on discipline would hardly allow them to suppose it unauthorized. One consequence of this event was imperfect accord between the ambassadors and the admirals, soon made apparent by cross action in regard of giving aid to a Turkish expedition of troops and stores to the eastward.

The French and English ambassadors, disregarding professional etiquette, promised, without consultation with the admirals, more aid than the latter had counted upon. General Baraguay d'Hilliers, for his part, offered to carry part of the troops in French ships, then wrote to his admiral on the subject. Admiral Hamelin refused to embark a soldier, and kept his word. Lord Stratford de Redcliffe, for his part, engaged for English steamers to tow some of the transports. He told the Porte to take that for granted, and instruct its officers to confer with Admiral Dundas on the matter. Admiral Dundas refused to tow a vessel, and also kept his word. The severity of the season and the scantiness of native means aggravated the disappointment. However, there was no help for it; the gallant admirals were not to be diplomatized out of the position their sense of dignity indicated as becoming.

The Turkish steamers, therefore, eight in number —frigates and corvettes—embarked on the 6th of February, 1854, all the troops, 5,000 for Trebizond, and 3,000 for Batoom; and early next morning, with the transport-craft, eighteen in number, some under sail, some in tow, proceeded into the Black Sea, in company with an Anglo-French steam squadron under the command of Rear-Admiral Sir Edmund Lyons. The patience of the soldiers, half of whom necessarily remained on deck, exposed to snow or rain, was exemplary, their endurance remarkable. Their apparel was flimsy, as usual in those days; their food innutritious, in accordance with custom when embarked. The military authorities had supplied them biscuit at the rate of $1\frac{1}{2}$ lb., with a handful of olives per day, per man, the bulk of their ration going to swell the Debboi fund;* and though in summer such spare diet may have some of the advantages claimed for it, seeing the way Turkish soldiers are crowded on board ship, in winter it impairs their health. We managed with difficulty to give them in addition, from the ships' stores, rice soup in the morning. All hands should have had a turn below at night, but that was easier for their officers to order than to effect. Wedged in one mass between decks, many were deaf to exhortations to move, and being sea-sick, the stimulus of blows, if resorted to, would have proved ineffectual. Twelve hundred accoutred soldiers agglomerated in a steam frigate, with a crew of 300 men, for several days and nights, wet, dirty, and sea-sick, made a picture of wretchedness, in the face of which one's own comforts, slight as they were, seemed a reproach. We cast wistful glances, thinking of the room on their spacious main decks, on our allies' line-of-battle ships steaming with a fair wind on parallel lines.

Severe, even in favourable weather, the distress of the troops on board ship, through overcrowding, till recently, has been painfully aggravated in heavy weather; and on the occurrence of an accident at times fatally. Four years earlier an 1100 ton paddle war steamer, bound for Trebizond with a mushir and 1,200 soldiers, lost her rudder off Eregli, when, as the first inconvenience, seas

* The equivalent in money of a reduction from the meat ration has formed the Debboi fund, the object of which has been the purchase of wholesome varieties of diet for the men. This fund has often been abusively used for other purposes, as gala clothing for musicians, &c. It has in some cases proved too strong a temptation for its trustee to resist. Since the accession of the reigning Sultan, Abdul Aziz Khan, the men receive their full rations in kind.

breaking over her fore and aft, drenched everybody on deck. She steamed at a venture, wind ahead, when the sea abated, and in 104 hours made the Crimea, fortunately at Caffa, having in the interval thrown overboard 100 bodies of soldiers frozen to death. With a supply of fuel and a temporary rudder, she continued thence her voyage, and on the tenth day from the date of her departure from the Bosphorus landed her human freight in a miserable state, many with frost-bitten hands and feet. But for her making land before the exhaustion of her coals, no one on board probably would have survived to tell the tale.

On the 8th, at 11 P.M. we anchored at Sinope, and next morning, after landing men and means for recovering the guns of the sunken ships, we proceeded on our course to the eastward, in sight of picturesque mountain ranges covered with snow. We passed near Tirazon and Tirepol, towns carrying on trade in fruit and wood with Constantinople, and at 7 P.M. of the 10th anchored at Trebizond. Having sent forward a fast steamer to announce our approach, lighters came off directly to land our troops. We disembarked a few hundreds, when a fresh breeze setting in from seawards prevented us from landing more. The soldiers had revived with the prospect of treading ground, and every man stood ready with his musket and knapsack. They bore the disappointment manfully. Morning broke calm and bright. We landed them speedily, and had the satisfaction before noon of seeing them in weather-tight quarters, partaking of a comforting meal. Only two had died on the passage; though, doubtless, the seeds of disease were implanted in many by that trying exposure. Speculation, however, on that head is vain. Ere three months had elapsed, a third of them had perished, some swamped in snow, others wasted in unhealthy encampments. Sending troops in winter to Erzeroom and Batoom, in want of ordinary means to wrestle with their direst foes, cold and wet, was gratuitously throwing them away. Regular, unlike irregular troops, cannot take care of themselves, and when their government fails in that respect, a standing army is a fearful drain on the population liable to serve. The mortality in the Turkish army and navy, chiefly from preventible causes, has balanced the general saving of life since 1838 by the absence of plague and the practice of vaccination in towns.

Our arrival relieved the inhabitants of Trebizond from their fears of a visit from the Russian fleet, which the departure of the combined fleets from Sinope had revived. That occurrence, however, had not weakened their confidence in the allies. The English, in particular, had a warm advocate amongst them in Hadgi Pir Efendi, a native of Trebizond, the most popular of the Ramazan preachers at Constantinople, drawing always crowds to the Conqueror's mosque to listen to his eloquence. The English, he averred, in reward for their goodwill for Turkey, would be kept apart from other unbelievers in the lower regions until an opportunity should offer for smuggling them into a corner of paradise: the Prophet, he said, had certainly granted a dispensation for Palmerston. The learned mollah's orthodox reputation ran comparatively little risk from the utterance of this heresy, because the Turks in general—seeing no priest, cross, bell, book, candle, or procession, seeing them neither pray nor fast—believe the English innocent of religion, and therefore open to receive the light; unlike the Greeks and Armenians committed by forms and ceremonies to obduracy. The word Protestant has that meaning with them. They call free-thinkers of any sect indifferently *protestan*, *fra-masson*, and *kyzil-bach*. Another mollah, with Mecca rank, Koran expounder to the imperial children, inquired of the author one day if the English did not worship the moon. People, whether Pagan or not, must worship some object, and what more natural, he thought, than for a nation of mariners to select a luminary whose beneficent light guided their ships in safety off their stormy coasts. A functionary, with less excuse for his ignorance, struck by the expression "please God" in an English memorandum, asked a learned Armenian if the English really knew God. "Certainly; they are Protestants." "Are Protestants Christians?" "Of course; they acknowledge Christ." "But are they Christians like your people?" "Not exactly; they are a sort of Christians." "Ah—I understand: the Persians are a sort of Mussulmans."

In the evening we left Trebizond, and next morning landed the remainder of our troops at Batoom. We found the houses occupied before the war by the French and English consuls receptacles for invalids from the camp at Tchuruk-sou. They were full of intermittent fever and dysentery cases. The surgeon, a Hanoverian, himself bearing the impress of the climate, complained of the normal want of bark—the essential drug. After many representations, he added, the medical board had recently sent him an ounce of the sulphate of quinine. Batoom was then garrisoned by 800 regular troops, and as many Georgian Bashi-bazouks; an athletic set of lads appropriately attired in native costume, armed with rifles, pistols, and camas, and habituated by the habits of border life to the varieties of military toil and devices. Two of them, remarkably handsome youths, were in chains for manslaughter, and were evidently not thought worse of for it by their comrades. Their leader Achmet Bey, the representative of an ancient family of Asia Minor, the Khasnedar-oglous, differed from them in appearance only by a cashmere vest and by handsomer mounted pistols. He was a fine specimen of that race of nobles, the Deré-beys, whose extinction or depression into unimportance formed part of the late Sultan Mahmoud's policy. His wife, also of gentle descent, with a family of six children, was residing with him.

At Tchuruk-sou, a few miles to the northward, we found the bulk of the troops under canvas, in sad plight from unusually wet weather. Many of the men had no great-coats, few had blankets, but each had a sedjadeh (prayer-rug). Fire-wood was scarce, and meat only procurable about once a week on the average. The state of the roads and the penury of the military chest deterred the peasantry from bringing supplies to camp. A diet of biscuit and pilaff, seasoned occasionally by a taste of meat, with scanty clothing under canvas in winter, soon deteriorates the best constitution. A long hut had been erected for the sick, but wanting stoves it was only a degree warmer than a tent. Warmth is at once the cheapest and most efficient restorative as well as the surest preventive of sickness, and is more necessary in Turkey than in any other part of the temperate zone. The upper and middle classes fastidiously wrap themselves in furs, and the lower classes, hardy as they are, dread chills with reason, seeing their fatal effects on man and beast in a variable inflammatory climate. Nevertheless, in the face of general conviction, the Turkish troops and sailors have been exposed to wet and cold since the formation of the *nizam*, as though their natures had become changed by enrolment.

In clothing its troops after a sorry European fashion, the Porte erred philosophically and financially. Much of the sickness of the army and navy since 1830 may be ascribed to the abandonment of the sash, turban and bag trowsers, worn by the natives from their infancy. Many recruits never became used to the privation; they remained sickly, and generally died—the practice of invaliding being of recent date—before the expiration of their term of service. The sash protects the loins and abdomen, chief inducts of disease, and supports the frame. The turban may be unrolled in the bivouack, to envelope the face or encircle the throat as well as the head; and on the march it may be arranged as the wearer likes, to screen his eyes from dust and wind. The bag trowsers and loose-sleeved vest facilitate the blood's circulation in sleep. In the old infantry dress, seen in the museum of ancient costumes at Constantinople, a man could march lightly, breathe freely, and sleep comfortably; the desiderata which ought to predominate in the mind of every designer of a military garb. The reigning Sultan, Abdul Aziz Khan, soon after his accession sagaciously flattered the national taste and increased with self-respect the efficiency of his troops, by the re-adoption of an oriental-cut uniform. In other respects also his Majesty's supervision has improved their condition, especially in regard of the quality of their food and raiment.

The foreigner, ignorant of the ways of the land, wonders how Turkish soldiers manage to serve and fight through a campaign under privations more than enough to lay up European troops in a week. His pointer, Rollo, would, if gifted with speech, moralize in a similar strain about his fellow quadrupeds, the flea-ridden, garbage-fed scavengers of Turkish towns. One explanation will serve for both. Weak infants and weak puppies, as a rule, in Turkey die; such as survive the ordeal of infancy or puppihood are sound in wind and limb, patient of summer sun or wintry blasts. We will leave the canine specimen in the enjoyment of his liberty, from which a soft rug with daily caresses and chicken-bones would not tempt him,—the redeeming point of his character,—and consider the training of the human specimen afterwards, of that valuable class from which soldiers are drawn. The Turkish peasant lad, who has known a mother's love but never maternal care, and whose father places more faith in the imam's *nooskha* (charm) than the hekim's skill, tends sheep or cuts wood on the hills all day in all weathers. In the evening he returns to the paternal hut, says his prayers after ablution, devours his meal off a wooden platter, washing it down with cold water, repeats his prayers, and then lies down, dressed, in a corner to sleep. In summer and autumn a few years later he sleeps out with his sheep; leading them from pasturage to pasturage, or to market, which may be three weeks' march distant. He is early taught deference for rank and age. Obedience is an instinct under Oriental rule. Resignation to whatever may happen is indelibly impressed on his mind. He is familiar with the company of fleas. Ramazan has accustomed him to bear hunger and thirst with cheerfulness. The oft-repeated tale of the pilgrimage to Mecca, the caravan hurrying on day and night, leaving its dying and dead on the road, gives him a vivid idea of the forced march of an army. He is therefore physically and morally prepared for military life, its hardships and self-denial. The soldier's first lessons, elsewhere irksome, come easy to him. Genuflexion, prostration, and reverent gesticulation several times a day under a roof or the sky, alone or in company, have given him suppleness, and command of his limbs. The warlike Prophet in making *namaz* (prayers) a gymnastic exercise may have had military organization in view. Any afternoon during Ramazan in any popular mosque at Constantinople may be seen many hundreds of individuals of all degrees performing in several ranks their complex *namaz* together, the imam giving the time, with a precision and uniformity scarcely attained by the highest trained troops. Put muskets in their hands, you think, and there would be a battalion of soldiers.

Neglected, in comparison with the army of the Danube, the troops on the eastern shore of the Black Sea and in Armenia were essentially good. All they asked for was bread and gunpowder. They were nerved by their Prophet's promises. Mohammed said,—"The sword is the key of heaven: a drop of blood shed in action, or a night passed under arms, is more meritorious than two months of fasting and prayer. Who dies in battle his sins are pardoned." Europeans in Turkey, during the late war, fancied the *morale* of the troops affected by arrears of pay. There never was a greater mistake. When men are inspired by a sentiment such considerations are of little account; for proof of which we need only look back to the attitude of British sailors in the Napoleonic war, when with deferred pay, they were ill-fed, ill-clothed, and ill-treated.

Attention anywhere to the comfort and solace of national defenders is of modern date. The Royal Family has the merit of the initiative in England: the Duke of York with one, the Duke of Clarence with the other service;* and in more recent times the solicitude of the Prince Consort for the well-being of the army has been exemplary. Few imagine the extent of naval improvement in one generation. One must have served for that since the general peace during that period, after the necessity had ceased, when a ship's company, without excitement or prize-money, received no pay abroad. Ships were then floating prisons, with scanty fare and tiresome work. Gazing wistfully on green hills and gay towns, the men had no leave given them; tantalized by the sight of boat-loads of fruit, they had not wherewith to buy a banana or an orange. The prayer-book, the articles of war and an old song-book were their library; a jig on the forecastle, a yarn on the booms and a bathe occasionally alongside, were their recreations. Their diet consisted chiefly of biscuit and salt meat at sea, varied with suet pudding on banyan days; biscuit and fresh beef, boiled with cabbage, in harbour, the liquid being dignified with the name of soup. Sick

* The administration of the navy by the Lord High Admiral, the Duke of Clarence, was signalized by three important measures:—1. The abolition of banyan days: 2. The exemption of petty officers from the lash: 3. The appointment of commanders (second captains) to line-of-battle ships.

or well they had no more enticing food; and but for the nourishment sent from the captain's and the officers' tables many men would have died of inanition after fever. And finally, on their return home, they were compelled, as it were, through the way things were arranged in the seaports in those days, to spend their wearily earned three years' pay in as many weeks.

Malaria in summer and autumn, and humidity in winter and spring, have always rendered Batoom and adjoining districts an objectionable station; and as soon as the allies commanded the Black Sea, troops ceased to be necessary there. But having taken Shekvetel, a small place on the Russian bank of the Tchoolook-sou, and subsequently Redout Kaleh, the Porte, to preserve those trophies, stationed permanently on a marshy coast several thousand regulars, with as many Bashi-bazouks, and on its own men failing, sent there the Tunisian contingent.* Too many for the defence of places unlikely to be attacked by the enemy in awe of steamers' guns, they were too few for serious operations inland. Selim Pasha marched from Tchuruk-sou in June, 1854, to dislodge the Russians from Uzughetti. At first fortune favoured him. Two battalions of Georgian militia and many Poles came over to his side. But he afterwards fell into an ambuscade, and got routed, with the loss of fourteen guns; whereupon, suspecting treachery, he ordered several Georgians and Poles to be treated as spies.

* The Tunisian contingent consisted of 7,000 infantry, 2,000 cavalry, and 1,000 artillerymen. 4,200 died at Batoom, 2,000 were invalided there; 3,800 remained in March, 1856, and returned to Tunis in the Tunisian squadron, which had brought them to the theatre of war.

On our return voyage from Batoom to Sinope a westerly gale dispersed the squadrons. With that wind, the Black Sea becomes suddenly disturbed, as by the up-heaving of an earthquake. In their caprice the waves washed away in the first hour the rudder of the *Faisi-bari;* the loss being revealed to us by the steamer's deep rolling, coupled with the helmsman's exclamation, "She won't steer!" in answer to a reproof. A more distressing accident could not have befallen us —distressing under any circumstances, but particularly in a ship ill provided for such a contingency. The water rushing through the stern windows flooded the cabin and main deck; and shot, 32 and 84 pounders, escaping from their racks, rolled about, imperilling the legs of every one on deck, till penned up in corners by hammocks and coils of rope. Our crew became, as usual, affected by sea-sickness. With difficulty, in the face of that leveller of distinctions, we roused hands enough to fasten in the dead-lights and additionally secure the revolving guns. Our blue-lights and rockets of distress burned to no purpose, for when morning broke, after an anxious night, we found ourselves alone. A rudderless paddle-steamer is unmanageable, caring no more for her sails than for so many pocket-handkerchiefs. With moderate weather she steams head to wind; with bad weather she keeps the wind abeam, labouring in the trough of the sea.

In the morning, the sea falling enabled us to steam head to wind to the westward as far as the meridian of Sinope. The gale then freshening up again, the vessel fell off as before into the trough of the sea, but this time with her head towards the Crimea. Notwithstanding that direction, we felt compelled to let the cranks slowly revolve from time to time to relieve the "scend" of the vessel, which her doubtful condition made apprehensive, and to mitigate her rolling, which threatened, in the opinion of her engineers, to distort the frame of her engine. A one-gun Russian vessel dancing on the tops of the waves would have had her way of us; we could not have cast loose a gun. Our efforts to turn the vessel's head to the southwards proved unavailing: we worked the port paddle with the head sails set, then the starboard paddle with the after sails set; we could not make it deviate two points either way. She would neither face nor recede from the wind, but remained a log in the hollow of the sea. Two of our consorts, a steam frigate and a steam corvette, passed us successively on the second evening, steering for Sinope. The former disregarded our signals, the latter obeyed them, and remained by us till 10 P.M.; then, apprehending we should require assistance beyond her means to afford, (so her captain averred in excuse,) she also made off out of the gale for Sinope, the rendezvous of the allied squadron. Much vexed at her defection, which filled the measure of our crew's discouragement, we consoled ourselves with the expectation of seeing a friendly steamer, perhaps under another flag, alongside of us in the course of next day.

Hassan Pasha, the port admiral of Sinope,—who in the Grecian war of independence made a running fight, in which he was wounded, and taken prisoner, with the *Hellas*, commanded by Lord Cochrane,—when informed of the *Faisi-bari's* situation, got under way in a steam frigate to proceed to her relief; but on finding the sea run higher in the offing than he expected, gave up the attempt and returned to the anchorage; whereupon Hambdi Pasha, the governor of Sinope, applied to the commander of the allied squadron for aid. The gallant admiral courteously expressed concern for the *Faisi-bari's* distress, but excused himself from sending one of his steamers to her succour, out of consideration for the Turkish steamers in port; to whom, he said, the honour of succouring their countrymen of right belonged. So, between inaptitude on the one and delicacy on the other hand, we might, in our character of a "known friend in distress," have fared badly, had we not at last succeeded in rigging a paddle over the taffrail fit to steer a 1600 ton steamer with. Our previous attempt in that line had failed through miscalculation of resistances. We had fancied ourselves able to manœuvre the paddle with the vessel in motion on an arc of a circle, and retain it at the required angle by hauling on the quarter and counter tackles fitted to it; in the course of which the apparatus gave way. Taught by experience, we secured the second paddle at a given angle with the keel first; then, letting on steam, gradually brought the vessel round against the sea. When nearly head to wind, several deep plunges checked her way and made it doubtful her passing the critical point. After some minutes of anxious suspense she passed it. The jib was then run up, and as she paid off, gathering fresh way with the wind and sea drawing aft, her crew with one voice gave thanks to Allah; while their captain—who, giving the affair up as a bad job, had predicted the rupture of the second as well as of the first paddle,—capered for joy on the quarter-deck as nimbly as his obesity would allow

We were now at ease, with our prow in the right direction. We worked our strained paddle tenderly; we aided its action by varying the speed of the engines, and heeling the ship to port or starboard as needful by shifting weights; and, making thus a course, we rejoined our friends at Sinope in the middle of the third night.

The pintals of the rudder-post having been drawn, the Sinope yard could do no more, through want of a dock, than replace the *Faisi-bari's* extemporized paddle with another, stouter, built on the same model. The boatswain of H.M.'s *Sans Pareil* assisted us to rig it with his runners and tackles; then, in tow of another steamer, we returned to the Bosphorus without further mishap on the 22nd February, 1854.

CHAPTER XIII.

Drifting into War—Insurrection of the Greeks, headed by Karaskaiki—Not supported by Russia—Policy of the Emperor Nicholas and the Empress Catherine—Repressive Measures of the Porte—The Egyptian Contingent—The Greeks calmed by Fuad Efendi—Hellenists banished by the Porte—Impolicy of that Measure—Intervention of the French Ambassador—General Baraguay d'Hilliers threatens to leave Constantinople—The Allies intervene in Greece—Indignation of King Otho and his Queen—The Hellenist warfare beyond the Frontier of Greece—Successes of the Ottomans at Czetate and Karakal—Turkish Enthusiasm—Call for the Bashi-bazouks—Their Arrival at Scutari—Reviewed by the Seraskir at Constantinople—Their picturesque Costumes—Bashi-bazouks headed by a female Chieftain—Sensation caused by Kara Fatima—She is received by the Seraskir—Popular Delusion as to the value of the Bashi-bazouk—Their Ideas.

Events were then rapidly marching in the teeth of diplomacy. The pen was giving way to the sword. With words of peace still on their lips, and irresolution in their hearts, the statesmen of the West were nerving themselves for the responsibilities of war. They had lacked the moral courage to adopt frankly the means to preserve peace, and had allowed themselves, quoting their own words, to drift into war. Greece overcame their last lingering hesitation. She thought the days of the Ottoman monarchy numbered; she claimed as her inheritance the imperial crown of Byzantium. The Thessalians and Epirotes, excited by a recent pressure for arrears of taxation, rose in arms; the Hæteria fanned the flame, and Hellas aspired to profit by the movement. Headed by Karaskaiki, son of the palikar of that name, distinguished in the war of independence, a body of Hellenists crossed the frontier, unavowed, but cheered on by the Hellenic court and nation. This was the disturbing element on which Russia, not misled by her agents, had counted; and which, wanting boldness for the occasion, she failed to support. Had she sent 20,000 men and a few batteries by sea to the Gulf of Bourgas—an easy feat, with the allied fleets in the Bosphorus—the insurrection might have attained formidable dimensions. Successor to the policy of the Empress Catherine, the Emperor Nicholas had not inherited her sagacious daring.

Instinctively alive to the danger of a raya movement, the Porte comprehended the necessity of energetic measures of repression, tempered to European proclivities. Two battalions, with a field battery, were forthwith despatched to Prevesa, to relieve Arta, then besieged by the insurgents. Four battalions, in part for that destination, followed them out of the Golden Horn a few days later; and Abbas Pasha, having furnished on demand a second contingent of 9,000 troops—who disembarked at Constantinople, blue with cold after a deck passage of a few days from Alexandria—4,000 of them were sent on immediately to Volo; where they landed, three weeks after the date of the application to Egypt for further aid, in time to disconcert a projected attack on that place. Part of that force, on its march thence some time afterwards to Yeni Scheyr, was surprised by a body of Hellenists in the pass of Kalabocca, and nearly cut to pieces. Its guns and tents were afterwards recaptured by Abdi Pasha. Fuad Efendi went, in the course of spring, as imperial commissioner to the disturbed districts, with instructions to calm the effervescence as much as possible by conciliation, and use force only when that failed; in which service he displayed his usual ability and much personal courage. Enlisting the zeal of the Moslems of Epirus on the side of order, he cajoled the rayas into quietude by promises (disavowed by the Porte) of remission of arrears of taxes; and thus the conflagration was before long confined mainly to Thessaly, where it smouldered, flaring up occasionally with brands thrown across the Grecian frontier.

Justly irritated by the disloyal attitude of the Hellenic Government, the Porte decreed the banishment from the Ottoman territory, within a limited period, of all Hellenic subjects. This decree was at once harsh and impolitic. The social distinction between Hellenists in Turkey, many of whom are natives with Greek passports, and Greek rayas, is shadowy, especially in the provinces. They are united by language, religion, habits, and sympathies. They intermarry. Their pursuits are similar. Hence exile would amount to severance from their friends and interests. Where could they go? They would go to Greece. They would embitter by their tale and by the aspect of their privations the anti-Turkish feeling there, and the ardent would swell the ranks of Karaskaiki. The French ambassador timely interposed his influence, though not on the broad ground of humanity. Taking a sectarian view of the case, General Baraguay d'Hilliers claimed, in virtue of France's right to protect the Roman Catholic religion in the East, exemption in favour of Catholic Hellenists;

dismissing from his mind her formal surrender of that assumed right in regard of Hellenists, on the establishment of the kingdom of Greece. The Porte, in a dignified reply, disclaimed all ideas of wishing to mix up religion with a police measure. The gallant general took offence. He threatened to leave Constantinople in three days if his demands were not complied with; and as he showed himself in earnest—his earnestness representing Redshid Pasha's fall or his own departure—it was deemed prudent to depute the seraskir to wait on and endeavour to pacify him. Better annul the decree, than allow the French ambassador to depart in dudgeon at so critical a conjuncture. Meanwhile Lord Stratford de Redcliffe, anticipating his colleague's success, claimed, as a diplomatic counterpoise, exemption for Hellenists connected with mercantile houses in England. In the end a compromise was made, whereby virtually the befriended and rich, who might work mischief, remained; the friendless, chiefly provincials, were exiled.*

While the Porte successfully dealt with domestic insurrection, England and France undertook to keep their spoiled child, Hellas, in order, with troops in Attica. King Otho, who, having accepted frankly *la grande idée*, deserved better treatment than he afterwards received from his subjects, was indignant at this infringement of his sovereign rights; Queen Amalie wept at being rudely woke out of a dazzling dream:—and thus ended the comedy of the Lower Empire, acted with unbounded

* The decree of exile was revoked in 1855. Within a year after the Peace of Paris more than a hundred of the exiled Roumeliote families returned to Turkey; their example having been followed since by about seventy Thessalian families, chiefly natives of Phthiotis.

applause at the theatre royal, Athens, in the spring of 1854. Nevertheless the chivalrous Hellenists, nothing daunted by the grecophobia of the Western Powers, continued the war beyond the frontier against unprotected villages, and indulged themselves in their usual way at the expense alike of Moslems and Christians. Some of them, intent on indoctrinating the monks with propagandist ideas, crossed the water to Mount Athos; but cut off from reinforcements by the vigilance of the Turkish Ægean squadron, they got only prayers and absolution for their pains, with free quarters in the monastery of Zographo.

On the Danube, fortune also smiled on the Ottomans. Brilliant successes at Czetaté and Karakal showed that their right hand had not forgotten its cunning. All combined to excite enthusiasm throughout the empire for "God and the Sultan." Benevolences of money and horses flowed in from various quarters. Ladies made up military under-clothing in their harems; and the mistaken call for Bashi-bazouk was rapturously responded to. The Bashi-bazouk—whom the Porte, not always keeping faith with them, agreed to furnish with rations for man and horse—left their districts in bands of twenty or thirty at a time, and traversed Asia Minor; living at free quarters wherever able. Collisions occurred between them and the inhabitants of several villages, reluctant to comply with their requisitions in the name of the Prophet. As the gathering began in winter, many companies were three months on the road, detained occasionally by snow. On reaching Scutari they used to be quartered for some days in the Selimieh barracks, for repose there and purification in the baths of the town. Whenever a few hundreds were assembled and ready for inspection, they were conveyed across the Bosphorus, and paraded through the streets of Tophana, Galata, and Constantinople, to the seraskiriat. The seraskir reviewed them and praised their zeal. The mufti of the Darishura recited a prayer for their welfare. Then, elated with the compliments paid them, they proceeded along Adrianople Street to the barracks of Ramis Tchiftlik, or Daoud Pasha, outside the walls of the city, to enjoy a few more days' *kief* with full rations at the Sultan's expense, before proceeding to the frontier. This leisurely progress was calculated to prevent the passage close upon each other of inconveniently numerous bodies of undisciplined armed men,—a precaution more necessary in Roumelia than in Anatolia. We saw individuals of all conditions among them, between the ages of sixteen and sixty, some older. Aged men, warmed by the enthusiasm of the hour, had disposed of their lands, and departed for the holy war. They were attired in the historic garb: sashed and turbaned, and picturesquely armed with pistols, yataghan and sabre. Some carried pennoned lances. Each squadron had its colours and its kettle-drums of the fashion of those, if not the same, carried by their ancestors who had marched to the siege of Vienna.

The frequent transit of Bashi-bazouk during the spring of 1854, made at length the Constantinopolitans indifferent to the motley exhibition, as well as doubtful of the wisdom of having evoked such gentry from their distant homes. The Bashi-bazouk, however, from Marash, who arrived among the latest, revived waning interest. They numbered about a hundred, all kinsmen, under their chieftainess, Kara Fatima, a single middle-aged lady, with a complexion tanned by exposure, and a countenance which indicated self-possession and the habit of command. From the hour of her arrival at Scutari nobody else was spoken of in the circles and cafehs of the capital; and in hopes of seeing her, the avenues along which she was expected to pass were crowded several days in anticipation. The novelty stirred the etiquette of the seraglio into manifestations of curiosity. When joined by the Bashi-bazouks from Adana and Konia, forming altogether a company of about three hundred, they were crossed over the water with unusual aquatic honours. Deemed worthy of an imperial regard, they were landed near the palace. Thence the streets of Fondouklu, Tophana, Galata, and Stamboul, with the "new bridge," and numerous boats lying off on either side, swarmed with spectators eager to see the amazon. Except on the passage of the "sacred camels," laden with the annual presents for Mecca, from Topcapou Saray to Bakché Kapousou, one has rarely seen a denser throng in the streets of Constantinople. Kara Fatima, with an ancient on either side, rode first, habited in the Damascene riding attire, and armed with sabre and pistols. Her Arabian, of pure blood, scarce showed any ill-effects from his long journey. Her followers rode in pairs after their lady, bearing themselves with dignity, and evidently esteeming themselves, as they doubtless were, truer believers than the spectators; who seemed highly amused by the scene, although somewhat scandalized by the appearance of a Moslem woman unveiled. Arrived at the seraskiriat, Kara Fatima and her near kinsmen alighted, and went upstairs to visit the seraskir. Riza Pasha received them courteously. He invited them to be seated on a row of chairs, in front of his sofa. He regaled them with coffee; but did not vouchsafe the pipe to provincials. After an interchange of compliments, they took leave with profound salaams, the lady alone kissing the hem of the functionary's garment. She remounted at the foot of the stairs; her followers gathered round her in the square; the mufti chanted the war hymn; they caracolled in review before the windows of the divan; and then proceeded joyously on their way to Daoud Pasha barracks.

The stimulus given to the Bashi-bazouk fever of 1854 was a weak deference to the popular delusion about the value of such a force. Much mischief, direct and indirect, ensued; by the withdrawal of hands from agricultural pursuits, by the unsettlement of men's minds, by idle consumption of rations, and by the exasperation often caused by their presence in Christian districts. Fervid Moslems, taking words in their literal acceptation, the Bashi-bazouks were not always capable of restricting the sense of the expression, "holy war." With them, non-Mohammedans were all in one category of anathema. They looked to the war as a means of reviving their waning dominancy over the rayas:—the latent aspiration of the nation.

CHAPTER XIV.

Attitude of Austria—She is invited to arm against Russia—Her ignoble Policy—The Western Powers shew no Sign of Earnestness—Sir John Burgoyne arrives at Constantinople—His Measures—Their Effect on the Turks—Russian Policy in War—Best Course for the Western Powers—Military Force of Turkey—How this Force might have been best used—The Turkish Army—Its former Organization—Its recent Alterations—The Soup-Kettles of the Turkish Army in old Times—The ancient Turkish Naval System—Reply of a Mufti on the Question of Foreign Aid—Secret of former Independence of Turkey—Machiavelli on Foreign Auxiliaries—The Allied Fleets leave Beikos—A "Benevolence" resorted to at Constantinople—Spontaneous Contributions of the Provinces—Sickness in the Army on the Danube—Deficiency of Medical Stores at Schumla, Rudshuk, and other Garrisons—Fraud and Venality—Inferior Quality of the Supplies—Fraudulent Contractory—Tenderness for such Characters immoral—Gravity of their Offences.

WHILE Turkey was contending alone with Russia, Austria, menaced by the press and courted by the governments of Western Europe, maintained an expectant attitude. The only resolve she betrayed was, by concentrating an army in the Bannat, in February, 1854, to be prepared to have, at all events, a voice in the fortunes of the Danubian Principalities. France and England had estimated Austria's morality by a low standard. They invited her to arm against Russia—the Russia who had saved her in 1849. They expected her to forget that debt; to forget also the manifestation of their sympathies with the Italians and Hungarians during that season of trouble. We may not ascribe Austria's soothing deceptive policy in 1854 to a sense of gratitude alone—as much of that, as weighed in the balance, was nearly allied to apprehension; but we regret, for the honour of human nature, her not having pleaded Russia's assistance in her hour of need in bar of the Western Powers' pretensions. The plea would have been unpalatable, as the assertion of a moral principle in politics often is; but it would have raised her in historic estimation. She would still have occupied the same position, but with self-respect and Russia's esteem. As it was, she endured the misery, without "the pride, pomp, and circumstance of glorious war." Forty thousand of her army of observation in Galicia are said to have perished of disease. Nevertheless, Austria's desire for the maintenance of peace—seeing the tendencies of Italy—was so ardent, that, with the best intentions towards Russia, she would, as the surest means of preserving it, have joined the league, in expectation of Russia yielding to the imminence of the danger, could she have discerned in the demeanour of the Western Powers an earnest of the will to strike hard while the foe was unprepared. She evinced this disposition later at Varna. But neither France nor England gave signs of earnest purpose. The idea—unshared by Austria—was abroad, that Russia's power was factitious; that her extended dominion had been obtained by fraud; that, in the scornful language of the day, she was a sheet of paper to be crumpled up with one hand.

The first visible and palpable sign of impending war

on the part of the Western Powers, was the appearance of General Sir John Burgoyne at Constantinople, as *éclaireur* for the British Government. He enjoyed a high reputation; but it had been acquired forty years earlier in the Peninsula. Having fixed on Gallipoli, as a proper place for the allied troops destined for the East to disembark at, with the view of "obtaining a sure base of operations against any Russian force which might hereafter move upon Constantinople, or against any direct attack on that city;" and having recommended fortifying the Isthmus of the Chersonesus, he went to Bulgaria, to gather notions about the army of the Danube. Accustomed to associate valour and discipline with stocks and shoe-brushes, he discerned no merit in the barenecked slipshod Turkish soldiers. Versed in the mysteries of Vauban, he looked upon the modest redoubts of Schumla and Silistria as little better than toys. It seemed to unprofessional people overcautious in the Allies commencing war by entrenching themselves at Gallipoli while the Russians were on the left bank of the Danube. It was calculated neither to deter the Czar by the prospect of energetic hostility, nor to encourage the Porte by the hope of zealous co-operation. Then reflecting Turks began to doubt the wisdom of Turkey having rejected the last chance of peace. But they were few: the nation had embarked in war, and was for seeing it out. The selection of so distant a base of operations betrayed inattention to the incidents of the war of 1828–29. Even then, with Turkey just emerged from an exhausting civil strife, and shaken to her centre by the throes of a social Moslem revolution, Russia had required two arduous campaigns to cross the Balkans.

The idea had been entertained of a Russian division crossing the Danube above Kalafat, to excite the Slavic races in Northern Turkey; but although those locally misinformed, making light of the seldom belied tenacity of Turkish troops, may have let their fancy outrun their judgment, the Powers interested, even if believing it feasible, felt guaranteed by Russia's doubt of Austria's neutrality from such bold strategy: little, moreover, in accordance with her genius. Russia had never in the course of her history seized victory by the forelock, and had rarely commenced war under favourable auspices. Unskilfully or unseasonably attacked, she had either evolved victory out of defeats, or, by an opportune peace, had retired a pace for a surer leap next time. Taught by that lesson, Western Europe should have commenced by striking heavy discouraging blows; which react from matter on mind, are difficult to rally under, and which in our days of publicity and rapid transmission of news produce on public opinion tenfold the effect producible when official despatches were the meagre record of passing events. That might have been accomplished by giving Turkey a principal, not a subordinate, part in the general war.

Turkey, when her allies were thinking of entrenching themselves in the Chersonesus of Thrace, possessed 150,000 troops under arms, with good artillery, the third division of redif in reserve, and 50,000 irregulars. Since 170 years she had not made so imposing a display. Her army had been collected silently and unostentatiously. It stood to its arms without fear of punishment, or hope of reward; but wanting a regular commissariat and organized hospitals and depôts—living from hand to mouth, so to speak—with no confidence in the administration, it was an army for the occasion. Enthusiasm creates but cannot maintain an army unaided by activity and success. "Forward!" should have been its motto. If rightly informed of the position in the spring of 1854, the Allies would have turned to account the energies of that devoted, afterwards contemned, army. Profiting by its enthusiasm and facile locomotion, they would have sent their own troops—detained first at Gallipoli, next at Constantinople—at once to Bulgaria, to give it moral support; and, if necessary, act by it the part of the Grecian auxiliaries of old with the Persian armies. Unincumbered by baggage, careless of comforts, patient under privations, it was just the force to co-operate with that novel and tremendous instrument of war, a steam fleet. While embarking 20,000 European troops, you might embark, convey 200 miles, and disembark 40,000 Turkish troops, in fewer vessels.

I speak of the Turkish army of 1854 relatively. I do not compare it, in its relation to contemporary armies, with its predecessors, whose battle-fields were in Hungary. The conditions were dissimilar. Halting between two systems—one dear to the nation, the other foreign to its instincts—the Turkish army no longer possessed the organization long peculiar to itself, which had rendered it often victorious over the imperialists in the sixteenth and seventeenth centuries, and redoubtable to the Russians in the eighteenth century; and it had not acquired the nerve of modern European armies—a body of high-bred disciplined officers influenced by honour, for whom death is preferable to shame. In former days, when Turkey was a vast camp, when every gentleman and yeoman slept with arms by his side and horses saddled in their stables, its military organization included special corps not admitting of improvisation, which give coherence to an army, and round which newly raised troops rally with confidence. Besides the enrolled Janissaries, the artillery, the bostandgis, and the yamaks, there were the djibedgis, guards of the reserve ammunition and the baggage, each man acquainted with a handicraft; the mounted tchiaushes, for police and courier service; the laghumdgis (miners); and the arabadgis, artillery and waggon drivers, composed of Bulgarians. When sick and wounded were left to fate, hospitals were supererogatory.

In puerile dread of every usage reminiscent of Janissaryism, *i. e.* of Ottomanism, in servile admiration of every European fashion, Turkey abandoned much of what was suitable in its own system and borrowed much of the unsuitable from Europe; and—singular coincidence—while travestying itself, Europe took up many of its cast-off habits. Its military garb, with slight variation, has been adopted by France for her zouaves, and will probably become the pattern for all armies; cannon of large calibre (of Turkish origin) are now cast in the foundries of every state; transport, army works, and police corps, in other days exclusively Turkish, are now considered essential by every war office; and the short stirrups and high saddle of the East, obviative of sore backs, are beginning to be faintly recognized as augmenting the rider's power over his weapon and steed. By engrafting modern instruction and tactics on her ancient system, reformed, Turkey would have united the strength of two eras without the weakness of either. One feature of the ancient system—a solecism in military practice — merits special notice. The soup-kettles of the Turkish armies, second only in value to the soldiers' weapons, did the duty of colours in other armies. Invested by military philosophy with the ideal value attached elsewhere to intrinsically useless emblems, they were rallied round with devotion, and the loss of any of them stigmatized the company to which they had belonged.

Similar remarks apply to the navy. The galiondji system,* at once solid and elastic, admitting of improvement in every sense to meet modern exigencies, harmonized with national habits and was singularly adapted for a navy restrictively employed on its own coasts.

Many orthodox Turks, desirous of naval, averted their eyes from the prospect of military, co-operation. The Sheick ul Islam expressing disinclination to it, and his assent being necessary, he was deposed and replaced by the mufti of the military council. The new head of the law answered allegorically the pregnant question, "Shall we

* The galiondjis, in their latter days about 5,000 in number, were a permanently enrolled body at Constantinople of seamen-gunners and seamen. The married men went to their homes at night, the bachelors lived in barracks They received each a ration, clothes, and about thirteen shillings a month. When a line-of-battle ship, for example, fitted out, two master gunners, each with a crew varying from sixty to eighty men, a bashrais (boatswain) with a crew of about eighty men, a sail-maker and crew, were sent on board from the galiondji depôt, with artificers from the dockyard. The remainder of the crew was drawn from the merchant service without regard to a man's religion, and as a cruise rarely lasted above three months, volunteers were always forthcoming. When the fleet fitted out it was manned by proclamation from the sea-bordering towns. The defect of the system lay in the somewhat exclusive control of the master-gunner and boatswain over their respective crews, which affected the captain's authority and impaired discipline.

avail ourselves of foreign troops?" "Hunters," he was reported to have said, "take dogs with them to pursue their game." The learned man had doubtless studied the Koran, but he certainly had not read the fable of Actæon. The prudence of the step, in a Turkish point of view, was doubtful. It was breaking a charm. The secret of Turkey's independence and greatness had been her isolation and her self-sustaining pride. Turkey had fought alone with Russia for above a century. She had fought unsuccessfully, had been defeated, had surrendered territory, but had never lost confidence in herself. Casting the blame of defeat on ignorant pashas, on want of concert, on a vicious administration, she had neither felt nor admitted organic weakness. Machiavelli, in his treatise on war, says: "Let a prince or a republic determine on anything rather than on calling in auxiliary troops, and above all let him or it beware of placing himself or itself at their discretion. Any treaty with his or its enemy, any concession however onerous, will be less fatal to him or it than this measure."

A French and an English war-steamer gave proof of their governments being at last in earnest by embarking, towards the end of March, two battalions of Turkish riflemen for conveyance to Varna; an imperial commissioner proceeded the same day to the Hellespont to be ready to welcome the allied troops on their arrival in Turkey; and two days afterwards the allied fleets again left Beikos; this time for Baltchik, to wait there the expected declaration of war by England and France. The allied admirals declined the company of any Turkish vessel, and virtually ignored the Turkish fleet by refusing to exchange recognition signals with it; assigning, in excuse for their unsociability, the necessity of its continuance in the Bosphorus for the defence of Constantinople.

About that time a council of Ulema and dignitaries was convened for the purpose of raising a "benevolence" from the civil, military, and naval authorities of the state above the rank of colonel, and from the wealthy denizens of the capital. Hitherto Constantinople had escaped this test of patriotism, while warmly applauding provincial liberality. Although termed voluntary, the gifts were often involuntary. Lists of names were circulated by authority, and no one ventured to signalize himself by writing down less than the expected sum; which, in the case of officers and employés, amounted to about ten days' pay. Flag and general officers and civilians of equivalent rank had already, during nine months, surrendered one-fifth of their pay to the treasury. In the provinces "benevolence" seemed more spontaneous than in the capital. Some lists, including sums from 100 to 10,000 piastres, indicated general contributory concurrence.* None, however, could escape the ordeal. Certain districts, remiss in responding to the appeal, were long afterwards invited to pay up arrears. Gradually, as enthusiasm waned, benevolence degenerated into requisition. Even the favoured capital was called upon for a second "benevolence" in the winter of 1854–55, for *hirkas* (wadded vests) for the troops at Eupatoria. The benevolent were rewarded by the publication of the subscription lists in the Turkish

* During the years 1854-55, the inhabitants of part of Turkey gave in money, under the head of *iané umumié* (benevolence), about 1,500,000*l.*; and in kind, as horses, cattle, corn, oil, &c., they furnished supplies gratis to an equal amount.

newspapers. Arabic, Kurdish, Turkish, Albanian, and Bosnian names grated harshly on the ears of the euphonious-tongued Constantinopolitans; who thus learned the heterogeneity of the Moslem population of the empire. By such means, in aid of the ordinary revenue, by a capitation tax of twenty piastres on males, by paying for supplies with promissory notes, by borrowing the orphans' fund, and by holding back more or less the pay of the public services, the Porte tided over the first year without a foreign loan.

But all was not rose-coloured. While fairly supplied for the shock of arms, the army of the Danube was in other respects ill off; sickness and other privations had, during the winter, decimated the garrisons along the Danube. The medical commission sent from Constantinople to the frontier in the spring of 1854 reported unsatisfactorily. At Schumla, the quarters of 25,000 men, they found only 200 drachms of sulphate of quinine, and a scarcity of lint, tourniquets, and bandages; similar deficiencies existed everywhere; and Rudschuk, garrisoned by 7,000 men, possessed no instrument for extracting a ball. The discrepance between the amount of medical stores charged to the Government and the amount in camp argued venality somewhere. The army surgeons declared that their stores never reached them in the amount stated. Their detractors affirmed that they trafficked with them for their own benefit. I do not pretend to adjust the balance, nor would the attempt be worth the trouble; but I may say that, whatever doubts may have existed about the quantity, none has existed about the inferior quality of the medicines supplied to the armies. A similar reproach applies to their food and clothing; most of the *pasterma* (dried meat) sent to the troops at Eupatoria in 1855 had to be thrown to the dogs. Unholy gains were made from such sources, with which honours were purchased as well as houses. No supplies issued from the stores in the capital reached their destination in their integity. Bullion made no exception to the rule; twenty millions of piastres (180,000*l.*) of the sums sent in 1853-54 to the army of the Danube were never satisfactorily accounted for.

The country where George of Cappadocia—transformed afterwards, according to Gibbon, into "the renowned St. George of England"—acquired wealth by supplying ill-cured bacon to the Roman armies, will never want apologists for the frauds of contractors nor panegyrists of their assumed virtues; and though none, like the "infamous George," may hope to attain ecclesiastical all may aspire to lay honours. At this we have no right to affect surprise. The Eastern Empire, whether under a Constantine or an Amurath, is in some respects immutable. But we have a right to feel surprise at the tenderness of western society for shortcomings which, setting human considerations on one side, may lead to national disgrace. Deteriorated medicines baffle the physician's skill; adulterated food and flimsy shoes disconcert the general's strategy. Society brands the individual who takes arms against his country with the name of traitor, and shoots him when caught, although he may never have had the opportunity to point a rusty firelock at it; yet refrains from applying the epithet to traders who undermine the health of their country's troops fighting her battles, by supplying inferior food and raiment, and who do not scruple even—relying on the indulgence accorded to the misdeeds of capital—to sell arms and ammunition to her foes. Of those traders—"all honourable men"—who sell preserved offal and spurious lime-juice to vessels bound on long voyages, we will only say with Dante, "Guarda e passa!" Their sin is grievous. When offences substantially alike shall be called by one name, the task of legislation will be lightened, and society be freed from the danger underlying it in the impression—daily gaining strength with education in men's minds—that crime is measured by a relative standard.

CHAPTER XV.

The Turkish Fleet eager to enter the Euxine—Employment for it suggested—Enthusiasm in the Caucasus for the Sultan—How to profit by it—Schamyl ruler of Daghestan—His Naib, Mehemed Emin Efendi, in Circassia—Their opposite Modes of Rule—Their Policy in regard to the War—The Caucasus the vulnerable Part of Russia—Mushaver Pasha's Proposal for employing the Turkish Fleet—How received by the Allied Admirals—An Anglo-French Expedition to the Caucasian Coast projected—Its Futility—The Turks best fitted to deal with the Circassians—A Turkish Steamer asked for to accompany the projected Expedition—Reasons for its Refusal—Views of the Porte.

During some days following the departure of the allies' fleets for Baltchik, the Turkish fleet, again alone in the Bosphorus, felt that kind of relief which is experienced in a quiet house on the departure of an exacting guest. With the closing of their friends' slaughter-houses and grog-shops, the air felt purer. But the sensation was transient. The Black Sea lay before them, and all hands sighed to follow the allies into it. They did not imagine, that the Russians, even if surmising the tenacity of its anchors wherever they might happen to be dropped, would think of slipping by the Anglo-French fleet into the Bosphorus to scare the fair inmates of the harems and ruffle the equanimity of the embassies on its banks. Still less did they give them credit for the bold conception of running with a choice squadron the gauntlet of the castles of the

Bosphorus during Ramazan—the season of drowsy days and festive nights; passing then, under strange colours, those of the Hellespont, into the Mediterranean, to intercept French and English transports steering eastwards, visit their co-religionists in the Ionian islands, salute Valette at a respectful distance, and finally seek a neutral port within or without the Straits of Gibraltar. Tranquil on that head, one of its officers, privileged in that respect, submitted to the Capitan Pasha a suggestion for the active employment of the Turkish fleet during the ensuing summer. There was appropriate work for it on the eastern shore of the Black Sea; which the Turks might but which the allies with the best intentions could not perform.

The Caucasians were then, like the Moslems of Turkey, at the boiling-point of enthusiasm for God and the Sultan. The spirit of Islam, normally lukewarm in Circassia, in parts tainted with idolatry, was roused, and for the hour rivalled the earnest fanaticism of Daghestan. To profit by the excitement, to unite the Circassians and Daghestanians in common action, was eminently worthy of consideration in a war undertaken to depress Russia. Left to their own inspirations, the Caucasians would effect nothing. Left in possession of the Caucasus, Russia would not be materially weakened by any terms of peace. Two men were then, in a different degree, prominent in the mountainous region between the Euxine and the Caspian. Sheick Schamyl, an austere Moslem—who might, if Mohammed had not declared the cycle of prophecy closed, have made himself to be regarded as a prophet—had long ruled theocratically in Daghestan. He possessed troops, forts, a police, and from time to time exchanged courtesies with Russia, as well as shot. With success, his views had extended. Aspiring to bring Circassia under his suzerainty, he had about ten years previously named Mehemed Emin Efendi his naib (vicar) there. Mehemed Emin Efendi, aided by Sheick Schamyl's prestige, had striven on his own account, and had gradually brought the turbulent tribes of Circassia more or less under control. But he failed to obtain the same result as his patron had obtained—cheerful obedience. Sheick Schamyl ruled with religion, his naib by intimidation, acquiesced in by the majority through the need of union for self-defence. That need ceased to be imperative with the commencement of war, and with it jealousy of the naib's ascendancy transpired. Feeling his authority menaced by tribal rivalries, the naib repaired to Constantinople to seek for imperial countenance. He obtained it, promised fealty, and returned to Circassia with the dignity of Pasha. Nevertheless, he had no more idea of rendering Circassia dependent on Turkey than on Russia, still less of subjecting it to the influence of the Franks; whose views, distorted by the partisans of Russia and of Turkey, were not to be counted upon.

There was little doubt, if the Circassians were given time for reflection, that their clannish notions would prevail over feelings of revenge on Russia or of love for Turkey. They had scarcely any more innate desire to be ruled by Turkish pashas than by Russian generals. Scheick Schamyl and his naib were aware of this instinct, and though at first carried away by the stream, they were unable to oppose the revived loyalty for the padishah, they hoped, on the subsidence of its ebullition, to bring the mountaineers to agree with them in the suicidal policy of remaining neuter during the impending struggle of empires. They reckoned on circumstances rendering the Caucasus again a barrier between Russia and the Turco-Persian empires: an Oriental Switzerland. They expected to see Russia disastrously beaten by the Allies. They would then be masters of the position, independent of Russia, Turkey, and Frenghistan. Our aim, profiting by the enthusiasm of the hour and the Sultan's name, was to frustrate this erroneous calculation by enlisting the Caucasians actively in the war; whereby, if nothing more had ensued, the Russian trans-Caucasian army would have been compelled to remain on the defensive. The position would then probably have been reversed. There was Russia's vulnerable quarter: the only quarter where a vital blow on her ambition could be struck; the only quarter where a result beneficial to England and to Turkey could be educed from the war. The Caucasians, the Turkish fleet, and the Turkish Asiatic army were the instruments to work with.

In his letter * to the naval chief, Mushaver Pasha proposed that the Turkish fleet, stored with military aid for the Circassians, should run along the coast of Anatolia to animate the inhabitants; tarrying some days on the way at Sinope, to practise the crews in disembarking and embarking and in the use of their arms. Thence proceed to Batoom to concert measures with the military authorities there; then take Soukhoum Kaleh, and make that port a base of co-operation. Afterwards, reduce the other Russian forts on the coast of Abasia and show its flag to the Crimeans - unseen by them in

* *Vide* Appendix I.

war for nearly a century. This project found favour. The fleet was ordered to prepare for sea; and the writer was directed by the Capitan Pasha to proceed to Baltchik to communicate with the allied admirals on the matter. This deference had been rendered necessary by the injunction laid on the Porte by the French and English ambassadors to abstain from undertaking any naval operation without previous consultation with the allied admirals.

The allied admirals evinced disinclination to discourse with Mushaver Pasha, on his arrival at Baltchik, about the Turkish fleet. They at length, however, yielding to his respectful persistency, agreed to confer among themselves on the mode of employing it during the summer; and having met for that purpose on board the *Britannia*, they invited him into the cabin to hear the result of their deliberations. He found assembled there Vice-Admirals Dundas and Hamelin, Rear-Admirals Sir Edmund Lyons and Jacqueminot, with a French and an English naval captain. He naturally expected the admirals would, at all events, go through the form of consulting with him on the subject of his mission, before framing a decision thereon. That was farthest from their thoughts. Without preface, they read to him a letter—written while he had been waiting upon their leisure outside—addressed to the French and English ambassadors, requesting them to advise the Porte to retain its fleet in the Bosphorus for its defence; excepting two line-of-battle ships required, in their opinion, at Varna, to aid in its defence against a possible attack by the Russian army. It rarely falls to any one's lot to hear men in a responsible position unwittingly cast a sarcasm on themselves. "If thus," their astonished listener might have asked, "why are your fleets in the Euxine? Is the order given you to retain all Russian ships in their ports a dead letter?"

Mushaver Pasha, treating as visionary the apprehension of the Russians menacing the Bosphorus, dwelt on the impolicy of letting the Turkish fleet, rawly manned, with a sense of depression to recover from, remain another year in port. The greater its inexperience the more necessity for its cruising. He instanced the disaster of the preceding autumn as having mainly arisen from the difficulty of keeping the sea. Circumstances, he observed, beyond the control of the allied admirals, might arise to send the fleet to sea the ensuing autumn, and it ought to profit by the mild season to abate sea-sickness and make sea legs. All present being nautical men, necessarily felt the justness of his observations. Rear-Admiral Jacqueminot first admitted it; his chief seconded him, and the result was further consideration of the subject; which ended in a resolution to write another letter to the ambassadors, recommending the Turkish fleet to be ordered to navigate off the coast of Roumelia, between the Bosphorus and the Gulf of Bourgas. This would be cruising certainly, but cruising to no purpose in regard of the object of the war; it would be only a degree better than remaining sequestered in port. Its proposed employment on the coast of Circassia found no advocate among either French or English; and though not rejected, the question was eluded by the expression of a unanimous opinion of the desirability of the Turkish fleet waiting the return of a projected Anglo-French expedition to the coast before going there itself. Time and opportunity were not considered. The admirals laid stress on the importance of the intelligence which they fancied their ships would obtain, and naïvely assigned the value of it to the Porte as a valid reason for the detention of its fleet during an indefinite period off a dangerous coast indrawing the Black Sea current with variable force.

Ideas gathered in a flying visit by strange ships were unlikely to add to the knowledge of the Porte on an intricate subject—the instincts and tendencies of the Caucasian races, derived from consanguinity and long uninterrupted intercourse. The ruling class of Turkey is Caucasian. The Tartar blood of the Ottoman family has been crossed out by Circassian connection. Slaves of the imperial house have at all times, since the conquest, filled high offices of state; and every notable harem has for ages been composed more or less of Circassians. The Turks might, therefore, without presumption, flatter themselves with possessing more knowledge of the Caucasus than the Allies' admirals were ever likely to obtain. Those gallant officers had, pardonably, no clear conception of the geographical features of that celebrated range whose lofty summit, Mount Elborooz, still shows, according to the Armenian legend, the notch scored by the keel of the ark grazing over it, before the waters abating allowed it to rest on Mount Ararat; nor, more pardonably, of its social and political features: for which, even now, it is doubtful if many marks would be obtained in a civil service examination by any one not specially crammed with Russian despatches, Tophana slave-dealers' reports, and Sheick Schamyl's reminiscences in captivity. They seemed to think their nautical envoys, intended to be set on shore at Vardan with an interpreter unacquainted with any Caucasian dialect, would ride in a few hours after breakfast to that sheick's head-quarters. A Tartar courier might, if not captured on the road, have reached it in a week. Talking against a fixed idea is idle, as idle as trying to cut glass with a knife: you see through it, but make no impression. Circassia seemed mentally reserved for the Anglo-French steam squadron, and laurels grew too rare on the shores of the Euxine to admit of sharing any which might be gathered with the Turks. The cypresses of Sinope were considered enough for them.

At the same time, if the unities of war had been studied, no one would have dissented from the proposition to leave fickle Circassia for the Turks to coquet with, while the allies wooed the stern beauty Sevastopol. The great actors on the world's stage have owed much to a correct casting of parts; to combining ably all their resources. The Eastern fable of the lion about to go to war is apposite. His vizir, the bear, advised him to leave the fox and the hare behind, as unlikely to render any service. His maned majesty replied: "They will both be serviceable: the fox will be my envoy; the hare will be my courier." Connected with the Circassians by the ties of religion, marriage, and adoption, skilled in the art of flattering the passions and ministering to the vanity of semi-barbarians, the Turks were appropriate agents to employ on the eastern shore of the Euxine. The admirals, nevertheless, signified their desire, in a letter to the Capitan Pasha, for a Turkish steamer to accompany their projected expedition to the coast of

Circassia. It found no favour in his eyes. Self-respect and policy alike opposed it. A single Turkish steamer in the wake of a foreign squadron would have lessened the Sultan's prestige in the eyes of the Circassians, as much as the sight of twenty vessels of war under the Turkish flag, in lieu of the Russian squadron they had been gazing on for a quarter of a century, would have increased it. The news would have rapidly spread to the remotest valleys of the Caucasus, and have electrified the dwellers therein. While a Turkish vessel might becomingly have displayed her flag with the allied fleets in operations against the common enemy, that conjunction on the coast of Circassia would have given weight to the reports industriously circulated of sinister designs on its independence.

Mushaver Pasha next proceeded to Varna, to see in what way ships might contribute, as proposed, to its defence. He saw they would have to fire over a cliff 60 feet high, with upsloping ground behind of equal elevation, to the spot where an enemy would sit down to besiege the town; and consequently, instead of being in a position to worry him, they would be disposed rather to move out of range of the guns of the redoubt he would not fail to plant on the edge of the cliff for their edification. But an attack on Varna by the Russians, lying in the circle of improbabilities, was not worth speculating about. He went again to Baltchik on the 10th of April, 1854; the day of the arrival there of intelligence of the declaration of war by England against Russia, in honour of which the English fleet manned yards and cheered. The allied admirals began to ponder over their first move; and the pasha returned to Constantinople to report his proceedings. His report in no way affected the views of the Porte, which were said to be approved of by the allied ambassadors. The Porte trusted in the allied admirals opening their eyes, on the completion of its preparations, to the importance of the proposed expedition of the Turkish fleet to the coast of Circassia.

CHAPTER XVI.

Arrival of the Vanguard of the British Army in the Bosphorus—Turkish and English Sentries at the Barracks in Scutari—Prince Napoleon and the Duke of Cambridge—Gloomy Presage in Constantinople—Reception of the Troops by the People and Authorities—Arrival of the *Fury* in the Bosphorus—Attack on Odessa by the Allied Fleets—Grounds for this Proceeding—Resemblance of Odessa to Brighton—What constitutes a Flag of Truce—Ultimatum of the Allied Admirals—Admiral Dundas's View of the Bombardment of Odessa—His desire to bombard Odessa more effectually—Odessa of no strategic Importance—War never aided by needless Severity—Moral and Physical Effects of wanton Aggression—Instances in Point—Popular Feeling in Russia and England excited by the War—Vicarious Retaliation—Blockade of the Danube by the Allied Admirals.

When the Turkish historian approaches in the course of his narrative the occurrences—beacon for old men hereafter to guess their ages by—of the month of April, 1854, he will pause for inspiration to guide his pen over that delicate page where truth clashes with national susceptibilities. On the 14th day of that month the vanguard of the British army of the East, the 33rd and 41st regiments, arrived in the Bosphorus, in the *Himalaya*, during a snow-storm. Next day they landed and found hospitable shelter in the Selimieh barracks. Female feet, those of soldiers' wives, then for the first time trod the area of a Turkish barrack; the like of which for space, symmetry and salubrity their fair owners had never seen elsewhere. Docile Arabians neighed welcome in their stables to restive Saxon chargers. Turkish and English sentries exchanged mute courtesies on the same post; and as the former, standing at ease, slouched and careless, watched the latter, ill at ease with stock and shako, pacing his measured walk, he may have doubted whether he were undergoing a penance or performing a duty. Other regiments followed in their wake in the course of a few days, and the unwonted bustle stirred the apathy—in harmony with the necropolis on its border—of the Asiatic suburb of Constantinople. The Crusaders led by "blind old Dandolo" had encamped on the same spot, and had gazed avidly from their tents on the same matchless panorama which greeted the eyes of Albion's fair-haired soldiers. Their Gallic comrades found congenial quarters on the other side of the water, in the region of theatres, cafés, and billiard-rooms.

Two imperial *yalis* on the Bosphorus, stored with luxuries, including the perfumes of the East and the wines of the West, with attendants, horses, and caiques, were placed at the disposal of Prince Napoleon and the Duke of Cambridge. The Prince went to his epicurean abode and enjoyed his *kief* there. The Duke, declining the *dolce far niente*, left his in a few days and went to Scutari, to live with his soldiers.

This gathering of the chivalry of the West spread a gloom over Constantinople. It seemed a warning, a portent. The ominous word *taksim* (partition) found utterance. The Constantinopolitans were awakened out of a dream of centuries. Their imagination had barely figured to itself foreign troops at Gallipoli: they started amazed at the reality in the capital. They asked each other, with bated breath, "why the Allies tarried at Constantinople? Why did they not proceed on to Varna? Had they not heard of the recent passage of the Danube by the enemy, and were they not come to defend Turkey?" Simple mortals! They had not read the decree of fate, that Russia should have time allowed her to balance her difficulties in the south through distance and want of steam-ships. They had not, in their faith in Him, supposed that Allah, having armed the Franks in their cause, would lead them to think of intimidating Russia with a splendid parade of fleets and armies.

Although the people looked coldly on the gallant strangers, the authorities seemed earnest in their endeavours to make them feel at home. Private houses were evacuated for the accommodation of officers; spirit-shops were licensed in the neighbourhood of the barracks; desecration of cemeteries was winked at; and, crowning mark of hospitable intent, the seraskir talked about alluring fallen houris from Galata and Tatavla, and lodging them in roomy houses with allowances for the solace of the soldiery. Deference to public decorum overcame his friendly zeal.

On the day of the landing at Scutari, H.M. steamer *Fury* arrived in the Bosphorus, having had the first shot of the general war fired at her from a Russian frigate off Sevastopol.

In that month also occurred the attack on Odessa by the allied fleets; which, as the first act of the drama, merits reminiscence. Odessa is, as most persons may know, a city as beautiful as Brighton; and as every person may not know, scarcely better fortified. The position of Brighton and Odessa is not dissimilar. Each stands on a cliff with open sea in front, and steppes or downs behind. Each is a bathing-place of fashionable resort; one from London, the other from Poland and Lithuania. Each contains young ladies' schools. Each exhibits a statue of its benefactor—respectively of George IV. and the Duc de Richelieu—erected by municipal gratitude. Odessa being a corn-mart has in addition an exchange, and rejoices also in an Italian opera and an imperial-founded Lyceum. When Russia obtained possession of the northern coast of the Euxine, a Tartar village, Hodja Bey, occupied a corner of the site of Odessa; and, pursuing the comparison, Brighton originated in a fishing village. Commerce in the one and royal favour in the other case transformed in a few years two hamlets into cities. The Prince de Joinville, in his noted pamphlet, dwelt *con gusto* on the facility of bombarding Brighton and other towns on the south coast of England; and the domesticated English felt shocked at the bare idea, foreshadowing recurrence to the practices of mediæval warfare. Had his Royal Highness contemplated indulging the French navy in similar practice against Portsmouth or Sheerness, he would have risen in the estimation of his readers.

The menace passed from Brighton and settled on Odessa.

April 20th, 1854, an Anglo-French fleet of twenty sail of the line, five of them with screw propellers, and many paddle steam frigates, cast anchor before Odessa, four miles off shore. The admirals in command demanded satisfaction of the governor for having recently fired on a flag of truce. Count Osten-Sacken denied the dastardly act; and his denial having been termed false, we will pause to investigate the case. An English war-steamer, on arriving off Odessa a short time previously, to bring away the English consul, sent a boat to the mole early in the morning, remaining herself under way. Said boat delivered her message or letter to a quarantine officer and shoved off. While rowing back to her ship one or more shot passed in her direction; fired, according to the Russian version, to warn the steamer, with her head inshore, to refrain from nearer approach to the town. Granting the baseness of firing on a boat under the circumstances (if that were done) it is open to doubt if she were invested with the character described. The simple display of a white flag does not constitute a "flag of truce." Other formalities are required. According to the laws of war, a boat with a parlementary flag lies on her oars at a convenient distance from the shore, until met by a corresponding boat. There ought to be nothing in her to indicate a latent intention of surveying; as a chart, a sounding lead, or a quadrant. She either delivers her message to the shore boat, or proceeds to the landing-place with it. In the latter case, she remains there as long as is necessary under surveillance, and is then re-escorted beyond gun shot. Were not this rule imperative, any cruiser might send in a boat anywhere with a white flag, on any pretext, make plans and take soundings of a roadstead, free from observation.

Having received their answer, the admirals sat down to frame an ultimatum. Their first draft contained a demand, in way of ransom from bombardment, for the release of neutral vessels in the port of Odessa, and for surrender of all Russian vessels, together with the artillery of the place; but on consideration of the improbability of a general parting with his guns, they restricted their demands to the release of neutrals and the surrender of the Russian shipping in the mole. They sent it to the governor, with a warning of the serious consequences of non-compliance. His Excellency returned no answer, but indicated his reception of the missive by letting the neutrals depart in peace. Chastisement was therefore decreed. In pursuance thereof at half-past six in the morning of April 22nd, four heavy armed steamers, with rocket-boats in attendance, opened fire on the mole-head battery at 2,000 yards' distance, and were reinforced two hours later by four similar steamers. Keeping under way, the squadron was manœuvred with admirable skill. Soon after noon the Russian fire was silenced, several vessels were in flames, as well as houses and stores adjoining the mole, and presently a powder-magazine in the vicinity exploded. The fighting squadron then desisted, to dine. After dinner the admiral made signal to the commodore, "Can you destroy any more?" which being answered in the affirmative, the firing recommenced at three o'clock, from the steamers and rocket-boats on the shipping remaining inside the mole; and in another hour they, with several buildings, were in flames. Only two guns replied to the repetition of the fire; they were at length silenced, and then the attacking squadron withdrew out of range.

In this action the Allies had one man killed and three wounded; and the Russians, sustaining a heavy loss, gave a foretaste of the courage under superior fire, afterwards shown by them on a grander scale. The allied steamers had discharged about 4,000 projectiles. Many, necessarily, from the extent of range, went over their mark into the city, one of them grazing the Duc de Richelieu's statue; and their impacts have been denoted since, by paint or inlaid stones, as honourable mementos.

Vice-Admiral Deans Dundas, in his despatch on the affair, gracefully took credit to himself for having spared the city of Odessa from bombardment, in deference to the Queen's expressed desire to have private property respected as much as possible; but as the press viewed the subject in another light, he repented of his forbearance, and on his return home the following year sought to clear his character from the imputation of mawkish humanity, by persuading a "friend" in the House of Commons to move for papers to show that his desire to revisit Odessa in the coming autumn, to bombard it effectually, had been frustrated by the reluctance of the allied generals to part with a division of the fleet. That reluctance saved us regret. Civilized, unlike barbarous warfare, glories in attaining its end with the least amount of suffering and injury to inoffensive persons and venerated things. It spares women and children, the sick and the aged: it respects churches, tombs, and works of art. Such objects in a city like Odessa are helplessly exposed to the capricious effects of a bombardment. The gunners fire in safety; their shells explode in the wards of the hospital, in the aisles of the church, in the galleries of the museum. Misled, the press saw in Odessa a place of strategic importance; whereas, situated at the extremity of the roadless steppe, open any day to a naval attack, it possessed none. The Allies were interested rather in its preservation, for the course of hostilities might have so turned as to render the possession of a city on the enemy's coast, to quarter an army in, of vital consequence. Shelter for modern troops is invaluable. Much of the misery and loss sustained by the French on their retreat from Moscow would have been avoided, had they respected towns and villages on their advance to that city.

War is never aided by needless severity or destruction of domestic property. Reflection and history combine to show a contrary result. The slaughter of defenceless crowds in Mesopotamia and Armenia by the hordes of Genghis Khan recoiled on the barbarians in consequent famine and disease. The destruction of the flourishing cities of the Palatinate by the armies of Louis XIV. brought down universal execration on the head of the crowned egotist, and sanctified the league forming against him. Wanton aggressions in war, like political oppressions in peace, are dragon's teeth, whence armed men surely spring, inflamed with bitter hatred, sooner or later. In a free country the press excites the ardour of the people, in a despotic country the enemy's acts shape public opinion. As long as the enemy directs his efforts against the obvious resources of Government, the people reason on the war, its causes and effects; but when he destroys private property with no apparent military object, passions are roused. The burning, for example, during the late war, of Kola, the capital of Russian Lapland, with its pinnacled wooden cathedral, the veneration of every Laplander, graved a deeper impression on the Russian mind than a thousand *Times* power could have stamped. Read by any light, hostile treatment of insignificant towns in the arctic zone could admit but of one qualification, arouse but one sentiment. We need not ask how we should feel on hearing of Lerwick in the Shetland Isles being thus treated late in autumn by an enemy's cruiser: we have only to turn back the page of history and read of the sensation caused by the destruction of Teignmouth by the French fleet in June, 1690. Faction was hushed by it; Jacobites and Orangemen for the hour were reconciled. Few persons can seriously think that molestation of open country towns, on the coasts of a vast empire engaged in a struggle for empire, can have a material weight in the balance. But it has a moral weight. It unites sovereign and people by the feeling of indignation. War, unadorned by chivalry, is so repulsive a spectacle, its details are now so immediately brought home to every hearth by the fulness and rapidity of news—the groans of the hospital blending with the shouts of victory—that were people unexcited by individual insult and suffering, or by the recital of acts of cruelty, they would be in a position to take a calm view of the subject, and enforce consideration of it upon their rulers, if necessary.

What occurred in the late war is confirmatory of this proposition. Neither English nor French property suffered by sea or by land; nevertheless, both in England and in France there was a peace party. Russian property, on the contrary, suffered largely; nevertheless, in Russia there was no peace party. Popular at first, the war became unpopular in France and in England; because, unstirred by individual misfortunes, the people were able to ponder over its inconsistencies and its cost. Unpopular at the commencement, the war became popularized in Russia by the razzias of the Allies in the White Sea, in the Gulf of Bothnia, and in the Sea of Azof. In England and in France, national impulse dwindled into state or class policy. In Russia, state policy expanded into a national sentiment; which, unhappily, has survived with peace. That war witnessed the revival of the practice, long disused in war between civilized nations, of vicarious retaliation. Because a military commandant had (presumedly) ordered a flag of truce to be fired at, commercial Odessa was menaced with condign punishment. Because a Greek partisan, ensconced in a dismantled redoubt on the left bank of an issue of the Danube, perfidiously shot Captain Parker, R.N., while rowing past in his gig, innocent Sulina, on the opposite bank of the river, was destroyed. Now there can be no doubt that such acts, if necessary, should have formed part of a scheme, and not have seemed dependent on the chance of an insulted flag or of a gallant young officer's death,—the assigned motives respectively. The destruction of Sulina was the stupid act of the war, since it injured friends alone. The Russians had already abandoned the islands of St. George and Leti, and had retired with their stores and matériel to Ismael. Not a Russian remained in Sulina. Its inhabitants were chiefly British, Ionian, and Turkish subjects, occupied in supplying the wants of merchant vessels and transporting their cargoes across the bar. Sulina then, when burnt to the ground by the allied admirals' orders, belonged exclusively to commerce.*

The allied admirals afterwards made another mistake detrimental to friends, in connection with the Danube. They declared that river blockaded; in order, using their words, to prevent supplies being conveyed to the Russian armies in the Dobrudsha, and they warned all vessels not to enter it.† They published that announcement to the world: then ordered their cruisers to seize all vessels leaving the Danube; such vessels being laden chiefly with cereals for friendly countries. About thirty vessels, *outward bound*, were accordingly captured by some of the Allies' steamers.

* Sulina was indifferently rebuilt during the Austrian occupation of the mouths of the Danube, which terminated in 1857.

† "In consequence of the Russian armies having crossed the Danube—having occupied the Dobrudsha, and taken possession of the mouths and north banks of the river Danube, We, the undersigned, being the vice-admirals commanding-in-chief the combined naval forces of France and England in the Black Sea, in order to prevent supplies being conveyed to the Russian forces, do hereby declare, in the names of our respective Governments, and do hereby make known to all whom it may concern, that we have established an effective blockade of the river Danube, including all the mouths of the said river having communication with the Black Sea: and we do hereby warn all vessels not to enter the said river Danube until further notice.

(Signed) "HAMELIN. J. D. DUNDAS."

CHAPTER XVII.

The Allied Fleets sail for Sevastopol, and an Anglo-French Steam Squadron for the Coast of Circassia—The Capitan Pasha proposes the Junction of the Turkish Squadron—Its Instructions—Presentation of the Turkish Admirals to the Sultan—Sefer Pasha and Behchet Pasha—Equipment of the Turco-Egyptian Squadron—Vice-Admiral Dundas counsels Delay—The Author's Opinion and Advice—Achmet Pasha's Objections—Mushaver Pasha requested to mediate with the Allied Admirals—His Memorandum for their Consideration—He joins the Anglo-French Fleet in the *Faisi-bari*—His Reception by Admiral Dundas and Admiral Hamelin—Objections of the French Admiral—Letter of Admiral Dundas to Ahmed Pasha—Dismay of the Circassian Pashas.

Four days after their attack on Odessa, the allied fleets sailed thence to cruise off Sevastopol, fixing their rendezvous forty miles west of that port. From that rendezvous, the Anglo-French squadron already spoken of steamed for the coast of Circassia, May 5th, 1854. The Capitan Pasha had already informed the allied admirals by letter, and verbally through the captain of an English vessel of war, of the proximate sailing of the Turkish fleet for the same destination, and had proposed the junction of the two expeditions. The Turkish fleet had been fitted for service on the coast of Circassia in a manner which reflected credit on all concerned. Communications opened with the Caucasians augured concert and co-operation on their part. "The appearance of the Turkish fleet off the coast," they said, "will be the signal for our rising from the Euxine to the Caspian." The fleet was instructed to join, in the first place, the Allies' admirals off Sevastopol, and after concerting with them a plan of operations on the coast of Circassia, proceed direct to Batoom; there embark 4,000 troops; and then, reducing Soukhoum Kaleh, make that place a depôt for stores, and the base of co-operation with the Circassians. In case of meeting with the Russian instead of the Anglo-French fleet off Sevastopol, it was to accept or decline battle, according to circumstances.

The Turkish admirals were presented to the Sultan, on the eve of their departure. His Majesty addressed them three sentences. He expressed his hope for cordiality between them and the Allies' admirals. The war, he said, was not of his making; but he supposed it necessary: moreover, wars had existed from the earliest period. He would pray for their welfare.

Sefer Pasha and Behchet Pasha, of Circassian origin, accompainied by Sheick Schamyl's envoy, embarked with suites of their countrymen in the Turkish fleet, with missions and gifts from the Sultan for Circassian chiefs. Sefer Pasha, better known as Sefer Bey, of a noble Anapau family, had been a renowned warrior in his youth, and had enjoyed much consideration among the Circassians. His renown led Russia, at the peace of Adrianople, to induce the Porte to retain him in Turkey. He had since resided at Adrianople, with an allowance from the Sultan. He had, nevertheless, maintained intercourse with his countrymen, and his recommendation had ensured honourable reception to any travellers professing an interest in their independence. Mr.

Urquhart, Captain Lyon, Mr. Longworth, Mr. Bell, and others, had availed themselves of it. In the spring of 1854 the Porte summoned him to Constantinople, gave him the rank of *ferik*, and invited him to return to Circassia in the Sultan's name. His satisfaction at this recognition of his merits was dashed with bitterness at the thought of his sequestration during a quarter of a century. His beard had grown white in the interval, his companions in arms were no more, another generation had since fought with the Muscovites, and he would in all probability be regarded with jealousy by the naib. Such was his language to us before we sailed. Nevertheless, he expressed hopes of gathering round him the sons of his ancient followers. Behchet Pasha had the merit of being one of Redshid Pasha's freedmen; and, though that would have but little weight in his native land, he was a courteous well-bred man, adapted for conferring the Sultan's distinctions with grace. About 300 other Circassians, traders or exiles, many of them with their families, embraced the opportunity of revisiting their country with *éclat* under the Turkish flag. Twelve European officers to instruct the Circassian militia, a field battery complete, with artillery officers, small arms, ammunition and other stores, were also embarked. Thus, full manned, and provisioned for four months, the Turco-Egyptian squadron, composed of eight line-of-battle ships, three frigates, four light vessels—corvettes or brigs—five steam frigates, and three steam corvettes, in all twenty-three vessels, mounting 1,100 guns, sailed from the Bosphorus in high spirits, May 6, 1854.

Pursuant to its orders, it stood to the northward in

search of the allied fleets, losing thereby, with regret, a fair wind to the eastward. The scanty stock of provisions laid in by its passengers, coupled with the want of comfort and abluent conveniences for the women and children, rendered a short passage desirable. When off Varna, May 8, it sent in a steamer to communicate with the town, and found there a letter from Vice-Admiral Dundas to its commander, Achmet Pasha, as follows :—

"*Britannia*, off Sebastopol, May 5th, 1854.

"SIR,—I have had the honour to receive a letter from his Highness the Capitan Pasha, informing me that a squadron under your command had been ordered to join and co-operate with the combined squadrons of France and England, and I hasten to acquaint you that it is the opinion of Vice-Admiral Hamelin and myself that it would be desirable you should cruise along the coasts of Bulgaria and Roumelia, between the Danube and the Bosphorus, until the return of Rear-Admiral Lyons from the coast of Circassia and the arrival of the combined squadrons at Varna, on or about the 20th instant, when further operations can be concerted.

(Signed) "J. W. D. DUNDAS,
"Vice-Admiral Commanding-in-Chief."

The assumption by the admirals to give directions to the Turkish fleet, before consultation with its chief or knowing the nature of his orders, was informal, if not offensive; while the enjoined delay, dependent on a contingency, might be indefinitely prolonged; and therefore their missive, if addressed to a man alive to the dignity of his position, would, instead of unsettling his mind, have received an appropriate answer. He would have regarded it as a release from the obligation to confer with them. Could Mushaver Pasha's opinion, in accordance with the wish of the majority, have prevailed in the council of naval and Circassian officers convened in the flagship to consider the subject, the fleet would then and there have squared its yards and steered for Batoom. With a prescience of the failure of the expedition if it remained within reach of the allied admirals, he advised its proceeding in the spirit of its orders to the coast of Circassia, and ventured to assure the commander-in-chief of the support of public opinion, ever on the side of enterprise, which would draw after it the approbation of the Porte. The fleet's destination was Circassia; and though it had been directed to join the allied admirals *en route*, that was a secondary consideration, or rather a formality, which they themselves might be said to have dispensed with. Achmet Pasha objected to this course, for fear of offending the allied admirals. The Porte, he said, would disown him in the right, on their complaint; would abet him in the wrong, on their approval. He and others had early made up their minds to subordinate every interest to the propitiation of any of the Allies' authorities; and it is fair to say their selfish calculation seldom proved erroneous. He also objected to the proposition next made, for the fleet (seeing the mischief of delay) to proceed on the letter of its orders to join the Allies at once. The foggy season, he said, was at hand; the Allies might increase their distance from Sevastopol; he might fall in with the Russians instead.

As a *mezzo termine* he, in concurrence with the council, requested Mushaver Pasha to proceed in a steamer to the offing of Sevastopol, show the allied admirals the orders of the Turkish fleet, disclose to them its stored and crowded state, and obtain their sanction for the continuance forthwith of its course to Circassia. None of them anticipated opposition from those distinguished individuals when made acquainted with the facts of the case. Mushaver Pasha accepted the mission, faintly encouraged by the altered circumstances under which he should again meet the Allies' admirals. When he had previously had that honour, at Baltchik, the Circassian expedition was in embryo; now it was developed into form and substance, and respect for their rank forbade him to assume without evidence an intention to mar the result of much cost and preparation for the sake of their consistency.

Leaving accordingly his ship hove to with the fleet off Cape Kellagriah, Mushaver Pasha steamed for the offing of Sevastopol; and on the way, that nothing pertinent to the matter might be omitted in his interview with the Allies' admirals, he noted down the following memorandum for their consideration :—

"*Faisi-bari*, at Sea, May 10th, 1854.

"The position of the Turkish army in Asia has excited anxiety, seeing the consequences that might ensue from its possible defeat. Persia, now waiting on events, might in that case, declaring war, march on Bagdad; the conquest of which would be considered more than an equivalent for the provinces wrested from her by Russia during the last half-century. Hereditary and religious associations are connected with Bagdad; and the power which shall hold that prize out to the Persians will be readily listened to.

"The Porte hopes to find auxiliary means of checking

the assumed advance of the Russian army of Georgia in the hostility of Circassia and Daghestan. Hitherto during the actual war they have rendered no service to the common cause, and have offered no more hindrance to Russia than they have done at any time during the last twenty years. Their attitude has been defensive; whereas the object is to render it offensive, and thereby influence Russia by the apprehension of a diversion on the flank or rear of her army in Asia. For this purpose it is necessary to unite the tribes under Sheick Schamyl's rule with the tribes ruled vicariously by him, and to supply them with military aid.

"With orders to proceed to the coast of Circassia, after consultation with the allied admirals, the Turkish fleet has left the Bosphorus. Sefer Pasha and Behchet Pasha with 300 of their countrymen, and several European officers to act as *talimgis* (instructors), are embarked in it. Those pashas bear the Sultan's firman, empowering them to act in his name, and are carrying *nishans* of merit and *berats* of rank to influential chieftains. In their opinion, unless the Caucasians operate timely in concert and with strategy, the Russian advance in Asia will be certain. There are embarked in the fleet a battery complete with artillery officers and 300 rounds for each gun, 500 barrels of gunpowder, 500 cases of musket cartridges, 400 cases of muskets, 2,000 pistols, 20 cases of cutlasses, 10,000 moulds of lead, 1,000 axes, 7 cases of flints, 300 soup-kettles, and 20,000 okas of salt, besides tents and bales of cotton cloth. Circassian merchants have also embarked with wares to reopen the trade, suspended for many years. Concurrently, orders have been sent to Selim Pasha at Batoom, for the embarkation of 4,000 troops in the fleet for conveyance to Circassia. It is anticipated that with the aid of 4,000 regular troops, the marines of the fleet, European military instructors, field-pieces, and other named munitions of war, the Circassians will be able to act offensively on the enemy's territory. At the same time Soukhoum Kaleh, after being reduced, will be garrisoned and its works strengthened, so as to render its port of due value.

"The Circassian pashas in and the superior officers of the Turkish fleet trust that the allied admirals will see with pleasure and advise its departure from the coast of Roumelia to the coast of Circassia without delay. Time is precious. The season for operations is rapidly advancing, and if the Circassians shall not be enabled to act soon, it is doubtful if they will be in a position to render valid service in the war. Defensive hostility will be of no avail. They must take the offensive, and for that they require excitement in gifts and promises, and the aid which the Ottoman fleet is bringing them.

"The Porte has been in communication with the Circassians on the subject, and the latter are daily expecting the Ottoman fleet as the signal for their gathering. If it do not soon make its appearance off their coast, doubts will arise in their minds of the Porte's earnestness."

May 11th, in the forenoon, making the land of the Crimea, the *Faisi-bari* tried speed with a large war-steamer, which thought her intent on breaking the blockade. Intent on that, she would have made Cape Aia early in the morning, and have run along shore, probably unnoticed, to Sevastopol. A Hamburgher crossing her bows was momentarily taken for a Russian, and was nearly having a shot fired at him by an impatient gunner. She ascertained from the stranger that the ships seen occasionally through the haze, half topsails down to windward, were the Allies. She then sighted Cape Chersonesus, spoke H.M.S. *Terrible*, and in the afternoon joined the Anglo-French fleet, hove to in a fog,—the fog fatal to H.M.S. *Tiger*,—twenty-five miles west of Sevastopol.

The rank of the allied admirals being coëqual, the first visit to either was, on the score of etiquette, a matter of indifference, admitting the indulgence of a natural bias.

Admiral Dundas, seeing the *Faisi-bari* alone, fancied her come in pursuance of his wish to join the detached allied squadron, and under this impression he cordially welcomed Mushaver Pasha on board the *Britannia*. "How many days' coal have you got?" he asked, and scarcely waiting for an answer told him to follow the squadron with all speed to the coast. But when he heard the object of the pasha's mission, the friend gave place to the admiral. His recommendation to the Porte about the Turkish fleet had been disregarded. His directions to its commander to cruise off the coast of Roumelia had been dissented from. That fleet had been placed under his orders, he said, and he would be obeyed. He listened impatiently to the perusal of the Turkish fleet's orders and the afore-cited memorandum. Giving no heed to the tenor of the former nor the argument of the latter, he reproached their bearer with being the cause of that fleet's Circassian destination, and expressed astonishment at his having dared to give advice at variance with his opinion. The pasha, asserting the policy of its destination, reminded the gallant admiral of the priority of his suggestion in that respect to the expression of the admiral's opinion thereon; and ventured to observe that although its commander was instructed to act in concert with the Allies' admirals, he might fairly expect to be consulted with, if only for form's sake. The deference for rank and age acquired by the habits of naval life enabled him to bear with equanimity a sally of official discontent, such as a worried first-lieutenant might have addressed to a truant midshipman. He was in a mood, seeing the importance of the issue between them, to exclaim with the Grecian, "Strike, but hear!" That would not have availed him. He might have been tapped good-humouredly on the shoulder; he would not have been listened to. The gallant admiral refused to discuss with him the affairs of the Turkish fleet before consulting with Admiral Hamelin; between whom and himself, he said, perfect accord existed on all subjects. Without his concurrence he decided on nothing. He would confer with him next day, and then give their joint answer.

Accompanied by an officer of the *Britannia*, Mushaver Pasha next rowed to the *Ville de Paris*. Admiral Hamelin received him with formal courtesy at the entering port, and having heard his colleague's message, delivered aside, conducted him into the cabin, to which he summoned the chief of his staff. Mushaver Pasha explained to those two officers the state of the Turkish fleet and the purport of his visit. He dwelt on the importance attached by the Porte to its Circassian expedition. He gave them a French translation of the orders of the fleet to read, and translated to them, *vivâ voce*, at their request, his own memorandum, which appeared to interest them. Admiral Hamelin admitted the policy of aiding the Circassians, but allowed his judgment to be warped by other considerations. He expressed apprehension of the Russian fleet pursuing the Turkish fleet to the eastward and causing another disaster. Thanking him for his solicitude about their safety (which seemed uncalled for), Mushaver Pasha expressed his doubt of the Russian admiral, even though a Paul Jones, being so demented as to leave his only port to run after the Turkish fleet, now become of secondary importance. That would indeed be playing the Allies' game. That consideration should be an additional reason for the Turkish fleet steering eastward, to become a decoy duck. He invited the admiral's attention to the dissimilarity between the cases, so marked as to destroy comparison. The Sinope squadron had been feeble, demoralized by cold and anxiety, and the allied fleets were then moored at Beikos, their governments at peace with Russia. Now, the Turkish fleet was comparatively efficient, the weather was mild, and the allied fleets commanded the Euxine.

Unable to controvert this matter-of-fact statement, Admiral Hamelin entrenched himself behind his original argument. If the Turkish fleet went to the coast of Circassia the allied fleets ought in his opinion to remain off Sevastopol, which was out of the question, as they were about to return to Baltchik for water. Serious responsibility, he repeated emphatically, would be incurred by him if during their absence the Russian fleet should track the Turkish fleet and bring it to action. He had, he said, received blame on account of the battle of Sinope, and he was disinclined to risk a repetition. The ascription of daring folly to the Russians was as gratuitous, as the motive assigned for intermitting the blockade, supposing one necessary, was specious. The Russians possessed then in Sevastopol eleven or twelve serviceable line-of-battle ships, and the *Vladimir* was the best of their steamers. With five line-of-battle ships watering at a time, the Allies would have had thirteen line-of-battle ships disposable, with several steam frigates, to maintain the blockade with. One thought of the tedious blockades of other days, with ships which would now be pronounced unseaworthy, on a strict allowance of nauseous cask-water: one thought of Nelson detaching four of his ships from off Cadiz to water at Tetuan. In those memorable days the practice was to cruise off an enemy's port with an inferior force in the hope of enticing him out: in the late war the practice was to appear off the enemy's port with a superior force and gibe him for remaining in. In conclusion, Admiral Hamelin said he would talk to Admiral Dundas on the matter: perfect cordiality on all subjects existed between them; they would consult together about the Turkish fleet, and then give an answer.

Having thus disposed of the public business, Admiral Hamelin abruptly took his visitor to task about a private affair more interesting in his eyes than the Caucasus—about a letter written by him five months earlier, by request, to an eminent person at Constantinople, on the advantage to be derived from the presence of the Anglo-French fleet in the Euxine, and the facility of its remaining in that sea with Sinope to water at: a copy of which had recently found its way to his hands. He brought this matter on the *tapis* with the remark, "We have seen your letter which sent us all into the Black Sea last winter"—a distinction assuredly not claimed for it by the writer. The gallant admiral commented with professional zeal on the indecorum of any person writing about his fleet, and his indignation thereat measured the position attained in its estimation by the French navy: a position above criticism. Mushaver Pasha, with great respect for that navy, a witness to its remarkable progress in a few years, could not take that view of the case. A more careful perusal of his letter, he observed in reply, would show that his remarks had applied to the French in connection with the English fleet, under the collective term "allied fleets;" meaning thereby that it was in good company. This seemed to the admiral a distinction without a difference. Any reference to the proceedings of a French fleet, though in a private letter, was an offence in his eyes grave enough to justify him in withholding thenceforwards his countenance from the author of it; and not content with that, he called upon Admiral Dundas afterwards to follow his example.

The gallant admirals, fearing perhaps to compromise the dignity of either by rowing in the fog to the other's ship, failed to meet according to promise, but came all the same to a perfect understanding with each other. On the third day, feeling the inutility of waiting longer, Mushaver Pasha, having dined in the interval with Admiral Dundas, took leave of him and of Admiral Hamelin in their respective flag-ships; receiving from the former, as their joint answer, the following letter for the commander of the Turkish fleet, with a verbal message to him to consider the anchorage of Baltchik reserved exclusively for the Anglo-French fleet:—

"*Britannia*, off Sevastopol, 13th May, 1854.

"SIR,—I had the honour to address you a letter on the 5th inst., informing you of the wish of Vice-Admiral Hamelin and myself as to the movements of the squadron under your command then about to enter the Black Sea, and I now enclose you a copy of it.

"Admiral Hamelin and myself still request you will be guided by the opinion therein expressed, and I have further to beg you will be pleased to make your future communications in writing, as *verbal* messages may lead to serious inconveniences and mistakes.

(Signed) "J. W. D. DUNDAS,
"Vice-Admiral, Commander-in-Chief.

"To Vice-Admiral Ahmed Pasha."

This laconic epistle found the Turkish fleet just emerged from the fog, co-extensive with the Euxine, in which it had been straying some days, and created a corresponding mental haze out of the elements of anger and disappointment. The allied admirals had addressed its commander-in-chief with scant consideration for his rank, and had characterized a mission entrusted by him to a flag-officer as a *verbal* message. Whose dog was he, to be treated in that way? The Circassian pashas were dismayed at the adjournment of the expedition; and the sickness among their countrymen and women, through confinement and privations, became aggravated by despondency. No allusion having been made in their letter to Mushaver Pasha, the allied admirals might officially ignore his mission. It therefore devolved on the Turkish commander-in-chief, in the interest of the Porte and his own responsibility, to confirm it in detail. He hesitated to take a step likely in his opinion to incense his supercilious colleagues, and counselled anxiously several days with his familiars before making up his mind to sign the letter * to that effect which he sent them.

Achmet Pasha's heart was not in the Circassian expedition. He agreed with Admiral Hamelin on the imprudence of the Turkish fleet going eastward, with Sevastopol unblockaded by the Allies, and he easily consoled himself for the tone of Admiral Dundas's letter. Though addressed to him, its sting was evidently meant for another. Lynx-eyed as a Persian in detecting a slight, he saw that, through irreverence or some other cause, Mushaver Pasha had forfeited the allied admirals' favour, and that he himself, if successful in acquiring it instead, would stand all the higher in the eyes of his own people—seeing him preferred by them to a Nazarene, one of their own race—and be able perhaps to make capital out of it at the Porte. On this prompting he acted. While he spat, figuratively, on their beards, and spoke disrespectfully of their mothers, for the "dirt" they made him (by his own account) eat in his interviews with them from time to time, he laid himself out in an Oriental spirit to win their smiles by any and every means; excusing his versatility by what he termed the exigencies of his position.

* *Vide* Appendix II.

CHAPTER XVIII.

The Allies' Fleets at Baltchik—How they watched Sevastopol—The Turkish Fleet kept at out-post Duty—What might have been done in the Summer of 1854—Powerful Force of the Fleets—Discourtesy to Mushaver Pasha—Conciliatory Compliments unacknowledged — Tidings of the Anglo-French Squadron on the Circassian Coast—Turkish Envoys and Munitions of War transhipped to Circassia—Precipitancy of the Measure—Indignation of the Turks — Disappointment of the Circassians — Admiral Sir Edmund Lyons' Report of the Circassians — Motives of the Allies' Admirals—Articles in the *Daily News*—Mortality in the Turkish Fleet—Its Cause—The Allies' Admirals object to its Cruising, and order it to lie at Varna—Remonstrance of the Turkish and Egyptian Admirals—Recall of the Fleet by the Porte—Views of the Allies' Admirals as to the Turkish Fleet carried out—Results of their Proceedings—Effect on the Circassians—The Allies' Admirals secure for Russia in War what she had not ventured to ask in Peace.

Within eight days of the date of the letter cited in the last chapter, the Allies' fleets returned to Baltchik. As they passed Kavarna, the Turkish fleet lying there showed them deep respect. It loosed its sails, drew up guards of honour on its poops, with bands playing alternately French and English airs, and sent its steamers to aid in towing them to their anchorage. Those fleets remained at Baltchik, with one short interval, until the ensuing September: a couple of their steamers looked into Sevastopol occasionally, and that inspection was humorously termed equivalent to a blockade. During that period the Russians may have conveyed munitions of war unnoted from Nicolaef to Sevastopol; and might, if they had had the wit, have sent their small frigates lightened and corvettes, useless at Sevastopol, into the Sea of Azof for its protection. The Allies' admirals refused to allow the Turkish fleet—solicitous of the honour for the sake of example—to lie in company with their ships, and practically commented on their professed anxiety for its safety by retaining it at the outer anchorage of Kavarna, seven miles to windward, in the way to intercept fire-ships, expected to be made use of by the Russians as in all their previous wars with Turkey. The Turks, thus left to themselves, did out-post duty for their allies with cruisers beyond Cape Kellagriah. There was no necessity for that precaution. The three fleets lay protected by the renown of the British navy. That ancient renown covered the Black Sea as with a mantle, and kept the Russians quiet.

Much might easily have been effected during those three precious summer months of 1854. In the first place, the Turkish fleet, carrying out the Porte's policy, might have laid the foundation of Caucasian independence. In the next place, a squadron of the allies' line-of-battle ships with attendant steam frigates, the bulk of their fleet off Sevastopol, might have silenced Kilburn and Okchakof forts; and then the steamers, ascending the Boug, might have fired the arsenal of Nicolaef, at that time unfortified and feebly garrisoned. War having found Russia unprepared, ill able to make front all round the compass, early maritime operations in the Black Sea would, in their reaction, have been sensibly felt in her vulnerable quarter, her southern provinces. The apologists for the inaction of the Allies' admirals at Baltchik during that summer have instanced their deficient means, by comparison with the means at the disposal of their successors the following year. Relatively with the preparedness of the enemy in 1855, they were equal; and they were far superior to any ever possessed by their predecessors in command of fleets in any quarter of the globe. While steam locomotion was yet a philosopher's dream, the British navy had ascended rivers in North America, sailing and warping, and had landed armies in Egypt in the face of gallant expectant foes.

The Allies' admirals, on their arrival at Baltchik, desired the commander of the Turkish fleet, Ahmed Pasha (who gave earnest of compliance), to come unaccompanied by Mushaver Pasha, when wishing to confer with them. There was nothing in the caution to take exception at; all that made it noticeable was its contrast with Admiral Dundas's refusal some months earlier at Constantinople to have an interview with the former, at the request of the authorities, unless in presence of the latter, "that his words," he said, "might not again be misrepresented." More significantly Admiral Dundas abstained, out of deference it was said for his French colleague's whim, from inviting Mushaver Pasha to an official dinner in the *Britannia*, given May 24th, in honour of the Queen's birthday; to which the captains of his own fleet, the flag-officers and captains of the French fleet, and the native pashas of the Turkish fleet with one Turkish bey were invited.

The invitations were sent to the Turkish fleet in a manner which gave immediate publicity to an exclusion little to be anticipated. A breach of the laws of hospitality or decorum is a momentous affair in the East, because it presages mischief for the object of it; and therefore speculation on what might follow after an Oriental fashion was excited among the Turkish officers, who, with exaggerated notions of their power, thought the admirals spiteful. Mushaver Pasha reassured some and disconcerted others by proceeding in a steam tender from Kavarna, in the forenoon of the said 24th May, to Baltchik, to pay his personal respects to Admiral Dundas as the Queen's representative in the Black Sea; and he recommended his colleagues to send their flag-captains to compliment him in their names. They sent them with sweet-offerings, they dressed their ships in colours, they fired royal salutes, and did not receive a simple "thank you" in return.

While we were thus loyally occupied in the *Britannia*, the imperial French steamer *Mogador* arrived from Circassia with the first intelligence of the detached Anglo-French squadron. It had looked at Anapa and Soudjouk Kaleh on the coast of Abasia, had landed two officers at Vardan to gather notions, had found Soukhoum Kaleh abandoned by the enemy and in possession of wild Circassians, busy extracting bolts from gun-carriages; and then, embarking a Turkish battalion at Tchuruk-sou, had occupied with it Redout Kaleh, as the Russians, who had already sent away their military stores to Kutais, were in the act of evacuating it.

The admirals, considering the occupation of Redout

Kaleh a signal advantage, resolved to follow it up "vigorously." With this view, they sent for the Turkish and Egyptian pashas, who were whiling away the time before dinner with the Mudir of Baltchik, and without preamble ordered them to transfer the passengers and munitions of war, embarked for Circassia in the Ottoman fleet, to an English screw line-of-battle ship and two Turkish steam frigates, for despatch that very evening to to Soukhoum Kaleh and Redout Kaleh; little thinking that stores landed at the latter place, *in Mingrelia*, had obviously slight chance of ever reaching Circassia. Remarks incidentally dropped by the admirals in disparagement of sail ships,—about the time they would take to traverse the Black Sea,—had indicated the prospect of some such mode of reconciling their duty by the Circassians (as they understood it) with the detention of the Turkish fleet at Kavarna; and therefore to meet that objection the pashas were advised to propose, in amendment, for the four Turkish steam frigates present to tow as many line-of-battle ships across the Euxine. No delay would have ensued therefrom. Thus handicapped, those steamers would have fairly kept pace with their consort the *Sans Pareil*. To no purpose. The gallant admirals could not, or would not, be brought to see the difference between an expedition and a consignment—the difference, in the eyes of a semi-barbarous people, between landing envoys, auxiliaries, arms and ammunition from a squadron with attendant pomp and circumstance, and dropping them like ordinary passengers and goods from crowded transports. Better far, but for appearance sake, have sent them all back to Constantinople.

The precipitancy of the measure was remonstrated

against: a respite only till next forenoon was prayed for, to effect the transhipment with due regard for the rank and sex of some of the parties, and for the safety of the ammunition. That reasonable prayer was refused. The two pashas were desired, within an hour of the dinner they had been invited to, to return to Kavarna and see at once to the business. Having to row back in their barges seven miles, they reached their ships hungry and weary, with gall in their hearts. One of them, usually reticent, exclaimed, in the midst of his scribes and domestics surprised at his return dinnerless, "Can I ever forgive this treatment!" Chafing under contumely, they carried out the irrational order: an order which they might, on the ground of policy and humanity, have declined to act upon. Pashas, military instructors, traders, women, children, field-pieces, small arms, gunpowder, provisions, and merchandise, were transferred, between 7 and 12 P.M. of the 24th of May, 1854, from a dozen vessels in the exposed roadstead of Kavarna to the said three steamers, with unavoidable confusion, damage and personal risk. No order of precedence or arrangement could be observed in the hurry of transhipment; no lists could be made of the goods hoisted in indiscriminately over the gangways, or handed *pêle mêle* out of the boats through the ports of the steamers.

Rarely has a more "fantastic trick" been played by "men dressed in a little brief authority." It made many sigh, if it did not make angels weep. Sefer Pasha and his colleague expressed becomingly their sorrow for such indecorous treatment. The European "instructors" swore loudly and declared the admirals worse than Turks. Women and children, roused out of sleep, screamed with alarm in the boats. Several artillerymen ashore lost their passage. Half the ammunition was necessarily left for another opportunity; much of the remainder having to be stowed, through want of room in the magazines, on the lower decks of the Turkish steamers thronged with a promiscuous crowd. The explosion of either on the passage should have caused no surprise.

Circassians of rank and others landed like adventurers, arms and stores cast on the shore to be scrambled for, could not be expected, even by the Allies' admirals, to produce the same result as if the former had disembarked with honours from a fleet, and the latter had been distributed with discernment. Sefer Pasha, returning to his country like a refugee, was long in recovering some of his prestige. The military instructors remained undirected, smoking their pipes at Soukhoum Kaleh, till they dispersed sick at heart. Behchet Pasha and others, landed at Ardler, turned their attention to pursuits of individual advantage. The presents and cloaks of honour intended for Circassian chieftains were appropriated by those entrusted with them. The stores melted away. The Caucasians, the parties chiefly interested, declared themselves betrayed as usual by the Porte. "The Porte promised us," they said, "the Turkish fleet with troops, and never sent it."

Four days after the *Mogador*, Rear-Admiral Sir Edmund Lyons arrived at Baltchik from the coast of Circassia, and as the proceedings of the Turkish fleet had been ostensibly made dependent on the information he might bring, we entertained hopes of being allowed to follow our friends, about whom some uneasiness was felt. The expedition had suffered heavy discouragement; but there was yet time for efficient operations. The Rear-Admiral reported the Circassians to be divided among themselves and clamorous for troops to act with them against the Russians,—the old oft-repeated tale. We had had in view to assuage their dissensions and give them the means of organization with military aid. He was as much opposed as ever to the Turkish fleet's Circassian destination; and thus supported, the Allies' admirals, throwing off the mask, definitively declared it inopportune. Then, with strange inconsistency, they desired the commander of the Turkish fleet to write to the seraskir at Constantinople a request for troops to be sent to Circassia. The seraskir's reply was reproachful. "With Roumelia in revolt and the Russians on the right bank of the Danube, we cannot spare troops for Circassia: we gave our fleet for that service, with orders to embark 4,000 troops at Batoom, and the Allies' admirals have detained it at Kavarna."

This was the only audible accordant note between the commanders-in-chief and the seconds in command of the Anglo-French fleet in the Euxine during the year 1854. Their motive was transparent. They ill brooked the idea of the comparison sure to be drawn by the public between the Turkish fleet active on the coast of Circassia and the combined fleets idle at Baltchik. One of the chiefs had, as we have seen, been already morosely affected by observations in a private letter, and the other had been painfully excited by articles in the *Daily News;* the indirect authorship of which he—misled by a pleasant guest who added one and two together and made the sum even—attributed to the writer of these pages, who had fortunately the opportunity given him to repudiate the charge in presence of the worthy admiral, before his informant and other witnesses.* Nevertheless, the acrimonious feelings naturally excited thereby never entirely subsided; so true is Solomon's remark: "The words of a tale-bearer are as wounds, and they go down into the innermost parts of the belly."

Timeo Danaos et dona ferentes.

The admirals, mollified apparently by its docility, graciously allowed the Turkish fleet about mid June to quit Kavarna and lie with their fleets at Baltchik. Encouraged by this condescension, the Turkish fleet, after a few days of neighbourly intercourse, proposed to part company and cruise off the coast of Anatolia. The inhabitants of that coast required encouragement; the coasting trade, exposed to a dash from Sevastopol, required protection; the fleet required fresh provisions, unattainable by it in competition with the fleets of

* The calumny alluded to in the text had its origin as follows:—A medical gentleman in London wrote to the author a request, on behalf of a patient connected with the *Daily News*, to recommend a correspondent at Constantinople for that paper. Knowing of no one in that line, the author applied to some friends at Therapia, who requested him to make the offer to Dr. ——. He accordingly sent the letter he had received to the literary doctor, with an intimation that if the post suited him he might put himself in communication with the editor of the *Daily News*. He heard no more of the matter; but has reason to believe the offer was not accepted. Quidnunes, on the assumption of its acceptance, jumped to the conclusion that the recommender influenced the writer. The request in question had been written *after* the publication of the offending articles in the *Daily News*. On their appearance at Constantinople, the author of these pages, thinking them harsh and unmerited, wrote in that vein to his brother in London, and begged him to mitigate their effect as far as he could among his friends in his clubs and at the bar.

wealthy European Governments. At Kavarna its crews had received only five ounces of meat per man twice a week, while vegetables, in default of which the Turk's health soon droops, were not procurable: *keshkesh* (pounded boiled wheat) served out for a while in lieu, proved deleterious; and the consequence of all was, in addition to a mortality on board at the rate of ten per cent. per annum since leaving the Bosphorus, eleven per cent. of the force, several hundreds of whom had to be invalided, were afflicted more or less with scurvy. This reasonable request for a cruise was unfavourably received. Nothing short of its quitting the Black Sea could assure the Allies' admirals of the Turkish fleet not going to the coast of Circassia when out of their reach. Equally averse from its presence in their sight, they ordered it to go and lie at Varna, an objectionable anchorage. At Varna the supply difficulty would have been enhanced, for the Allies' military purveyors were there with open bags of gold.

This order exhausted, for the moment, Oriental patience. The Turkish and Egyptian admirals thereupon wrote a joint letter to the Allies' admirals, in which they courteously requested to be informed of their motives for wishing thus to sequester twenty sail of men-of-war; reminded them of their own responsibility to the Porte, and proposed an interview with them; in answer to which the admirals, in an official letter, informed them of their having already requested the English and French ambassadors at Constantinople to make a communication to the Porte respecting its fleet, and pending the arrival of the answer, they begged to decline an interview. The terms of their letter, written before the junction of the fleets at Baltchik, did not transpire; but the result was the recall of the Turkish fleet, excepting two line-of-battle ships, already there for the purpose, which were ordered to lie at Varna to assist in the disembarkation of the Allies' armies' stores. The Porte thought that its fleet, doomed to inactivity, might as well lie in the Bosphorus with consideration and full rations, as in the Bay of Kavarna with humiliation and scurvy.

Thus circuitously, the Allies' admirals succeeded in carrying out their original views respecting the Turkish fleet, as intimated to Mushaver Pasha three months earlier at Baltchik. They carried them out to the very letter. They doubtless, in accordance with human infirmity, felt proud of their triumph. They had marred an ably designed expedition, promising success, which had sailed from the Bosphorus with four attainable objects in view. First, to make Soukhoum Kaleh the base of Caucasian operations; attempted seventeen months later, then too late. Secondly, to reduce other Russian positions on the coast of Abasia; abandoned a year later unmolested. Thirdly, to unite the Circassians by Moslem co-operation, and by the stimulus of imperial favours; also attempted fifteen months later with trivial means by the Allies' agents, then too late. Fourthly, to show the Turkish flag to the Crim Tartars, and open communications with them in anticipation of the invasion of the Crimea by the allied armies. Instead of cheering it on and aiding it, the Allies' admirals, in the exercise of their discretion, detained the Turkish fleet in the Bay of Kavarna, deteriorating there from day to day from inaction and disappointment. They had, moreover, overlooked an important principle.

Since the peace of Adrianople, the Turkish fleet had been excluded from the Black Sea, not in virtue of any treaty, but out of the Porte's deference for Russia's susceptibility in regard to Circassia and the Crimea. The Circassians and the Crimeans, unread, untravelled, connect the past and the present by ocular evidence. They distrust what they may hear; they may credit what they see. They knew traditionally that Turkey had been, in former days, a naval power. Russia willed their ignorance of her remaining one, to strengthen the sense of her ascendancy in their minds. The interest created by the presence of two Turkish brigs of war at Sevastopol, sent there in the autumn of 1850 to break the charm, showed the wisdom of her prevision. During three weeks 9,000 Russians and 10,000 Tartars visited them. Many of the latter came expressly from the ends of the Crimea; and some among them, aged men who remembered another order of things, were lachrymosely moved on finding themselves under the Turkish flag. This evidence of the vitality of religious associations indicated the enthusiasm which the appearance of a Moslem fleet at Kaffa, a Turkish settlement in the days of Crimean independence, would have evoked in 1854. What Russia had not ventured to ask for in peace, the Allies' admirals insisted upon in war: viz., the exclusion of the Turkish fleet from the only sea where its flag could give her umbrage, and where alone it could have a moral effect.

The Turkish fleet re-anchored in the Bosphorus, July 3, 1854. A letter followed it from Admiral Deans

Dundas to the president of the naval council, expressive of his desire for its crews to be sent to Batoom for military duty. No notice was taken of this singular proposition; but 300 men were appropriately sent to the Danube for boat and other nautical duties, making with those already there 700 sailors of the imperial fleet detached for service on that river.

CHAPTER XIX.

The Russian Army crosses the Danube—Prince Paskievitch lays Siege to Silistria—Its Governor, Musa Pasha, is killed—Gallantry of the British Officers Butler and Nasmyth—The Allies aroused to Activity—Conference with Omar Pasha at Schumla—Duke of Cambridge embarks with his Division for Varna—Quiescence of Omar Pasha—The Russians raise the Siege of Silistria—What the Allies might have done—Todleben joins the Russian Camp—Prince Gortchakof's Advice—The allied Armies ordered to the Crimea—Proposals of Austria—Her "Material Guarantee"—Plans of France and England—Reasonable Hopes of Success—Sevastopol no longer "a standing Menace"—Position of Constantinople—What is wanting to make it Predominant—Results of such Consummation—Feelings of the Turkish Navy—Exploit of a Russian War Steamer—The Turkish Fleet at Varna—The Town occupied by the Allies—Unceremonious Proceedings of the French—Disgust of the Inhabitants—Danger from Fire—Neglect of Precautions against it—Outbreak of Fire—Losses of the British Commissariat—No one to direct Operations—Conduct of European and Turkish Soldiers contrasted—Groundless Suspicions of Greek Treachery—Too late Precautions—Stormy Meeting of Turkish Notables—Angry Complaints against the European Commanders—Accessibility of Turkish Officials—Indignant Speech of an Efendi—Danger to the Shipping in the Bay—No Guard-vessels—Outbreak of the Cholera at Varna—Observations of the Disease—Inferences and Proofs—Assistance safely rendered by the Healthy and Well-fed—Danger of Mental Depression—Treatment of Cholera by the Turks—Danger from checked Perspiration—Why the Turkish Crews suffered less from Cholera—Superstitious Panic of Turkish Sailors—Heavy Losses of French Troops from Disease—Mortality at Kustengé—Sickness in the British Army—Its Causes.

In the meanwhile the Russian army, under Prince Gortchakof, had crossed the Danube at Toolscha; the spot where Darius crossed that river on his Scythian expedition. The most accessible point of the river for the disembarkation of an army, opposite Ismael, had been left invitingly bare of the means of resistance. Thence the Russians marched by Issatcha, Matchin, and Hirsova, the garrisons of which retired on their approach, to Silistria; before which they sat down, under the veteran Marshal Prince Paskievitch. The memorable siege of Silistria, characterized by moving incidents, had run its course. The envied martyr's death of Musa Pasha, its governor, mortally wounded by a piece of shell while in the act of stepping on to his *sedjadeh* to say his evening prayer, had sent a fervid thrill through Islam. "For him," said the Turkish Gazette, "the gates of Paradise opened wide." The gallantry of Captain Butler and Lieutenant Nasmyth, in sharing the vigils and perils of the Turco-Egyptian band entrusted with the defence of Arab Redoubt, had given every Englishman a personal interest in the siege.

The progress of the siege had aroused the Allies from their dream of Oriental repose; had dispelled the idea in their minds of the improbability of a shot being fired in anger by them. Marshal St. Arnaud and General Lord Raglan, accompanied by the Turkish ministers of war and of marine, had gone to Schumla to confer with Omar Pasha, had ascertained the danger of Silistria, had returned hurriedly to Constantinople, and had begun towards the end of May to send troops to Varna. The Duke of Cambridge embarked with his division, June 13. The presence of a fine Turkish army at Schumla, and the gathering of the Allies in the neighbourhood of Varna, influenced without doubt the result of the siege; but it ought not to be forgotten that neither moved a step to relieve the brave garrison, who had remained by their guns twenty-five days and nights. Straitened for provisions, Silistria was on the point of surrendering. Its governor had already informed the generalissimo of his inability to hold out another week. "God is great," was virtually the reply.

Omer Pasha's quiescent attitude at Schumla, making no serious attempt to disturb the besiegers, in a highly critical position between him and the Danube, is an enigma for a future Jomini to solve. All he apparently did was to allow Behram Pasha (General Cannon) to manœuvre himself with a brigade of infantry into the place a few days before the termination of the siege. But the Russians not suspecting scarcity in Silistria, the place being open for supplies, apprehending also the advance of converging armies from Varna and Schumla, when they would not have saved either their guns or baggage, raised the siege, June 18, and retreated with their entire matériel : more fortunate in that respect than their predecessors in 1828, who after four months' open trenches before Silistria, defended then chiefly by irregulars, left half their guns behind them, and abandoned nearly all the others in their retreat, harassed by the victorious garrison and by detachments from the Grand Vizir's army at Schumla. Had the Turks and the Allies followed up with like vigour Prince Paskievitch in 1854, they would have routed his army beyond the power of rallying. The Allies might afterwards have marched leisurely to Odessa, have there re-embarked in their fleets, or have continued their march by Nicolaef, Kherson, and Perekop to the Crimea. Although circuitous, that was the best road to Sevastopol.

A few days before the close of the siege of Silistria, an officer of engineers—so it has been said—joined the Russian camp, simultaneously with the arrival of an earnest request from Prince Mentchikof in the Crimea for an able engineer. Prince Gortchakof's choice fell on the stranger, Captain Todleben. Prince Gortchakof, the ablest of Russian strategists, advised, after the failure before Silistria, sending two divisions of the army of the Danube to the Crimea; but the Czar, in doubt about the Allies' intentions, would not consent to reduce that army.

Ten days after the raising of the siege of Silistria, the English and French Governments ordered the earliest possible embarkation of their armies for the Crimea. Whereupon Austria sent a military envoy to Varna to urge upon the allied generals' consideration the superior advantages likely in her opinion to be derived from an autumnal campaign in Bessarabia, professing her readiness, should they coincide with her view, to co-operate actively with them. She excused herself from co-operation if the Allies persisted in going to the Crimea, where it was observed their detention might exceed anticipation. She would be exposed in that case to be attacked by the Russian army of the west, without their being able to make a diversion in her favour. Paris was sufficiently remote from that army to be careless about its movements; but Vienna lay within a few marches of it, with discontented Hungary and fermenting Italy to think about besides. Austria, having thus proffered as much as she thought could be reasonably expected of her in her complex position, decided on armed neutrality. She had already been busy negotiating a treaty with the

Porte, signed July 14, 1854, for the joint military occupation of Moldo-Wallachia, with the faculty of marching troops into Bosnia in the event of the Servians and Montenegrins proving troublesome. The "material guarantee" thus entrusted by Turkey, with the consent of France and England, to Austria's keeping, became a guarantee for her that, end how it might, she would not be a loser by the war, and placed her in a position to verify the axiom that in every Eastern question she must sooner or later have a voice.

But France and England, confident in their resources, gave no heed to her schemes. They intended the Crimean campaign to be at once the commencement and the termination of the war,—to begin and end in the autumn of 1854. Counting on certain success, they were resolved to have the glory to themselves, to share it with no one else, and to show the world their ability with their forces then in Turkey to humble Russia. The Turkish army was not invited to join them, save a few indifferent battalions to amuse the Crim-Tartars with; the Turkish fleet had been turned out of the Euxine; Austria was made light of. The expectation of early and rapid success was not unreasonable. The English and French Governments had obtained tolerably accurate information about the Russian forces in the Crimea; they in no material respect, as events showed, misled their generals; and it seemed as if human means would be impotent to avert the anticipated catastrophe. They may be supposed to have said to them in as many words: —"Take 50,000 of the finest troops of Europe, supported by matchless fleets. Go to the Crimea, where a disaffected population is ready to welcome you. There you will find an army inferior in numbers and equipment, and an ill-fortified arsenal. Rout the former, reduce the latter, and return with laurels to eat your Christmas dinners."

On that hypothesis the expedition was judicious, and on no other; for when undertaken, Sevastopol had, through the agency of steam, ceased to be a "standing menace." The first screw line-of-battle ship which furrowed the Euxine dissolved the charm, and converted the menace into a bugbear. As long as the north-east wind, prevalent in summer, could chain a fleet two months together in the Bosphorus, Sevastopol commanded the Euxine, and cast the shadow of invasion over Turkey; but as soon as steam rendered egress as facile from one place as from the other, the balance was righted, if not inclined the other way. The Euxine possesses only two safe defensible harbours, Sevastopol and the Bosphorus, and for a steam fleet the latter is the best, since it has its port under its lee. The position of Constantinople, always unrivalled in a military and commercial sense, has gained by steam so much, that whenever the balance of power shall be permanently deranged, the seat of predominance will be that city—the natural capital of all the provinces of the Eastern empire linked with it by the traditions of fifteen centuries. All that seems wanting for that consummation is a government willing to rule on unsectarian principles, and adapt its policy to the requirements of the age. Mark the logical sequences. The Hellespont and the Bosphorus will be rendered impassable, and the fleets behind them become in their turn standing menaces for the Mediterranean and the Euxine. The fertile districts bathed by the

Propontis—the sun-lit lake of Constantinople—and its inexhaustible fisheries, will nourish treble the actual population of the capital. Fleets built and equipped at arsenals in the Red Sea and the Persian Gulf will command the Indian and Chinese seas. Emigration from Germany, Italy, and Western India, filling up voids in Roumelia, Asia Minor, and Mesopotamia, will re-cultivate neglected plains, rebuild fallen cities, and develop mineral treasures.

Seeing the daily passage through the Bosphorus of troops and military stores, its own arsenal building *shalans* to land them in the Crimea, the Turkish fleet felt humiliated by its seclusion at Buyukdereh. But its government was trammelled by deference to the behests of the Allies, and no press existed to espouse its cause. Unexpectedly its foe assisted it out of a false position. One day, July 19, a Russian war steamer, the *Bessarabia*, left Sevastopol and steamed across the Black Sea, then alive with thirty hostile steamers, to the coast of Anatolia; there captured two Turkish merchant vessels, one off Cape Kempereh, the other off Amassereh, laden respectively with Indian corn and coal; and, having replenished her bunkers from the latter, burnt them. She retained the captain and scribe of each vessel as evidence of her feat, embarked the crews in a coasting craft to go their own way, showed her colours off Ereghli and Kosloe, and then returned to Sevastopol. The caimacam of Ereghli, where the ejected crews landed, forwarded a report of the affair to Constantinople. Together with the news, at first regarded as a hoax, arrived accounts of the feeling of insecurity among the inhabitants of the coast; who fancied the Russian fleet at sea. The Russians had destroyed Turkish ships at Sinope, as though in defiance of the allied fleets at Beikos; they now burned Turkish vessels in the vicinity, as though in contempt for the allied fleets at Baltchik. The Turkish steamers being either absent or under repair, the author proposed to run down the coast of Anatolia with a frigate, to encourage the natives; but the Capitan Pasha expressed his apprehension of his falling in with a Russian squadron, Sevastopol, he said, being evidently unblockaded. Declining the responsibility, he desired him to wait on the Grand Vizir and confer with him thereupon. His Highness showed himself equally disinclined to risk a frigate; he would, however, he said, consider about sending the fleet to sea again: meaning rather, that he would concert an excuse to make to the Sultan for having consented to its recall; of which he appeared ashamed, with reason.

July 29.—The Turkish fleet again left the Bosphorus, each ship carrying two *shalans* lashed on either broadside, and four days afterwards anchored in the Bay of Varna, crowded then with shipping of all denominations. One of its line-of-battle ships, having exhibited dangerous leakage on the passage, was sent back to Constantinople.

Varna seemed then in hostile rather than friendly occupation. The best houses and private magazines had been taken possession of by the Allies without any remuneration to their owners. General Lord Raglan for his part, when spoken to on the subject, said he had served before in an ally's and an enemy's country and had always enjoyed free quarters. Foreign residents alone escaped the honour of furnishing quarters gratis.

An Ionian tried the question by refusing to surrender his house; on which the English consul was called upon to eject him, *nolens volens*, but excused himself on the plea of want of authority. The French were particularly unceremonious: they used to mark with chalk any house the aspect or position of which suited them, then desire the governor to give them immediate possession of it. Many sighs issued from latticed harems at their ungallant importunity. One day a staff officer, pensive as though meditating on a thorny enterprise, meeting the author in one of the streets, complained of the reluctance of the fair occupants of a house selected by him that morning to turn out, and requested his assistance. The Frenchman had never seen his face before, and on being referred to the governor, with the observation—"You should give the ladies two days' grace," looked as if he wished never to see it again. They chafed the temper of the military commandant, by making, without concert with him, a wide breach in the curtain of the sea wall to facilitate the disembarkation of their troops and stores. The inhabitants, irritable and sore, murmured reproaches against the habits of the foreign troops—their proneness to drink and quarrel, to deal with shops on credit—and soon began to admire wonderfully, by comparison, the order and docility of their own troops, who had landed at and marched through Varna the preceding summer, and had not taken the value of an apple nor disturbed the gambols of a child. One night at ten o'clock some French soldiers went to a Mussulman café, occupied as usual by sleeping guests stretched on the estrades, and demanded wine. The orthodox cavedji was shocked; he told them wine was not sold there, and requested them to retire. A quarrel ensued, in which one of the Turks was killed and several on either side were wounded. Other French soldiers coming in from the camp outside the gates on hearing of the scuffle, a serious fray on a more extensive scale nearly occurred.

Varna being the chief depôt of the stores and provisions of the Allies' armies, containing also much of their ammunition, demanded extraordinary precautions against fire, accidental or wilful ; but by the rule of contrary which prevails in Turkey, as well with foreigners as with natives, simple precautions were considered as needless as though the city had been constructed of asbestos. Strangers came and went as they pleased, free from police observation and passport investigation. Bashi-bazouks encamped or bivouacked in open spaces, cooking their food in currents of air. Rollicking camp-followers threw the lighted ends of their cigars right and left in the streets. Improvised cafés of boughs and laths were filled with drinkers, smokers, and brawlers, till late in the night. So, as was to be expected in a wooden town —its non-occurrence earlier being surprising—fire broke out one night, August 10. It blazed six hours, consumed the bazaars, many private dwellings and store-houses, and a large amount of military supplies. The British commissariat,—its difficulties thus early commencing,— lost that night near six weeks' rations of biscuit for the army, and much of its stored corn. An hour of intense anxiety was passed by all, watching and combating the flames shooting out their forked tongues at the powder magazines, and throwing sparks on their roofs. Their ignition and the destruction of Varna were convertible terms. Levelling adjoining houses and covering the menaced buildings with wet canvas ensured their safety. During the conflagration confusion reigned in the town. Many gave orders, no one commanded: a head was wanted. Marshal St. Arnaud was indisposed in his house, and General Lord Raglan was absent at Baltchik. Rear-Admiral Sir Edmund Lyons had come into the illuminated bay from Constantinople early in the evening, but after communicating with one of H.M.'s ships had steamed on to Baltchik with the rueful tidings. The field officer on duty, brave veteran, stood feeble on his legs on a heap of rubbish near the powder magazine, his voice unheeded amidst a Babel of tongues. The pasha sat smoking on a block of wood, in contemplation of a party of sailors busy in razing a knot of dwellings which threatened to lead the flames to the upper quarter of the town. The captains of the ships of war in port strove fearlessly and zealously, each on his own account. Aides-de-camp galloping about added much to the picturesque, but nothing to the useful. Prudence would have suggested placing the material means of the Allies at the disposal of the Turks, versed in the tactics for a burning town, and leaving them to deal with the fire while they maintained order with their own troops. As fast as store-houses became relieved of their contents, heads of wine and sugar-casks were stove in for the regalement of the thirsty and of the sweet-toothed. "Voici," said one of a hilarious group of zouaves towards morning, handing us wine instead of the water asked for; "voici quelque chose meilleure que l'eau: buvez, mes braves, ne craignez rien; le prophète ne regarde pas de si près." Frank soldiers and sailors spared dealers in the bazaars the trouble of removing their goods, and the rabble followed their example. As on other occasions when honour or loot was to be obtained, the Turkish soldiers and sailors were not invited to join: they neither robbed nor rioted.

About midnight the inverse process of tracing cause from effect was resorted to to account for the fire, which was afterwards ascertained to have originated in a French government store of spirits and stationery. The fire would benefit Russia indirectly, therefore her partisans had lighted it. Thus reasoned some persons of rank, who might have reflected on the improbability of incendiaries choosing a calm night under a full moon for their operations. They raised the mischievous cry of Greek treachery. Incontinently orders were given to arrest every Greek whom any one in authority might deem suspicious. Several individuals were beaten on the spot, others were reserved for a beating next day. Two or three, it was said, were tossed into the flames; though from personal knowledge I am only able to say that two narrowly escaped that fate through timely interference. There was no fair ground for imputing such a mode of carrying on war to Russia, still less for supposing the Greeks willing to spoil their profitable dealings with the Allies for her sake.

The morrow disclosed the usual scenes of desolation, increased by the too late roused vigilance of the Allies. They pulled down houses untouched by the fire to make wider spaces round the powder depôts: they threw the planks of those and previously razed houses—materials for reconstruction—into the sea; and they planted sentries in the streets to prevent the sufferers from searching among the ruins of their shops and dwellings for valuables. Precautions suggested by alarm are always exaggerated.

Next afternoon the medjlis of the city held a stormy meeting, presided over by the governor. The speakers inveighed angrily against their allies. They compared the Russians favourably with them. "The Muscovites," they said, "came to Varna after the irritation of a double siege; they remained there two years, gave nobody reason to lament their conduct, and left the town better than they had found it. The Franks have scarcely been at Varna three months; they have taken our dwellings and store-houses compulsorily, have covered us with opprobrium, and now the place is ruined by their carelessness." An angry notable, whose store full of wares had been consumed, reproached the pasha for having neglected to make representations to the Allies' generals about the inefficiency of their police. The pasha said he and the military commandant had warned them as far as they could of the risk of fire. "They are like sultans; it is difficult to obtain an audience of them. When we visit either of them we are referred to a dragoman; when we write to them our letters remain unanswered." The contrast between the accessibility of a Turkish and the inaccessibility of a European functionary astonishes Orientals. A ragged *fakir*, with scarcely a crust to munch, may walk up to a pasha's sofa: his tale will be listened to. This accessibility and the right of petition operate as a check on subordinate agents. Under the influence of pipes and coffee the effervescence of the company was subsiding, when an incidental allusion to the siege of Varna in 1828 nearly roused it again. A white-bearded *efendi* warmed at the recollection. "Talk of the late siege of Silistria," he said; "what is it compared with the siege of Varna! Varna possessed then only a few old brass guns and scarcely any of its existent works: yet we repulsed the enemy once and nearly repulsed him twice. Wallah!" he emphatically exclaimed, "that enemy behaved better to us than these——our friends."

Any one who, on the side of the aided, has noted the bearing of an auxiliary army would pray to heaven for any calamity to befall him rather than see his own country reduced to solicit such succour.

As on the land, so on the water. The Bay of Varna was crowded with shipping of many nations, under little or no surveillance. A vessel filled with combustibles might have anchored any day among them unquestioned, and her crew might have left in their boat at night after having fired her and slipped her cable. Many men-of-war and numerous transports, with two powder ships, were irregularly anchored in the bay; but there was not a cruiser in the offing nor a guard-boat service at night. A few fire-ships sent in with the prevailing north-east wind would have caused inextricable confusion and incalculable damage. Troop and store-ships were continually passing between the Bosphorus and Varna; nevertheless not a vessel was stationed off the coast to protect them from a dash such as the *Bessarabia* had lately made on the coast of Anatolia. The Allies' admirals at Baltchik were not insensible to that risk, as appeared by the following note from one of them to the Turkish admiral:—

"Baltchik, August 6, 1864.

"Do not omit to keep a small vessel between the Bosphorus and Varna, as the Russians may think of looking out for a merchant ship or a transport; as well as a steamer occasionally to Circassia. I have the *Wasp* there just now. I am keeping my force ready to embark troops."

This call upon the Turkish fleet to protect allied vessels was tantamount to an apology for its dismissal six weeks earlier. Marshal St. Arnaud spoke to us in the same apprehensive sense one day at dinner at his head-quarters.

At that date the Russian fleet was cruising off Sevastopol, and two days earlier four Russian steamers had been seen forty miles out at sea. The Russian admiral little guessed the game there was for Enterprise to play while the gathering was taking place at Varna.

During the month of August cholera tainted the allied fleets and armies. Frequent visits to the sick-bay of his ship, to relieve her crew of the apprehension of contagion which depressed them, familiarized the author with its features, and made him think, notwithstanding the fatal termination of some cases in thirty-six hours, the panic usually created by it unfounded. Further observation of the disease on a wider area at Constantinople, eleven years later, confirmed that impression in his mind. Three propositions seem demonstrable. 1. Cholera is not contagious in the literal sense of the term, by contact. Proof: the immunity as a rule of those who chafe with their hands the skin of patients in a state of collapse. 2. Cholera is not infectious through the medium of effluvia from the bodies of patients, where attention is given to ventilation and disinfecting processes. Proof: the immunity, with rare exceptions, of the doctors in attendance on cholera patients in properly organized hospitals, and of patients with other diseases under the same roof. The naval hospital of Constantinople was crowded during the summer of 1865 with cholera and cholerine patients, all of them sedulously attended; yet none of the medical officers—two of whom, Hassan Bey and Gosma Bey, displayed remarkable self-abnegation—took the disease. Similar remarks apply to the military hospitals, as well as to the civil hospitals improvised during that period. 3. Cholera attacks only those classes whose blood has been slowly poisoned by breathing for years foul exhalations in confined, ill-ventilated quarters, or whose occupations entail on them undue exposure to solar and atmospheric influences. Proof: the immunity of the easy classes, who can adapt their diet and apparel and their proceedings to the exigencies of an abnormal season; deducting those individuals among them who prefer brandy-and-water to barley-water, who swallow every nostrum advertised as "infallible," or who brood isolated over exaggerated reports, with their eyes mentally fixed on their stomachs. From these premises we may infer —with all deference for the opinion of learned members of the Cholera Conference, advocates of selfish isolation —that the easy classes, on the appearance of the disease in any place, may safely give themselves the satisfaction of mitigating by their example and advice the distress of their poor neighbours. When those in no danger flee away panic-stricken from salubrious dwellings, those in real danger, with open sewers under their windows and choked drains under their feet, may well imagine their case hopeless, and thus open the door to cholera's chief ally, moral depression.

The treatment of cholera in the Turkish fleet in August, 1854, consisted in friction,—the best remedy—chalk opiate mixture, and occasionally venesection. Doubtful about the lancet (which was not put in requisition by the Turks in 1865), I presumed, on the authority of the chief medical officers of the Allies' flagships, consulted *ad hoc*, to remonstrate against its use; but the doctors adhered to their view of its efficacy in some cases, and cited afterwards in favour of it the comparative large number of their cures, notwithstanding that official cupidity denied them means to nourish their convalescents suitably. Once the doctor of the *Nuzretieh* abstained from venesection out of an Oriental deference for rank, and although declining the responsibility I begged him to act on the dictates of his judgment, he would not swerve from his sense of the consideration due for it. He could not, he said, knowing the pasha's distrust in the practice, presume to bleed any of his suite. The patient was not bled, and died. On reporting his death, the doctor said, "If he had been bled, he might have survived." "You should not, as a good Moslem, speak thus," I observed; "the poor fellow's hour was come: bled or not bled, he must have died." This silenced, without convincing, the hekim. Medical study saps the dogma of fate.

Checked perspiration during a choleraic season is fraught with peril; and on this head it may not be amiss to observe that its recurrence is invited in most navies by the custom—partly a cause of the premature old age of man-of-war's men—of berthing a ship's company together, in summer as well as winter, on the orlop deck, in harbour,—a custom as injurious to the respiratory organs as it is disagreeable to the olfactory nerves. Perspiring from head to foot, vitally depressed by breathing foul air, a man, at the call of nature, runs half-dressed up to the head, and remains there, caressed by the cool breeze, longer than necessary. That grateful air bath may be his death. The larger the ship the greater the danger. Hence the vessels of the Anglo-French fleet most severely attacked in 1854 were three-deckers: the *Britannia* and the *Montebello*. The crews of the Turkish ships, debilitated more or less by scurvy and inferior diet, might have been expected to have had proportionally more cases than their Allies; nevertheless they had fewer, which may be attributed to the practice in summer of the men sleeping, with ample space between them, on their beds spread on the gun decks; and also to covered ship's heads. A slight chill might prove fatal, of which the author had melancholy verification. Thrice at night, one of his boat's crew sickened, and two out of three died. Alarmed, the remainder of the crew came one morning with deprecating salaams into the cabin, and delivered themselves to this effect: The cholera and a new coxswain had made their appearance together in the boat; there was evidently a connection between them, and they humbly requested his discharge. "Have you any other cause of complaint against Saly?"—"None: he is a good man, we all like him; but he has brought the cholera with him to the boat. Inshallah! you will send him away; if not, we shall all die." This hallucination was serious. Their request could neither be regarded as an infraction of discipline nor joked with as a morbid fancy. I adopted a middle course, and reasoned with them. I commented on their irreverence in ascribing to their fellow mortal more power than their Prophet had wielded. "If he is possessed with a djin (evil spirit—the lower classes in Turkey implicitly believe in djins,) "the person in the stern sheets is the most exposed to his malign influence, and as he has no fear, why should you?" This appeased them. But as their moral depression was predisposing, something more than argument was necessary. They were therefore ordered thenceforward to take their capotes with them at night, to put on when lying on their oars. The heat rendered this irksome, and they were then perhaps sorry for having spoken. On their return on board hot coffee was supplied them from the cabin. Thanks to these precautions, no other of the barge's crew suffered; and Saly, who had not admired the attribution of life and death given him by his comrades, retained his post.

One day the imams of the fleet embarked in one boat and rowed round every ship in succession, chanting supplications to heaven to deliver the faithful from the cholera. As the disease was then on the decline, they obtained much credit for the presumed efficacy of their intercession.

The French suffered disproportionately during the summer of 1854 by cholera and other diseases classed under that head: for cholera had then to bear the sins of absinthe. A Zouave regiment, 2,200 strong when it left Algiers, was reduced to 1,400 men by the end of

August; and the first division of their army, in its aimless incursion to the Dobrudscha, lost in a few days, from drought and heat combined, 3,500 men, including sixty officers. During their hurried march of nine hours, fleeing from an invisible foe, back to Kustengé, men dropped exhausted every hundred yards. None heeded them. Even a chef de bataillon, unhorsed by a sunstroke, was said to have been abandoned. At Kustengé the dead and dying lay, we heard, mingled in heaps. Steamer-loads of sick, brought away from Ovid's dreary place of exile to be encamped on the northern slopes of the Bay of Varna, long whitened with their tents, were more eloquent than despatches.

The sickness in the British army in Bulgaria during that lugubrious period may be fairly attributed as much to injudicious diet as to a disturbed atmosphere. The ordinary ration of one pound of meat per man per diem, having been increased to one pound and a half, gastric irritation naturally ensued more or less. A deduction of a quarter of a pound and an issue of rice in lieu, should have seemed preferable. Much animal food, even of a digestible kind, cannot be eaten with impunity in Turkey, where the climate is inflammatory, with exceptional action on the stomach. The assertion, repeated *ad nauseam*, of the troops requiring extra meat and porter to keep up their strength—men between twenty and thirty years of age, in weary idleness—induced the error. Nature had given them the principle of strength, and all she asked for was a suitable diet, cool and unexciting. Hygienic science slumbered in the British camp when it was proposed to counteract the action on the human frame of an increment of twenty degrees of atmospheric heat by an addition to the already liberal allowance of meat. Adherence to the routine, at variance with the universal practice of all classes in the south, of serving the men's principal meal at noon, proved another, if not the chief cause, of debility. Salt pork, or fresh killed ill-cooked beef, with biscuit and grog, is not tempting diet anywhere in any latitude; but swallowed under canvas, with the thermometer at 90 degrees, it is well calculated to produce intestinal derangement; and it is little flattering to cholera to call the dysentery resulting therefrom by its imposing name. In the cool of the evening, an hour before sunset, such diet would be comparatively wholesome; exercise would be agreeable afterwards, and refreshing sleep might follow—with the mosquitos' leave. As long as soldiers and sailors are compelled to eat indigestible food at unreasonable hours, the cry for doctors will not abate nor the consumption of drugs be diminished in either of the services. In the Turkish service, under normal conditions, the men have rice soup in the morning, a light repast of bread and olives at noon, and their substantial meal, composed of meat and vegetables, savourily cooked, or pilaf, is served towards sunset; and to this regimen, coupled with restrictions in regard of fruit, must be ascribed the exemption from cholera of the first regiment of the redif of the guard which lay encamped at Devna during the summer of 1854.

The foot fever and sore backs of some of the English cavalry, acquired during a few days' reconnaissance in the Dobrudscha, much animadverted upon at the time, originated in similar inattention to alimentary influences. Fed according to English rule, without corresponding care and shelter, the animals were unprepared for the call made upon them. Their riders, we fain hope, then learned that high condition is a relative term, varying with climate and circumstances. Equestrian tribes, the Arabs and Turcomans, deduct a quarter of their horses' barley, and stint their water, for two or three weeks before setting out on an expedition. Their horses are then in wind, without superfluous flesh to generate humours.

CHAPTER XX.

Embarkation of the Allied Armies—Rations of Turkish Troops—Quality of the Men—The Conscription in Turkey—Suleyman Pasha—The Turks averse from the Service—The Esnan—Their Losses at Varna—Nostalgia a real Disease—Tone of the Allies—Marshal St. Arnaud and General Canrobert—Lord Raglan Criticism of the Naval Commanders—The three allied Fleets at Baltchik—The French and Turkish Fleets weigh Anchor—Arrival of the English Transports at Baltchik—The covering Fleet—An Opportunity lost by the Russians—Influence of British Naval Renown—The Russian Fleet at Sevastopol—Appearance of the English Fleet—Advantages of Katcha Bay as a Landing-place—Two Modes of attacking Sevastopol—Error in choosing the Point of Attack—Probability of Success from the opposite Coast—Sevastopol exposed to a Surprise—The Flank March—The combined Fleets anchor at Eupatoria—Estimate of the Forces—Bat Horses of British Cavalry left behind—Newspaper Correspondents—The Question considered in relation to War—The French Press tongue-tied.

THE embarkation of the allied armies, originally fixed for August 14, 1854, was delayed from day to day by the prevailing sickness. Nevertheless, preparations for the event were not remitted. Wharves were run out into the sea, for men and horses to walk on board transit steamers; store-ships were loaded, and practice in landing artillery was made in a cove on the south side of the bay. Gradually, as the time drew near, the forces approached Varna from distant encampments by easy marches; and embarked, the greater part of them during the last week of August, without a mishap worthy of note. The English troops embarked in transports, the comfort and roominess of which soon produced a sensible amelioration of their health. The islanders felt at home on board ship. The French troops embarked in their own men-of-war, and in numerous small merchant vessels of various nations, ycleped and numbered for the nonce "transports;" and the more crowded they were the merrier they appeared. The Turkish troops were embarked in their own ships of war, with three weeks' supply of biscuit, flour, rice, and butter, for immediate use in the Crimea—the Allies undertaking to feed them afterwards: also a fortnight's supply of biscuit and rice for the voyage, at the rate of 150 dirrhems (seventeen ounces) of biscuit, and ten dirrhems of rice, with butter for cooking it, per day per man. The Turkish squadron carried in addition a siege-train with its ammunition; three French batteries, with eighty-six horses for each; twenty shalans (flat quadriform boats), and a large amount of stores and provisions for the French army.

The Turkish troops, ten battalions of 800 men each, more or less, were of inferior quality; being chiefly *esnan*.* Never before enrolled, the *esnan* battalions had

* Mussulmans in Turkey between the ages of nineteen and twenty-four, try their luck in the conscription lottery every year, in the districts where it can be enforced. Those who escape altogether are termed *esnan* (aged). They are aggregated to the *redif* (reserve) and are liable during thirteen years to serve *in war*. The redif is composed of soldiers who have served their time, five years, and are liable as such to be called out in war or on apprehension of war during eight years. The redif of each district is supposed to be called out once a year for exercise, under a permanent staff of officers.

This system works harshly in a country where the removal of a man fifty miles from his home amounts to exile, with ignorance about those dear to them, and it keeps a man's mind unsettled. The enrolment of the redif for service is always attended by considerable mortality.

left behind them families and fields on whom their thoughts dwelled. They had received three months' drilling at Scutari, and had been sent to Varna early in August; where two battalions of Roumelian *redif*, armed with percussion muskets, joined them. This contingent was under the command of Suleyman Pasha, who had passed the preceding twelve years of his life, with the rank of colonel of the guard, as superintendent of the imperial tannery at Beikos; the only variations of his duty in that period having been the surveillance of the Hungarian refugees at Kutaiah, and a mission to the Bey of Tunis: who impressed on his mind a high idea of his merit by giving him a *backshish* of 1,000 purses (4,500*l.*) A complimentary mission to a feudal vassal, who is bound by custom to mark his sense of the honour by liberality to the envoy, is a convenient way of rewarding a favourite. During the present reign, one of the Sultan's aides-de-camp received collectively in the course of a year from the Sheick of Mecca and the Pasha of Egypt, to whom he had been sent on missions, about 5,000 purses. Suleyman Pasha joined the expedition sorely against his will, ill-reconciled to it by promotion to the rank of *liva*. The Turks shunned this service, for they anticipated neglect when in the Crimea, both from the Porte and from the Allies. The health of the troops

The merit of the conscription, which is carried out as fairly as the habits of the country admit of, is due to Riza Pacha, who organized it about 1844. Previously the men had been pressed, and the term of service had been unlimited.

The Christian communities of the empire have been considered admissible to military service since the Peace of Paris, but they have been allowed to compound for it by the annual payment of nearly ninety millions of piastres (800,000*l.*), a sum equal about to the amount of the abolished kharatch.

under his command had deteriorated at Varna, through want of fresh meat and vegetables, which the ready money of the Allies monopolized. The destitution and penury of the government stores and chest at Varna were then complete; so much so that we were obliged, just before sailing, to make, through the governor, a requisition on the inhabitants for the small supply of rice and butter necessary to make pilaff for the troops on the voyage.

One battalion of the *esnan* being embarked in the author's ship, he learned its history; which did not differ materially from that of the others. When it left Scutari, August 10th, it was 820 strong, having arrived there 900 strong. Out of that number sixteen had died, thirteen had deserted, and thirty-two had been invalided at Varna; thirty-two had been left in hospital at Varna, and twelve died on the passage to the Crimea; making on the whole a diminution of fourteen per cent. in one month. The *redif*, and particularly the *esnan*, were always during the war more or less painfully affected with nostalgia; a veritable, often fatal, disease in connection with fatalism. The Turkish soldier on service has rarely means of communicating with his family. He broods over the forlorn condition in imagination of his wife and children in case of his death, news of which would not for months transpire in his village, unless by mere chance, such as the return of an invalided comrade. His arrears of pay, claimable by his heirs only within a year, might, through red-tapist obstacles, lapse to the treasury, or possibly become perquisites of office.

The tone and demeanour of the Allies on the eve of their departure for the Crimea betokened little ardour.

The chiefs seemed oppressed by the responsibility of leading an army into a country only a degree better known to them than Japan. Few supposed the Czar had left the pendent pearl of his empire in danger of being torn away at a grasp. Many expected to find there twice the number of troops actually encountered; in which case, observed a French staff officer, "pas un n'echappera, pas même le maréchal." The troops had the air of wanting confidence in their leaders' ability to meet a crisis. Marshal St. Arnaud, advantageously known as a dashing colonel of cavalry, had won his bâton by his services as minister of war during the coup d'état of 2nd December. He was moreover an invalid; with, however, a spirit to control disease in the hour of action. His second in command, General Caurobert, had conciliated imperial favour by storming with his brigade the barricades in the Faubourg St. Martin, rather than by his distinguished services in Africa. General Lord Raglan's name possessed only reflected military glory; he being reserved with his divisional generals, and from his sedentary habits personally unknown to his troops. The naval commanders-in-chief threw cold water on the expedition by criticizing its policy and dwelling on the lateness of the season: thereby laying themselves open to comment; for whatever their private opinion, the expedition once decided upon, they were bound to encourage and forward it by word and example. Even its warm abettors, their seconds in command, had misgivings while decorously advocating it: thus securing for themselves credit in case of success, and freedom from responsibility in case of reverses.

The French and Turkish troops were all embarked at

Varna, August 31st, 1854, and next day the three allied fleets rendezvoused at Baltchik, with Marshal St. Arnaud's head-quarters in the *Ville de Paris*. That day being Courban bairam, the Turkish fleet, dressed in colours, fired the customary salutes at noon. Its allies, hoisting the Turkish flag at the main, fired also a royal salute in honour of the occasion, from a French and an English ship. We lay at Baltchik, the French expressing impatience, till September 5th, waiting for the arrival of the rear division of the English transports from Varna, with head-quarters in the *Caradoc*. At daylight on the 5th, the French and Turkish fleets weighed anchor, and proceeded off Cape Kellagriah. They lay to there for several hours, in sight from Baltchik; then stood to the northward and eastward under easy sail. All the 6th and 7th of September we stood on and off, or lay to, out of sight of land, about the 44th, or between that and the 45th parallel, in a weatherly position for making a course to the Crimea. Lost in conjecture about the non-appearance of our friends, we began to apprehend the arrival of counter orders since our departure. A message brought by an English frigate dispelled that sick fancy. We afterwards learned that the absent transports arrived at Baltchik on the morning of the 6th; but we never satisfactorily learned the motive for the further delay of the English fleet at that anchorage. The single fact of the French and Turkish fleets, crowded with troops and encumbered with stores, being at sea without disposable steamers, should have seemed an all-sufficient motive for instant departure; at all events of the line-of-battle ships. They were not required at Baltchik, and might have come on under sail, like the

French and Turkish ships, leaving the steamers, which subsequently towed them, to accelerate the progress of the transports.

The covering fleet, including the *Napoleon* and the *Charlemagne*, the two best French ships, ought, in accordance with its chosen rôle, to have weighed anchor first, not last, from Baltchik, and have interposed itself between Sevastopol and the track projected on the chart for the army: no chance should have been left open for the enemy to profit by. He might have been assumed alive to the uncertain calamity of invasion, with his fleet on the look-out, and ready, as every fleet ought to be under similar provocation, to risk much to prevent it. Everybody conversant with the circumstances of the *trajet* across the Black Sea knows that any check would have caused the relinquishment of the expedition: all but relinquished as it was, if report spake true, when half-way over. On the appearance of the Russian fleet, accompanied presumedly by propelling steamers—supposing a diversion to have been attempted on the 6th or 7th of September,—the French and Turkish fleets must, as their least loss, have cut adrift the *shalans* for landing artillery from their sides, and have thrown overboard several hundreds of artillery horses, as well as the baggage and stores on their decks for which room could not have been found below. The wind during those two days being light and variable, they would not probably have been able, on the dictates of prudence for the sake of the troops, to avoid an action. The Russian fleet lost an opportunity of striking a heavy blow and acquiring much distinction. But its want of vigilance is accountable. How was it to calculate on the inversion of rule? on a transport fleet at sea, the covering fleet in port? As the name of the king was a tower of strength in the Middle Agės, so in the late war British naval renown was a fleet in itself. But it may be as well to remember that the shadow of a great name rarely serves twice.

The Russian navy may console itself for its non-observation of the first movements of the Allies from Baltchik, by the reminiscence of the noble part it acted in the defence of Sevastopol; but it cannot excuse itself from remissness; for had the Allies adopted any of the other plans which presented themselves for the reduction of Sevastopol, its fleet would have been sunk or captured, dishonoured in its country's eyes.

At 10 A.M., September 8th, our doubts were removed by descrying the van division of the English fleet. It rapidly advanced. Beyond, as far as the visible horizon from our mast-heads, the sea was covered with vessels, half obscured by the smoke of a hundred steamers. A Red Indian's imagination would have fancied a forest on the point of bursting into flame. At 3 P.M. the *Britannia*, towed by the *Retribution*, leading the fleet, passed under our stern. Crowds of steamers, some with men-of-war, others with transports, one or more, in tow, passed in close succession. They made a stirring spectacle—a novel exhibition of power. Alas! none of us anticipated how few of that gallant army would ever tread their native land again. Instead of joining us, and proceeding at once to the Crimea—which would have been a gain of three days—they steamed out of sight to the northward, and anchored forty miles west of Cape Tarkhan, the westernmost point of the Crimea. While the "covering fleet" lay thus at anchor in mid-sea, the *Caradoc*, escorted by steam men-of-war, made a reconnaissance of the coast between Sevastopol and Eupatoria.

The notabilities on board fancied, as we afterwards heard, the appearance of defensive works at Katcha Bay, which decided in the negative the question of disembarking the army there. This decision proved unfortunate. At the Katcha, wood, water, and forage were plentiful, while at "Old Fort" all three were wanting. It entailed also a more pregnant consequence. Landing in that bay would have ensured, in probability, adherence to the original intention of reducing the north side of Sevastopol, in sight from it, and wanting then the accessories to the "Severnaya Fort," which constituted, *long afterwards*, the strength of the position. Admitting the plea which has been urged of the hazard of an assault, a siege appeared an ordinary operation of given limited duration. The Russians have acknowledged, since the peace, its feebleness at that time, and have expressed surprise at our having turned away from it. In changing their minds, the Allies' generals betrayed a want of previous deliberation. There were two direct modes of attacking Sevastopol to choose between. The choice should have been irrevocably made before leaving Bulgaria; and, in accordance with it, the army should have landed north or south of the harbour, conveniently near the menaced point. The north side having been preferred, the pleasant valley watered by the Katcha, six miles from Sevastopol, near the high road to Bakchésaray, seemed an appropriate spot for the disembarkation. The siege-train, if wanted, might have been landed four miles nearer. The commanding position of the "Severnaya Fort" with respect to the harbour, had suggested that attack. That reduced, the fire from the north side would dominate the arsenal.

These may not, in themselves, be deemed theoretically sufficient inducements, in the absence of correct topographical information, to entirely justify landing an army, with numerous wants, dependent on shipping, on a part of the coast devoid of harbours; but the usual fair weather in September and October, the prevalence of north-easterly winds at that season making a weather shore, the engineers' low estimate of the Star Fort, and the time required to change the base of operations, more than sufficed to show the wisdom—the army being on shore—of adhering to the original plan. An error in the selection of the side of the harbour for disembarkation had been committed. Oral and written testimony of the perilous exposure of South Sevastopol to be carried by a *coup de main*, it being fortified (before steam had rendered invasion practicable) only against a naval attack, had not received due consideration. A hardily-executed attack from the south would have attained the object of the expedition before the date of the landing at "Old Fort:" thus surpassing the most sanguine expectations. Leaving Baltchik, say on the 8th September, and steering direct for Cape Chersonesus, 250 miles distant, the Allies would have reached the offing of Sevastopol on the 10th, designedly at daylight. Magnified by apprehension, the army would have been landed before night on the Heracleotic steppe. Immediate surrender might have been expected to have followed, to avoid an assault of no doubtful result; since, with the allied fleet ready to enter the harbour, the enemy could not have berthed his ships to fire on advancing columns. Setting aside, however, the effect of panic, supposing the army of the Crimea to have been concentrated in Sevastopol (an extreme supposition) and to have marched out, colours flying, a battle like that given on the Heights of Abraham would have been fought on, and have rendered otherwise memorable, the site of the Allies' subsequent dreary encampment. Victors and vanquished would have entered the city together. While thus peculiarly exposed to be carried by surprise, Sevastopol possessed, in the character of the ground before it, and its immense matériel, means for extemporizing, with short warning, a scheme of defence. Hence, with the probability of warning being given by it, the flank march, much extolled at the time, will finally be censured. An uncomplicated siege—a known quantity—on the north side, was abandoned for complex operations—an unknown quantity—on the south side; and a fertile position, whence an army could intercept communications between Sevastopol and Bakchésaray, was exchanged for a sterile corner of the Crimea pent in by a barrier of hills.

At 3 P.M., 11th September, we again descried a crowd of steamers N.N.E.; and at sunset the French and Turkish fleets anchored for the first time in thirty-five fathoms. Next morning, the other ships making their appearance, the three fleets joined company, and proceeded along the coast in picturesque confusion. Nonconformity of night signals — preconcert having been wanting in that as well as in other respects—and the passion of one of the admirals for using them, caused ludicrous mistakes the following night. On the 13th, in the afternoon, the combined fleet of men-of-war and transports came to anchor off the pretty, steppe-fringing, windmill-flanked town of Eupatoria. The sight of its minarets refreshed our Turks. How did the inhabitants feel? We tried to fancy ourselves in their place, but failed to conjure up an adequate sensation. In the evening the town was summoned to surrender, and a few ships were told off for firing on its white stuccoed walls and green venetian blinds. As the garrison consisted of only a few hundred invalid soldiers without artillery, the governor deemed compliance excusable. This hint of the military unpreparedness of the Crimea was confirmed by subsequent interrogatories.

We now contemplated in its aggregate at one anchorage our mighty host, and we might be acquitted of presumption in thinking the Crimea would be in our possession before snow should whiten its hills. Its means of locomotion, independent of wind, increased its might. None could say where the first blow would fall. There were present eight three-deckers, one of them screw-propelled, twenty two-deckers, including six with screw propulsion, seven frigates, two of them with screws, about thirty paddle war-steamers, and several hundred transports, many of them with steam; carrying 56,000 troops, including 1,400 cavalry, with twenty-two batteries and two siege-trains. The crews of the men-of-war, 35,000 strong, were trained to the use of great guns and small arms. On one side there were 90,000 land and sea troops, able by their command of the sea to draw supplies and reinforcements in three weeks from Western Europe, in three days from Turkey. On the other side there were about 60,000 land and sea troops, separated from Russia by the roadless steppe, with a disaffected population to control. Nothing, apparently, was wanting to the efficiency of the British army, save its bat horses, left behind through alleged deficiency of transport: a weak excuse, since the English fleet, unencumbered by troops and stores, might have embarked them, and many hundred horses besides, with a month's forage; and in the unanticipated event of the enemy showing fight have thrown them overboard. Officers, devoid of means of carrying with them some of the comforts which are necessaries to men accustomed to them from their childhood, became thereby often unable to perform their duties properly *off* the battle-field, and fatigued men delayed the march of the army.

Recognized "correspondents," uniting in their correspondence the graphic details of the early chroniclers with the graceful narrative of the panegyrists of Louis XIV.'s progresses, formed part—not the least important part—of the expedition. They wielded their power, save in one or two instances, generously, and on the whole impartially. They performed their duty by the public conscientiously. Their courage and self-abnegation, uncheered by honours in prospective, praising others themselves unpraised, were exemplary. Nevertheless, the compatibility of their avocations with the obligations of an army on service remains questionable with many. I doubt it. I am disposed to think that if a nation wishes to have an army like those armies which have in all ages won empires and defended empires, it will dispense with correspondents. The province of journalism is to indicate abuses and deficiencies during peace, and advocate amendment: in which respect the British press has not been remiss; but defects in war should be left to cure themselves, as they will do, by a slower, perhaps, but more salutary process. The special correspondent, in his single-minded earnest endeavour to perform his task loyally, does not reflect that, in exposing ills which have a different hue in civilian and professional eyes, and in giving expression to dissatisfaction at hardships perhaps unavoidable, he may be engendering a cankering evil, felt rather than seen—lax discipline. He is also liable, unwittingly, to excite jealousies, and even — a matter of deeper import—enhance a reputation, on the faith of which a man may be appointed to commands above his real capacity. There are men in every army as in every fleet ready to apply to "correspondents" Hamlet's words in regard of players:—"Good my lord, will you see the players well bestowed? Do you hear, let them be well used; for they are the abstract and brief chronicle of the time: after your death you were better have a bad epitaph than their ill-report while you live."

The French during the war went to the other extreme. Not content with excluding "correspondents" from their camp, they tongue-tied the press wherever able. Even some mild strictures on their operations in the Crimea in the *Journal de Constantinople* were offensive to them; and the Porte in consequence, on the demand of the French chargé-d'affaires, placed that journal under the censorship of the French commandant at Pera for its military articles.

CHAPTER XXI.

The Fleets anchor off Old Fort—Aspect of the Shore—Prompt Disembarkation of French Troops—Their Alertness—Prince Napoleon—French Soldiers under Canvas—Disembarkation of the British Forces—The Soldiers landed without Tents or Knapsacks—Their Bivouac under heavy Rain—Defective Organization—Results of needless Exposure—Altered Conditions of Invasions created by Steam—Landing of Cavalry—Tartars come into Camp—Their Joy at Sight of Moslem Troops—Their Account of the Force of Sevastopol—A Spy—Complaint against the Zouaves by a Tartar—How disposed of—Combined Forces of the allied Armies—Characteristics of each Army—The Turkish Commander returns to Constantinople and is banished—The English Tents re-embarked, and the Army bivouacked for three weeks—Ill Effects of this Exposure—Prince Mentchikof's Forces—His Aim to create Delay—His Position liable to be turned on both Flanks—March of the French—The British storm the Hill-side of the Alma—Steady Calmness of their Advance—" Forward " the only Order—The Crisis—Victory.

SEPTEMBER 14th, 1854, anniversary of the entrance of the French into Moscow, forty-two years earlier, the combined fleets commenced at 3 A.M. getting under way for " Old Fort ; " a locality seventeen miles from Eupatoria, and twenty-eight miles from Sevastopol. The continuity of the reddish cliff characteristic of the west coast of the Crimea is interrupted at Old Fort by two strips of beach, one mile apart, having inside of each a marsh, residue of the overflow of the sea in a south-west gale. By 6 A.M. all the ships had left Eupatoria, and were steering for the landing-place ; except the "covering fleet," which made an offing. The English transport fleet and war-steamers anchored off the northern beach, joined later in the day by the commander-in-chief with the remainder of the fleet, and simultaneously the French and Turkish fleets anchored off the southern beach. The French intimated their desire for the disembarkation of the Turkish troops to be delayed till next day, that the boats of the Turkish fleet might assist in landing their troops.

The aspect of the country from our thronged decks was cheerless. Save a child at the door of a cottage of a solitary hamlet a mile and a half inshore, and a few Cossacks *en vedette* on the brow of the nearest cliff, there were no signs of life. About 8.30 A.M. the disembarkation commenced under favourable circumstances. The weather was serene and cloudy, the water smooth as glass, and the shore accessible. The fore feet of the boats touched the beach, and the soldiers landed dryfoot. The artillery and horses were landed easily from shalans. The Cossacks remained tranquilly at their posts, their leader taking notes, until the first division of the French army was half-way towards the shore; when they galloped off with the portentous news. Rumoured invasion had become a reality. By noon, 10,000 French infantry, twenty guns, the staff horses embarked all at Varna in one steamer, and a few spahis, were on Russian ground. The spahis captured in the course of the afternoon fourteen country carts conveying flour to Sevastopol; the drivers of which confirmed the intelligence obtained at Eupatoria, of there being no Russian troops anywhere near. They had been thus employed for two months.

The French soldiers landed each with six days'

biscuit, four days' meat, and one day's water; and with that addition to their packs they stepped out briskly, with the air of men bound on a pleasure excursion. One of their chiefs, standing on the shore in an historic pose, attracted notice by his likeness to a celebrated portrait. I approached, with recollections of the tale of Austerlitz, Wagram and Jena, and entered into conversation with General Prince Napoleon. His Imperial Highness was meditating over an interesting problem—the cooking of his dinner—and proposed to find the solution in the above-mentioned hamlet; but on a bystander remarking that the Cossacks, a voracious ubiquitous race, might descend in a cloud of dust and carry it off, he wisely decided to remain inside the lines. Towards sunset the chief of the French staff sent to the Turkish fleet to land its troops, for no other apparent object than that of making a display. We reminded that officer of the intimation given in the morning; we could not get the tents ready for pitching at that hour; and we were disinclined to expose needlessly sickly troops to the impending rain; we would land them in the morning with their tents and provisions. This was agreed to. That night the French army slept under canvas, every officer and man in his appropriate tent; and next morning a stranger might have fancied them encamped there during a month. No one seemed out of place, or out of humour. The soldiers were drying their clothes or cooking their food before their gipsy-like tents; the officers in groups were breakfasting or smoking in front of their tents; the blithe vivandières had a smile or a word for every one, and the Field Marshal was sitting on a camp-stool before his marquee, enjoying the sun and reading a newspaper. I exchanged a few words with his Excellency, and rejoiced to remark an improvement in his health; which, however, wås illusory. Apart from the camp, the butcher, in a white apron, surrounded by a flock of sheep brought in by Spahis, was busily employed in his calling. "Are those sheep paid for?" I asked. "No, we never pay for anything in an enemy's country." "But the Tartars are our friends." "C'est égal."

The disembarkation of the British army was, on the whole, less felicitous. The passage of the troops from their transports to the shore,—a facile operation with numerous boats and two light steamers,—was rapid and continuous; but then appeared the want of comprehensive arrangement and attention to details shown by the French. The landing of staff horses being inconveniently delayed, an important part of the generals' functions, surveying the ground, remained in abeyance for some hours. A general, typified by the centaur, is only half himself without his steed. The troops were landed without tents; some regiments without their knapsacks—a grave omission, pregnant with mischief, the occurrence of which still, after the lapse of many years, excites regret. Rendered sensitive, by their sojourn in Bulgaria, to atmospheric vicissitudes, the troops could better have spared half their rations than their tents. Heavy rain descended the first night, and beneath it the British army bivouacked, minus head-quarters and part of the cavalry. Tents should have occupied a high place in the consideration of those entrusted with the responsibility of landing the troops: which implied landing them with all needful appliances, not setting them on shore like

Caffres, with only the clothes they stood in and their arms. Some regiments remained a month without tents; and as for knapsacks, when finally landed at Balaclava, many men could not find their own. The excuse about the tents was that, having been stowed in bulk in transports' holds, they could not be disinterred upon occasion. "Why were they thus stowed away?" ought to have been sternly asked. They might, together with the knapsacks, have been distributed according to brigades in ships of war and told-off transports; the crews of which should have had the charge—the gratifying charge—of pitching and striking them. By such an arrangement the army need not have passed a night, except on the flank march, without cover. The slightest canopy may prove invaluable to a sleeping man: a muslin tissue, interposed between him and the expanse on a starry night, may be the difference of health or sickness. Imperious necessity alone should have exposed the tenderly-nurtured British army, unaccustomed to shift for itself, to bivouac in autumn; especially the first night after leaving the shelter of comfortable transports. That dreary night sent more than a thousand men to hospital, and implanted the seeds of disease in thousands more. Many officers of advanced age never recovered from the effects of that exposure. Fortunately, the rain ceased in a few hours; but had it lasted (as sometimes happens in those latitudes early in autumn,) from twenty-four to thirty hours, it would have rendered the army invalid.

An elaborate plan had been drawn up for landing the army in the face of the enemy; but none had been thought of for the distinct, the probable, case of landing it on an undefended coast. What must be done promptly in the one case, may be done leisurely in the other. The order of landing cavalry and infantry may, if convenient, be reversed. Attention had not been given to the altered conditions of invasion created by steam. Viewing the facility now-a-days for an invader to steam right or left a few hours' march from his expected place of disembarkation, the general entrusted with the defence would prefer a central position, free to act according to circumstances. There being no signs of an enemy, the cavalry, profiting by the calm weather of the first day, should have landed at once: they were the most required to reconnoitre and gain intelligence; but roughish weather coming on next day, great part remained on board till the 16th. Cavalry cannot, like infantry, be landed in a fresh breeze or at night. Early disembarked in force, the cavalry might have cleared the neighbouring villages of Cossacks; and, thus encouraged, the Tartars would have rendered valuable aid: they might have furnished means to enable the army to march with tents and baggage unanxiously in any direction.

Several Tartars came into camp the day after the landing with stock for sale. Double-humped Bactrian camels drew some of their carts, and it was amusing to watch the devices of the soldiers to conciliate these stately animals, beside which the plumed Highlanders were in pictorial keeping. This beautiful breed perished, it is said, in the Crimea, during the war, from overwork. The Tartars manifested great joy at sight of Moslem troops, and, speaking a Turkish patois, soon established friendly intercourse. The inherent superiority of the Ottomans was admitted. The natives salaamed the pashas reverently; the latter promised protection, and

19—2

both parties seemed to anticipate the addition of the Crimea in a few weeks to Sultan Abdul Medjid's dominions, and the wooing of Tartar maidens for the harems of Constantinople. The Tartars described the guns at Sevastopol as innumerable, but the troops as few and indifferent. The native population was unarmed; no man being even allowed, they said, to carry a long knife. One of them, a pedling trader from Eupatoria, in fraternization with a knot of Turkish soldiers, seemed a fit subject for interrogation to the French *chef d'état major*, who asked me to interpret for him. The inquiry ended by handing him over to a guard for detention only. Shooting a spy is as a rule folly: it rarely deters others; whereas hope and wine may extract valuable information.

Some of the Spahis, in a distant reconnaissance on the 15th, intercepted a carriage with some ladies: a drosky with an officer, and several invalided soldiers. Unconscious of the invasion, the ladies were taking an airing; and if of a romantic turn of mind, they were doubtless pleasurably surprised by the apparition of a party of Arabs politely brandishing their spears by their carriage sides. That night we observed several fires in the direction of Sevastopol, on the presumed line of the Allies' march. Next day the *codja bashi* of a neighbouring village came to the French camp to complain of a party of Zouaves (some of whom, we heard, had remained in the Cossacks' hands), for having twisted the necks of sundry fowls and expressed their admiration of the fair sex in an unorthodox style. "The Tartars," he said, "are heart and soul for the Allies; but if such irregularities are committed they will make common cause with the Russians." The marshal pacified the old Tartar, and threatened to send similar offenders in future on board ship in irons. But he too well knew, from his African experience, the value of that daring corps, to allow their propensities (habitually winked at) to stand in the way of their services. Foremost of the forward in battle, gayest of the gay under privations, the Zouaves set a cheering example in the Crimea. If any one of the survivors of those landed at "Old Fort" considers himself overlooked, he may console himself with the reflection of having merited the Legion of Honour,—merited it, it may be, more than his favoured comrade, the imperial guardsman.

The allied armies landed at "Old Fort" consisted of 26,000 English including 1,200 cavalry with 60 guns, 25,000 French including 200 Spahis with 66 guns, and about 7,000 Turks. They were reinforced by the end of the second week in October by 14,000 French and English troops; barely sufficient to fill up the vacancies in the ranks up to that date from deaths and sickness. While the army lay at "Old Fort" some definite knowledge was obtained about the enemy; to whom the intention was ascribed of making a stand on one of the three rivers on the road to Sevastopol. The troops manifested no impatience at the delay. The French were careless, the English meditative, and the Turks listless. Neither the French nor the English commander-in-chief—one in pain, the other pensive—evinced active interest in the army. The Turkish chief's thoughts floated between the vision of a Crimean pashalik, and the hope of revisiting Constantinople with a whole skin: the latter weighed in the balance. Soon after the commencement of actual hostilities, auguring no speedy termination to them, he gave himself sick leave and with a colonel (a Pole) in the same temper returned to Constantinople; where, after a while, they were tried at the instigation of the Allies, degraded, exhibited ironed to the troops at the seraskiriat, and exiled to Cyprus for seven years. Their sentence, couched in defamatory language, was aggravated by its publication in the Turkish Gazette. Turkish officers on service, with their hearts elsewhere, have no recognized mode of getting out of their difficulty. They have no "papers" to send in; medical certificates are hieroglyphics, and leave of absence is unknown in war. They are expected to remain at their posts, to be shot at and face cold and disease with their men—no great demand upon them, seeing the personal advantages and prospective rewards of an officer.

On the 18th September, in expectation of marching on the morrow, the English tents were ordered to be struck, and, excepting one for the lieutenant-general, two for the commissariat, and six for the hospital of each division, were sent to the beach for re-embarkation. Circumstantially privileged, the artillery officers carried their tents with their guns. The rest of the English army bivouacked the ensuing three weeks; and to this exposure, at the season of hot days and chilly nights, may be traced the cause of the sudden failure of the health of the troops at the commencement of winter.

Next morning, at 7 A.M., the allied armies commenced their march towards Sevastopol; on the road to which, at that hour, we descried a village in flames. The fleets, weighing anchor simultaneously, proceeded a few miles to the southwards, and re-anchored off Cape Lougoul, where the Alma flows into the sea. After a short day's march, and a dallying skirmish between Russian and English cavalry, the armies lay down for the night, in anticipation of a battle on the morrow.

Prince Mentchikof in the meanwhile had not been idle. He had collected troops from all parts of the Crimea, leaving in Sevastopol only a few veteran batta lions, with the artillerymen of the forts. With 32,000 infantry—6,000 of whom had just joined him after a forced march from Kertch,—2,500 cavalry and 70 guns, he made his stand on an elevated plateau south of the valley of the Alma, with guns in position on its northern ridge. To create delay, to afford time for strengthening the north, the menaced side of Sevastopol, was his object. Although presumptuous—like all Russian generals in the late war, till taught by many bitter lessons the difference between man and man—he had not the presumption to expect to drive the invaders back to their ships; for among them he knew were the British Guards, "feared by their breed and famous by their birth," and choice regiments from Algeria. All he could hope for was to impede their advance on the city; and it would appear from what has been said uncontradicted that he counted on holding them in check many days. He had overrated the strength of his position: one condition of its strength being that it should be attacked in his own way; in which, as it happened, he was partly indulged. His position had the inherent defect of being open to be turned on either flank. A turned position is obviously weak; because, the original plan being deranged, other combinations, requiring presence of mind and tactical resources, become necessary, and are difficult to make in the face of modern artillery and rifle practice. Unable to approach near the sea—any doubt of which was removed on the 20th September, by the dispersal of a body of Cossacks by shells thrown from French ships—the Russian left was exposed to be turned, as well as its right. The French showed this. Marching along shore, their right covered by the sea, they arrived first at the foot of the acclivity, and ascending it by a carriageable road, with smart opposition from some guns dominating it (which the Zouaves charged and drove off in gallant style), they turned the Russians' left, and came on equal ground with them. Had the English, diverging from their line of march, similarly turned the enemy's right, his position guns laid for ascertained ranges would have been placed in jeopardy: and for him there could only be an artillery fight. He had little else than cannon to rely upon; for in presence of the Allies' rifle-armed infantry, his infantry, in dense formation, unable to come to close quarters, were virtually unarmed with old-fashioned muskets in their hands; and therefore it is doubtful if Prince Mentchikof, with both flanks turned, could have withdrawn his army in coherent order from the field of battle. Russian officers have said, since the war, that if the English had turned their right, their retreat on Bakchésaray would have been cut off. But this manœuvre required preconcerted accordant movements, non-existent through divided command.

Seeing the impetuosity of his ally with inadequate forces, General Lord Raglan, impersonation of calm courage, thought only of getting into action by the shortest road, guided by the hottest fire. Then was witnessed the acting of one of the finest pieces of manhood acted on the military stage—the storming of the hill side of the valley of the Alma. The English infantry, never before under fire, their strength impaired by the bivouac and the march, showed themselves animated by the spirit of their fathers on other fields. Calmly and resolutely, resolved to do or die, each man's elbow touching his neighbour's elbow, sending an electric touch of confidence through the line, every gap in the ranks instantly filled up, they marched steadily along the shot-torn road, to the order—the only order given—"forward," repeated by every general, re-echoed by every officer, silently responded to by every soldier. A smouldering village in their path deranged their ranks, but only till it was passed on either side. The passage of the river detained them longer; but having slaked their thirst and climbed its further bank, again they formed as on parade, under a withering fire, and again to the word "forward" advanced; then with cheers they rushed up the steep acclivity, down which, one-third of the way, Russian infantry, leaving the cover of their guns, descended to meet them. There was a wavering in the column of attack, a pause of indecision in its commander. But it was of short duration. All instinctively felt that the crisis of the day was arrived. Officers and sergeants stepped to the front; two batteries came into play; the deadly rifle cleared the arena.

CHAPTER XXII.

The Battle of the Alma fruitless—A Victory without Trophies—The Victors sleep on their Laurels—Their pleasant Despatches—Aged Officers—Few Troops in Sevastopol—Ineffective Fire of the Forts—The Object of the Crimean Expedition frustrated by Delay—Military Council in Sevastopol decides to obstruct the Entrance of the Harbour by sinking a Squadron of Ships—Review of the Position of Affairs—English Troops suffer from Diarrhœa—The allied Armies march to the Balbec—The Russians sink their Ships—An English Officer of Engineers—Capture of Russian Baggage—The allied Army reaches Balaclava—Its Dependence on the Sea disadvantageous—Artillery Engagement between Steamers and Batteries—Bad Practice of Russian Gunners—Death of Marshal St. Arnaud.

Like a tree in blossom which, suddenly blighted, bears no fruit, so was the battle of the Alma. An exaggerated view of the success caused so much daring to remain unproductive. Beaten in three hours from his chosen position, disconcerted by the rival valour of the Allies, and astounded at the effect of the minié rifle, Prince Mentchikof retired in order, with his colours, cannon, and baggage. Nevertheless, unprepared for a reverse, confident at the outset of repelling the attack, he had remained on the ground too long. By retreating half-an-hour earlier he would have sustained comparatively slight loss, while inflicting nearly as much on the Allies, who suffered chiefly on their advance. Good part of his own loss was incurred by the fire of the English artillery and of the French infantry on his retiring columns. The

Allies had gained a victory, but without trophies. They occupied the disputed field, and no more. Their dead lay mingled with the Russian dead in the proportion of one to four; but no captured batteries, no shattered tumbrels, no groups of valid prisoners, indicated a defeat involving dislocation of the component parts of an army. Had they, viewing the battle of the Alma simply as a brilliant prelude, pursued the enemy the same evening with their forces which had not been engaged—the English fourth division and cavalry, and two French divisions, the main body following after a few hours' repose—they would have gained a complete victory; decisive not alone of the fall of Sevastopol, but of the Crimea. With a river to cross eight miles distant, without a reserve, in the midst of a disaffected population, the Russian army, far from showing fight again next day, must have abandoned its cannon at the Katcha: its cavalry might have got away, but its infantry would have had to surrender or disperse. At all events it would have ceased to be an army. Whereas by virtue of its discipline and its moral impassibility, with three days' grace to recover in, it remained the army which had fought at Alma, less six or seven thousand men killed or wounded—and its presumption: the latter a gain.

The allied generals, as if under the impression of hearing no more of Prince Mentchikof and his "serf soldiers"—as if expecting Sevastopol to send her keys to their camp—slept the night after the battle of Alma on laurelled pillows, and next day sat down hopeful to write their despatches. Paragraph by paragraph, from the lofty announcement in one that the Emperor's cannon had spoken at last, to the graceful reminiscence in the other of the naval officer who had carried a telescope by the general's side, all was pleasant reading in them; and we may not wonder at the elated public in France and England, confirmed in their opinion of the hollowness of Russia's power, having blushed for their betrayal of anxiety about the capture of Sevastopol. They now derided the "easiness of the affair."

Care of the wounded and respect for the slain, alleged as the reasons, were inadequate to account for the inaction of the army on the field of Alma, seeing the assistance at hand in the transport shipping. The exigencies of age had pardonably something to do with it. Sexagenarian generals and quinquagenarian colonels could hardly be expected to be eager to run over the country after a hard day's work: like aged mettled hunters, they wanted rest. A distinguished officer observed to me the day after this battle, "In the morning I am forty, in the evening I am eighty."

In the opinion of some, the time had arrived for the fleets then at anchor off the Alma—one bearing the British flag, another a flag bathed in the halo of military and longing for naval renown, and the third a flag deeper tinged with the blood of Sinope—to finish with a blow what their comrades on shore had well begun; and in anticipation of it, apparently, Prince Mentchikof advised, after his defeat, obstructing the entrance of the harbour with sunken ships. The difficulties of the enterprise had been diminished by the operations of the allied armies far more than can be arithmetically expressed. Instead of a numerous garrison, arrogant and confident in their resources, there remained in Sevastopol on the 21st of September—by the testimony of deserters and prisoners

—only the dockyard brigade, a few veteran battalions and the siege artillerymen; who, dejected by the message reversing hope from the field of Alma, were not, the Prince may have thought, in a position to offer more than a feebly desperate resistance to thirty sail of the line, besides frigates, aided by steamers, mounting collectively 3,000 pieces of heavy calibre. The gunners in the frowning forts of Sevastopol had not assuredly enjoyed more sea-target practice than the gunners of the batteries of Portsmouth and Malta. Their guns were worked clumsily with handspikes and fired with matches. Uncertain at a distance, their fire would have been languid against ships' rapid and accurate fire at close quarters. When attention shall be paid to guns and gunnery on shore as well as afloat, the question of ships versus forts will cease to be vexed; but as long as things are so managed that men fire guns in batteries for the first time on the approach of an enemy, that enemy may fairly assume that appearances are sometimes delusive.

The delay of the army at the Alma showed inconsideration on the part of the allied commanders of the object of the Crimean expedition. Undertaken late in the season, without preparation for a winter campaign, its real object, less military than political, had been to elicit, by the moral effect of a great (by many deemed impossible) success on the suspensive mind of Europe, the expression of a unanimous opinion adverse to Russia, in the fairly grounded hope of cutting short thereby the war unwillingly commenced. And doubtless the early fall of Sevastopol—averted by remissness resembling the effect of predestination—would have been accepted by Europe as unequivocal evidence of her weakness, and have created an undefinable sense of apprehension in Russia, thus suddenly struck in her vaunted stronghold: whereas its remarkable defence, the energy displayed in supplying its wants, and her military organization, have increased the impression of Russia's innate vitality; especially in Turkey and in Central Asia. The natives of those countries beheld with amazement the power threatened with the loss of Bessarabia, the Crimea, and the Caucasus, in one campaign, resisting with dignity four nations backed by the genii steam and gold; holding in check 160,000 of their troops on the spot where they had landed, unable to obtain food for man or beast from her territory; and while opposing a titanic attack in the Crimea, able to restrain the Caucasians, intimidate Persia, and strike heavy blows in Turkish Armenia.

While the allied armies lay complacently on the field of Alma, anticipating no other, a scene of another character was enacted at Sevastopol. The important council sat, whence emanated the decision to sink a squadron of ships at the mouth of the harbour; derived from the persuasion of the impossibility, with the north side indifferently fortified, and the south side open, of resisting a combined land and sea attack. Apprehending an attack by the allied fleets, the Russians could neither have unmanned any of their forts nor deranged the order of battle of their fleet. Freed from that apprehension, they would be at liberty to station elsewhere the gunners of all but the outer sea batteries, employ ships' crews on shore, and moor ships in suitable berths for firing on advancing troops. The deliberation on the subject must have been painfully diversified by conflicting views.

Possibly some of the naval members derided the idea of an attack by the allied fleets. But although the masters in the art of war have at all times mainly owed success to divination of their opponents' designs, the question at issue involved too mighty a stake—an empire's prestige—to admit of leaving it in the circle of probabilities. Admiral Nakhimof may have considered improbable the magnificent spectacle of the allied fleets entering Sevastopol harbour in order of battle, but Prince Mentchikof must have viewed it as possible. A sense of immediate security was required. That would be insured by the obstruction of the harbour's mouth, and that overcame the prescience in the nautical mind of ultimate defeat thereby. Assured delay outbalanced problematic success.

A corresponding end alone justifies a great sacrifice: and it may still be doubted by some if the defenders of Sevastopol acted wisely, all circumstances considered, in destroying a part and imprisoning the remainder of their fleet. The object in view was to obtain a pause of tranquillity, leisure for throwing up redoubts. The question was, would the allied fleets, going in before the allied armies were ready to attack, frustrate it? This admitted of answer only by the process of deduction from conjectural premises; which, seeing the incalculable importance of postponing for a season the fall of Sevastopol, seemed hazardous to trust to. The Russians' game did not admit of a single doubtful move. Nevertheless we should not allow ourselves, while admiring the grandeur of the act, to overlook the violation of a principle. Among the conditions of the defence of a maritime town attacked by sea and land, the command of ships free to emerge from its harbour, to take advantage of the chances which weather and other circumstances may offer, ranks high. With their fleet disposable, the Russians would have rendered Kamiesch untenable, unless the allied fleets had remained always in force off the harbour. Taught by the consideration evoked by the experiences of the war, one might now construct steam locomotives which would render the effective blockade of a port impracticable. In no other way could the issue of the siege have been different. Steam transports brought troops fresh from England and France respectively in one-fifteenth and one-twentieth of the time required to march troops despondent and fatigued from Moscow to the Crimea; and the Allies were enabled to increase and vary their obsidional means at will, while similar means on the side of the defence were on the decrease. For although open to receive food and ammunition from the north, Sevastopol was closed against supplies of projectiles; and hence the siege finally resolved itself into a trial between its resources and the resources of Woolwich and Toulon. Whoever should plant the heaviest and most numerous guns and mortars in position would win.

During their bivouac on the Alma the English troops suffered much from diarrhœa, brought on by exposure to hot days and cool damp nights. Many died there, and numbers were embarked for Constantinople. The exertions of the medical officers, admired by all, could not make up for the want of administrative arrangements to meet the unfailing accompaniment of war. Before the English invalids were all embarked, the allied armies marched from the Alma. They lay, September 23rd, on the

Katcha, and next morning marched to the Balbec, within four miles of the north side of Sevastopol. On the morning of the 23rd the Russians executed their aforementioned project. They sunk one three-decker, four two-deckers and two frigates, attached to each other head and stern by chains, across the mouth of the harbour, between the southern shoal and the north shore; leaving a narrow passage for steamers near the latter. A deserter having given information the day before to the admirals of several ships lying plugged ready for immersion the event created no surprise. No great importance was attached to the sacrifice. Qualified by most as an act of desperation, few only regarded it as an earnest of determination,—of a step by step defence. As though at the last moment fearing impediment, the Russians fired shot from Fort Constantine to accelerate the immersion of the squadron.

The allied generals, deeming Fort Severnaya too strong to be carried by assault, continued their march on the 25th September, from the Balbec towards the head of the harbour. An aide-de-camp of Marshal St. Arnaud galloped back to the mouth of the Katcha to inform Admiral Hamelin of the flank movement, with directions to send the *materiel* of the army to the southwards. Finding him a boat to go off to the *Ville de Paris*, I walked up to a signal-station on the south side of the river, whence the news of the defeat at the Alma had been transmitted to Sevastopol. While enjoying the prospect, and musing on the eventful drama just commenced, I was joined by three English officers just landed from a transport newly arrived from England. One of them, in a convalescent state, carrying a small carpet-bag, inquired the direction of the army. The army was already miles away: its trail had disappeared; the sunbeam no longer flickered in the dust of its columns. The weather was sultry, and fearing the walk would prove too much for his strength, I urged patience, and recommended his companions, about to return on board their transport, to try and assuage his ardour. We spoke in vain. He set out alone on foot, and reached his corps, the engineers, safe: as I afterwards learned incidentally. He was a right-hearted fellow, whose name, only heard once, I have not remembered. He thought neither of the chance of sinking under fatigue nor of meeting with stray Cossacks; and though the latter risk was imaginary, it was then apprehended. He only thought of duty. No staff officer, no "correspondent" was by; only, apparently, a weather-beaten Turkish officer. Another officer, in rude health, for riding back from head-quarters over the same ground with an escort, was mentioned in despatches as having performed a remarkable feat, and received promotion accordingly. This is one of many instances in the late war of the difference between record and reality.

After a straggling march through woods, infantry, cavalry and artillery intermingled, the allied army emerged into the open country in the nick of time for its advanced squadrons to capture part of the baggage (including a welcome supply of wine and cigars) of the Russians marching from Sevastopol, by Khutor M'Kenzie, to Bakchésaray. This palpable invitation to follow up Prince Mentchikof and complete the battle of the Alma was not accepted. Away from the fleet, the army felt like a child separated from its mother. Turning to the right, it descended the heights, closing behind its rear-guard, and never halted till it reached Balaclava; the garrison of which, 140 in number, Greeks under a Russian colonel, surrendered, after the honours of a few shot. The sense of dependence on the sea injuriously predominated. Every confident invader, trusting in his star—to wit, William the Conqueror, Henry V., Cortez, and Napoleon (in Egypt)—has viewed the main duty of his fleet over on landing him. An apparently grave misfortune in our case would have turned out a signal advantage. If bad weather had forced the allied fleets to quit the coast temporarily after the battle of the Alma, the army must then, in self-defence, have marched on Bakchésaray and Simpheropol. The exultant Tartars would have supplied all its wants, and Sevastopol, isolated, have fallen of itself.

While the allied armies were circumventing the city, the allied fleets, at anchor off the Katcha, detached six steamers, half French half English, to engage the Wasp and Telegraph batteries. Taking up their stations in line of battle, they opened a heavy fire, which was duly responded to; but as the greater part of the shot mutually fell short, none striking the objects on either side, exercising the guns' crews was the only advantage gained. After an hour of such pastime, the firing ceased on both sides. Presently the commodore, his men being reposed, made the signal "Prepare to renew action," and experiments of the long range were repeated. Tired of splashing the water, the enemy left off first, and then the admirals recalled the squadron. This is a specimen of the "incessant bombardment of the Russian forts along the shore from the Balbec to Sevastopol," in which the admirals are said, by an "eye-witness," to have employed their steam frigates. A few days afterwards, the gunners of Fort Constantine edified the allied fleets by their practice at an Austrian merchant vessel, laden with forage for the English army, drifting in a calm across the harbour's mouth. Of numerous shot fired within easy range, one or two only struck her. Abandoned by her crew, who took to their boat and were picked up by an allied steamer, she drifted into a cove on the south side of the harbour, and lay there screened from shot. An English steamer brought her away at night; she then received back her crew and proceeded to Balaclava.

The rejunction of the allied armies and fleets was saddened by the sinking state of Marshal St. Arnaud's health. With the hand of death in his vitals, he had persevered, cheerful to the last; setting an example of chivalry and devotion. Having, as has been beautifully said, "bidden Death wait for Victory," he yielded, rather than gave up, the command of the French army of the East to General Caurobert, on the 28th September. Conveyed on board the *Berthollet*, he there, nearly speechless, took leave of his noble colleague, and died on the passage to Therapia, where he had left his wife. If funereal pomp could mitigate that lady's grief for her husband's descent from a pinnacle to the common level, it was not denied her. His remains lay in state for three days in a *chapelle ardente* at the French embassy at Therapia; they were visited by members of the Porte and of the diplomatic body; and the French steamer which carried them away to France was accompanied by two Turkish steamers with music as far as Seraglio Point.

This melancholy event changed the order of the allied armies. The English became the right, the French the left wing; the former with Balaclava, the latter with Kamiesh, for their base.

CHAPTER XXIII.

Harbour of Balaclava—Neglect, Confusion, and Waste—Mistaken Confidence in the speedy Fall of Sevastopol—Bird's-eye View of Sevastopol—The Malakof—Fortune's Favours disregarded—Talk with some English Soldiers—Corporal Wheeler's Bravery at the Alma—Soldiers should judge of their Comrades' Deserts—Partial Allotment of Good-Conduct Badges—Honorary Awards should be made on the Instant—Practice in the French Army—Colonel Todleben's Promptitude and Energy—Leisurely Proceedings of the Allies—Confidence of the Engineers—Comment of a Moslem—The Cossacks regain Sway over the Tartar Inhabitants—Russian Cavalry reconnoitre—The Allies' Siege-works completed—Guns in Position—First day's Attack by Land and Sea—The Enemy's Fire—Advance of the allied Fleets—Firing ineffective because of the Smoke—The Aim at long Ranges uncertain—Nelson's Maxim—The *Agamemnon* and *Sans Pareil*—Effective Fire of the Wasp Battery—Low earthen Redoubts with heavy Guns very formidable—Tactics of the French and English Admirals.

THE tiny harbour of Balaclava, nestled in a bosom of rocky hills, affording shelter to the frailest bark from the roll of the southern gale, is the realization of a smuggler's dream. Unheeded by commerce in the interval between the periods of oar and steam locomotion, it resumed, with the arrival of the Allies, and soon surpassed, the animation which had characterized it in the days of Genoese supremacy in the Euxine. A fleet of men-of-war and transports lay in it, side by side, like the galleys of olden times. The pretty town on its southern shore, lying in the shadow of lofty heights crowned with remains of mediæval fortifications, among which part of the marines of the fleet subsequently encamped, yielded accommodation for the heads of departments. General Lord Raglan fixed his head-quarters in a pleasant house near the water, and in front of his windows lay her Majesty's ship *Agamemnon*, with the flag of Rear-Admiral Sir Edmund Lyons. The disembarkation of the military stores, provisions, and the siege artillery, immediately commenced; and in a few days the 5th Dragoon Guards, who had arrived out too late to join the flank march, were landed in high condition.

With some forethought, Balaclava and its environs would not have degenerated,—one into a sink of filth, the other into a swamp of mud. Confusion and waste would not have become its characteristics. The buildings in it would have been disposed for hospitals and magazines, and the forage stacked in the neighbouring vale have been husbanded. But no one anticipating a long sojourn in the Crimea, *laissez aller* was the word. Streets became sewers; the harbour a receptacle for offal; hay was trampled into dung. Speculators on the wants of the army were allowed to settle down in the town. Anybody who pleased abstracted doors, window-frames, and rafters for fuel. Vessels under any flag entered and left the harbour unvisited. Confidence and carelessness rivalled each other. From the Commander-in-Chief down to the junior ensign, everybody spoke and acted as though under the impression that Sevastopol was only waiting to be asked—only required gentle compulsion, to surrender with honour. The reports of deserters of the resolution of the garrison to sink their ships, destroy their édifices, and leave only wreck and ruin for the Allies to hoist their colours on, were considered weak inventions. Even the daily departure of vehicles from the city with women and children was not viewed as an indication of the temper inside. The road of these commiserated fugitives passed some distance along the cliff, off which men-of-war lay at anchor, before turning inland to Bakchésaray. Beside one of the carriages, between it and the fancied danger—the ships' fire—we saw a lady one day riding on horseback. Confiding in man's honour, she knew that her fair person protected that carriage—which conveyed, presumedly, her children—more surely than the proudest Russian rampart.

Shortly after the occupation of Balaclava, leaving my ship off the Katcha, I went to that place, and thence to the front of the English lines. Seated on a stone near enough to note the agitation inside, I gazed long and attentively on Sevastopol as it appeared in the last days of September, white, bright, and symmetrical,—on its duplicate sea-batteries reflected in the water, on its colonnaded Athenæum, on its domed and spired churches, on its spacious barracks, broad streets, and venetian-blinded houses, on its blue harbour: on which, at that hour, boats were rowing and steamers paddling, and in which vessels of all denominations, from the first-rate to the yacht, were anchored. I looked across a straggling suburb, along open streets, down to the water. No battery, no redoubt intervened. Looking down, my hand above my eyes to exclude the opposite shore, the vista was bounded by a three-decker, moored off Dockyard Creek, heeled on one side for firing on the approaches to the town. Steamers also were in position to fire in the same direction. Looking towards the right, I saw on a hillock a solitary white tower, with a few guns mounted en barbette, and numerous labourers at its base laying the foundation of the Malakof redoubt.

The failure of the engineers to discern, until the ensuing April, the key of the position in the Malakof, is the reason assigned for the neglect of the allied armies to seize it on their arrival south of the city. The immediate occupation of that hillock, obviating the construction of forty miles of entrenchment, would have decided the question then as well as a year later; and few can doubt the ability of the Allies, neglecting less material points, to have entrenched themselves on it and on the Mamelon, how warmly soever opposed by the garrison; which was not reinforced till the end of September, and then only by a few battalions of the army beaten at the Alma. I do not know on whom the ray of light dawned; I only know that when it emerged from the night which had long obscured the operations of the siege, the post of honour on the right—involving the reduction of the Malakof, grown by that time into a fortress—had been ceded to the French. Fortune had ardently wooed the Allies since their disembarkation in the Crimea; if she turned at last, who should term her fickle? At the Alma she said, "Follow the repulsed Russian army and disperse it." On the flank march she repeated, "Follow it to Bakchésaray, isolate Sevastopol, and rule in the Crimea." She whispered the allied fleets, "Enter Sevastopol before it is closed to you, perhaps for ever." And she pointed significantly to the White Tower on the Malakof hill. Fortune does not like to have her advances rejected. The loss of 200,000 lives, and the expenditure of 200,000,000*l.* sterling showed her sense of the slight.

While I was wishing some guns of the siege-train, in part parked a mile in the rear, might be brought forward to disturb the ant-like labour of the Russians at the foot of the Malakof hill, a red-jacket came down from behind a bit of old wall in advance of the advanced post, and first by signs, and then (finding "bono Johnny" able to speak intelligibly) by words, invited us to retire out of view: the white umbrella in Anastasius' hand screening our heads from the sun, might, he thought, attract the notice of some aspiring artilleryman, and draw fire in that direction. We returned with him to his observatory, and there enjoyed half-an-hour's talk with an unaffectedly brave set of English soldiers. My telescope afforded them a keen and novel pleasure. They looked through it eagerly by turns at the city, doomed in their as in their superiors' eyes to fall like the walls of Jericho. After listening with delight to their animated yet modest recital of the deeds of their regiment at the battle of the Alma, I inquired who amongst them had the most distinguished himself. With one voice they shouted, "Corporal Wheeler, to be sure." "Sergeant Wheeler, of course, now?" I interrogatively observed. "No, indeed: who was there to speak for him?" was the equally unanimous but less cheerful reply. He had been judged by his peers and found worthy. I mentioned the gallant corporal's case afterwards to officers of rank, who seemed to view it much as his comrades had done: overlooked, and no help for it. Having mislaid a memorandum of the incident, I cannot recall to mind the number of the regiment. "Who was there to speak for him ?" is a compound of all ever said or written about the delusion of recommendations. His colonel, it might be said; but suppose his colonel to have clannish sympathies with the men in the regiment from his part of the United Kingdom ? The captain of his company, it might be said; but suppose the captain's eye to have lighted more favourably on his own faithful servant ?

I incline to the opinion ascribed to the Duke of Newcastle, of the fitness of soldiers to judge of conspicuous merit among themselves, and am disposed to agree with his Grace in thinking that the verdict might be safely entrusted to them; giving their colonel the right of veto. The popularity-hunter and the time-server would have no chance of winning their suffrages gathered on the morrow of the action. With their blood still warmed by the excitement, with their eyes still glistening with recollections of gallant feats, they would not wrongly award the palm. Less favourably situated than the officer, who, if passed over, may successfully urge his claim, the private must resign himself to neglect; fortunate if he abstain from seeking consolation in drink. Distinction could hardly now-a-days be conferred upon an officer less deserving than a co-equal in the same field; but as much cannot be vouched for in the case of soldiers. Out of six distinguished conduct badges sent to the — Foot before Sevastopol, three were (as was currently reported) bestowed upon field officers' servants excused from trench duty; and of similar distinctions sent to the — Hussars, one was said to have been given to the hospital sergeant, another to the orderly-room clerk.

On the publication of the first distribution of the Victoria Cross, a letter appeared in *The Times* from a private, claiming for himself performance of the service for which a sergeant had received that cross. Such a delusion, if there were one, could not have survived if the award had been made at the time. The faculty accorded to the commander of a French army to confer, subject to formal approval, the Legion of Honour on the spot, attains nearly the desired end: as nearly perhaps as human nature admits of. Leaving, for the sake of discipline, the right of discernment with the chief, it precludes the idea of favouritism. Favouritism could not well be shown in the face of the army soiled with the blood and dirt of the strife; or if shown, would be eloquently reproved by its silence. Of all the modes of conferring distinction, despatch mention is the most open to criticism. Associated with the personal character and sympathies of the chief, it is equivocal; written in the privacy of the cabinet, to come to light only on publication, it is final. It originally derived value from the presumption of the Commander-in-Chief being, in practice as well as in theory, the ablest and bravest man of his force, with a mind above low influences. Even if deserved in the particular case, it has not the merit of encouragement; since all feel that those only in the eyes or the thoughts of the chief, or of his prompters, are in the way of honourable record.

On the appearance of the allied armies before Sevastopol, its governor had apparently only the alternative of burying himself beneath its ruins, or of capitulating on disastrous terms. Colonel Todleben himself, while asserting the feasibility of making a prolonged defence, must have added mentally "with time for preparation." His prayer was for three weeks' delay. That interval was accorded to his genius. While the Russians, heart and soul in the cause, toiled day and night in throwing up redoubts on salient points, the Allies worked leisurely and routinely at their lines. The trace of their first parallel, more than 1,000 yards distant, made every Russian in Sevastopol cross himself in thanksgiving.. The facility of the battle of the Alma, unphilosophically considered, had impressed the Allies with contempt for the enemy. "Let him do whatever he likes," said their confident engineers, "in three days·we will level their works: that will strike terror; and the place will then fall without bloodshed." This assurance reconciled all to the delay in opening fire. The army had won its spurs; it longed for home; and though ready to march through fire and gore into Sevastopol, it deemed its conquest sweeter without further loss of life and limb. This feeling was natural. Serving an abstract cause, appealing neither to the heart nor the imagination of the many, and only vaguely to the reason of the few, the army had gained as much as. nascent ambition could fairly desire. It had achieved European fame; promotion and honours were ready to be showered upon it. The fall of Sevastopol, anticipated as the corollary of Alma, would confer no more; and therefore it is not surprising if most concurred in the engineers' opinion about the friable nature of Russian redoubts, and underrated the temper of men nerved by religion and patriotism.

With this disposition prevailing, the engineers were allowed to have their own way. General Lord Raglan pursued his usual avocations at Balaclava as composedly as when seated at the Horse Guards. In the cool of the evening, he and the Rear-Admiral used to ride to the front to note the progress of the works, then return to a late dinner. Which feeling predominated, satisfaction for the past or confidence in the future, it would be difficult to decide. Croakers, if there had been any, would have been answered in the words of Henry the Fifth before the battle of Agincourt. Thus, psychologically, the escape of Sevastopol from early capture is explicable. A pious Moslem some months later, explained it reverently: "You are always saying, 'We will take Sevastopol,' but you always neglect to add *inshallah* (please God). When you say *inshallah*, you will take it." We did afterwards in effect utter that potent word, by using the intellect given us by God; and had we done so at the outset the Turk would have had no reason for doubting our reliance on Him.

In the meantime, indications of the value of time were not wanting. During those precious three weeks, the Cossacks began to recover their sway over the Tartars; some of whom had manifested a reprehensible feeling. We met a party of them one day near a Russian village, laden with priestly robes and holy ornaments, which they had taken from the church, and were carrying for sale to the Turkish boats watering at the mouth of the Katcha. Purchasing the articles for a trifle to save them from desecration, we warned the sacrilegious plunderers to keep their hands off such spoil for the future. The Cossacks also invested Eupatoria, where many thousands of Tartars had taken refuge, and where in the sequel they suffered cruelly from disease and want. After the peace, the survivors and others were conveyed to the Dobrudscha, given land there, and located in villages; the principal of which is named

Medjidieh, built at the Sultan's expense. Russian cavalry reconnoitred Balaclava one day, but retreated before a party of Scotch Greys and Horse Artillery. On the other hand, the Allies sent some steamers to Yalta, to try and procure a supply of wine; but without success. They took, however, some coals on credit from Prince Woronzof's house, giving his steward a receipt for them; a noticeable circumstance, as being the only example, we believe, during the war, of respect for private property. The right of coal, however, wherever found, to be thus classed is doubtful, since in a steam era it is evidently a munition of war.

By the 16th October the Allies had completed their works. The English had about eighty guns in position, including several eight and ten-inch ship guns, served by a naval brigade, and two "Lancaster" guns, throwing spheroidal shot, with a range of 4,500 yards; the performance of which disappointed expectation. Excepting the latter, planted further off, the average distance of the guns from the enemy's lines was about 1,200 yards; the extent of range being erroneously considered compensated for by their calibre, as compared with that of guns used in previous sieges. The guns mounted in the French batteries against the western face of the town—then and long afterwards the real attack—were more numerous and nearer. Disinterestedly — anticipating victory whether joined by them or not — the Allied generals had on the 14th invited the fleets to share in the honour of the attack. Taken by surprise, the allied admirals met at Kasatch to deliberate on the proposal. Adverse to it on principle, doubting the prudence of risking damage to the fleets with the armies dependent on them, they nevertheless, in deference to the generals' invitation, agreed to make a diversion; which, by obliging the enemy to man his sea batteries, would be so much abstracted from the land defence. They left it to the generals to decide if the fleets should go in on the first or the second day of the bombardment or on the third, the presumed day of the assault. According to the original programme, the enemy's lines were to be fired at two days and the morning of the third day, and then to be stormed; but confidence increasing as the hour approached, expecting to finish the affair in a few hours, the generals decided on a combined land and sea attack the first day.

The allied armies opened fire on Sevastopol at half-past seven on the morning of October 17th, 1854, and sustained it vigorously during several hours. The enemy replied from corresponding batteries, erected in the same space of time; and as his guns were served by seamen,—part of those noble crews who bore the brunt of the siege with the loss of four-fifths of their number, including their admirals,—his fire was rapid and well directed; and though inferior to the English, was superior to the French fire. Various explosions in their batteries, from which most had been expected, caused the French to cease firing at 11 A.M.; and therefore—the project of assault having been subordinated to their success—the destructive fire of the English batteries, sustained till half-past 2 P.M. against the Malakof and Redan works, led to no result. The enemy repaired his damages during the night, and by morning was ready to renew action.

The allied fleets at the Katcha commenced getting under way at 10 o'clock on the forenoon of that day,

October 17th, each ship with a propelling steamer lashed alongside; and proceeded in succession towards the mouth of the harbour; the French in advance, led by the screw liner, the *Charlemagne*, which, approaching within range of Fort Alexander, began the engagement by skirmishing with it before anchoring in the line. Warned by the fate of his predecessor, who had been superseded from the command of the fleet for having arrived at Beshika Bay *after* the English fleet, Admiral Hamelin, better inspired, went into action *first*, with the signal "France observes you," flying at his mast-head. This felicitous distinction justified the paragraph of his despatch, expressive of his sense of the honour acquired by his fleet in the action. None of the other circumstances of the day could have been fairly viewed by him as congratulatory.

Anchored in the French line, I was enabled to form an idea of the situation, and to feel how nearly the sublime and the ridiculous are allied. I admired the beautiful and sustained regularity of the fire of my seconds ahead and astern, as well as of my own ship, and I regretted the want of a defined object to test the excellence of their gunnery. We were, most part of the time, as though firing *feux de joie* in a fog. Wrapped in smoke after a few rounds, the bulk of the ships did not see the forts, save occasionally looming in the haze, nor did the forts see more of them than their masts. The ships were not targets; they were butts for missiles flying through space to hit or miss as fate directed. As one of them flew by the noses of some of us leaning on the poop-rail of the *Teshrifieh*, making all our eyes blink as one, and the men on deck fancy our heads were off, I thought we could not have lost them on a more unsatisfactory occasion. The Russians had given their guns in general too much elevation. The firing from the fleets was also uncertain; and although the guns' crews, working joyously, flattered themselves they were dismounting guns and bringing down masses of granite at every broadside, inspection next day of the mischief done dispelled the illusion. It had apparently been expected that the aim once obtained from anchored ships would keep of itself: a miscalculation at long ranges. At long ranges the effects of oscillation on the longitudinal axis, unnoted by the pendulum—caused by the running in and out of the guns—of deflection of shot by windage or other causes, and of unnoticed quoinage slip, become sensible. There is more practical philosophy in Nelson's axiom, "not to fire till you see the whites of your enemy's eyes," than modern sea-gunners seem to be aware of. Several of the English ships were more exposedly, if not more usefully, placed. The *Agamemnon* and the *Sans Pareil* screwed as near Fort Constantine as respect for the environing shoal admitted of; and two other line-of-battle ships and a frigate engaged some redoubts on the cliff north of the harbour. After fighting gallantly several hours, the former drew off with much personal loss and some material injury, withal less than the amount sustained by some of Lord Exmouth's ships at Algiers,—direct evidence of the inexpertness of the Russian artillery at the commencement of the war, the result of parsimonious issues of powder and shot in peace. The Wasp battery and co-aiding redoubts, with skill derived from occasional practice during the summer at inquisitive steamers, told a more significant tale. Unhurt themselves, save by the explosion of a shell in the former thrown by a distant steamer, they drove their opponents out of action in an hour; one of them leaving her anchors behind her, and the other two so much disabled as to have to leave the Euxine for a dockyard. Profiting by this hint, the Russians afterwards raised similar works on cliffs within the harbour. Low earthern redoubts armed with heavy guns are formidable coast defences. At 800 yards ships are distinct objects from them, themselves being indistinct in the smoke at less than that range.

At sunset the deafening cannonade, in which 700 tons of shot had been discharged—in augmentation for the most part of the marine stores already deposited at the bottom of the harbour—ceased, and the allied fleets returned to their anchorage off the Katcha. They did not carry with them even the satisfaction of having exploded a powder magazine or ignited a store-house. As they turned their sterns to the forts, the Russian fire acquired intensity, and did not cease until the last ship was out of range. The terror of the fleets was removed by that day's exhibition. Thenceforward, during the siege, the enemy had nothing more to apprehend from them than the periodic apparition of a steamer firing random broadsides within gunshot at the harbour's mouth. The Russian artillerymen termed this nocturnal visitor "the Phantom."

The tactics of the French and English admirals were in contrast on that day. The former conformed his practice to his theory. Having objected on principle to a serious attack, and proposed only a pompous diversion, he kept his ships together, exposing none designedly more than others. The latter, with similar views, higher coloured (according to a pamphlet written by a friendly hand*) exposed part of his fleet to the risk of being cut up in detail. He allowed his two most valuable his sole screw ships to engage a double tier fort near enough for its fire, if ably directed, to be destructive, and too far off for their own fire to be effective; and he pitted three others against mischievous redoubts of no interest to the besiegers.

* The naval attack could be no more than a mere diversion. . . . . To have exposed the allied fleets to the danger of being crippled or destroyed, would be to risk an imminent and fatal disaster for little or no adequate advantage.—Brereton.

CHAPTER XXIV.

Partial Failure of the Expedition—Feelings of the allied Generals—Hints of Winter unwelcome—Illusory Hopes of speedy Success—Castrametation neglected—The British Lines—Turks driven out of Redoubts—The Russians repulsed by Highlanders and routed by Heavy Cavalry—The Balaclava Charge—Russian Sortie from Sevastopol repulsed—Wreck of an Egyptian Ship and Frigate—Sufferings of the Turkish Troops—Neglect of them by the Allies—Turkish Hospital at Balaclava—Deaths from Dysentery and Overtoil—Oriental Indifference to unseen Sufferings—Fatalism and Selfishness—Lord Raglan interposes—A Ship Hospital fitted out for Turkish Sick—Lord Raglan's Appreciation thereof—The Hospital Ship sent back to Constantinople—Rations of Pork and Rum not available by Mohammedans—Other Supplies not regularly Issued—The Turks destitute of Money.

On the evening of October 17, 1854, the Crimean expedition had failed: that is, the force embarked six weeks earlier in Bulgaria, and since reinforced, to take Sevastopol, had shown itself unequal to the task. It had set foot on the promised land; it had fought its battle of Hastings, or of the Pyramids: but there ended the parallel. No London, no Cairo, awaited submissively the victor. Its numbers had to be trebled, its matériel varied and quadrupled, a railway constructed, and nearly a year had to elapse before the object was attained; and when Sevastopol at last fell, few of the officers, few of the soldiers, originally landed in the Crimea, remained to share the triumph. The armies were then commanded and the engineering operations directed by other men:

not more talented, not more experienced in the art of war than their predecessors, but who had the fortune to be "les hommes du lendemain." The sun set that evening on the keenest disappointment recorded in history: on the reversal of the most remarkable foregone conclusion ever arrived at by hope. Salutes were fired, bells rung, and bumpers quaffed in Western Europe for the fall of Sevastopol, on the authority of a random telegram; and when the error transpired, the rejoicings were considered simply anticipatory of the event by a few days.

Crowned as victors by public opinion, sensible of the effect of suddenly chilling the warm expectations raised by the battle of the Alma, the allied generals shrank from avowing the truth, even to themselves; much less to those who had staked their reputation as statesmen on the event. They had not the fortitude to look the position in the face. Impressed with its reality, they would have profited by the few remaining weeks of fine weather to entrench the camp, make roads, and prepare huts, to enable them to wait unanxiously for spring and reinforcements. Depressed, the Russians had resisted a combined land and sea attack: elated, would they apprehend another attack by the same forces? Hints given by those who knew the climate, the sudden transition of balmy autumn to icy winter, were unwelcome. "If you talk in that strain we will have you thrown overboard," said jocularly an influential officer to one who said it would be well to think betimes on the prospect of the army wintering on those bleak heights. Hope of reducing Sevastopol before Christmas, notwithstanding the increased confidence of the garrison, overruled doubt, and incredulity prevailed at head-quarters in regard of hostile reinforcements arriving in time. Russia's ability to march troops and forward supplies over the steppes, measured by the western standard, caused erroneous calculation then and thenceforwards. The batteries of the Allies and of Sevastopol continued to fire at each other with equal results from dawn to dusk, and it soon became evident that for every Russian gun disabled there was another in store.

Castrametation, the art sedulously practised by the Romans, one of the causes of their uniform success, had formed no part of the studies of the British Staff; or if it had, the theory was not put in practice. The lines of the British army, uncovered from Inkerman heights to Balaclava, temptingly invited the enemy, now beginning to gather on the plain of Baidar. His first attempt, or rather feeler, occurred near Balaclava; where, on a low ridge, in advance of the lines, three redoubts had been thrown up, and were entrusted to the keeping of *esnan*, —Turkish militia. This exposed and dangerous post, above 2,000 yards away from any support, requiring the staunchest troops of the army to hold, if worth holding, was entrusted to men under depressing influences; men not long enrolled, and never in action. Ignorant and suspicious, in a strange army, they may have fancied themselves placed there by the "infidel" to be sacrificed. In this mood they were surprised at daylight of the 25th October, 1854, by the advance of a body of infantry, cavalry, and artillery. Those in the first redoubt attacked resisted with gallantry; those in the others, obeying their *khismet*, abandoned them and fled towards Balaclava, pursued over the intervening plain by cavalry. The 93rd Highlanders turned out, with cavalry and artillery, to cover the fugitives, and the former drawn up in one line fired a harmless volley. The detonation sufficed; its effect was as good as though fifty saddles had been emptied. Halting a few hundred yards off, the Russians wheeled to the right, and, unnoticing the Heavy Brigade, were charged in flank and routed with loss of life and credit. In the harbour all was commotion. Transports got up steam ready to go out, and men-of-war laid their guns to fire up the valley. Thus far all went well; and had the logical sequence of the capture of the redoubts been admitted all would have remained well. But Lord Raglan seeing, from an eminence whence he had watched the fray, the Russians carrying off the guns left in the redoubts, sent an order (which admitted under ordinary conditions of two readings) to the commander of the cavalry, to recover them by a vigorous charge. When it reached the lieutenant-general's hands the guns were irrecoverable save by a battle; and with that conviction he should have galloped up to the commander-in-chief, to explain the gravity of the position, presumedly unnoticed by him. *He* had not been ordered to charge: he had been directed to order a brigade to charge; and therefore no personal consideration stood in the way of his discharging an important part of a second's duty,—that of preventing, by timely caution or action, the consequences likely to flow from an erroneous order. Various examples might be cited of the exercise of such discretion. Had Nelson obeyed his chief's signal at Copenhagen to cease action, the Danish batteries would have crippled his retiring fleet. Had General M'Mahon carried out his instructions at Magenta, victory would have graced the

Austrian standards. The bearer of Lord Raglan's order, Captain Nolan, had written a work on the superiority of cavalry to every other arm; he was eager to prove his theory; and when asked what there was for the Light Brigade to charge, pointed to an army. Suiting his actions to his words, he placed himself in front with the advancing squadrons; where, before he had gone far, a fragment of shell terminated his brief promising career. The single view of the enthusiast ought not to have affected the circumspection of the general. Appropriately made, the memorable charge, resistless as a torrent, would, like Kellerman's charge at Marengo, have decided a battle had one been raging; but, under the circumstances, it was only a rare spectacle of courage and discipline,—fruitless: deplored by two, admired by three armies. In olden days the Turks used to open a battle by hurling a self-devoted body of cavalry (*serden ghetchdi*) at the enemy, and their reckless valour often made confusion in his ranks, their own army standing ready to profit by it: the survivors each received a pension for life. Unexcited by opium, uninspired by fanaticism, the Light Brigade charged home; but no army stood ready to second their headlong daring: no exceptional distinction awaited them. The charge of Balaclava was, individually and collectively, the valorous deed of the war. The Light Brigade saw destruction before it; yet not one drew his rein, not one swerved from his path. They charged through a storm of grape and shells up to the enemy's batteries, sabred his gunners, and cut their way out again through masses of cavalry supported by infantry. Every one who rode out of that fiery circle merited a special cognizance.

The disputed guns remained in the enemy's hands, and the redoubts in charge of his Cossack vedettes. Afterwards the English lines were bounded by the next interior ridge, breastworked and ditched, with batteries at intervals to cover the approaches to Balaclava; the exposure of which to a *coup de main* General Liprandi's attempt had disclosed. Encouraged, the Russians made a vigorous sortie next day from Sevastopol, and were repulsed by the British fourth division. During the ensuing ten days nothing occurred to vary the monotonous booming of the siege-guns; shot returned for shot, with equal injury to the works on either side. The first breath of winter, however, a cold warning gale, swept in the interval over sea and land, proving fatal to the Moslems. An Egyptian line-of-battle ship and a frigate, on their passage from Eupatoria to Constantinople, were totally wrecked, October 31st, on the coast of Roumelia —the former near Midia, the latter near Kilia; with the loss of above 1,000 men drowned, including the estimable Hassan Pasha commander of the Egyptian division. The change of temperature with the gale developed dysentery among the scantily clad, low fed, morally depressed Turkish troops; who merited more consideration than they received from the Allies, by whom they had been brought to a barren land. They early discovered *quanto sa di sale il pane altrui.* With sorrow we write it: the neglect of them was ungenerous, the disdain for them insulting. Yet there was a nobility about them deserving respect. When subsequently offered remuneration for forced labour they resented it, saying they had come there to fight and work in common, not to work exclusively. They passed the winter on unequal terms with the Allies. They were as the potter's vase contending with the iron vessel. They had neither extra clothing nor food; nor money to buy even tobacco with. They received neither praise nor sympathy from their countrymen. There were no commodious transports, with surgeons, beds, and restoratives, to convey them when sick to Constantinople. They had no press to stimulate their rulers; no philanthropists among their countrymen eager to run thousands of miles to administer to their wants. The hovel denominated their hospital at Balaclava presented early in November a deplorable spectacle. About 400 men, some groaning with abdominal pains, some breathing thick at the point of death, were strewed on the damp mud floors of unglazed rooms, the doors and windows closed to exclude the cold air.

> Qual sovra il ventre e qual sovra le spalle
> L'un dell' altro giacea, e qual carpone
> Si trasmutava per lo tristo calle.—*L'Inferno.*

They lay dressed as brought in from camp, without beds, covering, or attendance. The doctor, an Armenian, had no means of alleviating their sufferings: he had not even utensils to heat sufficient water for drink, far less for purification. Many were thus early dying every day, and the deaths rapidly augmented in the course of the winter, through overtoil in the British lines as night working parties.*

Seeing there was nothing to be done for them at Balaclava, where the Turks were regarded as pariahs,

* General Sir Colin Campbell, on being asked by the engineers, on the 18th January, 1855, for more Turks to work on the lines, answered that 2,000 had died, 2,000 were sick, and the remainder unfit for work.

the author impetrated from his chief a steamer to convey the worst cases to Constantinople. Out of 158 invalids embarked in her 75 died on the passage. It was giving them a chance: that was all. He then, seeing the difficulties in the way of attending the sick on shore, wrote to the naval council at Constantinople a recommendation to station hospital ships, one at Balaclava another at Kamiesh; but scepticism in regard of a protracted siege, aided by official routine, prevailed. No sufficient reason appeared to induce the naval authorities to go out of their way for the sake of the army. Oriental indifference to unseen woes also prevented consideration of the subject. Moslems, high and low, like other mortals left to their own promptings, are careless about sufferings not appealing to the senses; and this indifference prevails in the East more than in the West, through the want of publicity and the habitual reluctance of those in power to probe the ills of society. A man of rank in the East rarely visits prisons or hospitals, and when by chance he makes himself remarkable that way a veil is thrown over some things. Fatalism also plays its part. That terrible dogma, repudiated for self while accepted for others, often reconciles a Moslem chief to the consequences of neglect of the sick. "Their hour was come; no human agency could have availed," is the answer to reproaches on that head. This argument does not come seemly from men who seek medical aid for the slightest ache in their own persons, and who in their last hours summon doctors to their couch in the hope of deterring Azrael, who stands mocking in the doorway behind them.

Two months later (anticipating the narrative) the

adjutant-general of the army wrote to the author, in Lord Raglan's name, to inform him of the sad state of the Turkish troops under his orders, and to request his assistance in relieving it. On that showing, the Capitan Pasha ordered a 60-gun frigate to be disarmed and arranged for a hospital, with a steam tender in connection to convey necessaries to her, and bring away sick in excess of room. She was fitted with 300 beds complete. Two physicians, two surgeons, and two apothecaries, with an ample supply of medicines and comforts, were embarked in her. Due appreciation of this aid appeared in the following letter from the adjutant-general to the author.

"Camp before Sevastopol, Feb. 7th, 1855.

"SIR,—I am directed by Lord Raglan to thank you for your efforts to promote an arrangement which his lordship considers of so very much consequence. The numbers of sick at Balaclava have always exceeded very much the number you say that frigate will accommodate; and, in order to meet this difficulty, it will be the more necessary that the steamer to be employed in conveying the sick from Balaclava to the Bosphorus should be constantly making trips for that purpose. Much suffering and the saving perhaps of lives may result from the efficient working of the plan now set in motion."

Fate, mysterious agent, which often dims clear eyes, frustrated this healing arrangement. Towed to the Crimea by her Majesty's ship *Terrible,* proceeding there with a batch of Croat labourers for the army, the hospital frigate remained ten days in the offing of Kamiesh, waiting the pleasure of the British authorities, and was then sent back to Constantinople by order of the naval commander-in-chief, on the plea of want of room for her either at Kamiesh or Balaclava. Large vessels were then lying in those harbours for the accommodation of a few officers, and a berth might have been found for one more, exclusively for the service of humanity. Everything conspired against the Turkish soldiers in the Crimea in the winter of 1854-55. Many a gallant decorated English or French soldier would have sunk under their privations. Many a sneer would have been spared had a charitable thought been given to the effect of destitution and isolation on body and mind. One day the pasha in command at Kadykeuy spoke to the author about the slender rations issued to his troops: each man, he said, received a daily allowance only of biscuit and rice, without butter to cook the latter into pilaf, and fresh meat about once a week. Had he represented the case in the right quarter, I asked. He had not: he declined doing so; and the tenor of his remarks showed an indisposition, in common with other pashas serving with the Allies, to say or do aught likely, in his opinion, to make him seem troublesome. The loss of a thousand men was not to be named in the same breath with the loss of the English general's smile. An offer to speak officiously on the subject was thankfully accepted, provided no allusion were made to our conversation. The pasha's version, corroborated elsewhere, of partial treatment, was unwelcome at head-quarters, and was met by an assurance, conscientiously made, that equal rations were served out to all under Lord Raglan's orders, English and Turks alike. Theoretically equal, practically they were unequal. Pork and rum, declined on religious grounds, were not issued to the Turks. The commissariat was the gainer by so much; and the issue of an additional half pound of biscuit was advocated in lieu of them. With more wit, the Turks would have accepted the "unclean thing" and the "fire-water," to give or sell to their Frank comrades; who would then have regarded them more benignly. The courteous secretary did not exactly approve of official interference with "regulations," to suit "Turkish prejudices," and suggested an appeal rather to the feelings of the commissary-general. That tender-hearted functionary was unlikely I thought to heed officious pleading —an indifferent voucher—but certain to comply cheerfully with an order. Finally, a promise for the desired issue, conditional on the amount of biscuit in store, was given, and on inquiry, fulfilled. Tea, coffee, sugar, &c. —appropriate articles—always abounding in store, were never regularly issued to the Turks; who were more dependent, with their pay in arrears, than others with silver in their pockets, on the commissariat for comforts. The hucksters in the Crimea, unlike the *bakkals* of Constantinople, gave no credit. Whence arose this indifference about the Turks is difficult to say; unless one might trace it to the habitual bearing of Anglo-Saxons towards an "inferior race." It did not certainly proceed from economic motives. These could never be attributed to an administration which brought cavalry regiments from India, liberally entertained on their way by the Pasha of Egypt, to gaze on the siege of a fortress in the Crimea, and enriched its supply agents in Roumelia and Asia Minor by the overflow of a lavish expenditure.

CHAPTER XXV.

Russian Reinforcements—Prince Mentchikof tries to raise the Siege—His Choice between two Courses—Russian Plan of Attack—Conflict at Inkerman—Merits of the respective Troops—Perilous Position of the British—Timely Aid of the French—Russian Retreat—Loss of the Assailants—A Prisoner shot by his Captor—Temptation to a British Sentry—Medals for Balaclava and Inkerman — Theory of Distribution of War Medals — "Urgent private Affairs"—A noble Example—Violent Hurricane—Loss of Transports—Force of the Tempest—Cossacks come to the Rescue—Damage to Ships of War—Captain Christie, R.N.—Court-martial ordered upon him—The Case of the *Prince* Transport Ship—State of Anchorage at Balaclava—Rear Admiral Boxer and Captain Christie yielded to Clamour—Posthumous Honours awarded them.

Within three weeks of the opening bombardment of Sevastopol, that is, on the 2nd of November, 1854, General Danneborg's division arrived from Odessa, at Bakchésaray, by forced marches made with enthusiasm by the troops. They are said to have marched that distance in twelve days : a remarkable feat even with the aid of transports, to bring on wearied men and the knapsacks. Another division reached Sevastopol the following day. Thus reinforced, Prince Mentchikof, giving his troops barely time to recover from their fatigue, resolved to make an effort to raise the siege. He would have acted more judiciously by waiting, his strength concealed, for his best ally, cold. Summoning a council to deliberate on the choice between attacking the British position at Balaclava, its base and depôt, weak by nature, but covered since General Liprandi's attempt by batteries on commanding eminences; or the heights of Inkerman, strong by nature, where its right wing lay in careless security; he decided on the latter, as offering the fairest chance of immediate and ultimate success. In possession of these heights, he would flank the southern approaches to the city, and be in easy communication with the garrison. The project was hazardous, requiring tried and trusty troops to carry out: one of those in which a commander hardly dares to look at the reverse of the picture. Repulsed, he would have to retire down a steep declivity, across a valley, under fire. On the threshold of war, with the traditions of former campaigns—when field-pieces were unprovided with tangent scales, and percussion locks were unknown—generals had to learn the risk of exposing retreating troops to the fire of modern artillery and rifles during the extent of their range.

The Russian plan of attack was good, the execution faulty. While the garrison of Sevastopol, making a sortie, should occupy the French on the left, and a strong division menace Kadkeuy, the relieving army in two columns was to ascend the heights by two ravines and meet on the plateau above. Through the inherent difficulty of night operations, the columns meeting at the foot of the hills ascended by one ravine, whereby their dense masses had not room for deployment. Fewer men at first would have proved more efficient. Screened by mist, the advanced guard, infantry and artillery, gained unnoticed the shoulder of the hill early in the morning of November 5, and nearly surprised the sleeping camp.

Warned just in time, by the vigilance of Colonel Codrington, of the enemy's approach, the outposts fell back, formed, fired; again fell back, reformed; and thus gave time for a few thousand men, soon reinforced by every disposable man, to assemble. What followed none with a due regard for accuracy would venture to describe. It was a *mêlee*, a struggle, a fight hand to hand, foot to foot; but not a battle involving command and manœuvres. Generals and soldiers were commingled—were shot down side by side. Captains fought like privates, privates fought like captains, each man striving like a knight for his own honour. No orders were given; but words of encouragement resounded on all sides—now to attack this battery, now to recapture that gun; now to charge on the right, now to stand firm on the left. Wanting preconception and arrangement it was in regard of pluck and manhood the repetition on a small scale of the stand made at Waterloo.

All troops have their peculiar merits. The French, with eagles displayed, drums beating, and generals waving their embroidered hats on the points of their swords, charge brilliantly, checked by no surmountable obstacle. The Russians, with stoical fortitude, stand for weeks to be struck down in entrenchments, five hundred a day, by a fire which can neither be avoided nor replied to. The Turks, cold and hungry, remain unrepining by their guns till their last biscuit and their last cartridge are expended. The English excel on the open, when grape answers grape, and bayonets cross. We doubt, divesting ourselves of national predilections, if any other troops would have held the position at Inkerman till such time as the French, having repulsed the vigorous sortie on the left, were free to send a division to their aid. Nor did it arrive too soon. Onwards dashed the Zouaves and the Chasseurs d'Afrique into the midst of the fray; their shouts and the British cheers making wild and welcome harmony. Again, as at the Alma, shattered, mowed down by ranks, the Russians showed the force of their discipline, and retreated in order, carrying off every gun. The resolve of the Russians to leave no trophies in the enemy's hands impaired the action of their artillery in every battle. They halted under a bright sun, on the slope of the hill, on the opposite side of the valley which they had crossed in the morning mist; and before sunset some battalions marched into Sevastopol. We heard the cheers in the city for their arrival, simultaneously with the cheers in the French camp for the return of the Zouaves from the field of battle, strewn with the bodies of their comrades.

The Russians lost at the battle of Inkerman nine or ten thousand men, killed or wounded. Some of the latter remained on the field of battle, hid among bushes, a week before the searchers discovered them; having supported life in the interval with the biscuit and water which every soldier carries with him into action. The "Odessa" regiment had, it is said, 1,400 men killed or wounded, out of 2,200, being probably the heaviest loss sustained by a regiment in one battle.

Livy's remark on the Roman army surprised by the Volscians is applicable to the army surprised at Inkerman: "Militum etiam sine rectore stabilis virtus tutata est."

That heady fight darkened one man's nature. Near the field of battle we addressed congratulations to a party of soldiers returning to camp. Their spokesman vaunted of having killed one hundred men for his share of the day's work. "How do you know?" "No doubt of it; I have fired away all my ammunition, and I rarely miss my aim." "Did you take any prisoners?" "I took one." "What have you done with him?" "I shot him." "Why?" "Because he was troublesome." And shifting his rifle from one shoulder to the other, he marched on; little thinking, by his complacent mien, that in the scales of eternal justice one prisoner's life will weigh down a hundred lives taken in fair fight.

Riding back in the evening to re-embark in a frigate in the offing of Balaclava we saw in a sequestered glen an illustration of discipline resisting temptation, in the juxtaposition of a British soldier and a cask of spirits. "This," he said, "is a cask of rum abandoned in the night by its carrier. I was planted sentry over it this morning. I have been forgotten in the turmoil of the battle. I am hungry, tired, and thirsty. I expect to be left here all night." We gave notice of his position to the nearest post; and then riding on overtook after dark an illustration of reversed expectations, in a body of Russian prisoners toiling through the mud escorted by Turkish infantry.

The battles of Balaclava and Inkerman led to medallic confusion, and inclement weather developed nostalgia under the designation of "urgent private affairs." Infantry miles away from *the* charge claimed the Balaclava medal: cavalry out of sight of *the* struggle claimed the Inkerman medal. The difficulty of drawing a line is usually urged in excuse for indiscrimination, but in the above-cited cases the line of demarcation seemed self-drawn. When evanescent none should be traced, for it is better to honour many too much than one too little. The mode of distribution during the late war has made medals a geographical, clasps an equivocal distinction. A medal guarantees the wearer to have been in a given locality within a given period, but a clasp does not indicate as surely his having shared in the battle commemorated by it. We do not mean that as a rule it should be conferred only on those actually or likely to be engaged: that would be inconsistent. Some of your best troops may be ordered to hold a distant pass, or a bridge, to the last man, which if attacked and carried, would expose the flank of the army to be turned; and your engaged forces are encouraged to persevere by confidence in the arrival of reinforcements on the march, guided by the cannon's roar. Yet a sophist might ask, if that be not the limit where are you to stop? On the issue of the Turkish war-medals to the army and navy, the enrolled artisans of the ordnance department and the dockyard murmured at their exclusion from the distinction. "Without us," said the former, "your troops could not have taken the field." "Without us," said the latter, "your ships could not have gone to sea." Our own view, hazarded with diffidence, of a sensitive matter, is this: When a medal records an elaborately designed operation of war—an epoch in history—all concerned in it should be considered worthy of the distinction; and equity, we think, was lost sight of by witholding the Crimean medal from the crews of the transports employed in conveying the British army to the Crimea. When given for a battle in which the component parts of an army have concurred, or have been liable to concur, one way or the other—in action, in reserve, in charge of baggage, or in a preconcerted march—everybody, far or near, has an equal claim. But when it is commemorative of a chance rencounter, child of error or of surprise, combatants alone seem legitimate recipients of it.

Contemporaries confer distinction, posterity awards fame. There can be slight doubt that the Count de Thoulouse and Provence, the Duke of Normandy, the Count de Chartres, the Viscount de Melun, with other nobles and gentles, who, variously inspired, abandoned the famous siege of Antioch, were rapturously welcomed to their ancestral halls by their friends and partisans, who might reasonably have despaired of seeing them again; that banquets were spread and tournaments held, and that troubadours sung jocund lays in honour of the gallant Crusaders. There can be little doubt that private affairs were distressingly urgent in the twelfth century, when an absentee's property was exposed to despotic violence, clerical avidity, and rabble lawlessness; and that suspense about all whom a man held dear must have been painful, when news from home depended on the chance arrival of a retainer of the house, or of a friendly pilgrim. There can be little doubt that trifling ailments grew often, under indifferent leechcraft, into grave indisposition, and that the Genoese and Pisan traders failed at times to supply the crusading army with necessaries, let alone luxuries, twenty miles away from a stormy coast. But neither these nor other considerations seemed to our great historian adequate to excuse him from commenting in caustic language on the motives which made them leave their comrades when cold and wet, woe and want, beset the camp. Will the historian, describing the third phase of the revolution of the Orient since the Hegira, speak more daintily of nobles and gentles who—with luxuries on the spot, with no misgivings about their rights and properties, and with postal communication twice a week with home—seceded from the siege of Sevastopol when winter set in; leaving in sorrow and suffering the soldiers who had helped them to win their honours, and who would have felt comforted by their continued presence among them? Likening no one in the allied armies to Bohemond or Tancred, he will speak approvingly—glancing perhaps askance at the portrait of Godfrey de Bouillon—of one noble, who, though he had attained his highest distinction, a field-marshal's bâton, and had every comfort and solace adapted to his advanced age awaiting him at home, remained at his post until relieved by death. Time, rolling on, will efface the aberrations of his military career; and he will be remembered as one of the true race, keeping steadily in view the beacon which has guided England with augmenting renown through ages of varied fortune—the beacon Duty.

A few days after the battle of Inkerman, a tempest from south-west (bar. 29·38)—such as blows in the Euxine twice or thrice in a century—burst, November 14, on the allied armies, sweeping down their tents, and on the allied fleets lying off Balaclava, off the Katcha, and off Eupatoria; telling with direst effect on the first-named anchorage, where deep water and a rocky coast rendered escape from its violence impossible for vessels without steam to ease the strain on their cables, and with difficulty even then. Eight fine English transports, some laden with winter clothing, some with pressed hay—

precious cargoes—perished off Balaclava, with 460 men (all but six) of their crews. Inside the harbour two steamers were wrecked, one steamer was dismasted, and many other vessels were more or less damaged by the wash of the sea from side to side. At Eupatoria, a French and a Turkish line-of-battle ship, a French steam frigate, and eight transports were lost; and a Turkish steam frigate only avoided the same fate by slipping her cables and standing out to sea. At the Katcha, where we lay, fourteen transports (English and others) went on shore, and one vessel foundered at her anchors. From 8 A.M. till 6 P.M., the gale blew violently; the sea increasing from hour to hour, with hurricane squalls at intervals of rain, sleet, or snow. No one could stand on deck: whoever trusted to his feet alone was carried along it by the force of the wind. We gazed anxiously on each vessel successively as she parted from her anchors; we watched her borne helplessly from wave to wave, and when she struck and the first sea broke over her, there was a moment of breathless suspense. In general sound ships, grounding on a sandy bottom under wind-lulling cliffs, they held together till moderate weather allowed boats to approach and bring away their crews. Three of them were set fire to by their own people. One of them, the *Lord Raglan*, was afterwards got off, and her salvage was hailed as a good omen.

A detachment of Cossacks soon came to the beach. Their officers parleyed with the crews of the nearest stranded vessels under the cliff, and invited them to land, with assurances of good treatment. Some of the Cossacks, spurring their horses shoulder deep into the waves, made efforts to succour the crews of two small merchant vessels stranded off the valley of the Katcha, where the surf ran highest. Those hapless vessels went to pieces. Had the gale blown through the night with equal force the entire fleet would have been wrecked; but soon after sunset it abated sensibly (bar. 29·85), and though freshening up again at midnight, it was only a farewell squall; sending nevertheless two merchant craft on shore which had ridden out the day with their masts cut away. Next morning (bar. 30) found every man-of-war off the Katcha at her anchors, several more or less damaged. A Turkish line-of-battle ship had cut away her fore and mizen masts; an English steam frigate had been dismasted by collision with a drifting transport; and the rudders of five French line-of-battle ships had, as stated, been washed loose.

Self-imprisoned or sunk, there was no Russian fleet to come out and attempt to profit by the consequences of that fatal gale. Seeing the state of affairs on the 15th November, and the nervous excitement of the admirals indisposed to let their sail ships remain longer off the coast, we became confirmed in the opinion that nothing short of a sense of absolute necessity justified the defenders of Sevastopol in making a sacrifice which shut the chapter of accidents to them.

The wrath of the gale, as before said, fell on Balaclava. In the offing of that harbour the *Prince* and seven other transports had been dashed to pieces on the rocks. Captain Christie, R.N.—whom I had met a few weeks earlier at the mouth of the Alma, superintending with wonted solicitude the embarkation of invalids—had nearly shared their fate, through a high sense of duty; and he may have regretted an escape which reserved him to die in sorrow, under arrest, a few months later. In imminent danger, his ship, the *Melbourne*, rode heavily in a deep rolling sea, her masts gone by the board, her stern within a few hundred yards of rocks, to touch which and to perish were one and the same thing. Her master wished to slip her cables and steam for an offing, while the state of the sea rendered that possible; but Captain Christie withheld his consent, saying he would not leave the other transports in danger. His devotion was ill-rewarded. The press blamed him for the perilous position of the transports, and the Admiralty accredited the imputation by ordering a court-martial (averted by his death) to sit on him for the loss of the *Prince*. Contrary to the rule and custom of the service, the Admiralty ordered him to be tried for the loss of a ship which he neither commanded nor was on board of. Unaware of circumstances, the press imagined Captain Christie in possession of an independent command over the transports. Such was not the case. A commissioned officer on full pay he was amenable to the orders of any senior officer present; and though charged with the details of the transport service he had not authority to originate or alter the destination of a transport, nor to select the time for lading or unlading her. His suggestions on those points might or might not be attended to.

The *Prince* arrived at Balaclava four days before the gale, and coming to in deeper water than anticipated, with the ends of her cables unclinched, lost her bower anchors. Captain Christie, seeing her peculiarly exposed, with inadequate ground tackling, recommended the authorities either to receive her into the harbour or allow her to remain under way until it might be convenient to land her cargo. Both sides of the alternative were rejected. Want of room inside was alleged on the one hand, and the general's anxiety to have the winter clothing landed as early as possible was assigned as a reason on the other hand for retaining her at anchor outside. So she remained there with other transports waiting for means to land their cargoes. The means, two light steamers, were too often diverted from their legitimate object to carry unimportant messages to and from the fleets lying off the mouth of the Katcha. There should have been no illusion about the peril of the anchorage when the weather began to break and southerly winds might be expected. On the arrival of a transport at that season, the authorities at Balaclava should have cleared her at once, and sent her away to a safer anchorage,—especially if a sail ship. Before a southerly breeze might freshen into a gale, a sail ship would be exposed, when casting, to be thrown on the rocks by the swell before gathering way.

A Turkish frigate had gone to Balaclava a few days previously, with a supply of shot and shell for the army, and a detention in the offing of five days for what might have been accomplished in as many hours gave every one on board a keen perception of its insecurity: the faintest breeze from the southward raising a swell dangerous for boats. She need not, distrusting the anchorage, have remained there on an uncertainty, but did not like to disappoint expectation. Danger is a problem which in most cases has to be worked out: the party immediately interested is rarely allowed to assume its value: the apprehended gale may not blow home, the bristling fort may not fire true. If Captain Christie had gone away of his own accord with the transports, and the gale had held off or had blown from another direction, he would have laid himself open to censure for over-caution. No one remained longer at that season in the offing of Balaclava than his sense of duty prescribed. On the 12th, two days before the storm, of which there were already premonitory signs, the second in command of the British fleet left it with his division for Kamiesh roads; and with that prudent example before their eyes, those invested with discretionary authority at Balaclava might have taken upon themselves to let the transports go to sea or to another anchorage. The *Retribution* alone of the men-of-war, with the Duke of Cambridge sick on board, remained off Balaclava to brave the storm.

Captain Christie was not the only sufferer by the clamour excited by the general and local administration of the year 1854; not the only officer dropped by superiors bound to hold out a helping hand. Rear Admiral Boxer—whom I last saw at Balaclava, in the spring of 1855, toiling from morning till night in the task of creating order and enforcing police regulations—was another. One has no right to blame the press, guided by appearances, dependent often on partial information, for erring sometimes in regard of public servants; but one has a right to expect those in possession of justificatory data to denote unequivocally their dissent from an unfair verdict. Those officers had shared, one way or another, in the worry and anxiety of the Crimean expedition; and all knew they had striven, indifferently aided, with a zeal beyond their years. No one need feel disparaged by the expression of a doubt if any other officer would have been equal to the work—demanding exceptional energy and nautical experience—performed by Admiral Boxer at Constantinople in the winter of 1854-55. His exertions may be estimated by comparing the scanty means doled out to him in days of parsimony with the ample means ably used at the disposal of his successor in days of prodigality. His temper, it was said, ruffled philanthropists and speculators. Little wonder! A bishop in his place would have spoken irreverently. Admiral Boxer and Captain Christie were advanced in years. If deemed politic to yield them as peace-offerings to clamour, they should have been recalled—but recalled with honour—to pass the evening of their days at home, or in employments congenial with their age. Instead thereof, mortification was their lot. One was placed under arrest, an indignity which reacted on a weakened frame, and the other was superseded in the Bosphorus just as he had made the position tolerable and had been joined by his family, and was sent to pioneer anew alone in the slough of Balaclava. Both died in the fatal Crimea with the sense of injustice weighing on their minds; and then, in recognition of their merits, the Cross of the Bath was laid upon their tombs.*

* In the *Gazette* of — July, 1855, the names of Rear-Admiral Boxer and Captain Christie appeared posthumously honoured with the order of the Bath, respectively K.C.B. and C.B.

CHAPTER XXVI.

Dispersion of the Fleets—Preparations for Winter—Helplessness of English Soldiers—Obvious Precautions neglected—Available Resources of Constantinople—Mr. Filder, the Commissary-General—English Sympathy and Aid—Evils of Routine—The Army pampered—State of Things at Constantinople—Turks Amazed and Disgusted, but Powerless—Capitulations—Paralysis of Justice—Consular Privileges abused—Gibbon's Picture of St. Jean d'Acre realized at Pera—British Subjects abandoned—Turkish Jails—Public Buildings of Constantinople occupied by the Allies—The French dominate the City—Aspect and Bearing of the Ottomans—Separation of Turks and Europeans—Exceptional Cases—Russian Military Schools—Fate of Turkish Invalids—Turkish Naval Hospital—The Dockyard occupied by the Allies—Solicitude of a noble Eltchee for Russian Prisoners—An Ambassador at Constantinople—Military Hospital at Scutari—Sympathies of Miss Nightingale and Lady Stratford de Redcliffe—Soyer's Cookery—Sick Officers lodged in the Imperial Kiosk—Exertions of Colonel Moore's Widow—British Cemetery—French Hospitals at Constantinople—Mortality of French Surgeons—Boy Soldiers—Scurvy and Dysentery rife—Visitors—Invaluable Services of Sisters of Charity.

The storm of November 14th, 1854, blew away the last hope of reducing Sevastopol before Christmas. The fleets dispersed. The Allies' admirals, hoisting their flags on board steamers in Kamiesh harbour, sent some ships to Constantinople for repairs, others to France for troops. The French Euxine fleet was far different in composition from the fleet off Cadiz thirty years earlier, under the command of another Admiral Hamelin; regarding which the Duc d'Angoulême, in a letter to M. de

Villele, dated Manzanares, 30th August, 1823, wrote,—"Nous n'avons guère à nous louer de notre marine sur aucun point; elle nous coûte cependant soixante millions." The French navy in the late war may be said to have saved that amount in transport hire.*

The allied armies then began to think seriously about the mode of getting through the winter. Mature and intelligent organization enabled the French to meet the crisis with comparative facility; but the English, surprised, discovered their deficiencies. Accustomed to be cared for, cooked for, washed for, the English soldiers were unable to help themselves. They could only fight and eat: could do both right well; and the less distance they had to go for their foe or their food the better pleased they were: they preferred having either brought to them. Untaught, inexperienced, the Staff was unequal to its task. The machinery of organization existed, but motive power was wanting: as in an engine with leaky valves and priming boilers steam could not be kept up. Obvious measures of easy execution were neglected: such as cementing with stone and bridging with plank those parts of the thoroughfare likely to

* The imperial French navy, without ceasing to meet all the other wants of the service, co-operated as follows in the work of transport: 32 sail-of-the-line, 38 frigates, 21 corvettes, 24 transports, 17 small steamers, total 132 vessels, made 905 voyages, and transported either out or home, 273,780 men, 4,266 horses, and 116,681 tons of matériel.

The French war department chartered, in 1854-55, 66 steamers and 1,198 sail vessels.

The steam-packets (messageries) carried troops and stores twice a week.

The English Government placed at the disposal of the French Government 8 naval transports and 42 merchantmen, which carried to the East 38,353 men, 1,972 horses, and 6,624 tons of stores.—*Moniteur.*

become quagmires from convergent traffic, and forming limited depôts of provisions in the camp, to meet inability (from weather or other cause) to convey up the day's consumption from Balaclava. The artisans of the fleet might readily, with ships' spare sails and light spars, have stabled the cavalry; and ready-made *tchuls* (horse clothing) were to be had in any reasonable number at Constantinople. A requisition was sent to the commissariat at Pera towards the end of November for 2,000 suits of horse clothing; but unfortunately accompanied by directions to make them of a given pattern, so that with all the trade set on the work they were not completed under a month, when most of the horses were dead.

An army with unlimited command of money, in a locality by the sea-side, only thirty hours' steaming from the capital of the East—a city of commercial importance, with a million of inhabitants, dwelling in wooden houses, with nomade tastes—ought not to have been subjected to any privations. As encamped soldiers, heedless of the past, careless for the future, so in general live the Constantinopolitans. They eat hurriedly, in or out of doors, on a mat under a spreading tree, or on cushions in a gilded saloon; and sleep dressed, as ready by night as by day to go wherever summoned. Their houses are as airy as tents. They are ever on the alert for the enemy—fire. Their markets and auctions are held in the open air. They bury their dead as soon as the breath is out of the body, and forget them on the morrow. Wild dogs howl through the night in concert with the sentries' challenges. Lean cows browze in the outskirts. Dirt accumulates in the streets, till washed away by rain. Inanimate dogs and cats taint the lanes, till decomposed by the elements. Traffic is carried on in military fashion: strings of horses or mules convey food, fuel, and forage from one quarter of the city to the other; strings of camels, led each by a patriarchal donkey, bring in supplies from outside. Apart from the gorgeous mosques, the stately barracks, the marble mausoleums, the ornate fountains, the cypress-shaded cemeteries, all at Constantinople savours of a camp. There are always stored there, for the casualties of fire, plank enough to hut 60,000 men. Building materials are carried facilely up its steep hills and through its narrow lanes by a docile asinine race. With a timely appreciation of the congruous resources of Constantinople, the British army could have been as well sheltered in December 1854 as in December 1855, and at one-fourth the cost, with exemption from scandal. Artisans, labourers, donkeys, planks, and stoves might have been shipped in a few days, and the troops hutted within a month. *Yorghans* (wadded coverlids) and Salonica socks were procurable in the bazaars in any number.

Mr. Filder, the commissary-general, was made the scapegoat for all sins of omission; but Mr. Filder, wanting Atlas' shoulders, was unable to bear the load put on him. Not his fault that the troops six miles off were cold and hungry, through want of means to convey his supplies to camp, or of organization to march that distance to fetch them. In despair at last the army lay down and called upon Hercules. Hercules, grumbling and growling, bestirred himself; he made the air ring with his voice; he shook the ground with his club.

He stimulated torpor, directed energy, and shamed indifference. He called forth the might, he roused the sympathy of the nation. Reinforcements and supplies streamed out to the scene of war. France also made noble efforts. Turkey sent a reinforcement of 7,500 troops. So that the allied armies before Sevastopol, after all losses, exceeded in January, 1855, double the number originally landed in the Crimea. As much as England felt for her army, had that army reason to be proud of her. Such concord, such desire to assist brave men in distress, had never before been witnessed. Hams, jams, fur-coats, woollen comforters, worsted stockings, pipes, tobacco, preserved meats, potted game, plum puddings, offerings from all classes, sent partly in private yachts led by the Fairy cutter belonging to Major Lyon, were the visible tokens of homely affection; and they told a tale, on the moral of which statesmen may dwell.

A nation forgives a breach of national trust once, not twice. Since the general peace the English nation had given its rulers five hundred millions sterling for an army, and at the first heavy strain the machine gave way. Whole regiments nearly dissolved away through the operation of routine. By mid-January, 1855, the 46th Regiment, which had landed in the Crimea *after* the battle of Inkerman, 1,000 strong, was reduced to 150 valid men; and of the 63rd Regiment not twenty men remained fit for duty. The authorities, excited by the general outcry, sinned afterwards in the opposite sense. Overstepping the line of efficiency, they pampered the army, and rendered it, by reason of its wants, incapable of operating ten miles from the sea coast. The transport corps in the end numbered 18,000 animals, with a motley crew of drivers. They were to feed the army. Who would feed them ?

Shaken by the storm, the Turkish fleet—wanting repairs and necessaries,—returned to the Bosphorus the latter end of 1854. We found matters changed indeed since our departure five months earlier. In that interval Constantinople had been fully occupied by the Allies. The Turks, in stupor, were drinking the bitter waters of humiliation, were expiating the sins of their ancestors. Frank soldiers lounged in the mosques during prayers, ogled licentiously veiled ladies, poisoned the street dogs, part and parcel of the desultory bizarre existence of the East, shot the gulls in the harbour and the pigeons in the streets,—which till then, like the water-fowl in St. James's Park, had regarded every human face with confidence, mocked the *muezzins* chanting *ezzan* from the minarets, and jocosely broke up carved tombstones for pavement. Custom was disturbed in its cradle, prejudice was shaken to its roots. The Turks had heard of civilization : they now saw it, as they thought, with amazement. Robbery, drunkenness, gambling, and prostitution revelled under the glare of an eastern sun, or did mild penance in the shadow of a dozen legations ; to each of whom the withdrawal of a rascal from the station-house was a duty, the shielding of a miscreant from punishment was a triumph. The Sultan still sat in his palace, but his power was in abeyance. His ministers met at the Porte as usual ; but their councils were a formality : their monitors spoke from the French and English embassies. The Allies' troops had possession of the capital,—the English on the Asiatic the French on the European side of the

Bosphorus; and their guards patrolled Pera and Galata —sanctuary for a hybrid swarm from all parts of the Mediterranean, whose avocations the police were cautious in interfering with, for fear of drawing on themselves the wrath of some legation, by confounding an Ionian with a Hellenist, a Genoese with a Sicilian, or a Javanese with a Hindoo.

The necessity of framing capitulations in the sixteenth century—when human heads were struck off with as little ceremony as fowl's necks are wrung by the mistress of an Italian inn on the appearance of hungry travellers —for the protection of a few European traders, was a disgrace to Turkey; the strict enforcement of them in the nineteenth century, under altered circumstances, when it is difficult to get a murderer hanged, is a reproach to Europe. They were framed on behalf of limited associations, self-restrained by by-laws, and self-responsible for the conduct of their servants and employés: they are now enforced in favour of 50,000 Europeans of various nationalities and callings at Constantinople, and twice as many thousands or more domiciled in provincial cities, in pursuit, one and all, *per fas et nefas*, of one object—gain; and, though divided by clashing interests, united by the common bond of rancour against the dominant race. Probed to their source, the occasional outbreaks in Turkey called fanatical would be seen to be the natural reaction against the overbearings and insolence of foreigners and protected natives. Would you abolish the "capitulations?" asks the Levantine. Not altogether, so long as the separation of administrative and judicial functions in Turkey remains indistinct: but we would modify them in the interests of society by drawing a line between protection and impunity, between privilege and licence.

The interests of society do not require any Frank store or dwelling in Turkey to be an asylum for every kind of offender, long enough occasionally to baffle police action. A thief or a homicide may, as things are, run to a shop or a dwelling under the ægis of the "capitulations," and the policeman, witness of the deed, cannot follow him beyond the threshold without consular co-operation; which, never attainable under many hours, may, in summer, when people reside miles away from the city, be delayed for days. Two examples, of no distant occurrence, will suffice to show the working of the system. 1. A merchant's counting-house at Galata was broken into one fête day, its iron safe forced, and 5,000*l.* abstracted therefrom. With prompt action the police would have caught the suspected burglars red-handed; but the co-operation of their respective authorities was necessary, and was not obtained until the third day,—too late for the search then made in the rookery to be of any avail. 2. An Algerine was stabbed through the back one evening, at the entrance to Pera from the cemetery. His assassin, apparently a Sclavonian, fled along the gas-lit music-enlivened Frank promenade, *les petits champs*, closely followed by two cavasses, who were on the point of laying hands on him; when the guests at a café, before which the chase passed in full cry, interposed between the pursued and the pursuers, hustled the latter, and carried off the former in triumph. The deep murmur of the Moslems gathered round the victim, on hearing of the mode of the murderer's escape, was stilled by the arrival of a guard summoned *ad hoc*, and the prompt removal of the corpse to the mosque of another quarter dispersed the excited crowd. The interests of trade do not require each member of the consular legion in Turkey to have the privilege—in some instances much abused—of importing duty-free everything he pleases to declare for the use of his household; or the right of protecting in the obnoxious sense of the term every individual, of fair or ill repute, said to be in his service.

The picture, drawn by a masterly hand, of St. Jean D'Acre when it was the capital of the Latin Christians in Palestine, is somewhat apposite. "The population was increased by the incessant stream of pilgrims and fugitives. The markets could offer the products of every clime and the interpretation of every tongue. But in this conflux of nations every vice was propagated and practised: of all the disciples of Jesus and Mohammed, the inhabitants of Acre were esteemed the most corrupt. Nor could the abuse of religion be corrected by the discipline of law. The city had many sovereigns and no government. The Kings of Jerusalem and Cyprus, the Prince of Antioch, the Counts of Tripoli and Sidon, the Grand Masters of the Hospital, the Temple and the Teutonic Orders, the republics of Venice, Genoa, and Pisa, the Pope's legate, the Kings of France and England, assumed an independent command. Seventeen tribunals exercised the power of life and death; every criminal was protected in the adjacent quarter." Substituting the European governments represented in Turkey: to wit, Austria, Belgium, Denmark, France, Great Britain, the Hanse Towns, Hellas, Holland, Naples, Prussia, Portugal, Russia, Sardinia, Spain, and

Sweden, for the above-named powers, and making due allowance for assuaged manners and milder laws, we have seen, in several respects, the counterpart of Gibbon's picture in Pera and Galata. Cognizant of this state of things—unusually developed in 1855-56-57—the Secretary of State for Foreign Affairs, in a memorandum dated July 2, 1844, addressed to the consuls in the Levant, said: "If her Majesty's Government are obliged to abandon any attempt to place British jurisdiction in Turkey on a sound footing, the Porte may reasonably require that a jurisdiction should be renounced which is not enforced, but the nominal existence of which is incompatible with the security of the society at large."

An order in council, passed in that year with a remedial view, empowered consuls in Turkey, under certain circumstances, to abandon British and "protected" subjects; in other words, acquiesce in their consignment to life-long imprisonment in a Turkish jail.*

* The order in council empowered a consul to expel any one under his jurisdiction from Turkey after two convictions before a competent tribunal, the expelled person not to be entitled to British protection should he return to Turkey. Want had originally brought such individuals to Turkey, and want, supplemented by local ties, generally brought them back to it. Taken up for any offence after his return, an individual was at once, without inquiry, disowned by his consulate. He then became a nondescript. He was not a Turk, nor a raya, nor a European. His offence, if tried by the native authority, would probably have been atoned for by a few months' imprisonment in the Zaptie, which would have done him no harm; but in his quality of European he could not in virtue of treaty be tried without the concurrence of his consul. His consul's disavowal did not change his nature. The Turks solved the problem by dropping him into prison, leaving it to his consul to extract him therefrom. Had they drowned him in the Bosphorus his consulate would have been none the wiser. His death, when occurring, would not be reported to the consulate. Abandoned Ionians, in a hope-

The framers of that order little imagined the mode of its operation, combining cruelty with inefficiency; and were not enlightened on the subject by its executors. The praçtice was brought to light in 1857 by an English officer with Turkish rank meeting in the bagnio an Ionian in chains, there since twelve years, linked to a fellow-prisoner, other Ionians being in the same predicament, all of whom, but for that fortuitous rencontre, would to a moral certainty have died there. The jailors even considered that Ionian's case peculiarly hard: a hale man, thirty-five years old, he was likely to live long, without hope of liberation. The extreme sentence in Turkey, when blood is not demanded, being fifteen years in the bagnio, that man, with no recorded offence, might have lived to see three generations of murderers pass out before his eyes. A native of the United Kingdom, abandoned since four years, was subsequently lighted on in like manner in that dismal abode: he was found coupled with another prisoner, unable to converse with him through want of a common language. He gave direct evidence of his nationality, at first doubted, by saying, "Is it not a d—d shame, sir, that I, an Englishman, am chained here like a felon, without having been tried?" His case drew public attention to the subject of "abandonment," and led, with the liberation of the "abandoned," to the disuse of the melancholy practice in 1862. Many scores of Ionians, and some others, aban-

less state, were allowed by the prison authorities to be removed to the Greek hospital near the Seven Towers, where they were tended gratis.

England, Spain, and Naples were the only countries which abandoned their subjects. Spain is alone now in that respect. A jurisconsult might say that a person unable to surrender his allegiance could not forfeit his protection.

doned under the provisions of the said order in council, too rigidly interpreted, are understood to have wasted away unto death in Turkish jails. Those jails, in regard of natives, are simply jails, far better than several visited by the author in Naples and Cuba; but for "abandoned" Europeans, who, with dissimilar habits, have no local sympathies, they have been *oubliettes*.

The Allies had demanded and obtained nearly all the public edifices at Constantinople, including the naval, military,* and medical schools, for barracks and hospitals; leaving, in their liberality, two barracks for the native garrison and hospital room for about 800 men. The French thus obtained accommodation for 12,000, the English for 5,000 patients. By means of their establishments, selected with military judgment—hospitals or fortified barracks, as the case might require—the French dominated the city in every sense, outside and inside. They were quartered in the barracks of Daoud Pasha,† Maltepeh and Ramistchiftlik, on the eminences where Mahomet II. had encamped with his conquering army 400 years before. They occupied the palace of the Russian embassy in the heart of Pera, dominating the entrance of the harbour. They sat down in the Tash and Gumuchsouyou barracks flanking the approaches to Pera and overlooking the imperial palace. They planted themselves on Seraglio Point, and occupied the adjoining barracks of Gulhané. They encamped at Maslak and stationed guards over the bendts (reservoirs). They established themselves in the sensitive quarter of St. Sophia (where they had on one occasion a sanguinary

* The Military School was burnt down when in French occupation.

† Daoud Pasha barracks were burnt down when in French occupation.

fray with Tunisian soldiers) in a vast building near the venerable fane, dear alike to the Turk and to the Greek —trophy of conquest to one, memorial of empire to the other. And they built a hut camp along the course of the subterranean aqueducts, ready for a contemplated reserve army of 60,000 men.

The bearing of the Ottomans under this infliction, with gloomy prospects, darkened further by sinister predictions, was instructive to behold and impossible to depict. Once a great, always a proud race thus humbled by foreigners in the eyes of their rayas quivering with joy at their rulers' abasement, their faith gave them resignation to support it with dignity; their dread of ulterior consequences gave them strength to dissemble. Daily enduring mortifications more than enough to drive into wild excesses the population of a western capital, recalling the scenes enacted by the Crusaders on their passage through Constantinople, they conducted themselves with forbearance and urbanity. Their attitude betrayed not the dejection in their hearts. Moved by one impulse, under the apprehension of a great impending calamity, all ranks, high and low, instinctively concurred in the policy of abstaining from doing or saying anything to irritate their "guests." The war with Russia had become of secondary importance: the evacuation of their capital was uppermost in their minds. In this spirit they held aloof from the stranger; they avoided his haunts; and the slight social intercourse heretofore existing between Turks and Europeans soon ceased, or became formal. They attended not his military spectacles, nor encouraged him to witness their religio-civic ceremonies. The review of the English cavalry at Scutari had no Turkish spectators beyond the imperial suite; and the gathering at the mosque of Codja Mustapha Pasha in commemoration of the martyrdom of the imams Hassan and Hussein—the most characteristic of Moslem religious pageants, assembling both sexes of all classes, including royalty—was unchequered by a foreign uniform. Some few forgot their ideas of self-respect. One might occasionally see a grave official, who the year before had scarcely deigned to rise for the representative of a second-rate power, now advance several steps to meet the booted aide-de-camp of a general or the bustling dragoman of an embassy with an importunate message or an irksome demand, draw him with soft words to a seat beside him on the sofa, and give him the diamond-ringed pipe and Mocha coffee in a china cup within a gilded *zarf*. The Turkish proverb, "Honey flows from his lips while the blood is boiling in his heart" was exemplified in those days. The fair sex shared with their lords the feeling of repulsion. Not a *bonne fortune* left a souvenir of the presence of the allied armies on the banks of the Bosphorus.

While the French converted the Turkish military schools into hospitals, the Russians opened two additional military schools for the eventualities of the war.

We have debated in our mind if the Allies, in their laudable anxiety about their own sick, ever asked themselves what became of the Turkish sick, who were more numerous and more intensely diseased. They had deprived them of their hospitals and barracks, and knew that no others would be extemporized. We were not in the way to see the whole of that harrowing picture. We saw parts of it, and perused reports on the subject from the captains of

English transports in Turkish pay. Devoid of resources, with no public to stimulate their rulers, the Turkish sick, all more or less influenced by the dogma of fate, in general died where they had sickened. From time to time some hundreds of invalids by the sea-side, obstinately tenacious of life, were shipped in transports unprovided with necessaries, for conveyance to Varna or Constantinople, the only ports where relief awaited them. On one occasion 900 were embarked from Eupatoria, in the *Antelope* steamer, in so wretched a condition that twenty-six were found dead in the morning before she weighed anchor, and nearly a hundred died on her passage to Varna. More would probably have died, but for the solicitude of Mrs. Reid, the captain's wife. That worthy lady directed tea and coffee from her own stores to be given to them from time to time, and saw it done. Biscuit used to be supplied for the sustenance of men whose teeth were loose from scurvy.

The Turkish Naval Hospital avoided surrender, by the location of the French and English fleets' hospitals on the Bosphorus, respectively in an airy yali at Kandlidja and in the embowered imperial kiosk at Therapia. But in other respects the navy shared the common lot. We found on our return to Constantinople the dockyard, sole resource of four fleets for necessary repairs, in part a receptacle for Allies' commissariat stores, with consequent relaxation of rules conducive to safety; and the marine barracks occupied, through English influence, by Russian prisoners, who should rather have been berthed in a hulk, like their comrades in the hands of the French. The fire one night proceeding from a French depôt in the dockyard went no further; but the ejected marines spread mischief. Doubled up with the artisan brigade in their quarters, the agglomeration bred typhus fever, notwithstanding that additional windows and skylights had been opened in the walls and roof of the building. Several hundreds of the commingled corps died, and as many more were invalided to their villages. On the departure of the intruders for England, the marines regained possession of their barracks; but were, some months later, required to vacate them again, to make room for military stores sent from England for the "contingent." This was worse. The stores might have been housed more commodiously for the public service in vacant buildings by the water side, in embassy grounds, at Buyukdereh or Therapia. The naval authorities, reluctant to offend an eltchee of mark by refusal, were nevertheless indignant at this exaction. The marine barracks was also a depôt for naval supernumeraries. Apprehending further suffering, they officiously brought to his Excellency's notice the mortality consequent on the previous ejectment; and, although the letter addressed to him remained unanswered, it was tacitly acknowledged by a relaxation of the pressure, whereby the marines retained one floor of their barracks with its mosque.

The noble eltchee's solicitude for those prisoners grew, he said, out of a letter written him by the Czar Nicholas on their account: a plausible though inadequate reason for turning men in the Sultan's uniform out of house and home for their sake. His repetition of an irksome demand in favour of less interesting objects flowed from unconsciousness of the existence of people with feelings of self-respect outside a limited circle, and the difficulty of realizing privations by those who have never suffered any. Like an Oriental grandee, feared and flattered, an ambassador at Constantinople dwells in a pleasant house, secluded from plague, dogs and beggars, and like him may naturally say "Allah kerim" for the rest of the world. Armed cavasses guard his gates, ready at his behest to cut any intruder down; armed cavasses precede him in the streets to clear the way. Like the Oriental, he may be thoughtlessly unjust; no one remonstrates: he may indirectly inflict pain; no one repines, save in secret. His scorn is pardoned, his smiles are courted. The instincts of nature give way to the force of habit; and therefore one knowing the influences of the clime readily acquits the noble eltchee of all but inadvertence in the cited case. Others however, strangers to the Levant, came on the scene with the war; men with tongues in their heads and pens in their hands; and they, inferring duties from position, imputed to him at the outset indifference to the alleged wants of the Scutari military hospital. The inference was as illogical as the imputation was unjust. That hospital was in no way dependent on his countenance. Moreover, supposing it otherwise, as one can only judge of any thing by reference to a known standard, so, by comparison with the only hospital he had been in the way of seeing, the British seamen's hospital at Pera,* the Scutari hospital

* The old British seamen's hospital at Pera,—a self-supporting establishment, combining a maximum of expense with a minimum of relief—unable to bear the light reflected on it from the military hospital, ended its gloomy existence in 1856. Its successor, the British seamen's hospital at Galata,—a suitable stone edifice built by the Government,—is supported by a duty of 1½ penny per ton on British

in its decried state seemed replete with comfort and conveniences.

When we first saw it, the military hospital at Scutari had passed the stage of angry criticism. Its linen was clean washed, its dead were decently interred, its sinks were deodorized. Three simple accessories to comfort—the real medicine for disease induced by exposure—were still deficient: viz., bedside mats, unstinted bed-clothing, and sun-blinds. Wind circulating freer than agreeable to sound sleepers through broad stone-paved corridors made the patients laid in them sensibly aware of the atmospheric inconstancy of the Bosphorus, and daylight streaming in through lofty windows broke the precious morning slumber. The treatment early pursued, in ignorance of climatic action, was unsatisfactory. Native and foreign practitioners domiciled at Constantinople trust chiefly for the relief of complaints such as usually arrived from the Crimea to low diet and regulated warmth. Recovery then, in five cases out of six, ensues naturally. The hospital, reversing the process, gave its patients stimulating sustenance and let them lie chilly in bed; and therefore it is not surprising that during the winter of 1854-55 the average number of daily deaths was fifty, the maximum having been eighty. Rum in camp and port wine in hospital dug many graves. Routine at length listened to reason.

Under the eyes of the Court represented by Miss Nightingale, under the eyes of the House of Commons represented by Mr. Stafford, under the eyes of the press represented by Mr. McDonald, the hospitals of Scutari

shipping at Constantinople, and has a resident surgeon with requisite attendants: and like every such establishment under the Crown it is creditable to the nation.

and Kouleli,—owing much to Lady Stratford de Redcliffe's active sympathy,—progressed step by step, until they united the comforts of a sanatorium and a club, with reading and dining-rooms for convalescents; the former supplied with agreeable literature, and the latter with palatable food result of Mr. Soyer's gratuitous instruction. That renowned artist's soul was in his art. He had tarried on his way eastwards a day at Athens, and his feat of cooking a mutton-chop in the Parthenon remained his favourite recollection of the city of Minerva. He used to say there were three humbugs in the East, good-humouredly including himself in the triumvirate. Intelligent Soyer! He was no humbug; he was a practical enthusiast. He would have made cookery part of the scheme of national education; and many witnesses of the inexpertness of our soldiers in that respect in the Crimea, with consequent waste, will agree with him in thinking such teaching might benefit the poor more than some things pretended to be taught them. Sick officers were accommodated in the imperial kiosk * of Haidar Pasha, under the matronship of Mrs. Moore, widow of Colonel Moore. This estimable lady, following her gallant husband's example, died at her post. The remains of the brave who died near the Bosphorus repose in a cemetery, consecrated by the Bishop of Gibraltar, on the brow of a cliff overlooking the Golden Horn and the Propontis, between Scutari and Kadykeuy. This interesting spot, which merits a cypress plantation, is inclosed by wall and rail; it is under the charge of an English non-commissioned officer, and is indicated to the passing vessel by a granite column designed

* This kiosk was burnt down when in English occupation.

by Baron Marochetti. The remains of Khourshid Pasha (General Guyon), contested for by Christian and Moslem,* closed the long list. They were interred there, October 15th, 1856, by the chaplain of the British embassy, with Turkish (in default of British) military honours.

While the French hospitals in the Crimea might have advantageously taken example from the English hospitals there, their hospitals at Constantinople never required suggestion or stimulus from any quarter. Organized on the practice of former wars, with the improvements of modern science, and arranged in due

* General Guyon, a son of Captain Guyon, R.N., and a naturalized Hungarian by his marriage with a Hungarian lady, was one of that distinguished band of refugees who claimed Turkish hospitality in 1849. He received from the Porte then the rank of liva (major-general)—his rank in the Hungarian army—and a few years later promotion to the rank of ferik (lieutenant-general).

Having resided in Turkish fashion during the last year of his life in the orthodox quarter of Bozdan Kemereh at Constantinople, he was considered by the neighbours a "true believer," and therefore on his death the imams of the quarter came to his house to prepare the body for interment: but Countess Guyon put them off with fair words and sent for an English dragoman, who learned from the seraskir that although the deceased appreciated the merits of the Koran, he had died a Christian. The seraskir, seeing the incredulity in that respect among the inhabitants of the quarter, advised the removal of the body after sunset to Galata. This circumstance, coupled with the selection of the military cemetery at Scutari as the place of interment, suggested the propriety of applying to the commander of the British squadron in the Bosphorus for a man-of-war's boat to carry the body across the water and for a guard of honour. Compliance with this application was refused. General Guyon's body was therefore conveyed to Scutari in a Turkish man-of-war's barge, followed by two other man-of-war's boats with mourners, and was met at *Harem Skellesi* (the landing-place) by a company of the Imperial Guard with music, who escorted it to the gates of the cemetery, where they drew up in two lines with arms presented between which the funeral cortége passed. General Guyon's two sons were, after his death, placed in the *Collége Henri IV.* by Napoleon III.

time for the eventualities of a campaign, they met composedly the trials of the winter of 1854-55, and the heavier trials of the spring of 1856, when typhus fever prevailed. Eighty French surgeons died in them. The diseases were in general severer than in the English hospitals; owing in part to inferior food and raiment in the field, and in part to the comparative youth of the troops. Numbers were mere lads, appearing from their slight make younger than they really were. One day, among a group of convalescents airing themselves before the hospital at Gulhaneh, we remarked two lads under 18 years of age, as they said, who between them had given much flesh and bone to the moloch of war. What a prospect, we thought, for these poor boys! Virtual imprisonment for life in the Hôtel des Invalides. Ostentation lodges a disabled soldier in a palace: sympathy would nestle him in his mother's cottage with a pension.

The distressing complication of scurvy and dysentery was common in the French hospitals, and proved very fatal; while a liberal issue of anti-scorbutics rendered it all but unknown in the British army. Men used to arrive from the Crimea, barely able, from debility, to state their names: such were sent on immediately to France as the fairest chance of recovery. The French steam-packets from Constantinople to Marseilles carried twice a week from 160 to 200 sick or wounded soldiers, of whom many are reported to have died on the passage. The sick generally arrived from the Crimea in a state which necessarily rendered a bath the first process. The French hospitals being uncommented upon were less seen by the public than the English hospitals; which was to their advantage. Visitors might amuse convalescents, but they often seriously disturbed the sick. The sight of fashionably-dressed ladies and fine gentlemen in the wards constrained decent-minded men to regard conventionalities more than their condition advised. Free permission was given to visitors to perambulate the French hospitals, when a better motive than idle curiosity was assigned. Their organization was evidently the result of high professional knowledge joined with extensive practice. The familiarity of everybody with his duties rendered their performance easy. The intelligence of the attendants, a trained body, saved the surgeons much time and trouble : they made the preliminary arrangements for operations, and were adepts in the art of assuaging pain with pad and pillow.

The invalids derived inappreciable solace from the presence of Sisters of Charity amongst them. These self-denying women tended them as mothers and sisters are expected to attend sons and brothers. They fed those unable to feed themselves; they nursed the wounded with gentle hands ; they cheered the desponding by their gaiety; they smoothed the pillows of the sleepless. We saw many a poor fellow's eyes light up as one of those good spirits, noiseless and smiling, approached his bedside, if only to say a kind word and pass on to another. In our unworthiness we have been unable to elevate our thoughts to that frame of mind which leads women, many of them fair and young, to devote themselves, uncheered by fame, their names and garb conventual, to the service of humanity in its most repulsive form. They seemed to be ubiquitous. Wherever suffering lay there they were sure to be found. One stormy rainy day a French line-of-battle ship arrived in the Bosphorus with wounded Russians. Although we early went off to her, two Sisters of Charity had preceded us with a supply of lemonade, sugared wine, which they diluted with water on board, soft biscuits, and chocolate. We found them at their task, gay and smiling, administering restoratives to the wounded; who, excepting some who had suffered amputation, were lying or sitting on a sail spread on the main deck, in the dirty blood-stained clothes worn in the battle where they had fallen four days previously—the battle of the Tchernaya.

Only warm sympathy can overcome in the uninitiated the sickness of heart occasioned by these scenes. It was afflicting to behold those suffering men, some in a dying state, seeking relief by shifting their irksome position on the deck, or by leaning in various attitudes against gun-carriages. Fourteen had died on the passage. The lower jaw of one poor mortal had been shot away. He was sitting up, supported by an iron stanchion, his eyes staring with an expression of apprehensive agony, the forefinger of his right hand pointing to the ghastly wound. "Is there no hope of his death?" we inquired of a surgeon, feeling that to be the greatest blessing for him on earth. "There is," he replied, "when the reactionary fever sets in." He alone was passed by the good sisters: he could not swallow. When their jugs were emptied they repaired aft to replenish them; and on recommencing the distribution, misled by the resemblance of Russians to each other, they proffered the grateful beverage a second time to some individuals; but each resisted the temptation, and indicated his comrade in turn for it. As they had not calculated on so large a number, the captain of the ship furnished them with additional wine and sugar, so that each of the wounded received a refreshing drink of negus or lemonade, according to his state. Sister Bertha and her young companion, a novice, then stepped into their caik, and rowed to another similarly freighted French line-of-battle ship.

The wounded were landed next day, and conveyed, some to the hospital of Tash Kishlasi, some to the hospital of Gulhaneh. We saw them at the former, two days afterwards, laid in the same wards with French wounded, and receiving equal care and kindness. "They merit it," said our cicerone, a French sergeant, himself limping with a stick; "*les braves!* They have been fighting in defence of their country." Each prisoner in hospital received four sous a day, tobacco money. In one of the wards that day we witnessed an interesting scene. A French soldier, a handsome brown-bearded fellow, was lying on his back in bed; his left arm had been amputated, and his right arm, bound in splints, lay useless on the coverlid. By his side stood a Sister of Charity, feeding him. She had broken bread in suitable morsels, and lain them on his broad chest, and she held a basin of soup, in the composition of which eggs seemed to have a large share. All the while chatting, that he might not eat too fast, she alternately put a spoonful of soup and a morsel of bread into his mouth. When they were disposed of, she raised his head higher with her left hand, and with her right hand held a cup of liquid to his lips. Good sister, we thought, the recording angel is noting thee down!

Thirty-six Sisters of Charity died at Constantinople and three at Varna during the war, from the effects of their attendance in the French hospitals.

CHAPTER XXVII.

Result of the Battle of Inkerman—Council of War—The Army of the Danube transferred to the Crimea—The Russians attack Omar Pasha at Eupatoria and are defeated—Death of the Egyptian Selim Pasha—Omar Pasha's Tactics—What the Army of Eupatoria might have done—Omar Pasha with his Brigade at Sevastopol—Comment of the Turks on the death of the Czar—The Porte ill able to bear the absence of their Army in the Crimea—The Anglo-Turkish Contingent—Its European Officers—Proposal of the Porte rejected—Head-quarters of the Contingent at Buyukdereh—Life of Officers and Men—The Contingent transferred to Kertch—Skirmish with Cossacks—The Bashi-Bazouks—Their Cost.

The battle of Inkerman was remotely advantageous to Russia. That event, while it opened the eyes of the Allies' generals to their own position, closed them to every other consideration, and dwarfed the war, which demanded comprehensive strategy, to the siege of a town. Sceptical as those generals had been about the arrival of Russian reinforcements, they had now become no less apprehensive of further arrivals; and in sufficient force, perhaps, to render their own position critical. In this mood a council, composed of the military and naval commanders-in-chief and their seconds in command, met in the camp soon after that battle, to deliberate on the means of isolating Sevastopol. The vaunt attributed to General Caurobert, that no Russian soldier should leave the plain of Baidar except as a prisoner, had fallen into discredit. Eupatoria, already feebly garrisoned by English, French, and Turks, appeared a favourable point from which to make a telling diversion. An army operating from thence would, they thought, command the road from Perekop to Bakchésaray. Unable to spare troops for that object, the Allies' generals recommended the transfer of the bulk of the army of the Danube to the Crimea. The English and French ambassadors at Constantinople concurred in their view and backed their recommendation. The Porte consented: but consented unwillingly. No argument seemed valid in its eyes to justify the grave error of sending the best Turkish army, under a chief whose proverbial caution forbade the hope of enterprising co-operation, to a land where its deterioration would rapidly follow the difficulty (non-existent in its own provinces, where *ordou caimés* passed in exchange for bread, rice, and mutton,) of supplying its wants: and although no longer required in the valley of the Danube, there was fitting scope for its activity in Armenia, whence cries of distress were already heard.

No delay intervened. Under rain or snow, the lightly clad Turkish troops marched from their cantonments to the coast; and in four months, between mid-December 1854 and mid-April 1855, 60,000 men, 12,000 horses, and eighteen batteries were conveyed, with stores and provisions, from Varna and Sisepolis to Eupatoria. Cold rendered warm clothing indispensable, and to meet this want the Constantinopolitans were called upon for a "benevolence" of hirkas (wadded vests) for the army of Eupatoria.

Omar Pasha had scarcely established his head-quarters

at Eupatoria when that place was attacked, 17th February, 1855, by a Russian army of 30,000 infantry, 3,000 cavalry, and fifty guns, which hoped to snatch the honours of war on its march to Bakchésaray. Its ability to move in winter across the steppe was less surprising than its presumption in attacking 20,000 men on the sea coast, covered by entrenchments and supported by English gun-boats: one of which did good service in the action by dislodging a body of riflemen from a strong position, —the cemetery near the windmills. The Russians advanced tentatively three times to the attack, and then retreated, leaving 420 men and 300 artillery horses on the field. The Turkish soldiers, traditionally excited, cut off the heads of some of the slain and planted them on pikes on the lines of Eupatoria; but on this abuse of victory being pointed out to the general by European officers attached to his staff, he ordered their removal. The Turks had 103 killed and 298 wounded, including among the former the Egyptian Selim Pasha, who united experience and valour. An élève of Soliman Pasha (Colonel Selve) he had served under Ibrahim Pasha during his campaigns in the Morea, in Syria, and in Asia Minor. His death is supposed to have contributed to the inaction of the army at Eupatoria. Omar Pasha, wary in defensive, with no turn for offensive operations, was not the man for the situation. His favourite tactics, which had served him often in irregular warfare, consisted in raising redoubts or barricades and waiting to be attacked. Satisfied with the repulse of the Russians, he enlarged the circle of his entrenchments, and with Cossacks often in sight remained tranquil behind them. The agglomeration of numerous troops, refugee Tartars, and horses, within narrow limits under unwholesome conditions, bred fever and scurvy, and thus realized the Porte's worst anticipations.

The army of Eupatoria was negatively of service, by obliging the Russians to station permanently in observation of it a division of infantry and two divisions of cavalry; but in other respects it might as well have been in Arabia. Had that army gone in the spring of 1855 to the Asiatic frontier, Russia would (presumedly) have been reduced to sign away the Caucasus at the Peace of Paris, instead of acquiring then, for the first time, virtual recognition of her sovereignty over it. The Khans of Turkistan might now have been smoking their pipes, and the Ameer of Bokhara telling his beads, with confidence. Civilization would have then been spared the sad spectacle of the expulsion of half-a-million of Caucasians from their homes for the crime of having fought in defence of them for thirty years, and humanity the pain of seeing their misery traded on by cupidity and lust: the cupidity which conveyed the exiles from shore to shore in ill-conditioned vessels, as closely stowed as Africans in slavers,* and the lust which culled girls of all ages from destitute crowds in border towns of the Black Sea.

Omar Pasha, afterwards invited by the Allies' generals to share in the reduction of Sevastopol, joined

* A batch of 2,700 Circassians, male and female, embarked in three Greek vessels, measuring collectively 840 tons, were a fortnight on their voyage from Constantinople to Cyprus in September, 1864. More than 1,400 of them died on board; and of those landed in a state of exhaustion at Larnaca, only 300 were alive in January, 1865. The inhabitants of Larnaca did themselves no honour by their conduct towards those hapless refugees. This was the worst case; but there were others very bad.

them by sea with 20,000 men, on condition of exemption from trench duties. He did not long remain with them. He found himself in an ambiguous position. He thought himself slighted by generals of whose talents he professed a low opinion, and saw his troops despised by troops whom he did not consider superior. Deference he fancied was not paid to his experience; his advice seemed asked for form's sake only. So after the failure of the bombardment of April, he returned with his own brigade to Eupatoria, and there amused himself after his wonted fashion.

The mortification occasioned by the repulse of his troops at Eupatoria embittered the last hours of the Czar Nicholas. This startling demise made Turks reflect in the following strain:—"See," they said, "our Sultan has enjoyed himself as usual during the war, with his harem and his palaces, undisturbed by cares. His allies fight for him; he is well and prosperous. See, on the contrary, his enemy has toiled and fretted, Europe has banded against him, and now he dies broken-hearted. For whom has God declared?"

The Porte was ill able to sequester an army in the Crimea. The expense of maintaining it there, inefficiently, was the least objectionable feature of that misdirection of force. The cost alone of its transport from Bulgaria to Eupatoria absorbed 250,000*l.*, part of the proceeds of the first foreign loan made by Turkey, the commencement of a "facile descent:" a sum sufficient to have re-equipped the Asiatic army. Men had been miscalculated. The decrement of the Turkish armies since the declaration of war was already serious, telling on the demands for home service in Europe, Asia, and

Africa. The northern provinces, Roumelia, Mesopotamia, and Tripoli, all required troops. Thessaly and Epirus required military restraint. Montenegro, Servia, and the Grecian frontier invited military observance. Constantinople required a garrison to meet a possible outbreak of popular exasperation, as well as to furnish disposable troops for an emergency. The Asiatic army, weakened by several battles and disease, demanded reinforcements. Syria, Arabia, Anatolia, and the Archipelago, had been all but denuded of troops. Few of the above-named places were considered adequately garrisoned. Bagdad, temptingly alluring Persia, had only about 7,000 regulars. In Tripoli there were indications of the discontent of the Arabs breaking forth in insurrection; and it became necessary, on the evasion of their exiled sheick, Ghuma, from Trebizond, to send a reinforcement of five battalions to that province.

In this strait the Porte was further called upon to furnish 25,000 regular troops for an Anglo-Turkish Contingent. Unaware of the intention to collect them at the capital for new formation—believing them intended for immediate active service—the Porte acceded, though reluctantly, to the demand. Having acceded, it repented, but had not the firmness to state its reasons; feeling, perhaps, they would be unavailing. By the course pursued in regard of this corps, it seems to have been in contemplation to raise an Anglo-Turkish army after the Indian model; but if this vision had floated before the eyes of any person with influence to excuse the hope of its realization, slight reflection would have shown him that the Turks, with all their confidence in Great Britain, would never have consented to such an amalgamation of interests: nor, supposing obvious means adopted to render it comparatively popular, would other powers have remained silent thereon. No other power, however, had real motives for the jealousy which it excited, and which stimulated the premature desire for peace in certain quarters. The indisposition to furnish the Contingent, on national and religious grounds, felt by the Sultan, the Ulema, and the people, appeared from the outset. That of the army was natural. Officers who had served for years with their regiments in various grades were superseded by foreigners unknown to fame, with antipathetic notions derived from service in a land where natives are regarded as inferior beings.

Indian officers, accustomed to rule haughtily a subject race, were not the men (with few exceptions) to act judiciously with a dominant race, imbued with traditions of military renown. The soldiers they had graduated with were debarred the honours of the profession; the soldiers they were called upon to command carried each, in French phrase, a marshal's baton in his haversack. The seraskir (war minister) of that day had risen from the ranks. Those selected came out, not in the spirit of their comrades, Captain Ballard, Captain Ogilvie, Lieutenant Caddell, and Lieutenant Hinde, to identify themselves with the Turks; but with exclusive ideas, fostered by brevet rank, high expectations, and double pay. They were, nevertheless, a gallant set of men, eager for an opportunity to repeat on the Turkish the part they had nobly acted on the Indian stage. Things were so managed at the outset as to worry all parties. The Contingent officers, hurriedly sent from England, arrived at Constantinople with bed and baggage, expecting to find an army drawn up to receive them, and found less than a guard of honour. Their disappointment was keen, their position false. Thronging in no pleasant mood the thoroughfares, they talked of Turkey and the Turks as at Calcutta of India and the Indians. White scarves twisted round their foraging caps distinguished them at first in the crowd, and by that sign the sentries received orders to salute them. But the fashion, at once agreeable and becoming, was soon adopted by the Perotes, when the distinction ceased, and with it naturally the salutes. More than one puzzled sentry at the bridge head was called *eshek* (ass) by the officer of the guard, amidst the laughter of the bystanders, for having carried arms to a *pekin*—an itinerant dragoman or a broker's clerk—in mistake for a contingent officer. This was the beginning.

Aware of its error, and dreading the effect on the mind of the Constantinopolitans of the spectacle of a native force under foreigners who declined lending themselves to a slight illusion by wearing the *fez*, the Porte, when urged on the subject, too sensitive to avow the truth, cited, in excuse for delay, the expense and inconvenience of withdrawing troops from the provinces, and proposed, instead of bringing the men to the officers, sending the officers to the men, either in Europe or Asia, as might be preferred. Out of sight out of mind. The troops idly disseminated in Mingrelia and Lazistan might, with 10,000 men from Roumelia, have been collected at Trebizond; and thus formed, in the right place, the Contingent would have given effective support to the forces in Armenia. In presence of the enemy, officers and men would soon have come to understand each other's merits. No suggestion of the kind had any chance of being heeded. Her Majesty's Commissioner in Armenia, on the one hand, argued in disfavour of the services of the Contingent in that quarter; and the commander of the Contingent on the other hand considered it right, out of regard for his and his officers' credit, to reserve his force until organized in his own way on the shores of the Bosphorus. The former objected to be joined by a body of men bringing with them all he had been lamenting the want of in scores of despatches, and the latter did not reflect that with the money and means at his disposal, with unqualified support wherever he might be from every quarter, preparatory delay was unnecessary. In war, a game of chance and opportunities, one should make the best use of materials at hand; not wait for the attainment of an ideal standard of efficiency. General Bonaparte, pointing towards Italy, said to the ragged army of the Alps, "We will find clothes and shoes there." The Russian palace at Buyukdereh became the head-quarters of the Contingent, and pleasant heights in the vicinity the site of the camp of troops urgently wanted elsewhere. The Contingent officers, unaccustomed to heed social prejudices, lived in Buyukdereh and in camp as at a relaxed Indian station. The original mistake lay in giving officers to already organized regiments having a certain *esprit de corps*. Turkish troops only required, in the late war, to render them incomparable for service in their own country—a country beset with difficulties for European troops—a few able staff officers, a commissariat to ensure them their modicum of food, and skilful surgeons to tend them when seriously ill or wounded. Thus organized, chafing neither national pride nor regimental *amour propre*, the Contingent would have become an efficient corps at comparatively trifling expense; with a maximum of qualities for campaigning in Armenia and Trans-Caucasus.

Warily, at intervals, the Porte gave over troops to the Contingent, till the number reached about 12,000. Their comeliness improved with liberal rations, regular pay, and gentle exercise; but on the other hand their lithesomeness diminished. Some, moreover, learned to drink wine; and sundry disputes, involving on one occasion loss of life, between soldiers and the cultivators of adjoining vineyards—the question being who had the best right to the grapes—showed impaired discipline. After some months passed in the tranquil existence dear to Orientals, under canvas on breezy thyme-scented uplands, it was thought necessary to transfer the Contingent to some other quarter; for the most sanguine began to despair of its completion near Constantinople, and the most indulgent to desire fitter occupation for it. The dilemma was, where to send it? It would not suit everybody; it would not fit everywhere. The British commander-in-chief declined its company, on account of jealousies excited by the brevet rank of its officers. The Turkish commander-in-chief shunned the contrast between its comforts and the wants of his troops. After receiving various destinations from home, nine in all, the order of one day, sent by the electric telegraph—perplexing instrument in indecisive hands—being contradicted the next, Kertch was fixed upon as being a neutral out-of-the-way place. There it accordingly went, after the fall of Sevastopol, and was joined by the troops previously stationed in that quarter; making a total of about 18,000 infantry with some artillery and a few cavalry. Its own artillery remained at Scutari. The bulk of its cavalry followed, remained ten days in the roadstead, and were then, through unfounded fears about forage, sent to winter at Buyuk-Tchekmedjeh and Selivria on the Propontis.

Surprised at this destination, the seraskir asked, if not required at Kertch, why the cavalry did not go to Asia Minor, where they were required; rather than incommode the inhabitants of country towns, who were compelled to give up without remuneration their best houses for the accommodation of its officers. Deprived of this arm, invaluable in its position, the Contingent remained behind their fortified lines of Kertch and Yeni-Kaleh until the peace; watched by the Cossacks of the division on the isthmus of Arabat, who burnt large quantities of forage in the neighbourhood: the cavalry in Kertch were too few to deter them. One day a troop of Contingent horse, incautiously extending a reconnaissance, led on by a few Cossacks cantering a-head, were attacked unexpectedly by a superior body of cavalry previously concealed from view behind a hillock. Three of the former, including their gallant commander, Captain Sherwold, were slain in the skirmish, two mortally wounded, and forty-two captured. Next day a Contingent officer went with a flag of truce to the Russian camp, fifteen miles distant, to inquire after the prisoners. He found them well cared for, and saw the body of Captain Sherwold, bandaged with white linen and covered with a sheet, treated with due respect. In doubt of the captain's religion, the Russian general had invited a Greek and a Catholic priest to pray over it. The envoy also saw in the Russian camp some horses of the 10th Hussars, objects of peculiar solicitude.

The Contingent was the most expensive item of the war.

The Bashi-bazouks, addenda of the Contingent, fell under the same law of contrariety; being also retained from the theatre of war, to prepare them (so ran the phrase) for service. Raised as a suitable force, with nomade watchful habits, for confronting Cossacks, they were stationed, during the eventful summer and autumn of 1855, near the plain of Troy; where their pranks—exaggerated in recital to the prejudice of General Beatson who had campaigned on the Danube in 1854 with the few originally raised as an experiment—obtained for them unenviable notoriety. From that classic scene they marched, about 3,000 strong, across Roumelia and the Balkan, to winter quarters at Schumla; and the order acquired by them on the march showed the error of having kept such lads inactive. The Turks had no feeling about them: they only wondered at England thinking it worth her while to incur expense on their account. Independent of the first outlay, they are said to have cost about 40,000*l*. a month.

CHAPTER XXVIII.

Brussa destroyed by Earthquake—Strength of the Allied Forces before Sevastopol—Second Bombardment and its Effects—The Malakof the Key of the Position—French Forces predominant—Sevastopol as fortified by General Todleben—General Caurobert's Opinion—The Garrison short of Provisions and Ammunition—The Governor empowered to act on his Judgment—Generals Caurobert and Pelissier—Plans for cutting off Russian Supplies—Mr. Satler's Organization of Russian Transport Corps—Naval and Military Expedition to open the Sea of Azof—The Russian Garrisons of Kertch and Yenikaleh retire—Tokens of Amity from the Tartars to the Allies—Strange conduct of the Allied Troops—Destruction of the Museum at Kertch—Spoil shipped to Pera—Destitution of Jewish Families—Destruction of Property by the Allied Squadron in the Sea of Azof—The Russians evacuate Soudjouk and Anapa—Return of the Expedition to Sevastopol—Capture of the Mamelon by the French—High Expectations of Success—Combined Attack on the Malakof and Redan—Cause of its Failure—Bravery of the French and English Columns—Captain Peel and the Naval Brigade—Death and Funeral of Lord Raglan—Prince Gortschakof constructs a Raft-bridge for the Retreat of the Garrison—Russian Corps d'Armée defeated at Tchernaya—Loss of Men in the Siege Operations—Earthworks yield to a Vertical Fire of Shell—Rejoicings in Sevastopol on the Opening of the Raft-bridge—Final Bombardment of Sevastopol—False Attacks to deceive the Garrison—Their successful Result in the Surprise of the Malakof by the French—Resistance of the Russians—Repulse of the French at two Points, and of the English at the Redan—Evacuation of Sevastopol—Cause of Failure at the Redan—Masterly Retreat of the Garrison of Sevastopol—What the Allies had gained—Losses on both Sides—Total Loss of Russian Soldiers—The Siege of Acre in the 12th Century a Type of that of Sevastopol—Dissimilar Features.

Before the experiments mentioned in the preceding chapter and others were begun, and while war was waiting for spring, nature, as if to mock man's most gigantic efforts in destruction, overthrew in a few minutes (February 28th, 1855) by a gentle heave of the plain great part of the beautiful and venerable city of Brussa, resting-place of the remains of the first five Sultans of the Ottoman race. Mosque and church, bath and tomb, bazaar and khan, konak and cabin, fell together. The famous sulphur springs ebbed and flowed. The edge of the undulation reached, and slightly rocked, Constantinople. This dire disaster, mourned from the Danube to the Indian Ocean, aroused apathy and made resignation impatient. The wreck seemed ominous.

Careless about earthquakes, and uninfluenced by the conference of Vienna, the Allies had made strenuous efforts, since the commencement of the year, to reinforce their army and advance their lines, in the hope of reducing Sevastopol ere the violets should fade. By April, 1855, the English and French armies numbered 145,000 men; 500 guns were in position, with 800 rounds of ammunition for each; and a railway, novel instrument of war, had been laid down from Balaclava to the camp. All promised success. Letters, semi-official and private, written from the theatre of war, coincided in that sense. But the recently-appointed commandants of engineers had yet, like their predecessors, to learn the nature of a redoubt; had yet to witness the endurance of Russian soldiers. Slaves those soldiers may be, but not recreant. Put six ounces of meat a day into their mouths, serviceable arms into their hands, wearable shoes on their feet, give them more kind words, fewer blows, and less vodtka, and we should see a soldiery able to encounter both the troops of the West and the hardships of the East.

The second bombardment of Sevastopol opened on the 9th of April and continued until the evening of the 17th, with a daily expenditure of nearly 1,000 tons of shot and shell: it then ceased, through exhaustion. Although a higher application of the principle of force than the opening bombardment of the previous October, having lasted as many days as that had lasted hours, the result was scarcely more fructuous. The works of the Malakof and the Redan, twisted and torn by the iron storm, seemed shapeless mounds of earth; fascines and sandbags stood at all angles. But on looking narrowly through interstices, one saw remounted guns in position to fire on advancing troops; and while on the left the French batteries, at 300 yards' distance, had opened a breach twenty-five yards wide, in the curtain between the Quarantine battery and the Central bastion, inner batteries frowned warningly beyond. Many bold spirits, impatient and repining then, may in their hearts have applauded later the prudence which forbade the assault: in expectation of which the enemy had reserved fifty rounds per gun.

There was nothing left for the Allies but to sap nearer the enemy's lines, bring up heavier guns, and plant more mortars in position. The Malakof was now clearly recognized as the key of the position, with the necessity of taking preliminarily the Mamelon; which, long neglected by all parties, had been occupied and entrenched by the Russians only six weeks earlier. Thenceforward the Gallic element predominated in the siege. Of the six positions,—the Quarantine battery, the Central battery, the Flag-staff bastion, the Redan, the Malakof, and the Mamelon,—the French undertook to grapple with four.

This trial proved the strength of the works thrown up, under fire, by the genius of General Todleben, seconded by scientific officers of all arms and by devoted soldiers and sailors. They defied a threefold mightier host than the force Sevastopol had trembled before five months earlier, and showed that, under ordinary siege conditions, Sevastopol had been rendered impregnable. But if the defence was unique so was the attack. The facility of drawing supplies by sea from inexhaustible resources, indicated, with perseverance, a termination to the defence and no limit to the attack. Nevertheless, the failure of an eight days' bombardment of unparalleled severity had shaken the confidence of one of the allied chiefs; not in the result, but in the mode of attack. "Sevastopol," observed General Caurobert to the author a few days afterwards, "is an entrenched camp, defended by an army relieved at pleasure from outside; it is an exceptional place, for the attack of which the rules of war offer no example." General Caurobert saw no good reason for retaining all the allied forces in one spot, while in possession of a steam fleet able to carry 40,000 men at once in a few hours' run. He, it has been said, was for embarking part of the army and landing it further north, to make a diversion in the Crimea in co-operation with the army of Eupatoria. Isolated, Sevastopol would have fallen of itself. Indeed, it would soon have fallen; for there was not a month's supply of provisions in the city for 35,000 men: the number at which the garrison was permanently maintained. Their ammunition was nearly exhausted; little more than sufficient remaining, besides the fifty rounds per gun spoken of, for the infantry to fight a battle with. The army in the field was weak, and the towns in the peninsula were hospitals.

Fresh supplies of ammunition reached Sevastopol three weeks after the bombardment, and with them the governor received powers to act on his own judgment; either to abandon the place or continue the defence: as no more troops could be spared to reinforce him. He decided on the latter course; and the reception, three weeks later, of intelligence of the despatch of two more divisions to the Crimea, approved his judgment. General Caurobert's opinion, if given as stated, was overruled. Loved by his soldiers, and tender of their lives, General Caurobert seemed eminently fitted to lead an army through a dashing campaign. On the other hand, General Pelissier, stern, uncompromising, as ready to roast Arabs as chestnuts for the attainment of a military object, was the man to press a siege. Accordingly, the Arbiter of war having decided on Russia sustaining the least possible amount of injury by the war, in virtue of her opponents' determination not to swerve from their original plan of attack, the two generals changed places by imperial order. General Pelissier justified the decision. Week by week he circumscribed the enemy more closely, and 5,000 French *hors de combat* gave the measure of his exertions during the first month of his command.

Previous to the transference of command,—submitted to with a cheerful countenance by General Caurobert though with a wrung heart,—subsidiary means of straitening the enemy had been contemplated, and were afterwards carried out. The Russians were supposed to draw large supplies from the Sea of Azof, and the occupation of that sea had accordingly been decided upon. The Allies, with all Turkey to draw from, yet supplied their own armies with much cost and trouble; they naturally inferred from their own experience great difficulty in that respect for the enemy, and expected to enhance it decisively by cutting off that channel of supply. Their calculation was erroneous. Russia, in anticipation of that diversion, deferred unaccountably long, had organized the supply of her forces in the Crimea chiefly by land carriage; and although drawing supplies by sea as long as she was able, they were not depended upon for a permanent resource: nor, as it appeared, were they of sufficient importance to influence the result. Russia possessed in Mr. Satler, her commissary-general in the Crimea, as remarkable a man as General Todleben, each in his own line, and she gave him unrestricted powers. Mr. Satler, in addition to the ordinary army transport corps of 6,000 horses, organized six draught brigades of 1,000 pair of oxen each, two pair to a waggon, to bring provisions and stores from Perekop and Tchongar as they arrived there from the interior to Sevastopol and other stations in the Crimea, and to convey away sick and wounded to the hospitals. The dangerously wounded and seriously diseased were deposited chiefly at Simpheropol; the less afflicted were conveyed to Nicolaief and other places beyond the peninsula.

This vast movement shows demonstratively the connection between the defence of Sevastopol and the faculty of traversing the Crimea in every direction; and skilful diversional operations on the part of the Allies, with the aid of their steam fleet, would have deranged it. The diversion by turning the hills from the south, planned by the French Emperor in Paris, proved on trial impracticable. Mr. Satler — through whose hands 24,000,000*l.* sterling are said to have passed—kept the army in the Crimea well supplied; obtaining cordial co-operation from every quarter by prompt payments and by closing his eyes to the discrepancy between the amount of forage drawn for by colonels of cavalry regiments and of transport brigades and the number of animals in existence. The Russians, nevertheless, ought to have rendered the Sea of Azof safe, for the sake of the defenceless towns on its shores. They had forgotten the traditions of their wars in other days with the Turks, when they strove with flat-bottomed frigates for the mastery of that sea. The Cimmerian Bosphorus was ill fortified, weakly garrisoned, and a few insignificant steamers composed its naval defence.

After a false start, the combined naval and military expedition to open the Sea of Azof reached its destination towards the end of May, 1855, and landed 15,000 troops (English, French, and Turkish), at St. Paul, a few miles from Kertch, on which place they marched. Simultaneously the Russian garrisons of Kertch and Yenikaleh retired on Arabat. Those places immediately surrendered, or rather invited occupation. The notables of Kertch met the allied chiefs and tendered them bread and salt—an immemorial Tartar custom—in token of amity. In return, the Allies conducted themselves after the fashion of Arabs with a caravan. Making little distinction between public and private property, they destroyed government steamers and merchant vessels;

burnt planks enough to hut an army; threw corn and flour into the sea sufficient to feed for a month the refugee Tartars at Eupatoria, to whom the Sultan was then sending food from Constantinople where distressing prices ruled; and crowned their exploits by the dispersion of the unique museum—pride of the Crimea—of the Mithridatic era, wantonly breaking many of the relics in pieces. The nationality of the perpetrators of this act of vandalism is in dispute: all that is certain is, no Turk had a hand in it; nor in the subsequent rifling of tombs which Greeks, Romans, Scythians, Genoese, and Russians had respected. Chairs, mirrors, pianos, candelabra, &c.,—vulgar spoil—were shipped in Allies' transports on Frank or Levantine account, and sent to Pera; where they were afterwards seen, as reported, in various fashionable saloons.

Athens mourned her statues and Egypt her obelisks carried away by the Romans, and Spain sent maledictions after her pictures carried off by the French; but no one had cause to blush: the nature of the spoil condoned the act.

The Allies' proceedings ill-accorded with recognized rules of war. Kertch having come peaceably into their possession, its inhabitants with their property were entitled to respect; the more so on account of their sympathies; and its occupation having been decided upon, the care of stores and provisions became a military duty. Had their town been besieged, it would scarcely have suffered more injury at the hands of an enemy than their friends inflicted.* Many of the inhabitants were reduced

* At the termination of the Allies' occupation of Kertch, out of 2,500 dwellings, only 400 remained entire.

to beggary. Eighty-five Jewish families, for example, bereft of shelter and subsistence, were sent soon afterwards by the Allies to Constantinople, and there cast on the bounty of their co-religionists.

The navy followed suit. Fourteen steamers (French and English) entered the Sea of Azof, 25th May, with the laconism "Burn, sink, and destroy," for their orders. They acted up to them with zeal and discernment. Complaisant towns—Berdiansk, &c.—were let off with the destruction of their public stores; recusant towns — Taganrog, &c. — were shelled and rocketed. In a few days, in their rapid course from place to place, they destroyed ashore large quantities of corn, oil, and timber, chiefly private property; afloat, above 200 vessels. Disinterestedly they burnt corn-laden vessels at sea, instead of sending them to market to convert into prize-money. No corresponding result in distress at Sevastopol followed this stirring cruise, nor was its reduction facilitated thereby. An inconvenience certainly ensued. Expecting the Allies to pass the Strait of Yenitchi, and with their boats thread the mazes of the Siwash, the Russians thenceforwards abstained from forwarding supplies to the Crimea by Tchongar bridge, which had shortened the road from some of the supply districts by 100 versts. The Turkish galleys which in the reign of Sultan Ibrahim ascended the Don as far as Azof, burnt by the Cossacks on their approach, had made a milder visitation. The Allies were able in the end to boast of having swept the Sea of Azof of its last boat.

The presence of the allied fleets off St. Paul, where they tarried about three weeks, waiting the return of the flotilla, warned the Russians in garrison on the opposite coast to decamp. Accordingly, razing the works and disabling the guns of Soudjouk and Anapa respectively on May 28 and June 5, they retreated in order with their baggage towards the Kuban. When the Allies' admirals, apprised by a Circassian of the enemy's movements, reached Anapa, they found it had been already evacuated a week and was in possession of the Circassians.

Leaving a garrison in Kertch, and a few steamers in the Sea of Azof to keep the inhabitants of the coast on the alert and carry on war against the sturgeon fisheries in that sea, the expedition returned to Sevastopol, to be present at the projected attack on June 18th.

Since April the siege had made notable progress. Although still distant, the Allies' lines had been advanced considerably nearer, and the vertical fire from numerous mortars had acquired fatal intensity. The effect of a sharp bombardment on June 6th, followed up next day by the capture of the Mamelon by the French, and of the Quarries by the English—both with distinguished gallantry—indicated diminished resources on the part of the enemy, and allowed discouragement to be inferred. These successes, the extent of the preparations, the confidence of the engineers, and the ardour of the troops, excited unmingled hopes, and raised expectation higher than on any previous occasion. The expectation was equally shared in London and in Paris, then in electric communication with the Crimea. The initiated in these capitals into the designs of the allied armies, warned by the lesson of the previous October, were doubtless cautious of betraying their sense of confidence; but in the camp no reticence existed: champagne was laid ready for libations at head-quarters and at every mess; and the *Banshee* was ordered to be ready to start for Marseilles with the despatches. The armies were to be under arms before daylight of the 18th, the French and English assaulting columns in position, the Turkish and Sardinian troops in the field—to meet a possible flank movement by the Russian corps d'armée, supposed to be on M'Kenzie's heights—and the fleets, under way, out of gunshot, ready to go in on the fall of the southern defences to impede the retreat of the garrison. The French were to attack the Malakof, the English the Redan.

At daylight on the 17th, the French and English lines opened a heavy fire on the Malakof and Redan, and sustained it till evening; when the silence of the enemy's guns confirmed the generals in their intention to storm the defences next day. Suspecting, however, that the enemy might, according to custom, remount his guns at night, or have feigned exhaustion, Lord Raglan wisely proposed to open a preluding fire in the morning for a couple of hours, to try his strength; but General Pelissier, seeing no reason for that precaution, intimated his resolve to attack at three in the morning. Soon after midnight the troops were massed in the trenches, and as they lay in anxious expectation shells thrown from cohorn mortars dropped occasionally amongst them.

On a signal, to be given by General Pelissier from the Lancaster battery, the French divisions — right, centre, and left—told off for the assault, were to advance rapidly on the Malakof. With simultaneous action they might have carried it; but General Mayran, in command of the right division, misled by a chance rocket, marched prematurely. When the real signal flashed through the air, his division had already been exposed nearly half-an-hour to a warm fire from the enemy; who, warned by a French deserter, were prepared at every point: the General himself, in the meanwhile, being carried off the field mortally wounded. The other divisions then advanced, enveloped the Malakof, and fell by hundreds on the edge of the ditch. On no other occasion in the war did the French, losing that morning 1,600 men, display more resolute bravery. They persevered until further perseverance would have been temerity. Made in daylight and with concert, the attack would in all probability have predominated; made in darkness, with confusion, it was weak, and animating for the Russians.

The English attacking column, ignorant at the moment of their ally's discomfiture, left their trenches at daylight, 800 strong, as many thousands being in reserve, accompanied by a party of the naval brigade with scaling ladders led by the paladin Captain William Peel. With buoyant steps and stout hearts they traversed 240 yards of open ground, in face of grape and canister; and one of that resolute band (the author's nephew a youth fresh from Cambridge) though wounded continued to advance till checked by another missile at the abattis of the Redan. There fell his colonel, shot dead, with many other gallant men; while others, passing that frail barrier, found cover in rifle-pits. Their courage and valour were not altogether wasted on the sulphurized air. They drew on themselves, with heavy loss, the fire of the Redan away from the French, who were then retreating from the Malakof. Another column, operating on the left, made its footing good for a while in the cemetery at the head of the Dockyard creek ravine;

whence, ultimately, the first explorers of Sevastopol proceeded.

This grievous failure, result of divided command, disturbed Lord Raglan's equanimity; which was akin to Oriental resignation. Weakened bodily, and mentally depressed, the veteran sank ten days afterwards. He of the noble house of Somerset breathed his last on a camp bed, in a lone farm-house on the Heracleotic steppe, June 28, 1855. Mourned by his staff, who lost in him an indulgent chief, and attended by two armies, who had admired his serene intrepidity on the field of battle, his body was borne with military pomp to the *Caradoc* for conveyance to England. She tarried on her way at Constantinople to coal and there lay alongside a hulk, unnoticed and unnoted save by her coat of black paint. No minute-guns from the Allies' men-of-war in the Bosphorus, no colours half-mast, announced the melancholy cause of her arrival in the Golden Horn. The Porte wished to pay honours to the remains of Lord Raglan similar to those paid by it eight months earlier to the remains of Marshal St. Arnaud; but the proposal of Aali Pasha, the minister for foreign affairs, to that effect was declined.

Prince Gortschakof did not let himself be deluded by his success on June 18th: he knew he had only obtained a respite. Foreseeing the inevitable result, he had, on losing the Mamelon, the outwork of the Malakof, given orders to collect materials for the construction of a raft bridge across the harbour of Sevastopol, on the plan of General Bauchmaer, to ensure the retreat of the garrison; with purpose to maintain himself at all hazards till its completion, longer if feasible, in order to deter the Allies by the lateness of the season from an autumnal campaign in the Crimea. He made a vacillating attempt, on the faith of General Reed's report, to disturb the siege with a corps d'armée, sent, August 16th, against the French supported by Sardinians and Turks, who repulsed it with a loss of seven or eight thousand killed or wounded. Men had never been more idly sacrificed. General Pelissier was proud of the battle of Tchernaya. In his order of the day he congratulated his troops on having beaten the "vaunted Russian infantry;" but inspection of their arms * should have moderated his exultation.

The besiegers continued to push their approaches to the Malakof with animation; the enemy disputing the ground manfully step by step. During the last two months of sapping, their severest trial, the French had on the average 150 men killed or wounded each night. Science was no longer in doubt. The tentative process pursued during eight months had taught the lesson. It was simply recurrence to Vauban's practice: subdue the enemy's fire, and have your trenches sufficiently near to profit by opportunity. Vast formations of earth, disposed with art, the Russian

* Extract from a letter from the Crimea dated 20th August, 1855, about the battle of the Tchernaya:—

"An attempt seems to have been made by the Russian army to supply the want of rifles it laboured under. A number of their new rifles were picked up, and judging from their appearances they were equally as indifferent and quite as clumsy as their old muskets; they seemed for the most part to have been old muskets rifled and fitted with a sight after the Liége pattern. Probably there is no army in Europe so badly armed as the Russian. The Turkish army is immeasurably superior. The swords of the Russians seem as if made of the hoops of a barrel, one can bend them easily with the fingers; and their muskets are long, awkward, unwieldy things. They have no half-cock, and their locks are so stiff as almost to require both hands to lift the hammer."

works on the south defied horizontal fire, how well soever directed and sustained; but were powerless under a rain of shells with accurately cut fuses. The Russian admission of a daily loss of from 500 to 700 men killed or wounded during the last twenty days of the siege, showed the efficacy of the Allies' vertical fire. To protect themselves in some degree from it, they made bomb-proof burrows in their works: a choice of evils, since their batteries were thereby exposed to be unmanned at a critical moment.

The saving raft-bridge over the harbour being completed September 1, was opened that night with religious solemnities and civic rejoicings. The transport of archives, precious objects, and stores, immediately commenced from the south to the north side. A month would scarcely have sufficed to remove the immense matériel in the place. That interval was not granted.

Four days afterwards, September 5th, the final bombardment of Sevastopol opened from all points, and continued for more than three days. The 7th French parallel was twenty yards from the Malakof, with a spacious place d'armes: the nearest English parallel was 200 yards from the Redan, with a narrow place d'armes. Eight hundred guns and mortars were in position. In deception, to throw the enemy off his guard, the Allies from time to time slackened their fire, or directed it beyond the works, on the reserves. The Russians, each time deeming the assault imminent, left their retreats to man their ramparts; when shells again rained in amongst them with deadly effect. Shortly before noon, on the 8th, this manœuvre was repeated; but the Russians giving no heed to it, remained in their blindages eating their dinners. The device had succeeded. Ready, with all conceivable appliances, the columns of attack, the leader of each with his eyes fixed on his watch, waited silently for noon: then unseen, unexpected, they leaped all together out of their trenches, rushed forwards, and in a few seconds reached the ditch. The first regiment of Zouaves had the honour of leading the way. Some, jumping into the ditch, climbed up to the embrasures, and the eagle-bearer first appeared above the smoke and dust; others crossed it on planks thrown across by attendant sappers. In five minutes the French were within the precinct of the Malakof, with trifling loss. As they entered they met the enemy emerging like Troglodytes from the earth, and shot them down easily.

The Russians made desperate resistance from the basement of the White Tower, and at other points of the vast area of the Malakof. Disregarding lesser matters, General M'Mahon directed his forces to the narrow gorge—Todleben's only fault—and thus prevented the enemy, who made five attempts, from effectively bringing up his reserves. In the meanwhile the French engineers, running a sap up to the edge of the ditch, threw a bridge over it; along which the reserves passed continuously, till opposition ceased and the tricoloured flag floated triumphant. On all other points the Russians were successful. They repulsed the French with intimidating loss at the Central and Flag-staff bastions; and although the English, after running the gauntlet of a sweeping cross-fire, had gallantly carried the Redan—being left there unsupported, while expecting an attack from the enemy's reserve foiled at the

Malakof—they abandoned it, and made no attempt to reoccupy it. General Pelissier sent a message at 4 P.M. to his colleague to advise another attempt, prognosticating its success; on which General Simpson sent for two of his divisional generals to consult with; but on their joining him, it being then 8 P.M., further operations were deferred till morning: when, let alone the Redan, Sevastopol itself was evacuated. Disappointment ascribed backwardness to the English storming party on that day; but without reason. They were sent forward immethodically over a furlong of ground swept by the enemy's balls. The disposition for the attack inspired no confidence: no reserves appeared massed ready to support them. Nevertheless they followed their leader into the Redan, and did not follow him out of it until twenty minutes after his departure to seek reinforcements,—a step which none but a man of courage could have ventured to take. More could not fairly be expected from young troops. Had the French attack, with all the advantages of proximity and surprise, been thus languidly conducted, it would have failed even more signally.

The capture of the Malakof compensated for all failures. Aware that Sevastopol was no longer tenable, that further delay would compromise the safety of the garrison, Prince Gortschakof at once organized his retreat, and conducted it with a masterly hand. War has rarely witnessed a difficult operation more successfully performed. Preserving order amidst exploding mines and falling edifices, the dismaying scene lighted up by the flames of his ships, he gathered his troops in from the outposts, marshalled them on the shore, and abandoning some hundreds of wounded (in too sad a plight for removal), ten days' provisions, and many hundred pieces of siege ordnance, led them, in the grey dawn of the morning, over the tremulous bridge provided by his foresight. The sun rose on the 9th September on a deserted ruined city * and on the vestiges of a sunken fleet. The Allies had won the place, but were scarcely masters of it. They had driven the enemy from the field of battle, but could not sit down in it themselves. They had gained the power of destruction of everything remaining in it, but not of occupation, and the harbour remained impervious to their ships.

The loss on the 8th of September was about equal on either side. The Russians had 11,000, the French 9,000, and the English 2,500 killed, wounded, or missing.

During the war 180,000 Russian infantry and 20,000 cavalry passed Perekop; and 106,000 of that force were buried in the Crimea. Allowing for unnoted casualties by explosions and drownings, and for deaths beyond the Crimea from wounds received in it, we may estimate the Russian direct loss by the siege of Sevastopol at 125,000 men. The indirect heavier loss, by fatigue and sickness on the march from the interior to the Crimea, will never probably be known outside the Russian war-office. In addition, the Russian Asiatic army lost 40,000 men.

The nearest parallel in history to the siege of Sevastopol is the siege of Acre in 1189–91, alike

* At the termination of the war there remained, of 15,000 dwellings which had composed Sevastopol, 16 habitable houses, and 60 repairable. The rest was ruin.

tasking the might of three empires, alike holding Europe and Asia in suspense. Substituting Moslems for Russians, we read the siege of Sevastopol typified in Gibbon's account of the siege of Acre. The similar features are these: Acre was besieged by the united forces of France and England, with contingents from minor States, their wants being supplied from friendly Mediterranean ports; nearly invested by land—inversion of the Allies' disposition—the naval blockade could not be strictly maintained, and therefore, whenever bad weather drove the royal fleets away temporarily from the coast, supplies were thrown into the city. A few miles from Acre the Ccaliph lay encamped, intent on raising the siege, during the progress of which several battles favourable to the Crusaders were fought near Mount Carmel. One hundred thousand of the Crusaders perished in the siege. The intimate union between England and France began to cool at its termination.

The dissimilar features are as follow: at Acre the sovereigns of France and England and the Caliph were present with their armies; the chief honour fell to the English; the success of the Allies was complete; the defenders of Acre capitulated, paid 200,000 pieces of gold in ransom for their lives, freed all Christian captives, and restored the wood of the true cross. But the striking dissimilarity appears in the mode of following up the victory. Richard Cœur de Lion marched immediately, in the heat of a Syrian summer, along the coast, reducing Jaffa and Cæsaria on the way, to Ascalon. He fought the Moslem army every day, and routed it so completely, that at length Saladin remained alone in the field with his personal guards. The action at Koughil, near Eupatoria, September 29, between French and Turkish and Russian cavalry—in which the latter were defeated with losses in men, horses, and guns; and the reduction of Kilburn, 19th October, by the Allies' fleets, when the French iron-cased floating batteries made a successful début, were a poor set-off for the inaction of 150,000 matchless troops before Sevastopol in the balmy coolness of a Crimean autumn.

CHAPTER XXIX.

Critical Position of Kars—The Turkish Asiatic Army—Zarif Mustapha Pasha appointed to the Command—Battle of Kurekderah—Report of the English Commissioner of the Efficiency of the Turkish Troops and their Artillery—Report of the English Medical Officer on the Hospitals at Kars—The British Commissioner's Despatches—His Estimate of the Turks—Inadequate Grounds for his unfavourable Opinion—Zarif Mustapha Pasha and others recalled at the Instance of the Commissioner—Charge of want of Respect curiously disproved—The Porte unjustly reproached for not sending Supplies to Kars—Isolation of that City—The Decision to abandon it as untenable overruled by the English Commissioner—His Aim—The Question considered—The Asiatic Army concentrated at Kars—General Muravief encamps on the Arpa Tchai—Advance of the Russians—Brilliant Sortie from Kalafat an Example for Kars—General Muravief's Feint—He invests Kars—Successful Defences of Garrisons mainly due to Sorties—Instances cited—Russian Ravages—Protection of Kurdish Brigand Chiefs by the English Commissioner—Their Condemnation.

The lamentations of Kars, faintly heard in the intervals of the bombardment of Sevastopol, had been scarcely heeded by the Allies; although they may have apprehended the surrender of it, with the army, chief defence of Asia Minor. Whatever doubts may have existed about the prudence of occupying Kars, there could be none about the policy of preventing its fall, viewing the seasoned troops and valuable ordnance inside, and the effect of its re-echo. The eyes of Central Asia were concentrated on Kars. Whatever doubts may have been entertained of Russia's intention to act energetically in Asia, had been removed by the appointment of General Muravief, distinguished under Paskievitch in the campaign of 1828–29, to the command of the Trans-caucasian army.

The Turkish Asiatic army, with ill-luck from the commencement, had suffered more from its friends than its foes. Superior in the quality of its men, artillery, and small-arms, but ill commanded, it had gallantly fought in the first campaign three battles—the battles of Beyendir, Akiska, and Subahtan; and had lost the two latter through their generals' deficient knowledge of the art of war, coupled with divided authority. Those battles, costing the Turks 12,000 men in killed, wounded, and prisoners, and many guns, were nevertheless all but drawn. The Russians were unable to follow up their successes, and the Turks remained on the field. Various pashas, who had been proved incompetent, were then successively recalled, and Zarif Mustapha Pasha was appointed in March, 1854, to the chief command, with other divisional generals. The army, demoralized by the joint operation of his predecessors' incapacity and alien rivalries, was then at its lowest ebb of destitution. Fifty men a day were then dying at Kars. He reorganized the staff, reorganized the hospitals, and raising thus the tone of his army morally and physically, made it, in four months, again eager to be led under fire. The battle of Kurekdereh, fought early in August, within twenty miles of Kars, was lost by him, more, it is said, through the hesitation arising out of the rival plans of his foreign military advisers, than by the tactics of his opponent Prince Bebutof. The Russians, sustaining a heavy loss in killed and wounded, did not advance beyond the field of battle. The Turks rallied with sustained ardour, and within a few weeks were again in heart and spirits; according to a despatch written by her Majesty's commissioner in Armenia to the Secretary of State for Foreign Affairs. That officer inspected 12,000 of the infantry soon after his arrival at the theatre of war, and thus described them:—

"Camp, near Kars, September 26, 1854.

"In closely inspecting the troops as I rode through their ranks, I was struck with their healthy and soldier-like mien. I doubt if any army could produce better materials for working with in this country. Even from my horse I observed the brightness and good condition of their arms, and having expressed to the mushir my wish to inspect a certain number of privates taken promiscuously from each corps, his Excellency caused them to fall out as they passed him. I minutely inspected each man in succession. I found the greater proportion of the muskets and bayonets in good order. The greater proportion of them were flint firelocks, but three battalions of chasseurs were armed with the minié rifle, and seven battalions of infantry had detonating muskets." In the same despatch the commissioner thus speaks of the artillery:*—"The guns and the carriages were in an efficient state; and the horses, considering the season

* The artillery consisted of six batteries of horse artillery, 5-pounders, excepting one battery of 15 lb. howitzers; seven batteries of foot artillery, viz., five of 9-pounders, one of 12-pounders, and one of 24 lb. howitzers; one mountain battery—total 84 guns. The horse artillery had six horses and all the others eight horses per gun. Each heavy gun had 80 rounds, each light gun 120 rounds, of ammunition. In the magazines there were 400 rounds per gun.—*Gen. Williams' Report.*

of the year and the difficulty of procuring forage, were in tolerably working condition; although those animals had been cheated out of at least a third of their corn by the malpractices of the commander-in-chief and his generals of division. The harness will require considerable repair during the winter; but considering the constant exposure to sun and rain, it has been well cared for by its commanding officer, Tahir Pasha. . . . Everybody present in the late battle admits the efficiency of this arm, by which the enemy suffered most severely, and those guns which were taken by the Russians did not fall into their hands until they had inflicted severe chastisement on the attacking columns. . . . The small stores appear to be in very good order and ready for use. The ammunition is made up with great care and packed in boxes adapted for transport on mules or horses."

The English medical gentleman in his suite, in a report, dated 24th September, 1854, thus speaks of the hospitals at Kars:—"The number of sick at present in the army at Kars amounts to between 500 and 600, which in an army of 28,000, suffering from the effects of recent engagements and defeats, is not extraordinary. To these, however, must be added about 2,000 of the worst cases sent to the central hospitals of Erzeroom, a large percentage of which died on the road. The hospitals are large buildings, such as khans, mosques, &c., fitted up and furnished for the reception of the sick. These places are, on the whole, and considering the resources of the country, not ill-adapted for their present service. The beds of the patients consist of a good straw mattress, and a quilt stuffed with cotton; this quilt being enveloped in a covering of calico, which could be taken off and washed when necessary. The patients are supplied with clean shirts, calico drawers, nightcaps, and bed-gowns; in short, the bedding and body linen of the patients, as far as I observed, and considering the circumstances, are unexceptionable."

The commissioner, in a despatch to the Foreign Office of the same date, speaks from his own observation of the hospital at Kars:—"The beds are comfortable, the rooms as clean as the nature of the buildings would admit of, the kitchen and offices in better order than I had been led to expect; the patients were well cared for on all those points on which a military officer can be supposed to offer an opinion." He had previously in a despatch, dated Erzeroom, September 16, 1854, spoken of the military hospital in that town in the following terms:—"I found the sick and wounded much better lodged and taken care of than I had any reason to anticipate, and all the arrangements which meet the eye of the visitor show a regard to cleanliness and comfort which is very commendable. These arrangements are principally to be attributed to the care and attention bestowed on them by Emin Bey, the chief medical officer."

A general able to show his troops, artillery, and hospitals in the condition described at the end of two unfortunate campaigns, within seven weeks of a reverse, deserved credit for administration, and—taking men as they were in that day—support. The cited condition of the hospitals of Kars and Erzeroom was far superior to that of the hospitals of the army of the Danube. The afore-quoted reports seem irreconcileable with the charges of remissness and corruption, to the prejudice of the well-being of their men, brought against Zarif Mustapha Pasha and his seconds by her Majesty's commissioner. That distinguished officer was already known in the East, but less in a military than in a civil capacity. His estimate of the Turks, formed while employed on the delimitation of the Turko-Persian frontier, was unfavourable :—the inevitable consequence of his dependence on interpreters, drawn from classes prone from infancy to exaggerate in disfavour of the ruling class, and who, when conflicting opinions respecting them are deducible, invariably deduce the least flattering. He had seen the Turks with their rayas' eyes, he had heard about them from their rayas' lips, and had passed judgment accordingly. As well might an Algerine's sketch of the French, or a Hindoo's colouring of the English, be accepted as a genuine representation.

Thus impressed, the commissioner, face to face with proud susceptible men, unconsciously passed the faint line of demarkation between counsel and dictation. Strong in his integrity, he measured the authorities in Armenia by a higher than the national standard of morality :—an unphilosophical error, which made his remonstrances on certain points appear fanciful and irrelevant to the business in hand,—as fanciful as similar utterances in Marlborough's camp in the Low Countries would have sounded ; and he fancied, in the professional jealousy excited by his visitorial character, disrespect for his position :—singular hallucination, in days when the humblest individual in French or English uniform was caressed ! He, or those in his confidence, saw concerted fraud in every transaction; and trifles light as air—as the superscription of a letter carelessly or disloyally translated — became matters of grave import. Indications of latent power are ever watched for in the East, and when detected stimulate envy and defamation. As soon as it became known that the stranger in camp, himself above law, could convey praise or censure of any one directly to the British indirectly to the Turkish Government, his quarters became the focus of attraction for jealousies and ambitions. Undercurrents of intrigue set in, of a nature to affect the discipline of a firmer body than a Turkish army. Concord between individuals, the one exacting the other impatient and both distrustful, became difficult. Both viewing one thing in different lights, neither understood the other. One accustomed to the rule and routine of British troops, saw irregularity and disorder in the organization familiar to the other. The discrepance between the number of men and of rations—indicative of peculation to one brought up in a service where they are convertible terms—resulted from rations increasing in geometrical ratio with rank, and the customary distribution of bread rations to camp-followers and others having claims on the service; and if somewhat in excess of recognized practice, it need not, under the circumstances, have been closely scrutinized. Turkish generals during the late war had difficulties to contend with, such as officers drawing their pay regularly from the British Treasury and backed by the British authorities in Turkey, were ill able to form a correct notion of. They had their enemies at Constantinople; their letters were not always answered; their demands often seemed importunate. They had no "correspondents" by their side to set them right with the public when misrepresented. The fact of a body of officers without private means remaining long in arrears of pay was of itself a grave difficulty.

On the demand of H.M.'s ambassador, based on the commissioner's representations, the Porte recalled successively the Mushir Zarif Mustapha Pasha, and the feriks, Shukri Pasha and Husseyin Pasha; replacing the first ultimately by Wassif Pasha, who promised docility. The Porte thereby impaired its dignity in the eyes of the people, who were indignant at seeing men of rank condemned unheard on the *ipse dixit* of a foreigner. The evidence adduced in support of the charge against Shukri Pasha, while temporarily in command of the army, of want of respect for the commissioner, was disproved by a curious process;* and the charges against others might, if submitted to test, have been equally discovered to rest more or less upon imperfect or malignant information. Arslan Pasha (General Bystrzonowsky)

* The commissioner sent the superscription of a letter written to him by Shukri Pasha to the Foreign Office, in proof of his charge of that officer's intentional disrespect towards him. The Foreign Office sent the superscription to the embassy at Constantinople "as an instance of the disrespect shown to Brigadier-General Williams by the Turkish military authorities," with instructions to demand Shukri Pasha's recall. The superscription being translated at the embassy and found becoming, was sent back to London with that information. The Foreign Office then placed the superscription in the hands of Mr. Redhouse, its official interpreter. Mr. Redhouse summed up a critical report thus:—"From my own knowledge and experience, derived from many years' service in Turkey, I am bound to pronounce the original superscription to be, as far as it goes, a very polite and flattering specimen of the turgid mode in which letters are there constantly addressed, since many of the terms used in it are of a class more laudatory than strict etiquette demanded. . . . The terms actually employed are, under the system in use, as polite and deferential as language can make them."

and Shahin Pasha (General Breansky) were also recalled. Kerim Pasha, afterwards much distinguished in action, was complained of, but escaped recall by timely deprecation. The Porte was unable to comply with some of the commissioner's other demands.

Turkish history afforded no precedent of an Asiatic army looking to the capital for everything,—for necessaries, expected to be drawn, as in previous wars, from local sources. Asia Minor was not a desert; it was a fertile country with many cities. The Porte, when reproached for not sending supplies vià Trebizond to Erzeroom—along 180 miles of furrowed mule track, over two mountain ranges,*—then 100 miles further on to Kars, through defiles and over plains watched more or less by the enemy's cavalry, might have answered by citing the trouble of supplying the Allies' armies before Sevastopol. Lord Stratford de Redcliffe subsequently, in a self-exculpatory despatch, expressed the difference between giving and following advice, by contrasting the facility of taking a horse to water and the difficulty of making him drink: meaning that he had urged the Porte to forward supplies to Kars, but in vain. His Excellency had better have made a plain statement of the case and trusted in it to justify both himself and the Porte. Between November, 1854, and May, 1855, the route from Trebizond to Erzeroom was passable, as a rule, only by couriers and carriers with light goods, and not always by them. Between May, 1855, and the ensuing December a Russian army lay interposed between Erzeroom and Kars.

* The route between Trebizonde and Erzeroom traverses *Hodja-Bovnar-dagh*, at an altitude of 7,800 feet above the level of the sea.

Kars was ill selected for the station of the Asiatic army. Isolated on the extreme frontier of Turkey, 900 miles from the capital, 300 miles from the nearest port, Trebizond, and 100 miles from the nearest support, Erzeroom, it was a place at once difficult to relieve and to retire from. The Russian fortress of Ghumri, relatively impregnable, lay thirty miles from it in facile communication with Tiflis, the capital of the Transcaucasian provinces. Kars was a fitting base for offensive operations. With that view the Porte had given orders, carried out under the directions of Khourshid Pasha (General Guyon), for strengthening Kars with redoubts, and had sent there seventy siege-guns, with ample supplies of ammunition. But reverses in the field and other considerations indicated, the following year, to those on the spot the prudence of razing the works and removing the cannon—conveyed there with months of toil, and invaluable in a region 6,000 feet above the sea-level—to a securer place. If taken fortified, Kars would be an advanced post to Ghumri; if taken dismantled, it would prove a barren acquisition. The council of the army, after mature deliberation recorded in a note, decided on abandoning Kars as untenable, but their decision was overruled by the commissioner, who, having shown himself in possession of influence to procure the removal of pashas in disagreement with him, was deferred to. The council, aware of imperial embarrassments and topographical obstacles, placed no reliance on the arrival of reinforcements; aware, also, of the tendencies of the Armenians and Kurds, it may have apprehended encouragement to them by the sequestration of the army. Europeans in the late war never sufficiently dwelt on the grave fact of the Porte having, whether in Europe or in Asia, an internal as well as an external enemy to occupy its thoughts; and in regard of the former, its peculiar position counselled discretion in speaking of it. The council saw in the abandonment of Kars safety for the army. The commissioner aimed at saving both the army and Kars, one by the other. An eminent writer on the art of war, discoursing on the tactics for an inferior army anxious to avoid a battle, says: "Si vous vous enfermez dans une ville, votre perte est inévitable; car en vous enfermant avec votre armée dans une ville vous ne pourrez manquer d'être assiégé, et dans peu forcé par la famine de vous rendre." We will not try the value of these divergent opinions by the result, but by the doctrine of probabilities. Were the probabilities in favour of the arrival in time of succour on the scale required? An inspection of the map and consideration of the general military position would answer that in the negative. The overland route from Scutari followed by the warrior sultans in their Persian wars had ceased to be used even by tartars: the vast posting establishment along it had disappeared; the *menzil khans* had fallen to ruin. Shorter routes from the sea coast scarcely admitted of the passage of artillery. The inhabitants of the surrounding districts, even if paid for their services, were not likely to incur risk by attempts to supply an army resigned to inaction. Every authority in Armenia had reason to know, when the occupation of Kars was decided on in expectation of reinforcements arriving before the exhaustion of its provisions, that the available Turkish troops were detained in the Crimea indefinitely; save those demanded for the Contingent whose co-operation the commissioner objected to.*

The real question at issue was not whether succour might or might not arrive in time, but whether Kars was of sufficient importance to justify incurring the slightest risk of sacrificing an army for its sake. The advocates for its occupation might colourably argue that their expectation of holding out would have been justified if the *serdari ekrem* had operated, in their opinion, energetically; but this, at the best, was relying on a remote contingency; while, on the other hand, it might be as reasonably argued that if the Russians had undertaken a siege rather than an investment Kars would probably have fallen before that general left Constantinople. The vital question, however, for consideration was this: Was there anything in Asia Minor better worth preserving than the best army in it? Kars, without redoubts and guns, was an obscure country town, of no strategic value. The strategic value formerly belonging to it had been impaired by the territorial changes effected by the Peace of Adrianople. The capture of Beyazid by the Russians, July, 1854, had

* *From General Williams to the Secretary of State for Foreign Affairs.*

[Extract.]

"Erzeroom, May 8, 1855.

"With reference to the nature and composition of the troops to be sent to co-operate with the Kars army, I feel myself justified in warning her Majesty's Government of the danger which would threaten us were that force to consist solely of the Turkish Contingent about to be formed under British officers. No sudden influence can be obtained over men by officers ignorant of their language, manners, and habits; and however gallant and good those officers are, they would not, in my opinion, be so far seconded by the Turkish soldiers as to successfully cope with Russian discipline and combination in the open field."

circumscribed it still further. Kars derived importance in the late war, not from its position, but from its becoming an entrenched camp with the bulk of the Asiatic army inside. Wherever that army might have been stationed, the Russians would not have left it far in their rear. They wanted it, not Kars. There is a mountainous ridge, Sowanly Dagh, between Kars and Erzeroom, twelve hours from the former place. By occupying its passes, strengthened by redoubts, with a few troops, the Asiatic army, in communication then with the sea and the interior, would have equally held the Russians in check. The desire to send it supplies and reinforcements in detail as the means presented themselves would not have been controlled by apprehension of their falling into the enemy's hands. At the worst, the alternative of retreat from position to position was open to them. Long marches would not have been needed. No Russian general, with the possible movements of the Allies and the Caucasians on his mind, would have gone far from his base of operations; still less have disseminated his forces by the occupation of open towns, with a Turkish army in the field.

By the end of May, 1855, the Asiatic army, less 10,000 men at Erzeroom, Kiupri-Keuy and Hassan Kaleh, was concentrated in Kars. About 15,000 infantry, well armed, 2,530 cavalry, and fourteen batteries fairly horsed, composed it. The inhabitants of Kars, used to arms, like all Turks in frontier districts, furnished, in addition, 3,000 fighting men. The passes of Sowanly Dagh were unoccupied, the depôts of provisions on the way were unguarded, the communications with Erzeroom were unassured. Therefore, from that hour, the army, dependent on its own resources, was bound to watch for and profit by opportunities given by the enemy's carelessness or presumption.

General Muravief left Ghumri about June 1, and encamped on the Arpa Tchai (barley river) to complete his organization. Whereupon the military council in Kars proposed, in accordance with the rule of war based on expediency and humanity, sending away non-combatants to neighbouring villages, or to Erzeroom. Not deluding themselves with hopes of succour, they wished to economize their provisions. Their proposition was overruled. When it was subsequently entertained in October, the inhabitants declined to expose their wives and children to the nearly certain risk then of perishing of cold on the way or falling into Cossacks' hands. General Muravief thought he saw his foe in a trap. Promising his army possession of Kars without loss, he marched from the Arpa Tchai with about 20,000 infantry, 4,000 cavalry, and ten batteries, and appeared in sight of Kars on the feast of Bairam, 1271, corresponding to June 16, 1855. His cavalry drove in the Turkish outposts and advancing within range of the artillery of the place sustained a trifling loss. Two days later he encamped four miles south of Kars. From that position he sent, June 29, one-third of his force towards the Sowanly Dagh; thus rendering his plans doubtful. The detachment found at Yeni-Keuy, a place fifty miles from Kars, six weeks' supply of biscuit, wheat, and barley for the army. It destroyed part, brought away part, and having sounded the neighbouring country, rejoined the main body: which had been left unmolested during its absence.

The example of the garrison of Kalafat under somewhat similar circumstances should have inspired the garrison of Kars with confidence to make a sortie; which might have reversed the position of the opposing armies in Armenia. General Muravief, despising the enemy, had exposed his army to be attacked in detail. The sortie from Kalafat, the most brilliant affair of the war, has been little spoken of, through the absence of Europeans. Brief mention of it, therefore, may not seem out of place here. The Russians in the winter of 1853-54 concentrated considerable forces including three regiments of cavalry at Zetate, for an attack on the entrenched camp of Kalafat. The feriks, Ahmed Pasha and Ismael Pasha, entrusted with the defence, resolved to anticipate their movement. Accordingly, at 10 P.M., January 18, 1854 (the Oriental Epiphany), they marched from Kalafat with 15,000 infantry, one regiment of cavalry, and three batteries, expecting to surprise the enemy; but their intention having transpired, they found him ready to give battle. They attacked the enemy at dawn, routed him after a struggle of five hours, and returned to Kalafat with their wounded by 7 P.M. The defeated Russians retired to Crajova, and Kalafat was never again menaced. The combination of a twelve hours' march out and home, and five hours' combat, with twenty hours' continuous exposure in the valley of the Danube in the month of January, renders this sortie a remarkable event.

Towards the end of July, General Muravief again, as it were, laid a bait to allure the garrison out. Leaving fifteen battalions of infantry, one regiment of dragoons, and two regiments of Cossacks, at Komansoor, near Kars, he marched out of sight with the remainder of his force in the direction of Erzeroom. Driving in the slender garrisons of Kiupri-Keuy and Hassan Kaleh, which rallied at the entrenched pass of Deveboyounou, his vanguard halted at Hassan Kaleh, eighteen miles from Erzeroom; alarming that city enough to make the consuls in it pack up, ready for a start to Trebizond. General Muravief, intending no more than a reconnaissance in force, to ascertain the strength of the enemy in that quarter, went no further. He carried away 100 araba-loads of grain from the public store at Kiupri-Keuy, left detachments in the passes of Sowanly Dagh, and rejoined his division before Kars in the middle of August. Tranquil then about his rear, with his communications assured, he sat down in two camps; investing Kars by detachments of cavalry and Cossacks. Tartars with despatches easily escaped their vigilance. The Russian army now consisted of twenty-eight battalions of infantry, 5,000 cavalry, and twelve batteries. General Muravief had probably received incorrect information about the amount of provisions in Kars, or had measured an Oriental by the scale of a Russian appetite. Otherwise it is presumable he would have opened trenches before that place.

The undisturbed investment of an entrenched army during months, by an army in the field numerically about one-half superior, and inferior when disjoined as spoken of, is probably unexampled. Inferiority in cavalry, in part compensated for by three battalions of expert minié-armed riflemen, seems an inadequate explanation. Of the two modes of reducing a town—by force of arms or by dint of hunger—General Muravief chose the latter, and having a choice he was liable to err; but there being only one recognized mode of opposition, the garrison had no motive for hesitation.

All writers on the art of defence recommend sorties. Sorties harass the enemy; they oblige him to keep large bodies of men under arms; they cause him the loss of good officers, always on such occasions exceptionally exposed; they sustain the spirits of the garrison, and animate their partisans outside. All favourable defences have been mainly due to sorties. Londonderry, Limerick, Gibraltar, and Jellalabad, are familiar examples to the English. The two first had, like Kars, been extemporaneously fortified, and were garrisoned by troops comparatively inferior in numbers and organization: both made sorties and saved themselves. The garrison of the last, after an investment of five months, like that of Kars, sallied out and routed the Afghan army under Mehemet Akbar Khan. The sortie from Gibraltar against the Duc de Crillon's lines is ever memorable. The garrison of Candia,—Venetians and French—often renewed, resisted the Ottomans many years: withstanding sixty-nine assaults, they made eighty-three sorties, and finally capitulated on honourable terms. Sevastopol prolonged her defence till it became famous by sorties; and the date of the day of the decision, in February, 1855, to rest the defence mainly upon systematic sorties, is annually celebrated by the surviving engineers.

The object, as stated, of holding Kars to cover Asia Minor by retaining the enemy in one position, was frustrated at the outset by the passive attitude of the garrison. For, as we have seen, half the Russian army held Kars in check, while the other half traversed the country between it and Erzeroom, and was free to march in any other direction. The shame of abandoning the inhabitants and crops of the plains between Kars and Erzeroom to the enemy had been prominently put forward as a motive for occupying the former town. Nothing was ever more completely abandoned. The letters of the English consul at Erzeroom to the Secretary of State for Foreign Affairs, in August, 1855, show that the Russians had ravaged the country to that extent that "it would be difficult to estimate the immense loss of property which had been already incurred." He described all the villages as abandoned, and the cattle left at the mercy of the Kurds, who drove them off and then burnt the houses. The protection accorded to two Kurdish chieftains, Isdinshir Bey and Manzour Bey, formed not the least curious incident of the episode of Kars. Those noted brigands, long the terror of the country, were tracked by troops sent from Bagdad in the autumn of 1854, and their escape was cut off. In this strait a messenger reached the former from the commissioner, who had been led to believe him an oppressed man, with an invitation to surrender on the faith of his word for his personal safety. The Porte confirmed the guarantee, on condition of his being brought to Constantinople for trial. Tried before the Grand Council, Isdinshir Bey was proved guilty of the death of sixty individuals slain by himself. The council in its *masbata* (decree), signed unanimously, declared that in accordance with the laws of God and man he ought also to suffer death. The Grand Vizir professed himself unable to accept this decision, out of consideration for the British Government to whom the criminal's life had been promised, and advised reconsideration of it. The criminal was then, together with his lieutenant, Manzour Bey, sentenced to imprisonment in a fortress for life.*

* Early in 1858, Isdinshir Bey and Manzour Bey escaped from Widdin and sought for refuge in Austrian territory. Failing in that, they joined the Bashi-bazouks in the Herzgovine; deserted from them; went next to Bosnasaray, were there recognized, and reimprisoned.

CHAPTER XXX.

Council of War in the Crimea—Omar's Pasha's Proposals overruled—He returns to Constantinople—His Censures of the Porte and the Allies—He undertakes the Relief of Kars—Naval and Military Resources placed at his Disposal—Honours and an Estate bestowed on him—Darkened Prospects of Kars—Proposal to retire on Erzeroom negatived—Letter from Omar Pasha—Kars to be saved by attacking Tiflis—Omar Pasha embarks for Trebizond—General Muravief resolves to storm Kars—Vigilance of General Kmety—Gallant resistance of the Garrison—Defeat of the Russians—The English Commissioner thanks General Kmety—Who, however, is passed over without Mention—Exultation at Constantinople—General Muravief re-establishes the Investment of Kars—His Position—Omar Pasha at Soukhoum Kaleh—His Plan for relieving Kars—His unaccountable Delay—Selim Pasha sent to reinforce Erzeroom—Its Garrison—Selim Pasha's Despatches—Weak State of the Garrison of Kars—It surrenders to General Muravief—His Consideration for the vanquished—Effect of the Fall of Kars—Omar Pasha roused to Action—He defeats the Enemy at Rouki—His Caution—Abundant Supplies sent to him—Efficiency of his Troops—His leisurely March—Appropriation of Spoils—Deluge of Rain—Omar Pasha retreats to Redout Kaleh—Disappointment at Constantinople—Russia accepts the Ultimatum of the Allies.

Coincidently with the investment of Kars, a council was held in the Crimea, composed of the Allies' military and naval commanders. In that council Omar Pasha requested the allied generals to sanction the departure of a portion of the Turkish troops, then in the Crimea, to reinforce the army of Asia Minor. His arguments were overruled by the supposed necessity of retaining every man in the Crimea until the fall of Sevastopol. Omar Pasha, tired of acting a subordinate part, then quitted the Crimea and arrived, unheralded, at Constantinople, 17th July, 1855. Going, in disregard of etiquette, from his ship to the imperial palace, he accused the Porte to the Sultan of negligence and incapacity in regard of military matters. He also censured the allied generals; saying they were intent on ruining Turkey, by keeping her best troops in the Crimea to no purpose; and he averred their inability to reduce Sevastopol. This irregular proceeding hushed intrigue, and increased his temporary popularity.

The people looked to him to save Kars; and he undertook the mission. All the resources of the capital were placed at his disposal. He named his officers and selected his troops. Fourteen steam and fifty sail transports were taken up in the course of the autumn to ensure his supplies. His plan of campaign was approved of by the military advisers of the Allies' ambassadors. Time was the most precious material; nevertheless he tarried more than six weeks at Constantinople, enjoying a long ovation. He was invested with the Order of the Bath by the British ambassador, in the presence of the Sultan's ministers, with extraordinary ceremonial; a guard of honour of 100 English and 500 Turkish soldiers received him in the garden of the embassy, and the English guard-ship in the Bosphorus fired a royal salute. The Sultan gave him an estate, part of the succession of Khosref Pasha,—that remarkable individual, who, originally a slave of Selim III., had traversed with increasing wealth and honours the most troubled period of Turkish history, and died in 1854 at the age of 97. The Turkish minister for foreign affairs and the English and French ambassadors spread banquets in his honour. Finally, the ministers of war and of marine were replaced by two of his friends. Secure then of support, ministerial and diplomatic, he, towards the end of August, wrote to Wassif Pasha at Kars to hold out twenty days longer, with the certainty of relief. The tenacious pasha held out four times as long.

About the date of that letter the prospects of the garrison of Kars became darkened by diminution of forage. Without horses, Kars would become, *nolens volens*, a prison. Whereupon it has been stated the military council proposed, while yet a fortnight's supply remained, the garrison being still efficient, in good health and spirits,* to dismantle the works, leave invalids with surgeons to the clemency of the enemy, and retire, fighting their way if necessary, on Erzeroom by a circuitous route, partly through a hilly district difficult for cavalry to act in. But the commander-in-chief, it is said, declined the responsibility of abandoning Kars; and the arrival of Omar Pasha's letter enabled him to reprove the council complacently for having manifested distrust in the ability of the imperial government to succour them. Soon after the arrival of that letter, forage being nearly exhausted, most of the horses were turned out of the place; and thenceforward the garrison saw no prospect of escape save in winter or in Omar Pasha's

* "The health and spirits of our troops are most satisfactory. On the part of the enemy, on the contrary, I believe much sickness to exist."—*Gen. Williams to the Secretary of State for Foreign Affairs, Sept.* 14, 1855.

movements compelling the enemy's retreat before the failure of their provisions.

On the question being discussed of the mode of succouring Kars, some proposed for the relieving army to proceed direct to Erzeroom *viâ* Trebizond. The enemy would then be placed between two fires. But the seraskir and Omar Pasha said, "From Trebizond to Erzeroom the movement would be of long duration, and difficult, from the distance and the mountainous nature of the country; which is only traversed by mule roads, rendering the passage of artillery a work of great labour and of slow process." They decided in preference on the invasion of Georgia, in expectation of inducing thereby General Muravief to retreat, to cover that important province. This plan found favour with the Porte and the diplomatic circle. It especially pleased the Turks. Turks love the figurative. Omar Pasha, they said, will strike the serpent's head at its tail: Tiflis is the tail, and when he touches it the head before Kars will recoil.

With this avowed object, Omar Pasha embarked at Constantinople in a Turkish war steamer, September 1, 1855. Desirous of conferring with the allied generals, he proceeded, after a detour, to Kamiesh, and arrived there in time to co-operate, if he had pleased, in the fall of Sevastopol. He declined the honour. Forbidding the Turkish troops before Sevastopol to take part in the assault designed for the following day (the failure of which he predicted in a letter to Constantinople), he re-embarked on the 7th September, and steamed for Trebizond. Thence, after making hospital arrangements, he steamed on the 21st to Batoom and Redout Kaleh, to meet the division of his army coming from

Roumelia. The other division, completed with picked men from the regiments at Eupatoria, having been detained three weeks in the Crimea after the fall of the Malakof, reached their destination later.

General Muravief, on hearing of Omar Pasha's arrival on the eastern coast of the Black Sea, and soon afterwards of the fall of Sevastopol, which would leave the Allies free to send part of their troops to Asia Minor, knowing how much there was for an enterprising general to accomplish, felt his confidence shaken in his position before Kars and alarmed about the exposure of Georgia to invasion. Foregoing, therefore, his intention to win Kars by patience, yet loth to relinquish a prize on which depended Russia's prestige in Central Asia, he resolved as a desperate resource to try and carry the place by storm, then fall back on the menaced line. Accordingly, late in the evening of September 28, he summoned his divisional generals to his tent, and informed them of his resolve. Soon after midnight his troops left their camp and marched on Kars in three columns, the main object of their attack being the Tachmasp heights, the outwork and bulwark of Kars. Those heights were trenched and counter-trenched: resolute troops occupied them; the artillerymen were skilful; and Ismael Pasha (General Kmety) in command of them had seen much and varied service.

General Kmety's practised ear detected the distant measured tread of advancing troops. He sent word thereof to the town, and made due preparations to receive the enemy. His vigilance had saved the heights from a surprise. Disclosed by the moonlight, and exposed to a fire of shot and grape during the extent of the range of the Turkish guns, the Russians came on with cheers, rushed up the ascent, penetrated the outer line of defence, and were then checked by well-posted riflemen in interior redoubts. Exposed to a cross-fire of grape and musketry, they fell like game in a battue. Foiled in their principal assault, their subsidiary attack on the *Ingliz tabias,* chiefly manned by Karslees and Lazistan irregulars, was momentarily successful. They carried them; but were driven out again at the point of the bayonet by reinforcements, gallantly led by Captain Thompson, sent by the commander-in-chief from the camp. The battle remained long undecided; the daring of the assailants taxing severely the resolution of the defenders. Officers and men on both sides, animated by their respective leader's example, vied with each other in courage and devotion; and among the brave on the side of the defence, Kerim Pasha, Hussein Bey, and Lieutenant Teasdale, were observed. After a desperate struggle of seven hours, the Russians, bewildered, their leaders killed, fled in disorder, leaving 6,000 slain and some hundreds of wounded on the field of battle. The Turkish loss was insignificant by comparison; 362 killed and 631 wounded. The remnant of the assaulting columns rallied under cover of their cavalry, mournful spectators of the fray.

General Muravief's feelings at that moment may be easier imagined than depicted. All the possible consequences of his rash impulsive act must have rushed like arrows through his brain. There he stood with a shattered army, the fortress he was bent on taking intact before him, its defenders refreshed by victory, and the élite of the Turkish armies gathering in his rear.

After a pause, the Russians retired to their original position at Tchivilli; except a body of 3,000 men which halted at Ainali, one hour and a half distance from Kars, and four hours' distance from the main encampment. The garrison, by making a sortie the ensuing night against the detached force at Ainali would, in the opinion of a competent witness, have achieved further important success. "The least result of its dispersal," quoting the words of General Kmety, "would have been the impossibility of the enemy continuing the investment—shutting the garrison within a circumference of ten hours' march."

The omission of mention of Ismael Pasha (General Kmety) in the despatches addressed respectively to the British and Turkish Governments, announcing the battle of the 29th September, 1855, is noticeable. This omission was not the result of ignorance of that officer's services. After the retreat of the Russians her Majesty's commissioner repaired to the field of battle, and thus, it is said, addressed him:—"General Kmety, I thank you in the name of the Queen of England for your gallantry and exertions on this day." Corresponding mention of him in his despatch,* written the same evening, would have seemed becoming.

* General Williams, on the 29th of September, wrote a despatch to the Secretary of State for Foreign Affairs about the battle of Kars, in which no mention of or allusion to General Kmety is made. On the 30th of September he wrote a second despatch, with equal reserve in regard of General Kmety. Those two despatches, which left Kars on September 30, formed European public opinion on the subject. No one could deduce from them the existence even of General Kmety, the chief actor in the battle. On October 3rd General Williams wrote a third despatch, containing a detailed account of the battle, in which General Kmety's name appears with the names of others, but not prominently.

The news of the battle reached Constantinople a fortnight later, and excited rapturous exultation among all classes. Viewing the number of the enemy interred by the garrison, the Russian army was considered as good as annihilated, and Kars relieved by its own efforts. Honours and rewards liberally showered on the principal persons excepting General Kmety,* who, not having been mentioned in despatches, was not officially meritorious, showed the Porte's sense of the importance of the event, seemingly calculated to make a salutary impression on the Kurds and Armenians. The people, usually chary, were profuse of praise. They viewed the battle as their own, and they were justly proud of it. Depressed as they had been by the previous successes of the Russians in Asia, cradle of their power, they were now equally elated by the converse. Expecting the garrisons of Kars and Erzeroom to assume the offensive, and Omar Pasha to advance triumphantly, the Porte and people reckoned on a Turkish army wintering at Tiflis; and any one who ventured to hint a doubt thereon had no chance of being listened to for ten days.

The evening of the battle, General Muravief called in his circumlying cavalry outposts. Kars remained, in consequence, open during thirty-six hours, joyfully anticipating the retreat of the enemy altogether; of which he gave signs by sending away matériel and heavy baggage to Ghumri next day. But on receiving intel-

* General Kmety received promotion to the rank of ferik on his return to Constantinople, four months later. General Kmety, with his health enfeebled by his exertions in the war, passed the last two years of his life in England, and died in London in the month of April, 1865. His remains were interred in the Kensal Green Cemetery and a monument erected over them at the expense of the Turkish Government.

ligence of vacillation in Omar Pasha's movements, of indications of Soukhoum Kaleh becoming his base of operations, General Muravief re-established the investment; and maintained it, with diminished forces, regardless of Erzeroom in his rear and of the enemy on the Mingrelian shore.

Seldom, if ever, has a general been placed in a more arduous position, and one involving graver responsibility. It called for the highest faculty of generalship,—the faculty of estimating the military effects of time and distance, and of reading an opponent's plan of a campaign. Menacing at Redout Kaleh, Omar Pasha's presence at Soukhoum Kaleh would be comparatively innocuous. From Redout Kaleh his march to Kutais must have been viewed by Muravief as an affair of a few days; and even if, satisfied with an admirable base for a campaign in the ensuing spring, he had halted there, the apprehension of his advancing on the high-road to Tiflis would have sufficed to relieve Kars. Tranquillized on that account, Muravief prepared to hut his army.

The news of the battle of Kars found Omar Pasha, not according to his programme, at Kutais, but far away at Soukhoum Kaleh, disporting himself more like a young sultan after victory than a veteran at the commencement of a campaign. His motive for going there, whatever it was, involved self-contradiction. His avowed object before leaving Constantinople had been to relieve Kars strategically by the invasion of Georgia. He had stated the impossibility of relieving it in any other way, because "seeing that the roads are extremely bad, his army, with its artillery and munitions complete, would hardly reach Erzeroom (from Trebizond) in three or four months." On the other hand, "the road which leads straight from Redout Kaleh to Kutais is perfectly level and easy. The goodness of the road is favourable to the transport of artillery and munitions, and the march of a large army by this road will be rapid and free from difficulty." Such were the arguments brought forward to induce general concurrence with his plan for relieving Kars by threatening Tiflis. "This (the Turkish) army will be in the rear of the Russian army, and will march straight on Tiflis, which is the very soul of the Russians in the Caucasus; as soon as it has advanced a little, the Russians will evidently be obliged to abandon Kars and fly to the defence of Tiflis and Suram."

The first stage to Tiflis was Kutais (Colchis), twenty leagues distant from Redout Kaleh, with water communication nearly parallel the greater part of the way. The stream up which the *Argo* had rowed 3,000 year before, flowed sufficiently deep for the light steamers and boats of the flotilla on the coast. Redout Kaleh was the precise spot for commencing the campaign at. Troops had been stationed there and in the neighbourhood during eighteen months, in anticipation of Transcaucasian operations. The bare fact of Omar Pasha's presence there urged General Muravief to an act of desperation, which cost him half his infantry and rescued the garrison of Kars from the ignoble fate of being starved out without a redeeming feat of arms to excite public sympathy on their behalf.

Omar Pasha's delay at Soukhoum Kaleh was variously commented upon at Constantinople. His partisans fancied some deep design in it. His rivals hinted at treason. The public, still exulting for the battle of

Kars, gave little heed to it: ignorant moreover of localities, they were unable to estimate the gravity of the error. No pasha, probably, since the Vizir seduced by Catherine's jewels and promises on the Pruth, had unwittingly done Russia a greater service than Omar Pasha rendered her by deviating more that a hundred miles from the projected scene of operations, in a country where distance is measured by natural impediments, at a conjuncture when every hour was precious.

The Porte—finding Omar Pasha tranquil by the seaside, as though under the influence of a charm, and General Muravief abiding before Kars as though he had won, not lost, a battle—sent Selim Pasha with a battalion of the guards to reinforce the garrison of Erzeroom, *for its defence;* not, as has been pretended, to try and throw supplies into Kars. Had Selim Pasha attempted its relief, as certain enthusiastic parties expected of him, he would have lost both his troops and Erzeroom. This statement is due to a traduced officer. The problem was to send provisions for 30,000 mouths eight or ten day's march over devastated plains. Two thousand horses or mules would barely have carried a week's consumption. Where were those animals with drivers to be found? If found, how were they to feed and be sheltered at night on the road? Who was to escort them? The enemy must first have been driven from his intermediate positions and then defeated before Kars. The Turkish minister for foreign affairs, in a despatch to the British ambassador, had stated that, in the opinion of the Porte and of Omar Pasha, "to save Kars a force is required at least equal to the besieging army."

The garrison of Erzeroom, in November, 1855, consisted of about 1,000 cavalry, little better than Bashi-bazouks, four or five batteries indifferently horsed, and about 8,000 infantry. With this slender force, Selim Pasha has been censured officially and officiously by military men and civilians then at Erzeroom, for having declined to march to the relief of Kars in its agony, in the face of an enemy whom the garrison with undiminished health and strength had declined to encounter in the field. Had Selim Pasha, yielding to their importunities, undertaken such a quixotic expedition, Russia would have come to the conference of Paris with Erzeroom, as well as Kars, in her hands; with every gun and every regiment of the Asiatic army in her possession, and with the passes to the coast between Trebizond and Sampsoon in her occupation.

Selim Pasha has also been bitterly censured in a work called *The Siege of Kars*, for having by his "mendacious despatches" encouraged the garrison of Kars "to hold out to the utmost limits of human endurance;" but for which "they would, acting on a favourite idea of General Williams, have cut their way through the enemy while their strength allowed them to march." Whatever may have been the tenor of Selim Pasha's despatches, they ought not to have been deceptive. The pashas in Kars had means of knowing—did presumedly know (one of them being in direct communication with the English consul and staff officers at Erzeroom,) to a man and horse the force in that city; they knew the nature of the country, and were as well able as Selim Pasha to read Omar Pasha's strategy. It might have been judicious, while a few days' provisions remained, to have disabled the artillery in Kars, and have retired under cover of darkness in a direction away from the hostile camp; but it is presuming too much on credulity to expect any one to credit an emaciated army of infantry and dismounted cavalry—even if confident of being as well led as the Ten Thousand on their retreat over the same ground—with the idea of cutting their way through an enemy who had tranquilly invested them in their best days, undeterred from continuing the investment by one of the bloodiest repulses on record.

When succour was no longer calculated on, and when no military object was obtainable, the policy became questionable of prolonging a passive resistance, at the cost of women and children dying hourly of hunger, and daily executions of poor wretches, miscalled deserters, for endeavours to escape from starvation; until the garrison being on the verge of inanition, no choice remained but surrender nearly at discretion, with the works and matériel intact,—with seventy position guns, eighty-four field-pieces, and 24,000 stand of arms, including several thousand minié rifles which were turned afterwards in Russian hands against the Circassians; thus giving General Muravief a solid triumph, a triumph enhanced by his previous failure, and adorned by his consideration for the vanquished. His first act was sending provisions to the starving population of Kars: not an hour too soon. In nearly every house his commissaries found corpses; in one as many as eight. The position guns dragged to Ghumri, the field batteries driven to Tiflis, there parked in the square, and several thousand prisoners marched by detachments at intervals to Odessa, announced victory in more stirring terms than a gazette to the Caucasus and New Russia.

On the news of the fall of Kars transpiring in Persia, the Shah sent troops and munitions of war to the frontier of Bagdad.

Omar Pasha at length roused himself. Re-embarking with part of his infantry at Soukhoum Kaleh, he relanded at Tchamshirah, forty miles to the southwards; the remainder of the army proceeding there by land. He had lost a month. From Tchamshirah he marched coastwise to the Entischai, crossed that river, and then advanced inland with thirty-two battalions of infantry, four battalions of rifles, 1,200 cavalry, and forty guns; leaving 10,000 men to guard his depôts of provisions at various places. On the 4th November, 1855, he reached the Ingour at the ford of Rouki, five leagues from its mouth. He there first saw the enemy—nine battalions of infantry—posted on the left bank of the river, with field-guns in position. At noon of the 5th, fire opened on them from counter batteries established in the night, and with their attention thus occupied, troops, detached upwards and downwards, crossed the river at two other fords. Attacked on both flanks, the enemy gave way after a stout resistance, and retreated into the forest, leaving three guns and near 400 men on the field of battle. The Turkish loss was numerically trifling, but it included a promising young officer, Captain Dymoke, serving as aide-de-camp to Colonel Simmons, R.E.; who, with Colonel Ballard, an Indian officer in command of a rifle regiment, bore a prominent part in the action.

Now came into high relief Omar Pasha's characteristic quality—caution. He had still time, the serene autumnal weather of those regions being unusually prolonged in 1855, to make up in part for delay. The prisoners reported the Russians nowhere in force, the Mingrelians, though unfriendly, passive, and the country unorganized for defence by the process of devastation. He had only to advance. He could not have indirectly relieved Kars: the time for that had gone by; but he might have reached Kutais, the occupation of which would have enabled the Porte to style itself in possession of Imeritia, Mingrelia, and Gouriel (a fair set-off for the pashalik of Kars), and have given his troops comfortable winter quarters in the barracks and khans of that town, ready for further operations in spring. The zeal of his friends, the Seraskir and the Capitan Pasha, had sent him four months' provisions, winter clothing, 100,000*l.* in gold, and two light steamers for the navigation of the Phasis. The English Government had provided him a hospital staff in its pay. Too often in the East administration sacrifices a general: this time the general failed the administration. Twenty leagues separated Rouki on the Ingour from the corresponding ford of the Tchanniskal, and Kutais lay seven leagues farther; in all, a week's easy march for his troops.

Omar Pasha had under his command troops willing to march for a week on a few biscuits a day, seasoned with olives, and aided by gatherings on the road—troops able to dig entrenchments, cook their food, wash their linen, make shoes, and saddle-girths from hides, take care of their horses, and construct huts with branches and boughs of trees. Overlooking their essential qualities, he encumbered them with baggage, and made his advance conditional on the formation of depôts of provisions. Leaving the Ingour on the 7th November, he marched a few miles to Sugdidi, the capital of Mingrelia, already abandoned by its inhabitants and the Russians. He reposed there several days. He admired the Princess Dadian's palace ; and, partially relaxing his order to respect property, transferred from it to his own and friends' konaks, costly furniture, rare exotics, and carriages. The captains of the Turkish steamers which carried these trophies to Constantinople said, " Aib dir " (It is a shame). His next stage was Tachlis, on the Sieva. In that pleasant spot he halted several days to allow time to accumulate provisions ; and continuing his march thence at an episcopal pace, his advanced guard reached, on the 21st of November, the Tchanniskal, a tributary of the Phasis, the boundary between Mingrelia and Imeritia, at a point six leagues from Kutais. As far as the confluence of those rivers, perhaps some way up the former, provisions and stores might have been conveyed to meet him.

Simultaneously with his arrival on the Tchanniskal, the apprehended rain began to fall, to fall diluvially, as customary in those regions at that season. The stream lazily flowing knee-deep in the morning, became a heady torrent by night ; and in a few days the plain over which his guns might have trotted lightly was converted into a swamp. In this strait, with an unfordable river in front and a spreading morass in the rear, he received the intelligence of the fall of Kars. Deeming then all motive for perseverance over, and fearing to compromise the subsistence of his army by longer delay, he retreated, and led it in four days to Hopi, on a small navigable stream, fifteen miles north-east of Redout Kaleh. He encamped the bulk of his forces there, fixing his own head-quarters at Redout Kaleh. Sickness breaking out among his troops, by their exposure to wet and cold, sent many of them to hospital at Soukhoum Kaleh and Trebizond.

The news of the fall of Kars and the failure of the Mingrelian expedition reached Constantinople together, and created a painful sensation; for the public had just been reading hopefully in the Gazette the roseate despatch for the passage of the Ingour. All, impressed with grief and disappointment, seemed instinctively to feel the connection between the discredit of the campaign and the absence of zeal, and, but for the diplomatic cloak thrown round him, the Porte would, probably, in deference to the public sentiment, have invited the serdari ekrem to Constantinople to explain his reasons for having converted a four days' direct march from Redout Kaleh to the Tchanniskal into a six weeks' circuit by Soukhoum Kaleh and Sugdidi; which had rendered unavailing the devotion of the garrison and inhabitants of Kars, and had saved Russia from a damaging blow in her vulnerable quarter. The Porte—well entitled to say, "save me from my friends," — behaved with dignity. Bowing to the decree of Fate, it uttered no lamentations, expressed no vindictiveness; but alarmed about Erzeroom, it directed troops to proceed to that city from Eupatoria, and the gradual transfer of the army in Mingrelia to Trebizond, in preparation for a campaign in Asia Minor the ensuing spring.

Such was the position of affairs, gloomy for Turkey,

when the telegraph electrified the public of Constantinople, January 7th, 1856, by the announcement of Russia's acceptance of the Allies' ultimatum as interpreted by Austria. The announcement fell on the sarafs and speculators of Galata like a live shell among a company of gamesters.

THE END.

APPENDIX I.

Constantinople,
EXCELLENCE, *Mars* 22—*Avril* 1, 1854.

Je me permets la liberté de soumettre à votre jugement éclairé quelques idées sur l'emploi de la flotte Ottomane lors de sa prochaine sortie dans la Mer Noire, laquelle, soit dit en parenthèse, à cause de la ténuité des vêtements des matelots et de l'inexperience de la plupart des équipages, soit officiers soit matelots, doit être différée jusqu'à ce que le temps s'adoucit, ce que l'on pourra attendre dans une quinzaine de jours.

Vu la position de la flotte Anglo-Française dans les eaux de Kavarna, d'où elle veille les côtes de la Roumélie, et est à même d'observer les mouvements de la flotte Russe à Sévastopol, il serait, il me semble, inutile que la flotte Ottomane aille de ce côtè là. Elle saurait être mieux occupée ailleurs pour la cause commune.

Il y'a en outre une considération toute particulière qui mérite attention : c'est que la flotte ayant peu navigué depuis douze ans, elle pourrait faire mauvaise figure en allant se joindre à la flotte Alliée, sans avoir fait préalablement un court voyage. Par conséquent, s'il n'existe pas des raisons majeures contre, je suis d'avis que la flotte, en sortant du Bosphore avec un vent du midi, doive aller directment à Sinope. Elle devrait y rester quelques jours pour compléter son eau et pour remédier les défauts de grément et d'autres que le voyage aura immanquablement fait ressortir. Elle y aurait des facilités pour voir à l'armement et au conditionnement de ses embarcations à fin de pouvoir sans confusion débarquer, en cas de besoin, une partie de ses équipages pour coopérer avec les troupes de terre quelque part : s'approfitant de l'occasion, elle pourrait faire un exercise du tir de canon au blanc, et faire descendre ses équipages à terre pour les habituer au maniement de leurs fusils. Il pourrait se faire que dix au quinze jours seraient avantageusement écoulés dans cette manière là ; de plus, la santé des équipages, engourdis par un long ennuyant séjour a bord dans le Bosphore, s'ameliorerait.

Partant de Sinope, la flotte devrait alonger la côte de l'Anatolie jusqu'à Trebizonde, touchant en route, si l'on veut, à Sampsoon. Partout elle inspirerait de l'orgueil et de la confiance parmi les habitants des côtes. De Trebizonde elle se dirigerait à Batoom et à Tchuruksu, et se mettant en communication là avec les autorités militaires, ferait ce qui bon semblerait pour le service de la Sublime Porte. L'occupation de Sokhoum Kaleh nous serait d'une grande avantage. Ensuite la flotte naviguerait le long de la côte de l'Abazie jusqu'à Anapa, avec le but de s'emparer des forts (ou les détruire) que les Russes auront pu y garder, et d'encourager et d'aider les braves Circassiens, leur donnant des munitions de guerre et même des pièces de campagne avec des artilleurs. Ensuite elle côtoyerait la rive méridionale de la Crimée, à fin de faire des observations nécessaires et d'inspirer par la vue de son pavillon des sentiments convenables dans la population Tartare de la presqu'île.

Terminé ce petit course, la flotte irait sans ordre contraire rallier la flotte Alliée dans les parages où elle se trouverait.

Si dans cette intervalle une forte division de la flotte Russe sortât inapperçue de la flotte Alliée, la flotte Ottomane saurait bien, il faut espérer, y tenir tête.

Celle-ci n'est qu'une esquisse: si l'on en adopte le principe, la sagesse de votre Excellence y saurait faire les développements opportuns.

J'ai l'honneur d'être, &c.

(Signed) Mushaver.

À son Excellence Mehemet Pasha,

Grand Amiral de la Flotte Ottomane.

[Translation.]

Excellency, *March* 22—*April* 1, 1854.

I take the liberty of submitting to your enlightened judgment a few considerations as to the employment of the Ottoman fleet, on the occasion of its next cruise in the Black Sea, which (I would observe parenthetically) had better be deferred until the weather becomes more favourable, on account of the thin clothing of the crews and the inexperience of both officers and seamen. It is presumable that such a change in the weather may be expected in about a fortnight.

Considering the position taken up by the Anglo-French fleets in the waters of Kavarna, from which they can protect the coasts of Roumelia, and at the same time watch the movements of the Russian fleet at Sevastopol, I believe that it would be useless to send the Ottoman fleet in that direction, and that our ships might be better employed for the common good elsewhere.

There is, too, another point especially deserving attention. Our fleet having been but little at sea for the last twelve years, might possibly cut a bad figure were it at once to join the allied fleets, without having made a short preliminary cruise; I am therefore of opinion, if no reason to the contrary exists, that, sailing out of the Bosphorus with a southerly wind, we should steer direct for Sinope, and should remain there a few days to fill up our water and to repair any defects that may be discovered during the voyage thither. We should thus have an opportunity of seeing to the armament and to the fitting of our boats, so as to be able to land a portion of our crews without confusion, should it be necessary for them to co-operate with our forces on shore; we could also take the opportunity of practising with ball-cartridge, and could land and drill our crews.

A fortnight might be advantageously spent in this manner, and the health of the men, deteriorated by a long and tedious confinement on board ship in the Bosphorus, would certainly gain by the delay.

On leaving Sinope our fleet might coast along Anatolia as far as Trebizond, anchoring, if necessary, at Sampsoon. Its appearance would inspire confidence and pride amongst the population of the coast. From Trebizond it might proceed to Batoom and Tchuruksou, and placing itself in communication with the military authorities in those places, act as might seem best for the service of the Sublime Porte. The occupation of Soukhoum Kaleh would be very advantageous to us. The fleet might then hug the coast of Abasia, as far as Anapa, in order to obtain possession of or destroy any forts still in the hands of the Russians, and encourage and assist the brave Circassians by supplying them with munitions of war, and even with field-pieces and artillerymen to work them. It might then sail along the southern coast of the Crimea, collecting such information as might be useful, and inspiring, by the sight of its flag, loyal sentiments amongst the Tartar population of the peninsula.

At the close of this short cruise our fleet might join the allied fleets wherever they might happen to be, unless orders to the contrary were received by it. And if, during this interval, a strong division of the Russian fleet should escape to sea, unobserved by the allied fleets, it is to be hoped that the Ottoman fleet would be able to give a good account of it.

This is merely a sketch; should your Excellency adopt the principle of it, you will doubtless be able in your wisdom to fill up the outline which I have taken the liberty to submit to you.

I have the honour to remain, &c.

(Signed) MUSHAVER.

APPENDIX II.

EXCELLENCE, *Kavarna*, — *Mai*, 1854.

J'ai l'honneur de vous annoncer que d'après les ordres de mon Gouvernement la flotte Ottomane et la division Egyptienne a faite voile le 6 Mai pour la Mer Noire, avec ordre d'aller rejoindre les flottes Alliées, même devant Sévastopol, conférer avec leurs Excellences les Amiraux qui les commandent, et après s'être mis d'accord avec leurs Excellences, se rendre sur la côte de la Circassie, pour y débarquer S. E. Sefer Pacha, Behchet Pacha, quelques autres chefs des tribus Circassiennes, envoyés en mission en Circassie par la S. Porte, et y débarquer en même temps les munitions de guerre que mon Gouvernement a fait embarquer sur la flotte. Sefer Pacha et Behchet Pacha, chefs de tribus Circassiennes, et des personnes d'influence dans leur pays, parmi lesquelles se trouve l'envoyé de Scheik Shamyl près la Sublime Porte, accompagnés d'environ trois cents personnes, sont attendus par leurs compatriotes, avec lesquels ils ont été en correspondance. Le débarquement sur la côte de la Circassie de ces personnages, avec six canons tout montés, 7,000 fusils, 2,000 sabres, 500 barils de la poudre à canon, 500 caisses contenant des cartouches, 10,000 balles de plomb, une quantité des pierres à feu, 10,000 okes de plomb, 15,000 okes de sel, etc. etc., sera d'une grande utilité, soit pour l'armée de l'Anatolie soit pour la Circassie elle-même. C'est dans ce but aussi que mon Gouvernement, après en avoir fait part aux representants des puissances d'Occident, s'est décidé de faire cette expedition. Pendant que j'était en route, au large de Kalaghria, pour rejoindre votre Excellence, le consul Anglais à Varna m'a fait parvenir le 9 Mai la lettre que votre Excellence m'a fait l'honneur de m'adresser sous la date du 5 courant : lettre qui m'a mis dans l'embarras, parcequ'elle a mis mon ardent désir d'agir en tout de concert avec leurs Excellences les Amiraux en opposition avec les ordres que j'avais reçus d'aller trouver les flottes Alliés même devant Sévastopol, pour m'entendre avec leur Excellences sur la manière a faire le débarquement surindiqué. C'est dans cette circonstance que l'idée m'est venu d'envoyer auprès de leurs Excellences les Amiraux un officier supérieur qui possède ma confiance et qui m'a paru pouvoir faire plasir à votre Excellence. Après avoir conféré avec Hassan Pacha, le commandant de l'escadre Egyptienne, nous avons jugé convenable de vous députer Mushaver Pacha, pour exposer à leurs Excellences les Amiraux la position dans laquelle se trouvait la flotte Ottomane, à cause des personnages et des munitions destinés pour la côte de la Circassie. Mushaver Pacha, à son retour, m'a remis une lettre portant la date du 13 Mai, par laquelle votre Excellence me fait savoir qu'elle aurait mieux aimé que je m'adressasse à votre Excellence par écrit; en outre, Mushaver Pacha m'a dit que votre Excellence avait l'intention, si les batiments absens arrivaient à temps, de faire voile le 15 Mai pour venir a Baltchik, et que votre Excellence désirait que la flotte Ottomane mouillat at Kavarna, pour laisser libre le mouillage de Baltchik. Prêt à être agréable a votre Excellence dans tout ce que depend de moi, j'ai abandonné mon intention d'aller a Baltchik, et je viens mouiller à Kavarna pour attendre votre arrivée à Baltchik.

Je prie votre Excellence de vouloir bien communiquer la presente lettre à S. E. l'Amiral Hamelin, et de la considerer comme si elle était aussi adressee à son Excellence.

Je saisis cette occasion pour renouveller à votre Excellence les sentimens de la haute consideration avec laquelle j'ai l'honneur d'être,

Monsieur l'Amiral,

Votre très-humble et très-obeissant serviteur,

(Signed) ACHMET.

A son Excellence Monsieur le Vice-Amiral Dundas,
Comm. en Chef de l'Escadre Anglaise en Orient.

[TRANSLATION.]

EXCELLENCY,

I have the honour to inform you that, acting under instructions from my Government, the Ottoman fleet and the Egyptian division sailed on the 6th of May for the Black Sea, with orders to join the allied fleets, even if they should be before Sevastopol, confer with the admirals in command of them, and after having come to an understanding with their Excellencies, proceed to the coast of Circassia, to land there their Excellencies Sefer Pacha, Behchet Pacha, and other Circassian chiefs, disembarking at the same time a quantity of munitions of war which had been shipped by my Government on board the fleet.

Sefer Pacha, Behchet Pacha, chiefs of Circassian tribes, and other influential persons belonging to that country—amongst others the *envoyé* of Sheik Schamyl to the Sublime Porte—accompanied by about three hundred followers, are expected by their countrymen, with whom they have been in correspondence.

The disembarkation of these personages on the Circassian coast, with six guns complete, 7,000 muskets, 2,000 sabres, 500 barrels of powder, 500 cases of cartridges, 10,000 bullets, 10,000 okes of lead, 15,000 okes of salt, a quantity of flints, &c. &c., will be of immense service both to the army of Anatolia and to Circassia itself; a consideration which induced my Government, after having communicated with the representatives of the Western Powers, to undertake this expedition. Whilst I was at sea off Kalaghria on my way to join your Excellency, the English consul at Varna forwarded to me, on the 9th of May, the letter which your Excellency did me the honour of writing to me on the 5th instant: a letter which embarrassed me considerably, inasmuch as it placed my earnest desire to act in all things in concert with the admirals of the allied fleets in antagonism with the orders I had received to seek out their Excellencies even before Sevastopol, and to consult with them as to the best means of effecting the disembarkation of the men and munitions of war to which I have adverted.

It occurred to me in this difficulty to send to their Excellencies an officer of high rank, who possesses my confidence, and who seemed to me likely to be agreeable to them. After having consulted with Hassan Pasha, the officer in command of the Egyptian squadron, we thought it right to depute to you Mushaver Pasha, to explain to your Excellencies the position in which the Ottoman and Egyptian fleets are placed, by reason of the persons and the munitions of war destined for the coast of Circassia on board of them. Mushaver Pasha, on his return, handed me a letter dated May 13, in which your Excellency informs me that you would have preferred that I should have addressed myself to your Excellency in writing; Mushaver Pasha tells me, moreover, that your Excellency purposed, if the detached ships rejoined you in time, to sail on the 15th of May for Baltchik, and that your Excellency desired that the Ottoman fleet should anchor at Kavarna in order to leave the anchorage at Baltchik free.

Wishing to act as far as I can in all points in the way most agreeable to your Excellency, I have abandoned my design of going to Baltchik, and have anchored at Kavarna, where I shall await your arrival at Baltchik.

I beg your Excellency to communicate this letter to Admiral Hamelin, and to consider it as addressed also to his Excellency.

I take this opportunity of renewing to your Excellency the expression of the sentiments of high consideration with which I have the honour to be your Excellency's most humble and obedient servant,

(Signed) ACHMET.

To his Excellency Vice-Admiral Dundas,
Commander-in-Chief of the British Squadron in the East.

GLOSSARY.

AGA	An inferior title.
AIB DIR	It is a shame.
AIYAK-DIVAN	A mass meeting.
ALLAH KERIM	God is bountiful
AMAN	Pardon
ANGARIA	Forced labour (corvée)
ARABA	Waggon; any wheeled vehicle.
ARABADGI	A waggon or carriage-driver.
BACKSHISH	A present.
BAGNIO	Convicts' prison at Constantinople
BAIRAM	Feast of three days after the ramazan.
BAKALUM	Let us see
BASH-HODJA	A chief teacher, a purser in a ship
BASHI-BOZOUK	Irregular soldiers.
BASHREIS	Boatswain
BEEAT	Act of submission to the Sultan.
BENDT	Reservoir
BOSH LAKERDEH	Empty words, tall talk
BOSTANDGIS	Ancient seraglio guard (literally gardeners)
BOUYOUROULTOU	A vizir's order for safe conduct
CAABA	Ancient temple at Mecca.
CADI	A police magistrate; inferior judge
CAIK	A skiff
CALPAC	An ancient head dress.
CAPITANA BEY	Rear-admiral (not used now).
CAPITAN PASHA	Lord High Admiral
CAVEDGI	Coffee-house keeper.
CAZI-ASKER	Lord Chief Justice.
CODJA-BASHI	Chief of a rural municipality
COURBAN-BAIRAM	Feast of the Sacrifice.
DAMAD	Son-in-law (as used in the text of the Sultan).
DEFTERDAR	Accountant, paymaster.
DERBENT AGA	A chief of rural police
DERÉ-BEYS	Ancient Turkish feudal nobles
DIVAN-EFENDISI	Chief of a correspondence department
DICH PARASI	Teeth money.
DIRRHEM	Unit of weight.
DJIN	A spirit.
DJENABLERI	Excellency.
DJEBEDGIS	Ammunition guardians
DRAGOMAN	An interpreter

Efendi	An educated man; a gentleman; the title of the princes of the blood.
Eltchee	An ambassador.
Evcaf naziri	Minister of pious and charitable endowments.
Eshek	An ass.
Eski adet	Old custom.
Esnan	A class of militia.
Etmeidan	Meat-market.
Ezzan	Summons to prayers.
Fakir	A religious mendicant.
Fanar	Greek quarter at Constantinople.
Ferik	A lieutenant-general, or vice-admiral.
Fetwah	A decree of the Sheick Islam.
Firman	An imperial document.
Galiongi	Ancient man-of-war's man.
Ghazi	Victorious.
Ghioksou	"Sweet waters" of Asia.
Hegira	Commencement of the Moslem era.
Hadis	Oral sayings of Mohammed.
Harem Skellesi	A landing-place at Scutari.
Hæteria	Greek propagandist society.
Hashmetly	Magnificent.
Hatti-sherif	An imperial emanation of grace.
Hazretleri	Highness.
Hekim	A physician.
Hirka	Wadded vest.
Hunkiar Iskellessy	The "Royal Stairs" opposite Therapia.
Iani-umoumié	General contribution.
Imam	A parish priest; an army or navy chaplain.
Imaret	A refectory for theological students; soup kitchen.
Inshallah	Please God.
Jerreed	A blunt lance (for sport).
Kadaif	A favourite sweet dish.
Kalem	Public office.
Kapougi bashi	An honorary title given indiscriminately to civilians of ordinary degree.
Kapou Kiaya	Political agent at the Porte of a feudal vassal, or of a provincial governor.
Kesh-Kesh	Pounded wheat boiled.
Khademes	Royal domestics.
Kharatch / Kharadj	Graduated poll-tax on non-Mahommedan male subjects of the Porte (abolished in 1856).
Khismet	Fate.
Kief	Dreamy repose.
Kiathané	"Sweet waters" of Europe.
Kiatib	Scribe; government clerk.
Kiaya	Steward.
Kiosk	Summer-house.
Kislar aga	Chief of the black eunuchs.
Konak	A mansion.
Koub'alti	Ceremonial spot in the old seraglio.

Kourshaltai	Ancient Tartar national assembly.
Kutchek	Dancing boys
Kyzil-bash	Persian free-thinker : a disreputable term
Laghumdgis	Miners
Liva	Major-general or rear-admiral
Lokma	A sweet morsel.
Mahalleh	A parish
Masbata	A decree
Medjlis	A council
Medresseh	A college.
Mekteb	A school
Merkiemeh	Mussulman tribunal.
Mektoubdji	A letter writer
Menzil khan	A post-house
Misafir	A guest
Moalebbi	A sweet dish, like blanc-mange.
Moharrem	First month of the Moslem year
Mollah	A legal dignitary, judge of a city
Mooktar	A parish overseer
Muavin	An official assistant, less than a colleague
Muezzin	A caller to prayers.
Mushir	The highest Turkish rank (military and civilian).
Mudir	Governor of a town or hundred
Muderris	Koran reader in the mosque.
Muphti	Expounder of the Holy Law, a chamber counsel
Musteshar	Under Secretary of State.
Naib	A vicar or deputy.
Namaz	Prayer
Nazir	An overseer or superintendent
Nizam	Regular troops
Nooskha	A "charm"
Oda	A room
Okmeidan	Archery ground.
Orta	A company (of Janissaries)
Ordou caimés	Camp paper money (during late war)
Padishah	The sovereign of Turkey
Pasterma	Dried meat
Para	Smallest denomination of Turkish money
Pilaf	Rice cooked with butter
Ramazan	The Moslem fast; the ninth month
Raya	A non-Mohammedan subject.
Redif	Military reserve
Rushdieh	Progressing, advancing.
Sadr'azam	The Grand Vizier
Salathin	Royal founded mosques
Salian	Property-tax.
Sandjak	A flag; a military government; province.
Saray	A palace.
Sarraf	A banker.
Salaam	A salutation.

SEDJADEH	A prayer rug.
SELEM	Rural usurer.
SELYÉ BOUROUN	Cypress point, opposite Therapia.
SER-AKHOR	Master of the horse, head groom.
SERASKIR	Minister of War; commander-in-chief.
SEYAH	A roaming dervish.
SHALAN	A flat quadriform barge.
SHALLUM	The chief porter of the Tabernacle.
SHEVKETLY	Majestic.
SHIRKET HAIRIÉ	A promising company.
SHALWAR	Loose trowsers.
SINNI	A metal dinner-tray.
SERDEN GHETCHDI	A forlorn hope.
SOFTA	A theological student.
SOUREI FETHI SHEREF	The war hymn in the Koran.
SPAHIS	Hereditary yeomanry (non existent now).
TABIA	A redoubt.
TAÏN	Rations.
TAKSIM	A division; a partition.
TANZIMAT	Reforms.
TCHALGHIGILER	Turkish musicians.
TCHAMASHA AGASI	Master of the robes; first valet.
TCHAOUSH	A sergeant.
TCHIFTLIK	A farm; a country estate.
TCHIAUSHBASHI	Head of a police corps; ancient title of the minister of police.
TECHRIFATDJI	Master of the ceremonies.
TEKIEH	A dervish hall.
TIMARLEE	Ancient Turkish feudatory; timariot.
TOPCHI	A gunner.
TOPHANA	Gun wharf; ordnance department.
ULEMA	Wise men; a clerico-legal body.
ULUFÉ	A gratification.
VACOOF	A pious or charitable endowment.
VALIDEH SULTANA	The sultan's mother.
VIZIR	A first class functionary.
VLADIKA	The chief of Montenegro.
YALI	A residence on the shore of the Bosphorus.
YAMAK	Ancient garrison soldier.
YANGHEN VAR	There is a fire.
YORGHAN	A wadded coverlid.
ZARF	A coffee cupholder.
ZEM-ZEM	Holy-water at Mecca.
ZEYMEN	Ancient irregular troops.

London: Printed by SMITH, ELDER AND Co., Old Bailey, E.C.

CORRESPONDENCE OF LEIGH HUNT. Edited by HIS ELDEST SON. With Photographic Portrait. Two vols. Post 8vo. 24s.

LIFE AND CORRESPONDENCE OF MAJOR-GENERAL SIR JOHN MALCOLM, G.C.B., late Envoy to Persia, and Governor of Bombay. From Unpublished Letters and Journals. By JOHN WILLIAM KAYE. With Portrait. Two vols. Demy 8vo. 36s.

THE LIFE AND CORRESPONDENCE OF CHARLES LORD METCALFE. By JOHN WILLIAM KAYE. A New and Revised Edition. With Portrait. Two vols. Post 8vo. 12s.

LIFE OF CHARLOTTE BRONTË. By MRS. GASKELL. Library Edition. With Portrait of Miss Brontë. Post 8vo. 7s. 6d.

LIFE AND WRITINGS OF JOSEPH MAZZINI.
Vol. I.—Autobiographical and Political. With a Photographic Portrait. Crown 8vo. 9s.
„ II.—Critical and Literary Writings. Crown 8vo. 9s.
„ III.—Autobiographical and Political. Crown 8vo. 9s.
„ IV.—Critical and Literary Writings. Crown 8vo. 9s.

THE LIFE OF MAHOMET. With Introductory Chapters on the Original Sources for the Biography of Mahomet, and on the Pre-Islamite History of Arabia. By W. MUIR, Bengal, C.S. Complete in Four vols. Demy 8vo. £2 2s.

*** *Vols. III. and IV. may be had separately Price* 21s.

SIR CHARLES WOOD'S ADMINISTRATION OF INDIAN AFFAIRS. From 1859 to 1866. By ALGERNON WEST, Deputy Director of Indian Military Funds, and lately Private Secretary to the Right Hon. Sir Charles Wood, Bart., M.P., G.C.B., and the Earl de Grey and Ripon. Demy 8vo. 8s. 6d.

A VINDICATION OF THE MARQUIS OF DALHOUSIE'S INDIAN ADMINISTRATION. By SIR CHARLES JACKSON. Demy 8vo. 6s.

REMINISCENCES OF A BENGAL CIVILIAN. By WILLIAM EDWARDS, Esq., Judge of Her Majesty's High Court of Agra. Crown 8vo. 7s. 6d.

RECOLLECTIONS AND ANECDOTES OF THE CAMP, the Court and the Clubs at the Close of the last War with France. By Captain GRONOW. With Illustrations. New Edition, comprising the First and Second Series in one volume. Crown 8vo. 6s.

CELEBRITIES OF LONDON AND PARIS. Being a Third Series of Reminiscences and Anecdotes of the Camp, the Court, and the Clubs. Containing a Correct Account of the Coup d'Etat. By Captain GRONOW. With Coloured Frontispiece. Crown 8vo. 9s.

CAPTAIN GRONOW'S LAST RECOLLECTIONS. Being the Fourth and Final volume of Anecdotes and Reminiscences. With Portrait. Crown 8vo. 7s. 6d.

THE SPORTING RIFLE AND ITS PROJECTILES. By Lieut. JAMES FORSYTH, Bengal Staff Corps. Second Edition, Re-written and Enlarged. With Illustrations. Crown 8vo. 7s. 6d.

. CENTURY OF PAINTERS OF THE ENGLISH SCHOOL; With Critical Notices of their Works, and an Account of the Progress of Art in England By RICHARD REDGRAVE, R A (Surveyor of Her Majesty's Pictures and Inspector-General for Art), and SAMUEL REDGRAVE Two vols. Demy 8vo 32s.

HAKESPEARE COMMENTARIES. By PROFESSOR GERVINUS. Translated by F E. BUNNETT. Two vols. Demy 8vo 24s.

N SHAKSPEARE'S KNOWLEDGE AND USE OF THE BIBLE. With Vignette Illustrations. Second Edition, Enlarged Crown 8vo Elegantly bound, 6s.; with gilt edges, 7s 6d.

HAKSPERE: His Birthplace and its Neighbourhood. By JOHN R WISE. With Twenty-two Illustrations by W. J LINTON. Crown 8vo. Printed on Tinted Paper, and Handsomely Bound in Ornamental Cloth, gilt edges. 7s. 6d.

UR OLD HOME. By NATHANIEL HAWTHORNE. With a Photographic Portrait. Crown 8vo 5s

DYLLS FROM THE SANSKRIT. By RALPH T. H. GRIFFITH, M.A. Fcap 4to, cloth, gilt edges 10s. 6d.

OMPANIONS OF MY SOLITUDE. By the Author of "Friends in Council," &c. New Edition. Fcap. 8vo. 3s. 6d.

HE CLERGY AND THE PULPIT, IN THEIR RELATIONS TO THE PEOPLE By M. L'ABBE ISIDORE MULLOIS, Chaplain to the Emperor Napoleon III, and Missionary Apostolic Translated by GEORGE PERCY BADGER, late Chaplain in the Diocese of Bombay. Author of "The Nestorians and their Rituals." Crown 8vo 6s.

HE HISTORY AND LIFE OF THE REV. DOCTOR JOHN TAULER, OF STRASBOURG; with Twenty-five of his Sermons (*temp.* 1340). Translated from the German, with Additional Notices of Tauler's Life and Times, by SUSANNA WINKWORTH; and a Preface, by the REV. CHARLES KINGSLEY, Rector of Eversley. Fcap. 4to, cloth, 7s. 6d.; calf extra, 12s. 6d.; calf antique, 14s.; morocco, 17s. 6d.

HE INFERNO OF DANTE. Translated in the Metre of the Original. By the Rev. JAMES FORD, M A., Prebendary of Exeter. Crown 8vo. 10s. 6d. The Italian Text is printed on the opposite pages of the Translation for the Use of Students)

HE EARLY ITALIAN POETS. From Ciullo D'Alcamo to Dante Alighieri. (1100, 1200, 1300) Together with Dante's "Vita Nuova" Translated by D. G. ROSSETTI. Crown 8vo. 12s.

HE SOUL'S EXODUS AND PILGRIMAGE. By the Rev. J. BALDWIN BROWN, B A. Third Edition. Crown 8vo. 7s. 6d.

HE HOME LIFE IN THE LIGHT OF ITS DIVINE IDEA. By the Rev. J. BALDWIN BROWN, B A. Third Edition Crown 8vo. 6s.

HE MYSTERY OF PAIN. A Book for the Sorrowful. Second Edition Fcap. 8vo. 2s 6d.

THE BOOK OF WERE-WOLVES. Being an Account of a Terrible Superstition. By SABINE BARING-GOULD, M.A. With Frontispiece. Crown 8vo. 7s. 6d.

ICELAND; ITS SCENES AND SAGAS. By SABINE BARING-GOULD, M.A. With Thirty-five Illustrations and a Map. Royal 8vo, elegantly bound, gilt edges. 10s. 6d.

THE CONSCRIPT. A Tale of the French War of 1813. From the French of ERCKMANN-CHATRIAN. New and Cheaper Edition. Fcap. 8vo. 2s. 6d.

WATERLOO: A Story of the Hundred Days. Being a Sequel to "The Conscript." Crown 8vo. 6s.

QUEENS OF SONG; Being Memoirs of some of the Most Celebrated Female Vocalists who have appeared on the Lyric Stage, from the Earliest Days of the Opera to the Present Time. To which is added a Chronological List of all the Operas that have been Performed in Europe. By ELLEN CREATHORNE CLAYTON. With Six Portraits. Engraved on Steel. Two vols. Demy 8vo. 32s.

CAPITAL PUNISHMENT. Based on Professor MITTERMAIER'S "Todesstrafe." Edited by JOHN MACRAE MOIR, M.A. Crown 8vo. 6s.

CHRISTIANITY IN INDIA. An Historical Narrative. By JOHN WILLIAM KAYE. Demy 8vo. 16s.

A HISTORY OF PERSIA, from the beginning of the Nineteenth Century to the year 1858. With a Review of the Principal Events that led to the Establishment of the Kajar Dynasty. By ROBERT GRANT WATSON, formerly attached to Her Majesty's Legation at the Court of Persia. Demy 8vo. 15s.

JOURNAL OF A POLITICAL MISSION TO AFGHANISTAN IN 1857. With an Account of the Country and People. By H. W. BELLEW, Medical Officer to the Mission. With Eight Plates. Demy 8vo. 16s.

JOURNAL OF A DIPLOMATIC THREE YEARS' RESIDENCE IN PERSIA. By E. B. EASTWICK, Esq., late H.M.'s Chargé d'Affairs in Persia. Two vols. Post 8vo. 18s.

FOUR YEARS AT THE COURT OF HENRY VIII. Selection of Despatches written by the Venetian Ambassador, Sebastian Giustinian, and Addressed to the Signory of Venice, January 12, 1515, to July 26, 1519. Translated by RAWDON BROWN. Two vols. Crown 8vo. 21s.

HISTORY OF THE VENETIAN REPUBLIC: Her Rise, her Greatness, and her Civilization. By W. CAREW HAZLITT, of the Inner Temple. Complete in Four Volumes. Demy 8vo. With Illustrations. 21s.

*** *Volumes III. and IV. may be had separately. Price* 10s. 6d.

WATERLOO: The Downfall of the First Napoleon. A History of the Campaign of 1815. By GEORGE HOOPER. With Maps and Plans. Demy 8vo. 15s.

Lightning Source UK Ltd.
Milton Keynes UK
UKOW06n0223040316

269515UK00013B/71/P